Words Their Way

WORD STUDY FOR PHONICS, VOCABULARY, AND SPELLING

Donald R. Bear
University of Nevada, Reno

Marcia Invernizzi
University of Virginia

Shane Templeton
University of Nevada, Reno

Francine Johnston
University of North Carolina, Greensboro

Merrill,
an imprint of Prentice Hall
Upper Saddle River, New Jersey   Columbus, Ohio

Library of Congress Cataloging-in-Publication Data
Bear, Donald.
    Words their way: word study for phonics, vocabulary, and spelling
/ Donald Bear, Marcia Invernizzi, Shane Templeton; illustrated by
Francine Johnston.
            p.   cm.
    Includes bibliographical references (p. 373).
    ISBN 0-02-307490-6
    1. Word recognition.   2. Reading (Elementary)—Phonetic method.
3. English language—Orthography and spelling.   I. Invernizzi, Marcia.
II. Templeton, Shane.   III. Title.
LB1050.44.B43   1996
372.4'14—dc20   95-9580
                                                                      CIP

Editor: Bradley J. Potthoff
Production Editor: Sheryl Glicker Langner
Design Coordinator: Jill E. Bonar
Text Designer: Angela Foote
Production Manager: Pamela D. Bennett
Production Coordination: Linda Kauffman Peterson
Illustrations: Francine Johnston

This book was set in Century Schoolbook by Carlisle Communications and was
printed and bound by Quebecor Printing/Semline. The cover was printed by
Phoenix Color Corp.

 ©1996 by Prentice-Hall, Inc.
A Simon & Schuster Company
Upper Saddle River, New Jersey 07458

Printed in the United States of America

10 9 8 7 6 5

ISBN: 0-02-307490-6

Prentice-Hall International (UK) Limited, *London*
Prentice-Hall of Australia Pty. Limited, *Sydney*
Prentice-Hall of Canada, Inc., *Toronto*
Prentice-Hall of Hispanoamericana, S. A., *Mexico*
Prentice-Hall of India Private Limited, *New Delhi*
Prentice-Hall of Japan, Inc., *Tokyo*
Simon & Schuster Asia Pte. Ltd., *Singapore*
Editora Prentice-Hall do Brasil, Ltda., *Rio de Janeiro*

This book is dedicated to our families and friends.

Donald R. Bear
Marcia Invernizzi
Shane Templeton
Francine Johnston

The Authors

Donald Bear (right)

As Director of the Center for Learning and Literacy, at the University of Nevada, Reno, Donald works with teachers to develop word study activities. In the Center, he works with learners who experience difficulties learning to read and write. As a former preschool, third, and fourth grade teacher, he extends his experience working in residential settings with adolescents. He also is a consultant to many school districts and is an active member of the International Reading Association.

Shane Templeton (left)

Shane Templeton is Foundation Professor of Curriculum and Instruction at the University of Nevada, Reno, where he teaches undergraduate and graduate Reading/Language Arts courses. He has taught first and second grades, and English at the secondary level. His research focuses on metalinguistic awareness and on the development of orthographic knowledge.

Marcia Invernizzi (left)

Marcia Invernizzi is an Associate Professor of Reading Education at the Curry School of Education at the University of Virginia. Ms. Invernizzi is also clinical director of the McGuffey Reading Center where she teaches the clinical practica in Reading Diagnosis and Remedial Reading. Formerly an English teacher, Ms. Invernizzi enjoys seeking ways to incorporate word study in the context of literature and writing.

Francine Johnston (right)

As the illustrator for this book, Francine Johnston, now at UNC, Greensboro, also brings her special expertise gained from working at the McGuffey Reading Center at the University of Virginia. Her work in the center with children and teachers has allowed her to contribute generously to the book's visual presentation, as well as to the many activities included in the chapters that follow.

PREFACE

Words Their Way: Word Study for Phonics, Vocabulary, and Spelling provides a practical way to study words with students. Based on the research on invented and developmental spelling, the framework of this text is keyed to the five stages of spelling or orthographic development (Henderson, 1990; Templeton & Bear, 1992). Ordered in this developmental format, *Words Their Way* complements the use of any existing phonics, spelling, and vocabulary curriculums.

Text Features

One of the unique features of this text are the descriptions of more than 300 word study activities. These activities are set up to follow literacy development from emergent to more mature, specialized stages. Often presented in a game-like format, these activities are actually mini-lessons that draw upon what students concurrently are learning in developmental reading and writing. There is time provided in each activity for students to examine words and their patterns and to reflect on how words are organized, how they are spelled, and what they mean. We have chosen to include activities that especially interest students in words and can easily be integrated into the social contexts in which reading and writing activities occur.

Throughout the activities sections in this text, we have labeled some activities with a symbol **GA** to indicate how they are generic to each aspect of development. These are the activities that we use in each developmental stage illustrating how they can be adapted to fit the literacy continuum.

As you use any of these activities, you will probably create many of your own. If you want to share these, we'll try to include them—with proper permission and credit to you—in the next edition of this text.

Text Organization

The organization of the text and of each chapter is straightforward. The first three chapters present an overview of how words are learned, a discussion of development, methods for assessment and for getting started, and finally, a clear presentation of the principles of word study and how to organize word study in a classroom. Chapter Four outlines fundamental practices in word sorting.

The remainder of the text, Chapters Five through Eight, focuses on particular stages of literacy development. A description of each stage is then followed by a series of word study activities that best complements its development.

The organization of this text should facilitate using it in some different ways. If you feel the need to explore the nature of word study and the type of classroom organization and environment that eases an immersion into it, we suggest you begin reading this text at the beginning—with Chapter One. If, on the other hand, you are ready to jump right in and explore word study activities with your students, we recommend that you skim Chapters Four through Eight, look for activities related to the developmental levels of your students, and examine a few closely. Then try one or two out with a small group of students.

As you look more carefully through activities designed for more mature, specialized readers, you may find yourselves or some of your students getting really involved as we did. The more you learn about words—what they mean, how they are structured, and how they are used—the more your interest is sparked and you can demonstrate just how fascinating words can be in their meaning, history, usage, and connotation.

Acknowledgments

Words Their Way: *Word Study for Phonics, Vocabulary, and Spelling* is a community undertaking. You can see that many of the activities are credited to our students and colleagues. Edmund Henderson, our mentor at the University of Virginia's McGuffey Reading Center, was the first person to show us a number of these activities. Surely, many of these activities go back to Ed's training with Russell Stauffer at the University of Delaware. Many of the generic activities come from our own experiences. We are appreciative of all of this collaboration to create a rich word study resource for you.

Additionally, we gratefully acknowledge those colleagues and peers whose reviews throughout the developmental process helped us refine our work. They are Anne Hall, University of South Florida; Patricia P. Kelly, Virginia Tech; Beverly Otto, Northeastern Illinois University; Mary C. Shake, University of Kentucky; Terry Piper, Memorial University of Newfoundland; Ruth Beeker, University of Arizona; Edward W. Holmes, Towson State University; Eilene K. Glasgow, Pacific Lutheran University; and Melba M. Hutsell, St. Mary's University. We also thank our colleagues and our students at the University of Nevada—Reno, and at the University of Virginia. We offer you our sincere appreciation.

Donald R. Bear
Shane Templeton
Marcia Invernizzi
Francine Johnston

Contents

5 Word Study for Emergent Learners in the Preliterate Stage   92

8 Word Study for Intermediate and Specialized Readers and Writers in the Syllable Juncture and Derivational Constancy Stages   298

List of Activities

7 Activities for Within Word Pattern Students   **255**

1

How Words Are Learned

How Spoken Words Are Learned

> One afternoon at an elegant garden party, young Elbert heard a word he had never heard before. The word floated by like a small storm cloud. It was ugly and covered with dark, bristly hairs. With a swift flick of his wrist, Elbert snatched the word from the air and stuffed it into his back pocket. Forgetting about it, the boy went on his way. But the word waited patiently. When Aunt Isabella sang opera in soprano, the word made itself small and flew into Elbert's mouth like a little gnat. . . . [Later, a] mallet landed on Elbert's great toe. . . . Elbert opened his mouth to scream, but the bad word sprang out, bigger and uglier than before. Everyone at the party was shocked.
>
> *Elbert's Bad Word* (Wood, 1988)

How words are learned, whether good words or bad, remains a great mystery. But, as the story of *Elbert's Bad Word* illustrates, **social forces** exert a powerful influence. Whether at an elegant garden party, on the street, or in the classroom, words float by us like little clouds, nebulously understood at first, acquired in our speech and gradually specified.

Our brains are ready to serve us in learning language. This is because **biological forces** ensure that language learning is innate. Just as with Elbert's "swift flick of the wrist," there is coordination among thousands of muscles. This biological foundation of language underlies learning to read and write words (Lenneberg, 1967; Lieberman, 1991).

While biology ensures that we are *able* to learn to speak words, social and cognitive forces provide the experience needed to learn words. As Elbert reflects on his trouble with the "bad word," he seeks the help and advice of a word wizard to learn more socially acceptable expletives. The wizard tells Elbert that "Sometimes we need strong words to say how we feel. Use these and perhaps you won't get into trouble (p. 17)." Then, as Elbert consciously eats the substitutes, the "ugly word shriveled to the size of a flea and hopped on to his necktie (p. 19)."

How Written Words Are Learned

Like Elbert's, our students' word learning is socially motivated, biologically driven, and cognitively refined. In this section we explore **social, biological,** and **cognitive forces** which affect students' learning.

Social Forces

Like spoken vocabularies, written words are learned in context. Whether through shared book experiences, lap reading, or bedtime stories, written words appear in a social setting, and **social forces** provide the impetus to learn them. Teachers, parents, and other intimates are the children's models in the social habits of reading and writing for work, for recreation, and for information. The practice and experience of imitation provide the most powerful sway in children's learning.

Social forces and rewards create the urge for students to spend the time necessary to learn to read and write. The more feedback and encouragement extended, the more persistently children continue to imitate the literate behaviors of their role models.

Biological Forces

Language Forces:
Social
Biological
Cognitive

Unlike learning to talk, learning to read and write are not biologically preprogrammed (Liberman & Shankweiler, 1991). Nevertheless, biological forces do influence how we learn the written word. Every writing system has developed a match between the spoken and written word. The ability to make this match between the spoken and written word quickly and easily during fluent reading depends upon our unique biological endowments. When we read and write, our brain focuses our mind and eyes and ears on the language and ideas which underlie the written word. Children with speech and/or hearing problems or those who experience significant language delay find learning to read and spell especially tough going (Kamhi & Catts, 1991).

Cognitive Forces

Cognitive forces help children learn written words. In learning spoken language, children's knowledge of word meanings is initially incomplete and grows through experience with words in meaningful contexts. For example, the young child calls all four-legged animals "doggie" until horses and cows are known.

We call the form of written words **spelling,** or **orthography.** And as with spoken language, children's knowledge of the orthography is initially incomplete and grows through experience with words in an orthographic context. The same child later spells all long $\bar{a}$ words a–consonant–e until ai and ay words are known. Through processes of categorization, using rule-like criteria for determining similarity and difference, children extend their reach. Their knowledge of the orthography becomes more sophisticated with plenty of experience.

The Speech-to-Print Match

Readers and
writers match
speech with print.

Learning to read and spell is a process of matching oral and written structures at three different levels:

1. The global level at which the text is organized into phrases and sentences
2. The level of words within phrases
3. The level of sounds within syllables

For someone learning to read, there is not always an obvious match between spoken and written language at any of these levels. Mismatches occur because of the inflexible nature of print and the flowing stream of speech which it represents. Learning to make the match between speech and writing is a gradual process. In order to learn to read and spell, children must explore the structures of both written and spoken words at these three levels.

The Phrase and Sentence Level

Three Levels of
Language:
    Global
    Phrase
    Sound

In oral language, we can characterize the global level as **prosodic.** This is the "musical" level of language, usually consisting of phrases. And within these phrases speakers produce and listeners hear intonation contours, expression, and tone of voice, all of which communicate ideas and emotions. The musical pizazz and expression are found in the prosody of spoken language. For example, a rising note at the end of a statement indicates a question; precise, clipped words in a brusque tone may suggest anger or irritation. Oral language is a direct form of communication where there are partners who fill in gaps in the incoming message and who indicate when communication breaks down. Thus, oral communications tend to be informal and flexible, lacking the regimented sentence structures of the written word.

We talk in
phrases. We write
in sentences.

The prosody of the speaker's voice is not directly available in writing. Printed language can only approximate the richness of oral expression. Punctuation and word choice are the reader's cues to the emotions and intent of the writer. Written language must contain complete, freestanding messages in which meaning is clear. Further, written language tends to be more formal and carefully constructed, using recognizable story structures and literary devices such as "happily ever after" to cue the reader.

Young children are used to talking in phrases, and when they learn to read they must match the phrases in the familiar prosody of their oral language to the more formal structures of written language. In order to do this, they use their knowledge of the world, their knowledge of how stories are told in writing, and their developing knowledge of the conventions of writing.

Words in Phrases

A second level of structure students negotiate are the units of meaning we call **words.** The comprehension of words depends on context and position in the phrase or sentence. The meaning of the word "dog," for example, varies greatly in the following statements:

Collies are pretty **dogs.**
Carmen **dogged** the trail of the suspect for a week.
The **dog** days of August are hot and still.

What is a word?

While context and position are equally crucial for specifying words in both oral and written language, there is an additional variable involved in matching words in speech to words in print. In speech, words are not distinct; there is not a clear, separable unit in speech that equates perfectly to individual words. Because of this, when children try to match their speech to print they often miss the mark—it takes some practice to match words in speech to written words (Morris, 1980; Roberts, 1992). We discuss this further in Chapter 5, and the illustration on page 95 shows how a child tries to match speech to print.

Beginning
readers find the
words in phrases.
Beginning
readers learn to
match spoken
words with
written words.

This mismatch of meaning units between speech and print is most clearly illustrated through an "EKG" of speech called a **spectrograph.** This acoustic representation of speech reveals a surprising thing: We don't speak in words! There are no demarcations for individual words when we talk. The only break in a spectrograph coincides with phrases and pauses for breathing. These breaks always occur between syllables. A "word" is a term specific to print, and according to Malinowski (1952), cultures which have no written language have no word for "word." This remarkable state of affairs creates an enormous challenge for individuals learning to read.

Sounds in Syllables

In learning to read, students negotiate sounds within syllables. In speech, consonants and vowels are interconnected and cannot be separated (Liberman & Shankweiler, 1991). Yet the alphabet and letter sounds must be learned as discrete units. As children stabilize the match between print and speech at the phrase and sentence level, they come to discover the way the alphabet divides the sounds within syllables. Their first understanding develops through exploring the beginning sounds of words.

Orthography: How words are spelled; their spelling patterns

Later, once they understand how the alphabet represents sounds, children begin to view the writing system—the **orthography**—as a series of patterns which are organized at the level of the syllable. They see orthographic patterns organized around the **vowels:** first, they explore the short-vowel patterns (as in *cat, hat, rat*), and then the long-vowel patterns (*meet, feet,* and *keep*).

Eventually, students learn that syllables within words can have meanings all their own. They understand the meaning of prefixes and find meaning in orthographic patterns across similar words, for example *sign, signal, significant,* and *signature*. With plenty of experience, they discover that words share roots, for example, re**vol**ve, e**vol**ve, **vol**untary, and **vol**ition.

In the classroom, teachers and their students can explore these matches between oral and written language: At the phrase and sentence level, teachers read to children, tell stories, write them down, and act them out. At the level of words, teachers call attention to printed words, to their meaning, to their boundaries, and to their order within phrases. At the level of sounds within syllables, teachers help children categorize speech sounds into units that correspond to meaningful elements and patterns in the orthography. The word study in this book is designed to help your students match oral and written language structures at each of these three levels.

The Braid of Literacy Development

Literacy is like a braid of interwoven threads. Figure 1–1 illustrates how, from a developmental perspective, the braid begins with the intertwining threads of *oral language* and *stories*. When children are in settings which encourage literacy, a *writing* thread is intertwined as well. As children play with the threads of oral language, stories, and writing, they move into *reading*—and the threads of literacy begin to bond. Students' *orthographic knowledge* strengthens the bonding. The size of the threads and the braid itself become thicker as word knowledge grows. The aim of this book is to demonstrate how our exploration of word knowledge can lead to the lengthening and strengthening of the braid of literacy.

Literacy begins with oral language and stories.

During the primary years word knowledge is fundamentally **aural.** From the oral language that surrounds them—world experiences and stories—children develop a rich speaking vocabulary. As children have opportunities to talk about and to categorize their everyday experiences, they begin to elaborate what they know and to expand their oral vocabulary.

The *written* words students learn are words students already understand in oral language. The first written words students learn are usually their own names, followed by those of significant others. Words like *cat, dog, car,* and *I love you* represent animals, objects, and ideas dear to their lives. Later, students learn some of the terms that describe and refer to language, such as *word, sentence, beginning sound,* and *rhyme*. These "words about words" bring to the surface concepts only tacitly understood in speaking.

FIGURE 1–1 The Threads of Literacy Development

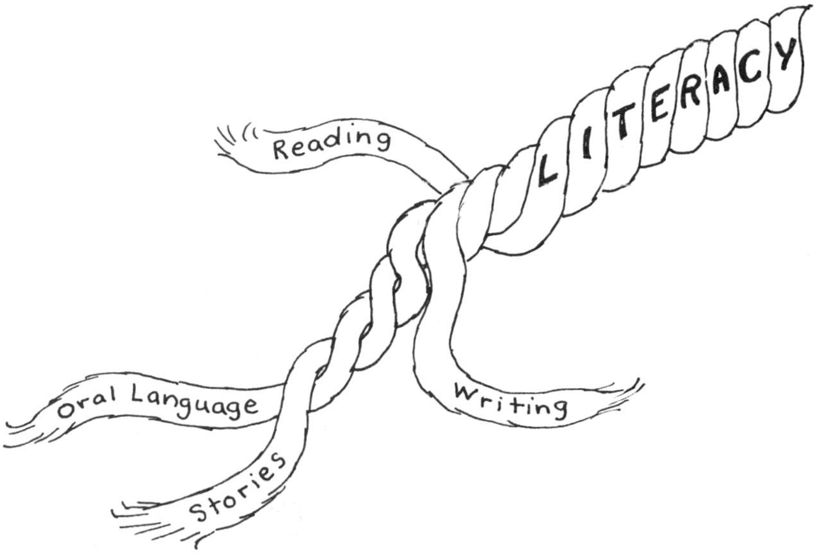

As students mature as readers and writers, they learn vocabulary from written language that they have not heard in oral language. In school, the emphasis shifts from learning written forms of concepts already understood to elaborating and expanding those concepts through print. By learning about the structure of written words, relationships are forged which extend students' overall understanding of words. Students find that the relationships among words—their sounds, their spelling patterns, and their meanings—are found in the orthography. Through a growing knowledge of the way words are spelled, students' vocabularies continue to swell.

Wherever purposeful reading, writing, listening, and speaking take place, words are learned along the way. Even more words are acquired when words are explicitly examined.

This book is about directing children's attention to ways in which written words create meaning. To facilitate vocabulary growth, teachers must know a good deal about the threads which join together to make this braid of literacy.

Facilitating Vocabulary Growth and Orthographic Knowledge

Preschoolers and elementary students play with words and their meanings. There are similarities in the ways learners of all ages expand their vocabularies. It seems that humans have a natural interest to find order, to compare and contrast, and to pay attention to what remains the same despite minor variations. Infants learn to recognize Daddy as the same Daddy with or without glasses, with or without a hat or whiskers. Auto mechanics learn to recognize carburetors despite changes in size or manufacturer. Through such daily interactions, we categorize our surroundings. Our students, then, expand their vocabularies by comparing one concept with another. Gradually, the number of concepts they analyze increases, but the process is still one of comparing and contrasting the elements of the words they read and speak.

Word study is active.

Some common strategies that learners use to explore words are described here in terms of **word play** and **word study**. The activities presented in this book build on what students do on their own. In the word and picture sorts, hands-on experiences are combined with observation and talk. Just as *Math Their Way* (Baretta-Lorton, 1968) uses concrete manipulatives to illustrate principles of combining and separation, so *Words Their Way* uses concrete pictures and words to illustrate principles of similarity and difference.

Word Play

Early word play is oral. Children naturally delight in the silliness of words and relish the opportunity to indulge in word play. One five-year-old lugged her cat across the porch to introduce her to a friend. "This is Catfish," she said. "She's half cat and half fish because she ate a fish! So now she's a Catfish!" Both children howled with laughter. Is this word play so different from adults chuckling that "efficient bureaucracy" is an *oxymoron? All* of us have a natural inclination to explore words and the concepts they represent, and teachers and parents help direct interest by modeling engaging ways to examine words. The games young and older learners play are the same; only the words and concepts are different. To foster this interest, teachers talk about words and promote an interest in word play through read-alouds of books filled with puns like *The Hungry Thing* (Slepian & Seidler, 1967), *The BFG* (Dahl, 1982) and *Amelia Bedelia* (Parish, 1981). Orally playing with words in the classroom helps pave the way for children to explore written words as they learn to read and write them. When this exploration is underway, students' natural inclination to categorize is developed in card games like Crazy Eights, Old Maid, and Go Fish. As they look for matches, they show an interest in order, and they develop plans to compare and contrast their words.

Play with words by
sound
image
concept

Words are
categorized in
word study
games.

Word Study

To enrich and expand students' knowledge, we start with concepts that are already meaningful. We help students enrich their conceptual thinking and vocabulary by simply *associating* words. For example, consider words and concepts associated with "growth": *development, evolution, ripening,* and *progress,* to name but a few. And from a slightly different angle, the idea of "growth" is also associated with words like *nutrition, sustenance, nourishment,* and *care.* With these words we can now talk about "growth" as well as what causes growth to happen. This type of expansion happens naturally in content studies in the classroom. Many teachers write these terms on a chart or on the board as the terms come up in discussions. Vocabularies expand as a function of understanding. By categorizing words, new concepts develop as extensions of old ones.

Everyday surroundings offer the best potential for concept development and vocabulary growth. Plastic animals, buttons, coins and rocks—all can be sorted by size, shape, color, or distinguishing feature. Teachers direct students to look at qualities of familiar objects and concepts that they had not thought of before. An exploration of caterpillars and moths, for example, can lead to a consideration of the concepts of life cycles and metamorphoses.

Another way to facilitate vocabulary and conceptual development is through **picture sorting activities.** Teachers use picture cards to make fundamental contrasts between concepts. Few five-year-olds, for example, have a concept of the geographical hierarchy entailed in the move from city to countryside, state to country, country to continent. Some may, however, have a concept of "our land" as an undifferentiated zone of familiarity. By driving some distance through "our land" from one city to the next, we can develop the vocabulary of cities within "our land": skyscrapers, traffic, apartment buildings, and stores.

Sort pictures by concept and sound.

These concepts can be contrasted with those noticed in the drive through the countryside: farms, mountains, woods, barns, and silos. Figure 1–2 illustrates a picture sort in which students sorted pictures to differentiate the vocabulary of "our land" into the two distinct conceptual groupings. Through experience and the vocabulary associated with that experience, new concepts emerge.

As children begin to read and write, they use these *written* words in similar sorts. This categorization technique elaborates conceptual development while casually reinforcing sight words. The word groupings in Figure 1–3, drawn from a five-year-old's personal collection of sight words, represents the conceptual distinctions she made.

Word sorting is a process of categorizing known words into groups of similarity and difference. As words are sorted, children *compare* and *contrast* across categories of their own creation as well as those of other students. In this way, students elaborate concepts underlying words they already know, and they make important distinctions among concepts and words. When they examine the structure of words, they discover orthographic distinctions and patterns.

Primary-aged children begin by sorting concrete objects and pictures until they acquire some facility and interest in the sorting process. When children have acquired a fair number of sight words, they sort written words in the same ways they sorted concrete objects and pictures of objects. Later, they sort by word elements dealing primarily with sound, such as alliteration and rhyme. The sorts in Figure 1–4 show how words sorted first by familiar concepts can then be sorted by beginning sounds.

FIGURE 1–2 Concept Sort with Country and City Pictures

FIGURE 1–3 Concept Sort with Words

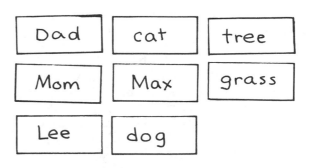

FIGURE 1–4 Concept Sort with Word Bank Words

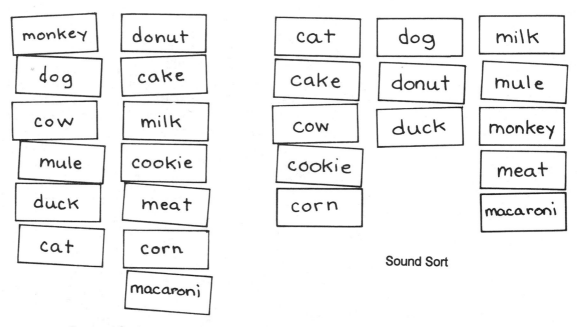

Concept Sort

Sound Sort

| Words represent concepts. | Students who are more advanced in their literacy development also sort words into conceptual categories. In reading *Stuart Little* (White, 1945), for example, a group of Ms. Brickhead's third graders sorted some of the vocabulary they encountered as follows: |

Weather Words	**Boat Terms**	**Birds**
squall	rigging	henbird
mist	bow	vireo
breeze	stern	wren
brisk	schooner	beak
ominous	helm	flutter
cloudy	staysail	breast
wind	mainmast	wing
sunshiny	capsizing	
	seafaring	

Later, these same words were classified by various structural characteristics. *Mainmast, staysail, seafaring, shipshape* and *sunshiny* were grouped together, this time based on a structural characteristic they shared—**compound words.**

| *Word study and vocabulary growth intertwine.* |

By fourth grade, for many students, vocabulary and spelling become so tightly intertwined that vocabulary and spelling are regarded as two sides of the word knowledge coin. Clearly, in students' word study at this level, vocabulary knowledge helps spelling, and spelling helps vocabulary. By categorizing words by meaning and by various orthographic structures, students acquire the knowledge for independent vocabulary growth. They learn how to direct their attention to the ways in which spelling elements combine to create word meanings.

Teachers encourage this natural progression by asking students to examine the structural components of words. Students categorize elements within words by the way letters represent sounds, the patterns within the words, and the meaning among these patterns. Let's look more closely at these three layers of information in the spelling system of English.

The Structure of Words: Layers of Information

| *Layers of English Orthography: Alphabetic Pattern Meaning* |

We examine three layers of English orthography to show a developmental progression from alphabet to pattern to meaning. Each layer provides information, and in mature readers and writers, there is interaction among the layers. First, we'll look at the three layers of information—alphabetic, pattern, and meaning—and then present a brief history of English orthography which shows this interaction.

Alphabet

| *The letters of the alphabet describe the sounds left-to-right.* |

Our spelling system is **alphabetic** because it represents the relationship between letters and sounds. In English, of course, this relationship is usually read in a left-to-right fashion. In the word *sat*, it is clear that each sound is represented by a single letter; we blend together the sounds for /s/, /a/, and /t/, and we come up with the word *sat*. In the word *chin*, we still hear three sounds, even though there are four letters. This is because the first two letters, *ch*, function like a single letter, representing a single sound. So, we can match letters—sometimes singly, sometimes in pairs—to sounds left-to-right and come up with words. This is the *alphabetic* principle in English spelling, the first layer of information, at work.

Pattern

| *Letters combine to form patterns: rat CVC fin CVC hop CVC* |

What about words like *cape, bead,* and *light*? If we spelled these words with single letters, they would look something like CAP, BED, and LIT—and of course these spellings already represent other words.

It is obvious that English does not have a single sound for each letter under all conditions. You know that single sounds are sometimes spelled with more than one letter or are affected by other letters that don't stand for any sounds themselves. When we look beyond single letter/sound match-ups and search for **patterns** that guide the grouping of letters, however, we find more consistency than we expected.

There is another level of information, therefore, that overlays the alphabetic layer. We talk about **patterns** or groups of letters that represent certain

New letters form
new patterns:

rate
CVCe

fine
CVCe

hope
CVCe

pronunciations within a single syllable. Some letters within a pattern or group have an affect on how other letters are pronounced. Take for example the -*ape* in *cape*; we say that the final *e* "makes" the preceding vowel letter, *a,* stand for a long-vowel sound. The *e* does not stand for a sound itself, but it plays a very important role. The -*ape* group of letters, therefore, follows a pattern which can be described this way: When you have a vowel/ consonant/silent *e* in a single syllable, this letter grouping forms a pattern that usually will function to indicate a long vowel. We refer to this pattern as the "consonant-vowel-consonant-silent e" (CVCe) pattern.

Another example is *bead.* Quite often, when we have a CVVC pattern in a single syllable, this means we have a long vowel sound—the second vowel letter is silent but serves to indicate that the first vowel letter is "long." We can then say that CVCe and CVVC patterns very often represent long vowel spellings.

The notion of pattern helps us talk more efficiently about the alphabetic layer as well; we can talk about the CVC pattern (*sat, chin*)—and we are able to notice that, regardless of how many consonant letters you may have on either side of the single vowel, the fact that there *is* but one vowel letter in that pattern means it will usually stand for a "short" vowel sound. (We'll see shortly that, as you learn more about words, your brain comes to operate in terms of these *patterns* rather than in terms of any specific letters. In the case of spelling, our brains can be much more efficient if they come to understand how these patterns work.)

Syllables follow spelling patterns, too. These patterns are described with the same "V" and "C" symbols. Let's consider two of the most common syllable patterns. First, there is the VCCV pattern. *Robber* is a VCCV pattern—as you can see, what we're referring to here is the vowel and consonant of the first syllable and the consonant and vowel of the second syllable—whenever we have this pattern, the first vowel is usually short. Knowledge of this pattern can help students figure out an unknown word in reading, and it can help them with the correct spelling of an uncertain word when they're writing: If a student is puzzling over whether "robber" had one *b* or two (because we *hear* only a single /b/ sound) and if the student is aware of the VCCV pattern, he or she could make a very good guess and write down *two* b's. Second, there is the VCV syllable pattern, as in *radar, begin,* and *limit.* Most of the time this pattern signals that the first vowel is long, but as in the case of *limit,* the first vowel can, on occasion, be short as well. Still, this pattern is an important one—as we'll see later on.

In short, knowledge about patterns within single syllables, and syllable patterns within words, will be of considerable value to students in both their reading and their spelling.

Meaning

Overarching both alphabet and pattern in sophistication is the layer of **meaning.** Groups of letters can represent meaning directly, and when students learn this, they will be much less puzzled by unusual spellings they encounter. Examples of these units or groups of letters are prefixes, suffixes, and Greek and Latin stems.

As one example of how meaning functions in the spelling system, think of the prefix *re-*; whether we hear it pronounced "ree" as in *re*think or "ruh" as in *re*move, its spelling stays the same because it directly represents meaning. Why is *comp**o**sition* not spelled *comp**u**sition*? Because it is related in meaning

Orthographic
knowledge builds
vocabulary.

to *compose*—the spelling of *compos* in the related words *compose* and *composition* stays the same even though the sound that the letter *o* represents changes. Likewise, the letter sequence *photo* in *photo*graph, *photo*grapher and *photo*graphic signals family relationships among these words—despite the changes in sound that these letters represent. By building connections between meaning parts and their derivations, we enlarge our vocabulary. This is a powerful feature of English spelling that very few people know. As you'll see, this interaction of spelling and meaning opens up a whole new frontier in exploring and learning about words.

Students invent and discover the basic principles of spelling, the three layers of information, when they read good stories, when they write purposefully, and when they are guided by knowledgeable teachers. In this book, word study is presented in teacher-directed activities in which students examine the spelling system. In the small group setting, teachers carefully organize students' word study activities, choosing the type of word study they present based on observation of their students' development. Word study activities draw a part of the learners' attention to the spelling system when they read and write. In a sense, word study gives students something to look for as they read and write. We believe that this word study is well worth the ten to fifteen minutes of time daily.

But how do we know where to begin word study? We find out where students are in their knowledge of the spelling system—in their knowledge of English *orthography*. Students' **developmental** knowledge of the orthography refers to what they know about written words: What words look like, how they sound, what they mean, and how they are used. A good deal of what students know about the orthography is revealed in their invented spellings. Students' invented spellings are windows to their orthographic knowledge. Research on invented spelling has shown that students learn the features of English orthography in a common progression. According to **developmental spelling theory,** teachers can use assessments of invented spellings, like the ones discussed in Chapter 3, to select the content of instruction in word recognition, alphabet study, phonics, vocabulary, and spelling.

In this book, we will present a broad scope and sequence of word elements that is compatible with children's growing levels of cognitive development and knowledge of written English. We will examine these levels of development in some depth in Chapter 2, because they underlie our informed judgment about what to teach and when to teach it.

Words Their Way

Word study is
based on
development.
Word study is for
conceptual
exploration.

When we say that we want to help students explore and learn about words *their* way, we mean that our instruction will be sensitive to two fundamental tenets:

1. Students' learning of spelling and vocabulary is based on their **developmental level.**
2. Students' learning is based on the way they are *naturally* inclined to learn, on their natural course of conceptual learning.

When we honor these two tenets we almost guarantee that our students will learn their way—building from what is known about words to what is new. *Words Their Way* is organized according to these two tenets, and we'd like to conclude by pointing out how the remaining chapters will reflect this organization.

Developmental Spelling Instruction

It is impossible to know exactly what to teach and when to teach it until we have a living child before us. An informed, developmental interpretation of children's efforts as they read and write show us which words they can read, and of those, which they might learn more about. There is more to pacing instruction than plugging students into an arbitrary sequence of spelling features. **Instructional pacing** must be synonymous with **instructional placing**—fitting the features of words to be taught to the students' understanding of what is to be learned.

> Word study begins with the known.

The instructional match we make between the levels of information contained in the structure of words and the synchrony of reading, writing, and spelling development is discussed in Chapter Two. In Chapter Three, we present a procedure for interpreting spelling errors to ascertain what children know about written words and what they are trying to learn.

We will discuss the principles and procedures for word study in Chapter Four. By focusing instruction on what children are trying to learn next, teachers ensure that students work within their conceptual reach. The word study presented in *Words Their Way* replicates the process of concept development.

Why Teach Spelling and Vocabulary?

When we say that instruction should be based on our students' *natural* inclination to learn, does this mean that there is no role for deliberate and explicit teaching of spelling and vocabulary? Of course not. We teach spelling and vocabulary primarily because we *have* to: Written English is not the same as spoken English. It is a rich, multilayered system based on a host of linguistic information pooled together in a living sea of speech. Written English is an alphabetic system which achieves greater economical proportions through the patterning of its letter combinations. These patterns can be recognized through categorization tasks which reflect the cognitive processes of concept development. English vocabulary—its meaning, its patterns of use and representation, its alternations in sound—all must be directly taught in relationship to the conceptual understandings of the learner.

Rather than a variety of surface-level activities designed only to ensure repeated exposure, our teaching tasks encourage active exploration and examination of word features that are within a child's stage of literacy development. Word study is *active,* and by making judgments about words and sorting words according to similar features, students devise their own rules for how the features work. The simple act of making judgments about words this way helps teach the relationships among a word's sound, its spelling pattern, and its meaning. Meaningful practice helps students internalize word features and become automatic in using what they have learned.

Chapters Five through Eight are the "teaching/learning" heart of the book. The type of instruction we've just described is reflected in these chapters as they present appropriate word study for each of the stages of developmental word knowledge. Now that we have looked at the nature of words and the spelling system that represents them in print, it is time to examine briefly the nature of these stages of developmental spelling knowledge and the type of reading and writing characteristic of each stage.

2

Words and the Development of Orthographic Knowledge

We have seen that there are three layers of information represented in English spelling:

1. **Alphabetic,** in which individual letters match up to individual sounds following a left-to-right sequence
2. **Pattern,** in which groups of letters function as a single pattern or unit to represent sounds
3. **Meaning,** in which groups of letters represent directly the *meaning* units underlying words

Developmentally, we see students progress in their strategies and awareness of these layers from alphabet, to pattern, to meaning.

In this chapter we will explore students' development of orthographic knowledge in terms of these layers of information. We can observe the development of these three layers of information in our students' spelling, particularly in their invented spellings. Notably, the order in which students come to understand and apply a knowledge of these different layers of information parallels the order in which the information appeared *historically* in the spelling system (Templeton, 1976, 1992). Students' knowledge of these layers of the orthography underlies their ability as mature readers and writers to read words efficiently and effectively as well as to write most words with little conscious effort. It is this broader level that we will consider first in this chapter—the overall interaction among word knowledge, reading, and writing as described in the **synchrony** model of literacy development. Then we will look more closely at each of the developmental stages.

> Three layers of information in the orthography:
> Alphabet
> Pattern
> Meaning

The Synchrony of Literacy Development

Developmental spelling theory suggests that invented spelling is a window into a child's knowledge of how written words work and can be used to guide instruction (Invernizzi, Abouzeid & Gill, 1994). Specific kinds of spelling errors at particular stages of orthographic knowledge reflect a progressive differentiation of word elements which determine how words are read and written. Insight into these conceptual understandings helps teachers direct children's efforts as they learn to read and spell.

The scope and sequence of our studies is based on this developmental foundation. When we do word study with students, we are addressing learning needs in all areas of literacy because we know that development in one area relates to development in other areas. This harmony in the timing of development has been described as the **synchrony** of reading, writing, and spelling development (Bear, 1991b). This means that development in one area is observed along with advances in other areas. All three advance in stage-like progressions which share important conceptual dimensions.

An understanding of these dimensions is crucial for effective literacy instruction. Figure 2–1 presents a model of how reading, writing, and spelling progress together. Later, with this model in mind, you will see how to assess students' development and progress. Word study activities are organized around this model; therefore, if you can identify your students by the stages described in this model, you will know which chapters contain the activities most relevant to your students' development.

FIGURE 2–1 Synchrony of Reading, Writing, and Spelling Development

Chapter Five *Preliterate*	*Chapter Six* *Letter Name*		*Chapter Seven* *Within Word* *Pattern*	*Chapter Eight* *Syllable Juncture &* *Derivational Constancy*	
Reading ⟶					
1) EMERGENT	**BEGINNING**		**TRANSITIONAL**	**INTERMEDIATE** **& SPECIALIZED**	

Pretend reading	Concept of Word
	Rereads pattern books
	  & dictations
	Reading is disfluent
	Reads aloud
	Fingerpoints
			Silent reading
			Stop fingerpointing
			Approaching fluency,
			  phrasal reading,
			  greater expression
				Reads fluently, with expression,
				  prefers silent reading
				Acquires a variety of reading
				  styles
				Experiences styles & genre	

(Ages 1-7)	(Ages 5-9)		(Ages 6-12)	(Ages 10-100)	
Writing ⟶					
2) EMERGENT	**BEGINNING**		**TRANSITIONAL**	**INTERMEDIATE** **& SPECIALIZED**	

Pretend
writing/drawing
	Syllabic
	Word-by-word writing
	Summarizes events & writes
	  retellings
	Volume increases from a few
	  words to a half page of writing
			Approaching fluency
			Greater planning
			  time
			More detail &
			  organization of
			  writing
				Fluent writing
				Building expression & voice
				Experiences different writing
				  styles & genre
				Writing shows personal
				  problem solving and personal
				  reflection	

Orthographic Knowledge and Spelling ⟶					
3) PRELITERATE	**Early** **Letter Name**	**Middle & Late** **Letter Name**	**Within Word Pattern**	**Syllable** **Juncture**	**Derivational** **Constancy**

Pretend writing	Spells
	  predominant
	  sounds &
	  then first &
	  last
	  consonants
		Spells
		  consonants &
		  vowels in
		  each syllable
			Spells short vowels
			  correctly &
			  experiments with
			  long vowels
				Learns how
				  syllables fit
				  together
				Studies
				  external/
				  inflectional
				  junctures,
				  prefixes, &
				  suffixes
					Studies
					  derived
					  forms in
					  bases &
					  roots
					Studies
					  internal
					  morphology
					  in syllables

Based on Henderson (1990); adapted from Bear (1992)

How Orthographic Knowledge Develops: Stages of Spelling Development

Because word study is based on stages of spelling, the word study activities presented in this book are arranged by stages of spelling. The order of word study and the principles which guide the selection of activities to match development are discussed in Chapter Four. Beginning with Chapter Five, there are four chapters devoted to instruction based on these stages. Knowing the stage of spelling of each of your students will determine your choices of appropriate word study activities. This section presents an overview of these stages to guide you to specific activities in later chapters.

The idea of stages is used to describe particular scenarios of students' orthographic development. Over the past 20 years we have established criteria to determine which phase of development students are in, and have worked with many, many teachers in using the guidelines discussed below and the procedures described in the next chapter.

> Word study is based on stage of spelling.

By conducting regular spelling assessments, perhaps three times a year, you can track your students' progress and development. (We discuss this assessment procedure in Chapter 3.) An important prerequisite, however, is to know something about the stages of spelling development.

Levels of Learning

For each stage, students' orthographic knowledge is defined by three functional levels:

1. **What students do correctly**—an independent or easy level
2. **What students "use but confuse"**—students experiment; where instruction is most useful
3. **What is absent in students' spelling**—spelling concepts are too advanced; instruction for what is absent is frustrating

(Invernizzi, Abouzeid & Gill, 1994)

> Functional Levels of Orthographic Knowledge:
> ✦ What students do correctly
> ✦ What they "use but confuse"
> ✦ What is absent

In the following discussion of each stage, a chart is presented which describes spelling development according to these three functional levels.

To determine what orthographic features and patterns to explore with each child, we focus on what they "use but confuse" because this will be where instruction will be of most benefit to a student. In Vygotskian terms, the level of awareness where students "use but confuse" is their "zone of proximal development" (Cole & Scribner, 1978). By studying the stages of spelling development, it becomes obvious what sequence the study of orthographic features should take. The stage of spelling a student is in guides instruction to particular word study activities.

History of Stages of Spelling

Edmund Henderson described six stages of spelling in 1981, but he began to study invented spelling with his students over a decade earlier. First at the University of Delaware and later at the University of Virginia, Henderson examined the specific spelling features children used to invent their spellings in the course of writing down their ideas. He and his colleagues found that children's spelling errors were not random and that they evolved over time (Henderson, Estes & Stonecash, 1972). About the same time, in Boston, Carol Chomsky and Charles Read were also looking at preschoolers' invented spellings (Chomsky, 1971; Read, 1971, 1975). There was a natural match in interests when Read and Henderson discovered each other. The discovery of

Read's work in the linguistic arena helped Henderson and his students make sense of the invented spellings they had been collecting. Henderson and Read explored and identified the common errors students make as they learn more about the orthography. Subsequently, these patterns of spelling errors have been observed across many groups of students, from preschoolers (Templeton & Spivey, 1980) through adults (Bear, Truex, & Barone, 1989; Worthy & Viise, 1993), as well as across socio-economic levels, dialects, and other alphabetic languages (Beers & Henderson, 1977; C. Gill, 1980; Stever, 1980; Temple, 1978). In addition, the phenomenon of invented spelling has subsequently been explored by a number of other researchers (e.g., Richgels, 1995; Treiman, 1985; Wilde, 1991).

By 1974, Henderson had formulated stages of spelling and orthographic knowledge. Ever since then, he and his students have refined these stages and have reworked the labels to reflect our changing understanding of the stages and to represent most appropriately what occurs at each level. The names of the stages we use in this book are descriptive of students' spelling behavior, and the names make it easier to remember the basic strategies that students use to spell:

Stages of Spelling

Preliterate
Early Letter Name
Middle and Late Letter Name
Within Word Pattern
Syllable Juncture
Derivational Constancy

Stage I: Preliterate Spelling

The emergent period of literacy development is a period of "pre's"—prereading, pretend writing, and preliterate spelling. In emergent reading, children pretend to read by rehearsing familiar story books and by reciting well known poems and jingles by heart. Likewise, emergent readers pretend to write. They may scribble or write in letter-like forms with all the seriousness and vigor of a stenographer. Their spelling may range from random marks to legitimate letters bearing no relationship to sound. Because of this lack of correspondence to sound, however, this stage of developmental orthographic knowledge is decidedly **preliterate.** The characteristics of this stage are presented in Figure 2–2.

Preliterate writing, like scribbles, does not meet the usual requirement that a written text have a direct correspondence to spoken language and that it be "rereadable." While there is great power to a picture, writing is different from a picture. Writing is based on oral language and the thoughts we can talk about.

We call what children write **graphs.** These graphs are not pictures, and this preliterate writing is non-phonetic; there are no *sound-symbol correspondences*. The size of the graph may be related to the length of the text, but there is no single match between the graphs and the sounds.

Preliterate spelling may be divided into a series of steps or landmarks. At the beginning of this stage, students produce large scribbles which are pretty much drawings. The movement may be circular, and children may tell a story while they draw. At the earliest points in this stage, there are no designs that look like letters, and the writing is not much different from a drawing. The marks are merely scribbles on the page. As you can see in Figure 2–3, the child has drawn large circles and called it writing. There is little order to the direction in the writing; it goes up, down, and around, willy-nilly.

Preliterate
Spellers:
   Scribble
   Write in letter-
   like forms

Gradually, and especially when they are sitting next to other children who write letters, and about the time they are able to copy their own names, children in the Preliterate stage begin to use letters and something that looks like script. And about the time they are able to draw "tadpoles" for people, they acquire the convention of **directionality** (left to right in English).

FIGURE 2–2 Characteristics of Preliterate Stage Spelling

	What Students Do Correctly	What They Use But Confuse	What Is Absent
Early	✦ Write on the page ✦ Hold the writing implement	✦ Drawing and scribbling for writing	✦ Sound-symbol correspondence ✦ Directionality
Middle	✦ Horizontal movement across page ✦ Clear distinction between writing & drawing ✦ Use lines & dots for writing ✦ Letter-like forms	✦ Use letters, numbers, and letter-like forms ✦ Writing may wrap from right to left at the end of a line	✦ Sound-symbol correspondence
Late	✦ Consistent directionality ✦ Use some letter-sound match	✦ Substitute letters which sound, feel, and look alike: B/p, D/b	✦ Complete sound-symbol correspondences ✦ Consistent spacing between words

FIGURE 2–3 Early Preliterate Writing

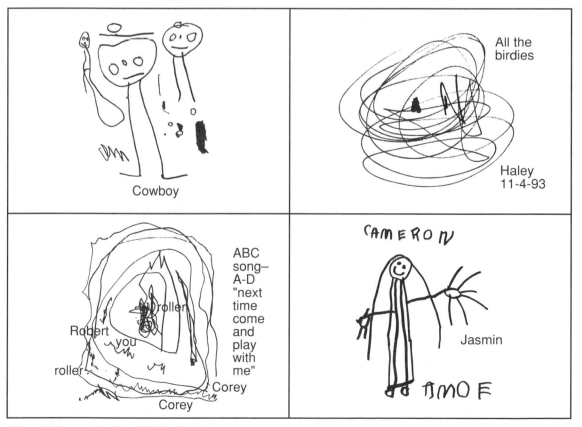

Cowboy

All the birdies

Haley 11-4-93

ABC song– A-D "next time come and play with me"

Robert you roller Corey Corey

CAMERON

Jasmin

AMO F

Adapted with permission from Bloodgood (1995).

Throughout this stage, children begin to learn letters, and particularly the letters in their own names. The writing by Carly, presented in Figure 2–4, is characteristic of a child in the middle of the Preliterate stage of spelling. When asked to spell a series of spelling words, she spelled the words by using the letters she knew best—the letters in her name. She is beginning to use letters to represent words, but there is no sound-symbol correspondence between what she writes and the sounds of the word. Many Preliterate spelling children develop a special relationship with the letters in their names as one of their first forays into the alphabet. As another example, there is Lee, who, upon entering pre-school, noticed that other children had names that used some of the same letters which make up her name. Perplexed and somewhat annoyed, she pointed to the letters that were also in her name. At that moment for Lee, it did not seem possible or fair that others should have some of her letters: "Does everyone else have an *e* too?" she asked.

Children in the Preliterate stage also begin to see the letters in their names in environmental print. Walking around the grocery store, Lee pointed

> Preliterate children learn directionality.

FIGURE 2–4 Middle Preliterate Writing

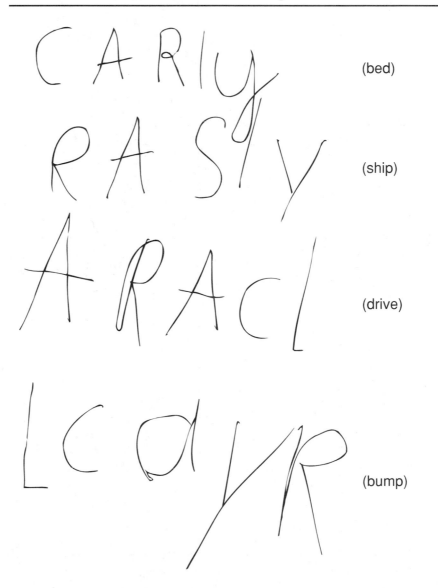

(bed)

(ship)

(drive)

(bump)

to the box of Cheer detergent and said, "Look Mommy, there's my name." At the ages of three and four, whenever Lee saw a word with two *c*'s in it, she said that that was her name. What many children do at this stage is make a simple match between letters across words. The principle that the letters in the alphabet represent sound is not yet something that Preliterate children understand.

Gradually, and as children are encouraged to write and draw their stories, they begin to tell you or write down prominent phonetic features—especially the initial consonants—of a word or two. Toward the end of Preliterate spelling, children become more interested in letters and sounds, and they may even start to memorize some words and write them over and over again; words like *no, Mom,* and *love* top the list.

Children in the Preliterate spelling stage begin to recognize the most basic visual characteristics of written text: that writing moves from left to right, top to bottom, and that the writing is somehow related to what they say. As with Lee and her own name, Preliterate spellers see simple visual patterns which letters make. Throughout most of the Preliterate stage, children do not know about letter-sound correspondences; at best, they may make a few letter-sound matches. The movement from this stage to the next stage hinges on learning the alphabetic principle: letters represent sound, and words can be segmented into sounds.

Students acquire a basic understanding of the alphabetic principle as demonstrated by their ability to segment syllables by sound. (The ability to divide syllables into individual sounds is called **phonemic segmentation.**) This becomes evident in **phonemic segmentation activities,** when students at the end of Preliterate spelling can say with some consistency that there are three sounds in a single syllable word which begins and ends with a consonant. In spelling and word study activities, students who have recently learned the alphabetic principle begin to compare words by their initial sounds and basic rhyming schemes.

There is a natural caution about heavy-handed phonic lessons which are not based on the students' developmental lead. Programs that expect *all* students to memorize, recognize, and produce the initial sounds of words can in fact be destructive and work *against* children's growth in literacy. The most teachers need to do with phonics during the Preliterate stage is to teach children to recognize and write the letters of the alphabet and to play with the sounds in words. When Preliterate children are exposed to directed instruction that *is* developmentally appropriate, their writing reflects this influence—and this signals the beginning of the end of the Preliterate stage of spelling. With a fairly stable knowledge of the alphabet, children analyze sounds in words. You will see in Chapter Five that toward the end of the Preliterate stage, students are introduced to sorts in which they categorize words by the way they sound. In many sound sort activities, students use picture cards to categorize words. Following many sound sorts, students draw pictures of words with the same sound. Letter sound study focuses on initial consonants through initial consonant sorts. In other word study activities, students play with the sound of simple rhyming patterns.

Stage II: Letter Name Spelling

The next stage of literacy development includes the beginning of both reading and writing. Children achieve a speech-to-print match and begin to read predictable pattern books, rhymes, and jingles. The familiar language patterns of these materials support students as they try to make the speech-print match. They use a finger to point to words lest they get off-track and lose the speech-to-print correspondence. Like their reading, their beginning writing is slow and disfluent. The writing of beginners is not only word-by-word, but sound-by-sound as well. They laboriously match letter names to the sounds they are trying to write. Because the beginning readers use the literal names of the letters when they invent their spelling they are called **Letter Name** spellers (Read, 1975). Letter Name spellers spell in a linear, sound-by-sound fashion, just as they read and write.

We have divided our discussion of the Letter Name stage into two parts: The first part covers the early phase of the Letter Name stage when students first write syllabically and then by spelling the first and last sounds. The second part of the stage spans the middle and late Letter Name periods when students begin to use a vowel in each syllable, and then begin to spell short vowel patterns conventionally.

Early Letter Name Spelling

Students in the early Letter Name stage are Beginning readers. They have recently acquired a "concept of word" (Morris, 1981, 1993)—how the stream of speech corresponds to the printed word—and they have begun to learn some sight words. Their choice of reading materials is limited to simple pattern stories and brief individual dictations like the one-sentence dictations written on Group Experience Charts in small groups.

The characteristics of this orthographic stage are summarized in Figure 2–5. What is crucial about this stage is that students use the alphabetic principle to spell. Students in the very early part of the Letter Name stage make letter-sound matches between the letter names of the alphabet and sounds in the words by writing syllabically, using one letter to represent the predominant sound for that word.

Early Letter Name children apply the alphabetic principle primarily to consonants. Often, students spell the first sound and then the last sound of single syllable words. For example, *bake* may be spelled *B* or *BK* by a student early in the Letter Name stage. The middle elements of syllables, the vowels, are usually omitted. Modern psycholinguistic research has shown that consonants

FIGURE 2–5 Characteristics of Early Letter Name Stage Spelling

	What Students Do Correctly	**What They Use But Confuse**	**What Is Absent**
Early	✦ Write syllabically spelling most salient feature of the syllable or word ✦ Uses several letters of alphabet	✦ Will substitute letters based on point of articulation ✦ Y for *when,* J for *drive*	✦ Beginning & end of syllables ✦ Vowels in syllables ✦ Some spacing between words
Middle	✦ Directionality ✦ Uses most letters of the alphabet ✦ Clear letter-sound correspondences	✦ Will substitute letters based on point of articulation	✦ Vowels in syllables ✦ Some spacing between words
Late	✦ Uses most beginning & ending consonants ✦ Clear letter-sound correspondences	✦ Continues to substitute consonants based on point of articulation ✦ BD for *bed,* YN or WN for *when,* SP for *ship,* JRF for *drive* ✦ Uses some vowels	✦ Consistent use of vowels ✦ Consonant blends & digraphs

are the "noise" and vowels the "music" of language (Crystal, 1987). Early Letter Name spellers attend to the noise and use the alphabetic principle to find letter names in the alphabet to spell the most prominent features in words—the consonants.

When students use the alphabetic principle, they find matches between letters and the spoken word by how the sound is made or articulated in the mouth. In our teacher training, most of us have learned about the sound system of articulation, and the work in spelling development has shown how important articulation is to children's spelling. It has been fascinating to learn that, during this stage, students use information about how sounds *feel* to make choices about what letters to use in their first spelling. The spelling of the first sounds in words like **dr**um, **v**apor, and **b**ump illustrate how articulation is used to spell.

J for *dr* & *F* for *v*. Many children substitute a J for the consonant blend *dr* and spell *drip* as JP. There is a good reason why students choose *j*: *dr* and *j* are made in the same way, except that the /dr/ sound is made with the tongue against the palate (the top plate of the mouth), and the /j/ sound is not made with the tongue on the roof of the mouth. A less obvious example is the substitution of an *f* for a *v* in words like *drive*. Like the *dr* and the *j*, the /f/ and /v/ sounds are made in pretty much the same way. Given that *f* is a much more familiar letter, students choose this familiar letter to represent the /v/. A bit of linguistic analysis on your part will show you how similar the sounds are: Choosing an *f* for a *v* is a logical mistake given the limited experience of the student in this stage of development. (A student's relative experience will influence choice; for example, a child named Virginia would perhaps learn the /v/ sound first and, as a result, begin *favorite* with a V.)

b/p Confusions. During this stage, students make similar errors based on the similarity between how sounds are made. For example, students at this stage may substitute a /b/ sound for a /p/ sound because they are made in the same way except for one feature—in making the /p/ sound, air comes out of the mouth in an explosive way, whereas with the /b/, there is no accompanying explosion of air.

Middle and Late Letter Name Spelling

Compared to children in the early Letter Name stage, Letter Name spellers are less hesitant in their reading, and by the end of the Letter Name stage, students can read many texts, even simple chapter books.

The general picture for reading throughout this stage is one of disfluency and reading aloud. As is discussed in more detail in Chapter Six, beginning readers sound disfluent, word-by-word, and unexpressive. In addition, they read aloud when they read to themselves, and they often fingerpoint as they read. They need support in their reading. A variety of support techniques and materials—dictations, pattern books and rhyme—are used so that these beginners can use their memory and understanding of the rhythm of language for support as they read through simple texts. What is unique about the middle and late part of this stage is that vowels are used to represent the middle vowel in syllables (see Figure 2–6). Students who use a vowel in each stressed syllable are solidly in the Middle Letter Name stage. For example, to spell the word *bake*, Middle Letter Name spellers use the letter name of this long vowel and spell *bake* as BAK. During this stage, students begin to see the differences between consonants and vowels, and they see that each syllable must have a vowel.

Reading behaviors of Letter Name Spellers:
✦ Disfluent reading
✦ Reading aloud
✦ Fingerpointing

Middle Letter Name Spellers: CAK for *cake* Concept of Word

FIGURE 2–6 Characteristics of Middle and Late Letter Name Stage Spelling

	What Students Do Correctly	What They Use But Confuse	What Is Absent
Early	✦ Most initial & final consonants ✦ A vowel in most syllables	✦ Uses letter name for vowels: CAM for *came,* LIK for *like* ✦ Substitutes letter name closest in point of articulation for short vowels: NAT for *net,* SEP for *ship*	✦ Long vowel markers ✦ Vowels in unstressed syllables: SISTR for *sister* ✦ Most consonant blends & digraphs
Middle	✦ Initial & final consonants ✦ Frequently occurring short vowel words	✦ Includes some consonant blends & digraphs	✦ Preconsonantal nasals: BOB for *bump*
Late	✦ All of the above plus: ✦ Regular short vowel patterns ✦ Most consonant blends & digraphs ✦ Preconsonantal nasals	✦ Regular pattern for a low frequency short vowel: COT for *caught* ✦ Spells some common long vowel words: *time, hope*	

Students in the middle of the Letter Name stage focus on vowels, and there is substantial growth in how they use short vowels. As you will see in the word study activities in Chapter Six, students study short vowel patterns before they study long vowels. Teachers know that attention is not directed to the vowel digraphs, or "silent e" words, (as in **beat and rate**) until students can spell words like *bet* and *rat* easily without conscious contemplation.

Letter Name spellers also use a phonetic spelling strategy in which they focus more on the letter-sound matches and less on the visual patterns. For example, in a difficult word like *caught,* early Letter Name spellers spell *caught* as CT or KT. Now, in the middle of the Letter Name stage, students insert a vowel and often spell *caught* as COT. To ask students to focus on <u>aught</u>, a difficult and infrequent visual pattern, is an overload, and in fact this vowel will be spelled correctly later on after some of the easier long vowel patterns are learned.

By the middle of the Letter Name stage, spellers have learned that syllables have vowels. They begin to understand the closed syllable, the Consonant-Vowel-Consonant unit (CVC). They will not necessarily know these terms, but they do show evidence of their implicit knowledge through their invented spellings. Over the course of the Letter Name stage, students make the match between short vowel sounds and the standard or correct spelling. With plenty of reading, they also learn the exceptional but frequent odd spellings of words like s**aid** and c**ome**. In addition, they learn about initial consonant blends and digraphs in English, and by the end of this stage, they are able to represent most initial consonant digraphs and blends correctly.

The CVC pattern is the fundamental short vowel pattern.

One of the hallmarks that tells us that a student is moving from the Letter Name stage to the next stage, **Within Word Pattern spelling,** is the correct spelling of words with m's or n's like *bu**m**p* or *bu**n**ch.* As you may know, n's and m's are referred to as **nasals.** They are made by air passing through the nasal passage and then by closing off the passage with the **uvula.** These nasals are called **preconsonantal nasals** because they occur in front of another consonant. Henderson recognized that the correct spelling of the preconsonantal nasal was a reliable and important event. This event is presented in the summary chart for this stage in Figure 2–7.

FIGURE 2–7 Characteristics of the Within Word Pattern Stage of Spelling

	What Students Do Correctly	What They Use But Confuse	What Is Absent
Early	✦ Initial & final consonants ✦ Consonant blends & digraphs ✦ Regular short vowel patterns & preconsonantal nasals ✦ Good accuracy on r-controlled single-syllable short vowel words: fur, bird ✦ Some infrequently used short vowels & frequently used long vowel words: like, see	✦ Long vowel markers: SNAIK/snake	✦ Consonant doubling: POPING, STOPED
Middle	✦ All of the above plus: ✦ Slightly more than half of the long vowel words in single syllable words: hike, nail	✦ Long vowel markers: nite/night ✦ Consonant patterns: SMOCK/smoke ✦ Inventive substitutions in frequent unstressed syllable patterns: TEACHAUR/teacher ✦ -ed and other common inflections: BATID/batted	
Late	✦ All of the above plus: ✦ Single syllable long vowel words ✦ May know some common Latin suffixes: inspection	✦ Low frequency long vowel words: HIEGHT/height ✦ -ed and other common inflections ✦ Represents some common Latin suffixes phonetically: ATENSHUN/attention	✦ Consonant doubling ✦ e-drop: AMAZZING/amazing

Stage III: Within Word Pattern Spelling

This third stage of spelling development occurs in synchrony with the Transitional stages of reading and writing. As described in Figure 2–1, Transitional learners approach fluency in both reading and writing. They move away from a literal application of the alphabetic principle and begin to chunk elements of written language structures: Their reading changes from word-by-word to phrasal reading fluency. With easy, independent-level material, students stop fingerpointing, and when they read to themselves, they usually read silently. From the beginning to the end of the Transitional stage, students move from needing support materials and techniques to being able to pick up many different texts and reading them independently—from the Sunday comics to easy chapter books such as *Freckle Juice,* (Blume), *Superfudge,* (Blume), and *Ramona the Pest* (Cleary). Likewise, students execute *writing* more quickly and with greater fluency. In *spelling,* Transitional readers move away from the literal application of letter names to include patterns—letter sequences which relate to sound and meaning. This stage of development has been called **Within Word Pattern** (Henderson, 1990). Knowledge of within word patterns affords greater efficiency and speed in reading, writing, and spelling.

As the name of this stage indicates, Within Word Pattern spellers take a closer look at the vowel within syllables, and they begin to examine patterns. As can be seen in the synchrony model illustrated in Figure 2–1, the Within Word Pattern stage matches the Transitional period of reading and writing. The Transitional stage can be a fragile period in a child's literacy development; with adequate time spent reading materials at independent and instructional levels, students take off with fluency and motivation—a positive trajectory. Without such practice, however, or if too much time is spent struggling with materials that are too difficult, students' growth at this stage is stunted, and they lose motivation.

As can be seen in Figure 2–7, the Within Word Pattern stage begins when students can correctly spell most single-syllable short vowel words. They also spell consonant blends and digraphs correctly and can read low-frequency short vowel words which they cannot spell. For example, Within Word Pattern spellers can easily read a word like *caught,* but as noted earlier, they will spell it as COT. The key factor during this stage is that *students experiment with long vowel patterns.*

Because students are experimenting with long vowels during this stage, word study is centered on long vowel patterns. Children in this stage have a sight reading vocabulary of probably 200 to 400 words. Whereas Letter Name children pulled words from their Word Banks for word study (see Chapter 6), students in the Within Word Pattern stage will work with words provided by the teacher. An important new feature during this stage is that students develop **word study notebooks** (see Chapter 7) in which they enter groups of words which they have sorted or which they have found to follow particular patterns.

At this point in their reading and writing development, students begin to think more abstractly. They begin to talk about what a story has meant to them, and the discussions of texts move easily beyond generalities and summaries (Barone, 1990). As they examine orthography, Within Word Pattern spellers show a similar level of abstraction in their thinking. They begin to work with the more abstract patterns of long vowels. In the Letter Name stage, a student's strategy is a *linear* one; each letter stands for a sound, and for the most part, there is a one-to-one correspondence between sounds and letters. During the Within Word Pattern stage, the "code" is expanded to include patterns for long vowels, like the CVVC pattern (n**ai**l, b**ea**k), the CVCe pattern (n**a**m**e**, t**i**m**e**) and the CVV pattern (h**ay,** t**ie**).

There is a concrete visual differentiation among many long and short vowel patterns. Although just three sounds occur in single-syllable long vowel words, students indicate long vowels by using *four* letters in their invented spelling. In the Within Word Pattern stage, students no longer assume a strict rule of one-to-one correspondences and develop a sense that patterns do not always have to be consistent with sound, as in, for instance, *have, come,* and *some,* which do not fit the long vowel pattern. With changes in the ability to reflect and to use abstract patterns, students also begin to think more about their spoken vocabulary. They can play with words in meaning sorts in the same way that they may arrange baseball cards. To foster this analysis, students keep lists of words arranged by topic. In this way, students' interest in vocabulary is easily expanded upon in the next stage of spelling development.

The focus for instruction is on what students are "using but confusing" at that moment, so teachers involve students in exploring long vowel patterns. Students begin with one vowel and spend some time examining the various patterns of that long vowel. After this thorough examination, they examine similar patterns in another long vowel. Comparisons are made across the two long vowel patterns; for example, the CVCe patterns in *name* and *line*. After

Within Word
Pattern Spellers:
Four letters for
three sounds:
NALE for *nail*

these comparisons, students examine some of the special patterns for the vowel being studied, as in *climb* and *kind* when they study the long i. Throughout the word study, students record these categorizations in word study notebooks.

Many of the words students learn to read and spell come from seeing these words frequently as they read and write. Students learn to read words they see frequently and whose patterns they can understand (Beck & McKeown, 1991). Students develop an appreciation for pattern with experience. During the Within Word Pattern stage, there is overlapping cognitive growth in written responses, writing fluency, and problem-solving. Within Word Pattern spellers work with the orthography and with the writing system at a more abstract level than the Letter Name spellers. The study of common single-syllable patterns is the focus throughout the Within Word Pattern stage. Students are not ready to study two-syllable word patterns unless they clearly and easily understand the differences between long and short vowel patterns.

| Long vowel patterns are more *abstract* than short vowel patterns.

Stages IV and V: Syllable Juncture and Derivational Constancy Spelling

The synchrony of literacy development is also evident in the last two stages of development where Syllable Juncture and Derivational Constancy stages correspond to the Intermediate and Specialized stages of reading and writing. If you refer back to Figure 2–1, you can see that Intermediate and Specialized learners read fluently. Their word recognition is automatic, and because of this, their minds are free to think as rapidly as they can read. This period of literacy development is generally accompanied by the ability to think abstractly. Intermediate and specialized writers are also fluent writers. The content of their writing displays complex analysis and interpretation. As noted in Figure 2–8, in spelling, these readers grapple with meaning units such as prefixes, suffixes, base words, and roots. Intermediate readers negotiate **affixation** (adding prefixes and suffixes) and the conventions of preserving pattern-to-sound relationships at the place where syllables meet. Accordingly, this stage of orthographic development is called **Syllable Juncture** (Henderson & Templeton, 1986). Specialized readers encounter the specialized vocabulary of Greek and Latin origin. This stage of orthographic knowledge is known as **Derivational Constancy** because this is when students examine how the derivations and spellings of parts of words remain constant across different words (Templeton, 1983).

The last two stages are presented together because many of their features overlap. For example, in both stages, there is an interesting interaction between *pattern* and *meaning,* and meaning has increasingly greater power. The level of meaning found in the Syllable Juncture stage is often centered on syntax or grammar and affixation. The meaning levels in the Derivational Constancy stage often focus on word roots and on the classical origins of polysyllabic words.

As Figure 2–1 shows, the reading stages which are in synchrony with the Syllable Juncture and Derivational Constancy stages of spelling are the Intermediate and Specialized stages. Intermediate readers read most texts with good accuracy and a good reading rate, both orally and silently. For these students, success in reading and understanding is related to familiarity and experience with the topic being discussed.

Students in the Intermediate stage acquire, through plenty of practice, a repertoire of reading styles. The same is true for writing. Intermediate readers orally and silently read most texts with accuracy and a fluent reading rate. Success in reading during this stage is related to familiarity and experience with the topic being discussed. Specialized readers have a broader experience base which allows them to make finer and finer distinctions in the use of reading styles among various texts. The same picture is evidenced in writing development. With purpose and practice, students develop and master a variety of writing styles.

During these two stages, students' reading and speaking vocabularies grow along with their concept development. The research in upper-level word study and development has highlighted the importance of reading in vocabulary development (Templeton, 1976). From adolescence on, except perhaps for slang, most of the new vocabulary students learn comes from reading. The meaning connection is central to this stage, and new vocabulary reflects the new subject areas which students explore (Templeton, 1992).

In spelling and orthographic development, these two stages have much in common: Students' orthographic development grows primarily from wide exposure to texts in new areas of study, what can be thought of as breadth, or from deeper excursions into familiar topics. As can be seen in Figure 2–8, both stages entail focus on multi-syllabic words, and they both are concerned with meaning. At this point in their development, students understand single-syllable word patterns; there's hardly a single syllable word they cannot read or spell.

FIGURE 2–8 Characteristics of the Syllable Juncture and Derivational Constancy Stages of Spelling

	What Students Do Correctly	What They Use But Confuse	What Is Absent
Early	✦ Initial & final consonants ✦ Consonant blends & digraphs ✦ Short vowel patterns ✦ Long vowel patterns ✦ -ed & most common inflections	✦ Consonant doubling ✦ Long vowel patterns in accented syllables: PERAIDING/parading ✦ Reduced vowel in unaccented syllables: CIRCUL/circle ✦ doubling + e-drop: AMAZZING/amazing ✦ Common Latin suffixes: ATTENSHUN/attention	✦ Occasional deletion of middle syllables ✦ Assimilated prefixes ✦ Root constancies in derivationally related pairs
Middle	✦ All of the above plus: ✦ Consonant doubling: stopping ✦ Doubling + e-drop: amazing ✦ Common Latin suffixes: attention	✦ Assimilated prefixes: ACOMODATE/accommodate ✦ Vowel alternations in derivationally related pairs: COMPUSITION/composition ✦ Consonant alternations in derivationally related pairs: SPACIAL/spatial	
Late	✦ All of the above plus: ✦ Long vowel patterns in accented syllables ✦ Doubling + e-drop (except where overlaps with assimilated prefixes) ✦ Most vowel & consonant alternations	✦ Same as above	

During these stages, students become aware of and develop the *spelling/meaning connection* (Templeton, 1983).

The Syllable Juncture stage represents a new point in word analysis when students consider where syllables meet—their **juncture.** In the previous stages, students could scan a single syllable word and come to quick closure as to where a word began and ended. In the analysis of single-syllable words, it was observed that when students look at words, they move from the first sound in the syllable and to the last sound and finally to the middle of the single-syllable word. The analysis of multi-syllabic words is more complicated, for there is more than one perceptual unit. For example, a two-syllable word like *clopped* may be divided into *clop(p)* and *-ed.* For easy words, and especially where the text gives plenty of contextual clues, this analysis is done at an unconscious or tacit level. The analysis of unfamiliar multi-syllabic words is more complicated, and to make the meaning connection, the students divide words into their syllables and then see how the syllables fit together.

In word study throughout the Syllable Juncture stage, students examine two-syllable words. Word study in the Syllable Juncture stage begins with the consonant doubling principle. A frequently occurring word like *stopped* may require very little processing time; recognition of this frequent word may be close to automatic. However, a word like *clopped* may call for slightly more analysis.

It is often at this time that teachers and students study plurals where the link between syntax and spelling is also obvious. They examine the various spelling changes for the plural suffix: *funnies, foxes.* Towards the middle of this stage, students come to see the convention of *-tion* and *-sion* as affixes for changing verbs into nouns. They also study other syntactic and semantic affixes like *-er, -or, -ian,* and more. Later, they look at less familiar endings like pat**ience,** broch**ure,** and correspond**ence.**

As word study proceeds in this stage, the examination of accent becomes a more central interest, and the meaning connection is made with numerous language systems. For example, notice how a change in accent on two syllables can affect the word's syntactic and semantic function:

con tract   "You signed the contract for a year."
       "He may contract the disease."

Beyond consonant doubling for suffixes (*-ed* and *-ing*), students examine consonant doubling in words like *settle* and *success,* and *occasion.* Teachers aim to take students from the naive view that the "spellings just look right" to a more metacognitive analysis of the junctures at which consonants are doubled. When students understand why some consonants are doubled, they begin to think about and study the meaning of prefixes. Students at this point have moved into the Derivational Constancy spelling stage.

After the common prefixes and suffixes are examined, students begin to examine the meaning of bases and roots. This is when the study of derivational morphology begins with students in the Derivational Constancy spelling stage. For example, it is not a big jump from seeing what *trans-* means from exemplars like *transportation, transport, transplant,* and *transmit* to looking deeper at some of the basic English bases like *ten* in **ten**nis, **ten**dency, **ten**et, **ten**ant, pre**tend,** and on and on.

In word study, teachers show students how to move back and forth between the spelling of a word and its meaning. Students begin to see how spelling tells them about meaning and how pronunciation can blur meaning. Students continue to work by analogy, moving back and forth between looking for exemplars and reflections on what the commonalities mean. A student who misspells *competition* as COMPOTITION may see the correct spelling more

Syllable Juncture Spellers:
  BARBAR for *barber*
  ALOW for *allow*
  Examine two-syllable words

Derivational Constancy Spellers:
  ✦ Spelling-meaning connection
  ✦ Examine Greek and Latin derivations

easily by going back to a base or root, as in *compete* where the long vowel gives a clear clue to spelling; and as noted earlier, there is *composition* spelled COM-PUSITION clarified by the long *o* in *compose*.

One of the exciting aspects about word study sessions at these advanced stages is that teachers do not always know the meaning connections themselves, and so there is a freshness that comes with the word study explorations. Here, word study is managed with the assumption that together students and teachers can explore the histories of words and that words are interesting. Word study sessions throughout these stages can begin with this basic question: "Did you find any interesting words in your reading?" And so, together the group is off exploring, studying the words students bring to the session. Teachers show their students that they themselves are excited by what can be learned about words, language, and ideas. As you will see, the word study activities in Chapter Eight are ordered in terms of development, but there is some flexibility in the exact order in which the affixes and roots are studied.

As in all word study, one of the foremost aims of word study at these last two stages is to teach students how to examine words. Sometimes the words that students examine are familiar but fascinating in their histories, and as the students study words, a new dimension is added to their vocabularies. As an example, growth in vocabulary knowledge was increased as the result of the following word study that ensued when a student brought the word *panacea* to a word study session.

This word is uncommon, and the student brought the word to the group because the meaning of the word was unclear to her. What was fascinating was how the word study came around to a simple word—*company*. The students and the teacher could see that both words had *pan* in them, and over the course of the session, students began to wonder if *pan* represented the same meaning in both words. Subsequently, they found out that there are four different meanings of *pan*, and that *company* can literally mean "to break bread with," where the *pan* in *company* means bread: simply stated, *com-* means "with," and *pan* in this word means "bread". At the beginning of this word study session, no one knew that *company* would be studied or that such a charming word story would appear.

| The Derivational Constancy spelling stage lasts a lifetime. | The history of the English language has many wonderful stories to tell; words can be our companions. The study of the history of the English language takes on more importance during the Derivational Constancy stage, and word study helps students to understand the meanings behind the vocabularies in specialized areas of study. |

The History of English Spelling and Children's Learning of English Spelling: Some Intriguing Parallels

We have been referring to the role of the history of English as it has impacted the development of the spelling system. We have also noted that students develop knowledge of the system in a manner that parallels this historical development. We hope you might be intrigued just enough to explore the historical foundation further—and to involve your students as well. We wish to highlight the parallels between historical development and individual development for two reasons: First, this comparison serves to emphasize the complexity that learners must negotiate; second, the comparison helps *us* as teachers appreciate the wonderful and instructive terrain that our students—and *we*—can explore.

The English language began about 450 A.D. when the Angles, Jutes, and Saxons—three tribes that lived in Northern Europe—invaded the British Isles. These invaders were a primitive lot, known to practice human sacrifice. The in-

Old English:
Begins
approximately
450 A.D.

vaders, however, brought the beginnings of the English language with them—what we now refer to as Old English—as well as the name by which the later English nation would be called, *Angle*land. Eventually the invaders settled down to more peaceful activities—primarily farming and raising livestock. Much of their language included words that had to do with these pursuits (words such as *sheep, dirt, tree,* and *earth*), and many of their words would come to constitute the most frequently-used words in the English language today. In fact, *all* of the 100 most frequent words in contemporary English come from Old English.

Around 600 A.D. St. Augustine arrived in Britain, and with him came Christianity and many Latin words associated with the church. Monasteries were established, eventually becoming cultural and intellectual centers. Because of this influence, English began to be written down, the first of the European languages to do so. Britain became the center of learning in Europe, providing a multitude of books for the rest of the Continent. Throughout the seventh and eighth centuries A.D., Anglo-Saxon England rose to cultural heights unmatched in Europe.

Another invasion was to interrupt this development, however. In the late eighth century, the Vikings landed and began a process of conquest that lasted well into the following century. Their arrival brought a large segment of Danish vocabulary into English (for example *want, skill, raise*). Their conquests were eventually halted by Alfred the Great, a legendary figure in English history. Among other things, Alfred encouraged the translation of books into English and instituted a widespread literacy campaign.

By the end of the first millenium A.D. the English language had grown over the course of some 500 years in its vocabulary, its structure, and its capacity to express meaning. It was the language of the intellect in medieval Europe. Suddenly, however, English as a written language practically disappeared for almost two hundred years. Yet another invasion, this time from the northwest of France, brought radical changes to the English language. In 1066, William the Conqueror invaded and brought the French language with him. This is the point from which most scholars date the beginning of Middle English.

Middle English:
Begins when
William the
Conqueror
invades in 1066

Norman French was used at court and in legal affairs. For years after the invasion, however, there was little intermingling with English. But with the passing of time, Old English and Norman French came together, and by the early 1200's, what we call Middle English began to appear. The French legacy remains in the English we speak today: some 40% of Modern English is from French (for example *nourish, commence, interrogate*). By the 1300's the demand for books increased because of the increased availabilty of paper, and with the introduction of the printing press in England in 1476, the market was even greater. About the same time, the Renaissance had brought a rediscovery of the Classical languages, Greek and Latin. Many new words would soon be created from Greek and Latin word elements—these elements lent themselves to combination (as we'll see in Chapter Eight)—and this was particularly useful because the "Voyages of Discovery" of the late fifteenth and sixteenth centuries introduced so many new objects and ideas that needed to be named.

Spelling, however, had become a topsy-turvy affair. It had been fairly standard by the time of the Norman invasion, but the influx of French began to change that. Later on—with the spread of books—the professional scribes, and later the printers, had quite a degree of flexibility in how they spelled words. It would not be until the middle of the 1700's—the period of English we call Modern English, that English spelling would finally be standardized. This would be the result of the publication of Samuel Johnson's *Dictionary of the English Language* in 1755.

Before we leave Middle English, however, we should note an important phenomenon that would have implications for the way we spell English today and for children's learning of conventional English spelling. This phenomenon is called the *Great Vowel Shift*. While it would take a great deal of space to explain why it occurred, we can look at its effects more easily: In a nutshell, the long and short vowel sounds that a letter represented in Middle English changed by the time Modern English began (around 1500). In Middle English, for example, the long and short sounds for the letter *e* were ā and ě ; the long and short sounds for the letter *i* were ē and ĭ. One of the effects of the Great Vowel Shift was to change the long vowel sound of these letters to our present-day ē for the letter *e* and ī for the letter *i;* the short-vowel sounds of these letters, however, stayed as they were in Middle English. (Later, in Chapter 6, we will examine children's invented spellings during the Letter Name phase of development, and we will see that at some point they match up long and short vowel sounds very much as they were matched in Old English.)

Scholars divide Modern English into two periods: Early Modern English (1500–1700) and Contemporary English (1700–present). We have already noted that, because of the Renaissance, Greek and Latin came to influence English; this continued even more intensively during Early Modern English. While new words were created from Greek and Latin elements, many other existing words came to be *re*spelled to reflect what scholars believed were their historical roots in Latin and Greek. For example, *dette* was respelled *debt* (related to Latin "debitum"); *sithe / sythe* was respelled *scythe* (the *c* was inserted to reflect the Latin "cisorium" meaning "to cut").

Early Modern English: New words created from Greek and Latin word parts

The rich language heritage of Early Modern English was used to its fullest extent in the writings of Shakespeare in the later sixteenth and early seventeenth centuries; indeed, these writings have profoundly influenced the nature and the vocabulary of English. During the time of Shakespeare's life the English language in fact grew at an incredible rate, more so than at any time before or since. It was also during this time that the first *spelling* books appeared, and they helped to contribute to the standardization of English spelling that was for the most part completed by the time of Johnson's dictionary in the middle of the eighteenth century.

In this brief overview, we have left out a number of quite fascinating bits of information. Nonetheless, we hope you have gained a general idea about the evolution of English spelling over the last 1500 years. And we hope that, throughout the rest of this text, this overview will help you appreciate the implications of the parallel between the sequence in which students learn about English spelling and the historical development of English spelling: Once children know what "words" are, they expect that spelling represents sounds in a straightforward left-to-right manner—just like it was done in Old English. Somewhat later, they learn the more complex vowel patterns—patterns that came into the language with the French language after the Norman invasion.

Children's spelling development parallels historical development.

Now let's examine this phenomenon more closely. Henderson (1990) compared the spelling strategies of Letter Name children to those of the Anglo-Saxons: both follow an alphabetic strategy. Templeton (1976) described how children in the Middle Letter Name stage categorize long and short vowels the way these vowels were categorized in early Middle English, before the Great Vowel Shift. Moreover, Letter Name children learn first the conventional spelling of short vowels—historically, it is interesting that the spellings of many short vowel words in modern English are older than the spelling of similar long vowel patterns: for example, *pet* is easier for children to spell and came in earlier than *piece; bet* is easier for children to spell and came in earlier than *beat.* (Actually, we can go even farther back—so many of the CVC patterns have their origins in the Indo-European language, the mother of over half of the world's languages, including English and almost all of the European languages.)

During the Within Word Pattern stage, students' growth in orthographic knowledge reflects the influence of French during Middle English. During the fifteenth century when scribes experimented with the spelling of different long vowels, they borrowed the *ai* from 12th century French, as in *plain* and *saint.* Also, *ea* was used to spell the vowel in words like *deal, meal,* and *meat, reason* and *ease* to distinguish the vowel sound in these words from the short *e.* By the seventeenth century, however, the original sound that *ea* represented was pronounced the same way as present-day short *e.* (Modern French preserves the sound differences in *ai* and short *e,* as in the spelling of *raison* and *aisle.*) Other examples in which spelling has stabilized but the pronunciation changed, here over 400 years old, include the spelling/pronunciation mismatch in words such as *bread, earth, great,* and *heart* (Scragg, 1974). English has also used the French grapheme *ie* in *piece, brief, relief* with the same effect.

Later still, students learn about the ways in which spelling represents *meaning* most directly, despite changes in pronunciation, as in the consistent spelling of the element *-jud-* in the words *judge*, pre*jud*ice, and ad*jud*icate. Cummings (1988) refers to this as the "semantic demand" on the spelling system, and observed that, historically, "the rise of the semantic demand . . . *is repeated in microcosm* in the development of any individual's writing and reading skills" (p. 14, emphasis added). Learners come to understand, in other words, the role and influence of the many Greek and Latin words and word elements that became a part of the spelling system during the Renaissance and into the sixteenth and seventeenth centuries.

Words—their structure and how students learn about them—are of tremendous significance in literacy development. These first two chapters have established why this is so. Now it's time to turn our attention directly to our students and determine how we can establish where they are developmentally and how we can organize our instruction to address most effectively the features of words they will need to explore.

3

Getting Started

THE ASSESSMENT OF ORTHOGRAPHIC DEVELOPMENT

At the beginning of the school year or when a new child enters the class, teachers need to know what the instructional goals should be for each student. Teachers assess to plan an effective program of word study which helps students learn to read and write. So, how do teachers learn about students' literacy development? Particularly, how do teachers learn about students' orthographic knowledge—the knowledge they have about the writing system? Teachers read and write with their students, and from reading and writing together, teachers make informal assessments of students' orthographic knowledge.

As we discussed in the previous chapter on stages of development, the guidance to plan students' word study programs comes from observing invented spellings and from these, assessing orthographic knowledge. This chapter presents a method to assess students' orthographic development throughout the year, to monitor their growth, and to plan word study instruction. The information in Box 3–1 also presents you with some practical guidelines to use as you perform your assessments.

Spelling-by-Stage Assessment

In the following writing sample of a child in kindergarten, we can learn a good deal about her developmental level. Sarah called this her first restaurant review. While it appears to be a menu, she posted it on the wall the way she had seen reviews posted in restaurants.

1 CRS KAM SAS	(First course clam sauce)
2 CRS FESH	(Second course fish)
3 CRS SAGATE	(Third course spaghetti)
4 CRS PUSH POPS	(Fourth course Push Pops)

There is so much we can learn from this writing: Sarah sees a practical use for writing, she has written quite a long and complete message, and she enjoys writing and displaying her work. She has a good grasp of how to compose a list, and she is beginning to understand menu planning.

If we concentrate on just the spelling, we see what she knows about the orthography, what she is using but confusing in English spelling, and we can make some preliminary statements about the type of word study that would be beneficial.

Box 3–1

Five Guidelines for Assessment

There are a few guidelines to keep in mind as you think about assessment and organizing instruction for word study in the classroom.

1. ***Work from a developmental model.***
   Use the developmental model in Figure 2–1 by reading from top to bottom across the literacy behaviors of reading, spelling, and writing. Look for corroborating evidence to place students' achievement somewhere along the developmental continuum. This model helps to generate expectations for students' development using an integrated literacy approach. For example, a students' reading behaviors should be in synchrony with the range of writing behaviors.

2. ***Use informal diagnostic teaching.***
   Instead of relying on standardized tests and test results reported in grade levels, use informal diagnoses and diagnostic teaching practices as part of your daily teaching. After watching students sort and write, you can determine what students are learning about the orthography. By watching while teaching, you can gather information, and based on the developmental model presented in Chapter Two, make sense of what students do in their spelling and word recognition.

   Look across a variety of literacy behaviors to understand students' development. There are many ways to observe students while you teach. In addition to the observation of students as they sort words, and spell, consider these examples:

   Teachers learn about students through their oral reading fluency and expression.

   Teachers learn about students at the beginning of the year with learning and literacy interviews, writing samples, and reader response activities.

   Throughout the year, teachers learn about students by talking with them, and by trying to solve problems together; these problems can be part of low verbal situations such as working puzzles or playing checkers, or highly verbal situations, such as Directed Reading-Thinking Activities (DRTAs).

3. ***Welcome surprises for what they say about individual children.***
   The expectations you develop by using the model illustrated in Figure 2–1 may or may not be seen in a student's performance. Expectations are one thing; what students can do and what they want to show may not match expectations based on the developmental model. The mismatches observed between reading, writing, and spelling development are most interesting, and informative.

   There are students who are out of synchrony in their development. This is true for the notoriously bad speller who is a capable reader. When there is indeed a mismatch between reading and spelling, you can help a student improve his or her spelling and regather a developmental synchrony by pinpointing the stage of spelling development and then by providing developmentally rich instruction which addresses the student's needs. Using this assessment and the developmental model, you can develop individual educational plans for students, and plan for small group instruction accordingly.

4. ***Do not assess students at their frustration levels.***
   The frustration level is the level at which students are very far from being correct in their work, and where even your assistance would

Guidelines for
Assessment:
♦ Use developmental
  model
♦ Use informal
  diagnostic teaching
♦ Welcome surprises
♦ Don't assess at
  frustration level
♦ Start with what
  students can do

not be sufficient for them to learn. While there may be times when you dip into students' frustration level, this is no place to collect meaningful information about development. You should take a common sense approach here: How well does anyone do when under extreme pressure to perform, and, in this case, when the speller knows that he or she is not doing well? And how realistic a reflection of proficiency is this performance anyway? Part of the frustration a student experiences comes from not having the structural, cognitive background to support a reasonable guess. Clearly, in spelling, students' frustration work can put you off the developmental track, for so often work performed at the frustration level contains a fair amount of "spitting at the page," where students spell by plugging in letters.

5. ***Start with what students can do and track progress over time.*** In the diagnostic process, focus on what students' errors reflect about what students know. For example, if a student spells *peat* as PEET, you will know that she has moved beyond the simple linear approach to spelling; otherwise she would have spelled *peat* as PET.

The assessment must be conducted on a schedule that is helpful. Assess informally throughout the year to track progress and help explain students' development to the next teacher. To most successfully assess your students' development and progress you should conduct informal spelling assessments three or four times over a school year.

Three steps in
spelling-by stage
assessment:
♦ Collect spelling
  sample
♦ Analyze for
  stage
♦ Plan
  instruction and
  monitor growth

What do we learn about her orthographic knowledge from this sample? We see that she has learned many of the consonants and that she is experimenting with short vowels. The substitutions are entirely predictable given the recent research on spelling development (Templeton & Bear, 1992a). Other than in the word *course,* she has placed a vowel in each syllable. The letter *R* in CRS is a natural influence at this point in development, and it is common for students who are also learning that short vowels will be impacted by the *r.* Given the sequence of development presented in the previous chapter and summarized at the end of this chapter, we would say that Sarah is in the Letter Name stage of spelling.

At the beginning of Chapters Five through Eight, the way to assess for each stage of development is discussed in detail. Then in each of these chapters there are a series of activities for instruction. For Sarah, the activities presented in Chapter Six on Letter Name spelling will be most useful.

To find word study activities for students, we first determine their stage of spelling, and then examine students' spelling in terms of the stages developed by Henderson. There are three steps in this assessment process:

1. Collect a spelling sample that includes several invented spellings
2. Analyze the spelling sample for stage of development (see Figure 3–1)
3. Monitor growth and plan instruction

Collect a Spelling Sample

To determine stages of spelling, the obvious first step in the assessment process is to document the way students spell. The quality of students' spelling can be examined in daily writing the way we examined Sarah's. We can also examine students' spelling by using the inventories presented in this chapter.

These spelling inventories are quick and easy to administer. We explain that this information helps us see what students know about words, and this

FIGURE 3–1 Sample of a Student's Spelling Paper

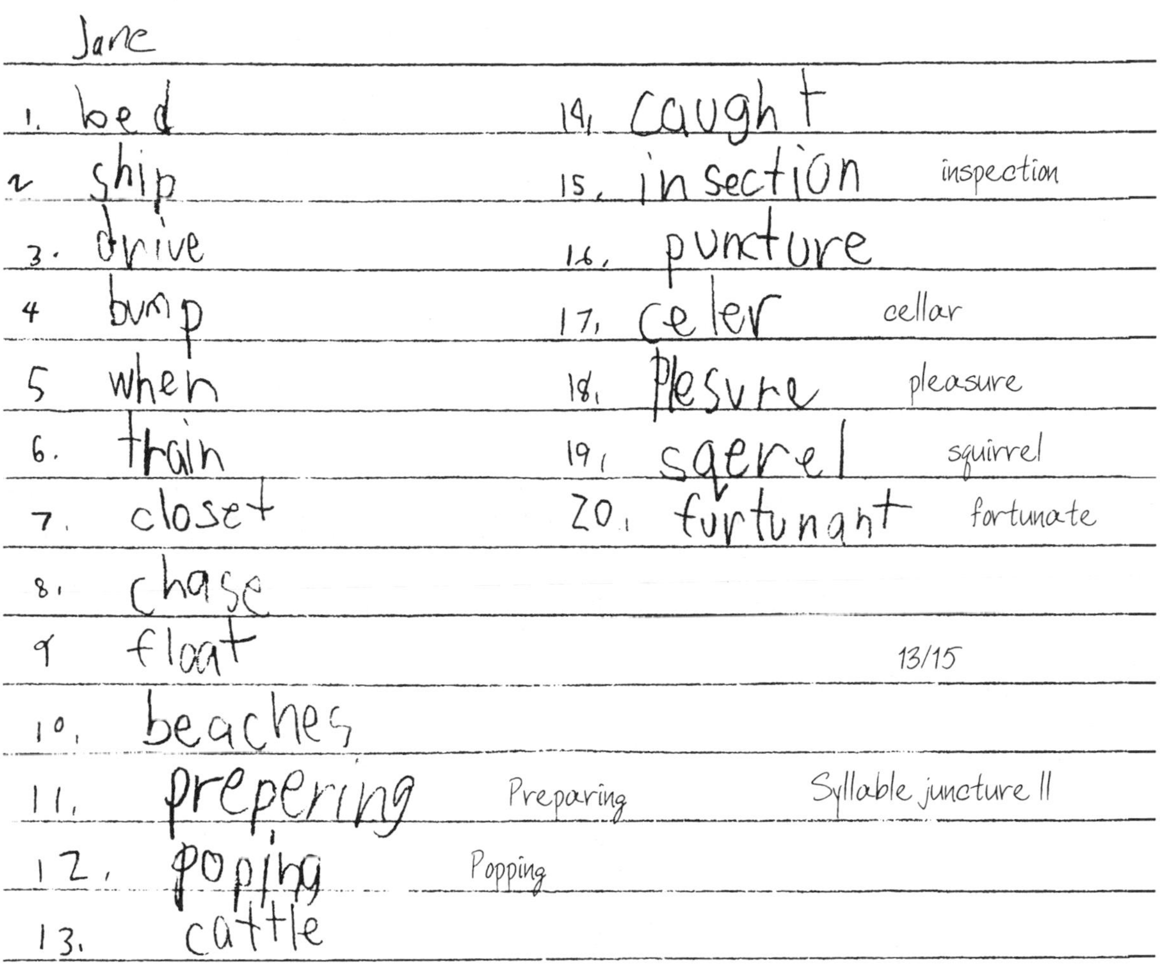

Jane

1. bed
2. ship
3. drive
4. bump
5. when
6. train
7. closet
8. chase
9. float
10. beaches
11. prepering   Preparing
12. poping   Popping
13. cattle

14. caught
15. insection   inspection
16. puncture
17. celer   cellar
18. plesure   pleasure
19. sqerel   squirrel
20. furtunant   fortunate

13/15

Syllable juncture II

information helps us think about instruction in our class during the year. These lists have been specially designed to obtain a significant number of invented spellings, a sample large enough to determine a spelling stage.

Invented spelling from student writing can be used effectively to determine students' development; the invented spelling samples collected in the inventories need to be compared to the invented spelling in the students' writing.

Sometimes, teachers and students may be uncomfortable with any kind of testing. In these situations, simply collect a broad sample of the students' writing and study the spelling in those samples.

Sometimes, samples from students' writing do not contain enough invented spellings because some students believe that what they write in their stories should be spelled correctly, and they limit their word choices to words they can spell. As we saw in Chapter Two, the orthographic features students use but confuse show us where to focus instruction, so be sure to have a sizable sample of invented spellings.

In the classroom, look at spellings across several samples—journal entries as well as spelling inventories. Then compare the invented spellings from the inventories to invented spellings from students' writing to make sure students are performing at a similar level in both types of writing.

It may be easier to go through the assessment process with a small group first. In this way, teachers who have not analyzed invented spellings before can go through the steps of administering the list, analyzing development, and planning instruction for a small group before trying the same with the whole class.

Analyze the Sample for Spelling Stage

The second part of the assessment process is to analyze students' work to determine a level of spelling development. Based on the stages of spelling discussed in the previous chapter, a spelling-by-stage assessment process is presented in this chapter. Students spell the words on one of several qualitative spelling inventories. This spelling sample documents students' development at one point in time. The analysis of students' spelling is made easier by the checklist and the error guides which show what stage of spelling a student is in.

Monitor Growth and Plan Instruction

The last part of the assessment process is focused on using this information to monitor students' growth and to plan and organize instruction. Upon completing the spelling-by-stage assessment, it is clear how to organize small groups and what orthographic patterns to study in small group word study sessions. This assessment process steers teachers to the developmentally appropriate word study activities presented in Chapters Five through Eight. The chart at the end of this chapter outlines the stages and should be used as a guide to find word study activities for your students.

Implementing Spelling-by-Stage Assessment

The spelling-by-stage assessment is at the center of the assessment process described in this chapter. The spelling-by-stage assessment is used to determine and place students in a stage of spelling development. As we discussed above, the assessment begins with the administration of a spelling inventory (Step 1); which is then analyzed qualitatively for what students use correctly, what they use but confuse, and what is absent (Step 2); and then a plan of instruction is developed to meet each student's needs (Step 3).

The inventories are not tests or part of students' grades. Teachers administer these inventories three times over the school year (e.g., September, January and May) to check students' progress and to plan word study according to development. These spelling-by-stage assessments create student profiles and can be included in student's portfolios.

15-point scale divides spelling stages into thirds for word study.

One advantage of the spelling-by-stage assessment presented here is that there are gradations created within each stage. A 15-point scale shows gradations within each of the stages of spelling development. For example, the Within Word Pattern stage is divided into thirds: late Within Word Pattern, middle Within Word Pattern, and early Within Word Pattern. The gradations within each stage make the assessment of orthographic knowledge more refined than just a stage designation.

The 15-point scale also makes it possible to resolve scoring differences between raters. For example, a teacher who says that a student is in the late Letter Name stage is quite close to a teacher who determined that a student was a beginning Within Word Pattern stage speller. In the following section on organizing instruction (Step 3 of the assessment process), the gradations make it easier to group students for instruction.

The spelling-by-stage assessment has been used for 14 years by classroom teachers, and, with some training, such as the training provided in this chapter, teachers' spelling-by-stage assessments are reliable. In several studies, spelling-by-stage assessments have been highly correlated with scores on standardized spelling tests. In one study, teachers who were involved in an hour and a half training session learned to make spelling-by-stage assessments with good accuracy. Interrater-reliabilities are usually quite high (>.90), and the correlation between the spelling-by-stage assessments and the number of words spelled correctly is equally high. Moreso than the number of words spelled correctly, or grade level that spelling measures, the spelling-by-stage analysis leads you to a developmental assessment which guides word study instruction (Bear, 1992).

Where Do Inventories Come From?

Throughout the course of our work with Edmund Henderson at the McGuffey Reading Center, we learned to develop effective spelling inventories. The lists we used in our diagnostic work were quite long, with 20 to 30 words per grade level, through eighth grade (see Schlagal, 1992). These words were chosen for two reasons: because of their frequency of occurrence, and their orthographic patterns. Some words occur frequently (such as *bed*), and others do not, such as *indictment*. The frequency of occurrence is based on the number of times the words were found in children's books as well as their own writing (Jacobson, 1982). The words were also chosen because of their orthographic patterns. For example, a word like *train* will show us which students use the alphabetic principle characteristic of students in the Letter Name stage (TRAN), compared to a student who uses patterns typical of students in the Within Word Pattern stage (TRANE).

> Spelling inventories are arranged from easiest to hardest.

As part of research studies, many of Henderson's students developed shorter lists. In the classroom, these shorter lists have been used to obtain a general picture of students' development. The 25-to-30 word lists presented in this chapter have been used since 1981, and thousands of samples have been collected (Bear, 1992; Bear, Templeton & Warner, 1991). These samples have provided information about the frequency and types of errors for these words. While lists presented in this chapter do not test for all spelling features, the words do cover the crucial orthographic features for each stage of spelling. This makes it possible to analyze the words students spelled correctly as well as the invented spellings to determine a spelling stage.

The words in both the elementary qualitative spelling inventories and the upper level inventory are arranged from the easiest to the hardest words; for the elementary list, *bed* has been the easiest word, and *emphasize* has been the most difficult word for first through sixth grade students to spell correctly. The same ordering has been used in the development of the upper level spelling inventory presented below. In a study of 456 middle school students, 95% of the students spelled *inspection* correctly, and only 19% spelled *emphasize* correctly. The words in these lists cover a wide range in difficulty levels.

Elementary Spelling Inventories

The 25-word elementary spelling inventories presented in Figures 3–2 and 3–3 are used through sixth grade. By April, every kindergartner should have taken the inventory, and by October, every first grader. Certainly by second grade, all students can participate. Given its extensive use and its broad applicability from K-6 grades, the spelling inventory in Figure 3–2, Bear I, beginning with *bed, ship,* and *drive,* is given the greatest attention in this chapter.

In the lower elementary grades, teachers conduct invented spelling lessons to show students how to write down how they think the words are spelled. Lessons like the one modeled in Box 3–2 below are used to help students who are hesitant to invent.

To track students' progress, teachers administer a spelling inventory at the beginning of the year, in the middle of the year (usually in January), and again at the end of the year (see Bear, 1992). The same inventory can be used as long as these words are not taught directly or assigned in spelling tests. The second inventory in Figure 3–3, Bear II, is used as an alternate form.

FIGURE 3–2 Elementary Qualitative Spelling Inventory: Bear I

Elementary Qualitative Spelling Inventory
Spelling-By-Stage Assessment

This is a short spelling inventory to help you learn about your students' orthographic knowledge. The results of the spelling inventories will have implications for reading, writing, vocabulary and spelling instruction.

Instructions: Let the students know that you are administering this inventory to learn about how they spell. Let them know that this is not a test, but that they will be helping you be a better teacher by doing their best:

Possible script: "I am going to ask you to spell some words. Try to spell them the best you can. Some of the words will be easy to spell; some will be more difficult. When you do not know how to spell a word, spell it the best you can; write down all the sounds you feel and hear."

Say the word once, read the sentence and then say the word again. Work with groups of 5 words. You may want to stop testing when students miss 3 out of 5 words. See the text for further instructions on administration and interpretation.

Have students check their papers for their names and the date.

Set One

1. bed   I hopped out of *bed* this morning.   *bed*
2. ship   The *ship* sailed around the island.   *ship*
3. drive   I learned to *drive* a car.   *drive*
4. bump   That is quite a *bump* you have on your head.   *bump*
5. when   *When* will you come back?   *when*

Set Two

6. train   I rode the *train* to the next town.   *train*
7. closet   I put the clothes in the *closet*.   *closet*
8. chase   We can play run and *chase* with the cats.   *chase*
9. float   I can *float* on the water with my new raft.   *float*
10. beaches   The sandy *beaches* are crowded in the summer.   *beaches*

Set Three

11. preparing   I am *preparing* for the big game.   *preparing*
12. popping   We are *popping* popcorn to eat at the movies.   *popping*
13. cattle   The cowboy rounded up the *cattle*.   *cattle*
14. caught   I *caught* the ball.   *caught*
15. inspection The soldiers polished their shoes for *inspection*.   *inspection*

Set Four

16. puncture   I had a *puncture* in my bicycle tire.   *puncture*
17. cellar   I went down to the *cellar* for the can of paint.   *cellar*
18. pleasure   It was a *pleasure* to listen to the choir sing.   *pleasure*
19. squirrel   We found the tree where the *squirrel* lives.   *squirrel*
20. fortunate   It was *fortunate* that the driver had snow tires during the snowstorm.   *fortunate*

Set Five

21. confident   I am *confident* that we can win the game.   *confident*
22. civilize   They had the idea that they could *civilize* the forest people.   *civilize*
23. flexible   She was so *flexible* that she could cross her legs behind her head.   *flexible*
24. opposition The coach said the *opposition* would give us a tough game.   *opposition*
25. emphasize   In conclusion, I want to *emphasize* the most important points.   *emphasize*

Administering a Spelling Inventory

These spelling inventories are as easy as any spelling test to administer and should take no more than 15 minutes to complete. The spelling lists and the basic directions for administering the inventories are presented in Figure 3–2. These lists can be reproduced and used by teachers in a school to create a school profile, and to help track students' progress over several years. (School-wide assessments are discussed in more detail below.)

FIGURE 3–3 Elementary Qualitative Spelling Inventory: Bear II

net
trip
crime
dump
then

chain
forest
trail
soap
reaches

comparing
topping
battle
fought
intention

rupture
stellar
treasure
confident
tempest

Directions for administering these inventories are presented with the lists. It is best to administer the elementary lists to students in small groups. The second time a spelling inventory is administered, students in second and third grades are comfortable with invented spelling, and they can take the inventory quickly and easily as a whole class. Again, these spelling inventories should take no more than 15 minutes to administer.

Create a Relaxed Atmosphere

Students need to know why the spelling inventory is being administered; they need to be encouraged to relax and do the best they can. It is easier to create a relaxed environment working in small groups. Sometimes children are particularly uptight about taking what they see as a test. Therefore, it is important to emphasize to students that their work will help us be better teachers, and that this is not a test that will be a part of a grade. Be direct in an explanation for having them spell the words: "Your work spelling these words will help me be a better teacher. Your work will help me understand how you are learning to read and write and how I can help you learn." For secondary students, teachers often say to students that as long as they try their best in spelling these words, they will earn an "A" for the assignment. Once these things are explained, we find that students are able to give the spelling a good effort.

Spelling inventories are not part of grading.

When a student is extremely frustrated and upset, ask the student to spell the word to you: "You've worked hard writing and spelling. I'll be glad to do the writing, if you will spell to me. I'll be your secretary by writing down what you spell." Most students welcome this invitation. Some students approach all writing tasks with some trepidation. When a student has a death grip on the pencil, it is best to back away and look elsewhere for spelling information. In contrast to the death grip, some students write so lightly or so tiny that their writing can not be read. Like the death grip, this is another sign that it is time to ease the pressure the student is feeling.

Ask students to spell the words the best they can.

Box 3–2

"Spelling The Best We Can": A Lesson to Encourage Invented Spelling

Students have to be comfortable spelling words they may not know how to spell. The ability to invent spellings is important to their writing. A hesitant writer who labors over spelling words will lose the reward of expressing new ideas. Getting ideas onto paper is easier when there is some fluency in the mechanical aspects of getting the letters down on the page. Students who are willing to risk being wrong by inventing their spelling have an easier time getting their ideas down.

To help students feel more comfortable writing, before the spelling assessments, conduct a few lessons either in small groups or with the whole class. The theme of this lesson is "How to spell the best we can." Lessons like the one to follow can be conducted over several days. Each aspect of the lesson should be repeated a few times.

A Discussion to Encourage Invented Spelling

Scaffold students—show them how to spell words they do not know how to spell.

We're going to do a lot of writing this year. We will write nearly every day. Sometimes our writing will be drawings and pictures. At other times we will write stories and write about what we see and do with words. When you are writing, there will be times when you will not know how to spell a word. This is part of learning: If we already knew how to spell all words, we wouldn't need to learn.

When we want to write a word, and we don't know how to spell it, what might we do? Student responses usually include:

Ask the teacher.

Ask someone.

Look it up.

Skip it.

We often explain that one thing they can do is to "write down all the sounds you hear and feel when you say the word. Write down all the sounds and go on. We can work on the spelling together later, but for now, get the ideas down."

A second part of this lesson is to spell a few words together:

We may begin, "Who has a word they want to spell? What is a tough word you don't know how to spell?"

A child may offer, "Ninja turtle."

"That's a great one. Can we keep to the second word, 'turtle'?

Assuming that they agree, we will ask them to say the word 'turtle'.

"Turtle."

We begin then to examine the orthographic features: "What's the first letter at the beginning of *turtle?* Say the word, again, and then tell me."

"Turtle. T."

We write down an upper case *t*. Then we may ask a few students what the next sounds are that they "hear and feel".

After a few minutes, we may generate several spellings of *turtle:*

Teacher-guided lessons help students invent spellings.

Tl

Trtl

Terdl

Tertul

Finally, we talk about what we do if we can only figure out one or two sounds in a word. "Start with the sound at the beginning. Write the first letter and then draw a line." Here, we would write *t* with a line: T__

Occasionally, a child will be hyper-critical about another student's attempt: "That's not the right way to spell it!" We cannot tolerate someone being criticized for earnest effort, so we are careful to handle this criticism firmly. We may say: "The important thing is that you have written your

Can students
reread invented
spellings in their
writing?

word down, and that you can reread what you have written." Then we direct the group's attention back to the board: "On the board here, there are four spellings of *Turtle*. They all could be correct." We may remind students that they are learning, and that there will be times when we don't know how to spell a word and so we spell the best we can. "We do learn over the years, and you will see your writing improve the more you write. In June, you will be surprised to see how much more you can write."

One lesson to discuss invented spelling will not suffice, so plan to conduct similar lessons over a two-week period. Some teachers take the time to talk about **standard** and **nonstandard spellings** in a script like this:

"When you do not know how to spell a word, write down all the sounds you hear and feel when you say a word. When you write in this way you use invented spelling. Another word for invented spelling is nonstandard spelling. When you know the spelling of a word, you use standard spelling. As learners, we often use nonstandard spelling until we learn the standard spelling."

Observe how
students
approach the
spelling task—do
some have a
death grip on

Ask students to write the words down the page. (Inevitably, a few younger students write from left to right.) Also ask students to make only two columns on any page.

After the initial instructions, say each word twice. It is common practice to say the word in a sentence, and sentences are provided for the first elementary list and the upper level spelling inventory. However, for most words, saying the word in a sentence is time consuming and may even be distracting. There are a few words for which the context of a sentence will be helpful. For example, *cellar* is used in a sentence to differentiate it from *seller*.

Occasionally, after spelling an entire list, and if there is time, students are asked to place a star by the words which they think they may not have spelled correctly. And if there is still time, they are asked to take a second try at the words they starred. Throughout this reexamination, students show their willingness to reflect on their work. Their notations and successive attempts are additional indicators of the depth of students' orthographic knowledge.

With younger
students,
administer the
spelling inventory
in small groups.

Lower elementary students may copy from each other when they are uncomfortable inventing spellings. It is easier to see if a student is copying when the inventory is administered in small groups. Students can be asked not to copy, and lessons can be conducted which show students how to spell words they are not sure how to spell. Since there will be many opportunities to collect corroborating information, there is no reason to be upset by copying. If it is clear that a student has copied, make a note to this effect after the papers have been collected.

Can You Read Students' Handwriting?

After collecting the papers, or while walking around the room, teachers should look for words they cannot read. Without making students feel that something is wrong, it is appropriate to ask them to read the letters in the words that cannot be deciphered: "I am having a little trouble reading your writing. What you wrote is fine; I am just having trouble making out the letters. Can you tell me the letters in this word?" There will only be a few papers that should cause much difficulty in this regard.

How Many Words Do Students Spell?

As noted in the directions of the elementary spelling inventory, teachers look at the students' papers after each set of five words. Once familiar with analyzing students' spelling, teachers can scan the papers after each set of words to see whether or not to continue. The inventory can stop as soon as a spelling stage can be determined.

For example, spelling can be discontinued after five words when students are in the Preliterate stage. Anywhere from five to 10 words should be enough for Early Letter Name spellers. At least 10 words should be used for Letter Name spellers and from then on, a full 20 to 25 words should be collected for an overview.

Play it on the safe side and discontinue the spelling when there is enough information. The administration of the inventory can be spread over a few days; for those who need to continue, subsequent sets can be administered in groups on another day.

A similar provision for discontinuing the assessment is noted in the upper level spelling inventory. We have found that a sufficient number of words has been collected when a student misses five out of the first eight words. By walking around the room, teachers can see if there are several students who have missed this many words. If so, on subsequent days, teachers can move students to small groups and use the elementary inventory with those who had so much difficulty with the upper level list.

There are times when teachers want to use a longer and more detailed spelling list. For example, a teacher may want to obtain a full inventory of the students' knowledge of short vowels or consonant blends and digraphs. The list for the elementary grades presented here does not attempt to measure each feature. For example, the elementary list helps teachers look at long vowels generally, and does not even have a single syllable word for long *i*. A more complete list can be found in Schlagal (1992) and Templeton (1991b).

Analyzing Students' Papers

We have developed several tools to analyze students' spelling of the elementary and upper level spelling inventories. The analysis begins with scoring the papers, but then the focus is on a qualitative analysis. In this qualitative analysis teachers look at students' papers to see the whole picture of students' development.

Three forms can be used to analyze students' spelling inventories and to determine a stage of development:

A checklist
An error guide
A 15-point scale for interpretation

The most structured analysis occurs with the use of the checklist. Referring to the error guide will remind you how to classify particular invented spellings. And the 15-point scale is used to remind you what the point scale is for the stages of spelling. With some practice, you can stop using the checklist and error guide and just refer to the 15-point scale as a reminder of the stages. Using these forms, there are four steps in a qualitative analysis of students' spelling:

1. ***Ask: What does the student know?***
   To find patterns, use the checklist presented in Figure 3–5.
2. ***Ask: What does the student use but confuse?***
   The chart of errors by stage in Figure 3–6 is helpful here.
3. ***Determine a stage.***
   "What stage of spelling is this student in?"
   The error guide and the checklist help with this decision.
4. ***Determine a level: Early, Middle or Late?***
   The scale in Figure 3–8 is a good visual aid here.

It takes some practice to gain confidence and speed analyzing students' papers. But, teachers have become accurate in their analyses with an hour or

Side notes:

After 5 or 10 words, scan the papers.

To Assess Orthographic Knowledge:
♦ What does the student know?
♦ What does the student "use but confuse"?
♦ What is the stage of development?
♦ Is it the beginning, middle, or end of the stage?

two of practice. With one pack of class papers, a teacher can see the differences in students based on the developmental scheme presented in this book. The analysis of a class of 28 students takes between 20 and 40 minutes, depending upon how advanced the spelling is and how comfortable the teacher is in determining a stage of spelling for each student.

When working with a pack of student papers, keep the error guide, the checklist, and the 15-point scale in sight. The determination of the students' development can be recorded in two places: Directly on the students' papers and on the class profile. Sometimes teachers work with a partner to compare assessments and to decide how word study might be organized.

Count The Number Of Words Spelled Correctly

Before determining a stage of development, take a moment to correct the papers by writing the word beside each error. Date each paper for future reference, and then count the errors and report the ratio of correct to total. For example, if the student spelled 20 words and spelled 16 words correctly, write 16/20.

Reversals are studied qualitatively.

Reversals present a small problem. Reversals can be counted as errors, but the qualitative analysis must be made and the reversals should be seen as the letters they were meant to represent. For example, ɔat is considered a correct spelling for *cat*, and a spelling of *ship* with the correct letters but with the *s* written backwards should be counted as correct. These letter reversals occur with decreasing frequency through the Letter Name stage. By the Within Word Pattern stage, reversals are rare. Notes about students' reversals can be made on students' profiles in their portfolios and planning guides, when it is a problem of extreme frequency or when they occur with regularity in the Within Word Pattern stage, the time when we would predict that reversals would cease to appear.

Now it's time to look at each paper and determine a stage of spelling for each student. A few ways to determine students' spelling stage are offered here.

The number of words spelled correctly is related to stages.

The correlation between the number of words spelled correctly and the spelling-by-stage assessment has been reported to be quite high. As a matter of fact, this correlation between stages and the number of words spelled correctly led us to think that the Spelling-By-Stage Assessment would be useful, and reliable. Both scores are highly related to standardized reading achievement measures at all levels, from kindergarten through postsecondary levels (Bear, 1992).

Students who spell 1–5, or *bed* through *when* correctly are usually considered to be through with the Letter Name stage, and they are playing with long vowel patterns, and at least in the beginning of the Within Word Pattern stage. Students who spell words 1–10 correctly, or nearly so, are in the beginning of the Syllable Juncture stage. Lastly, students who spell most of the words from 1–20 correctly are in the Derivational Constancy stage. A summary of these ranges is presented in Figure 3–4.

Even though the words are arranged by difficulty, students' growth is gradual and they do not move absolutely from one stage to another, abandon-

FIGURE 3–4 Ranges of Development Based on Number of Words Spelled Correctly

Number of Words Spelled Correctly	Range of Development
0	Preliterate – Letter Name
1 – 5	Letter Name – Within Word Pattern
5 – 10	Within Word Pattern – Syllable Juncture
10 – 25	Syllable Juncture – Derivational Constancy

FIGURE 3–5 Qualitative Spelling Checklist

Qualitative Spelling Checklist

Student _____ *Observer* _____ *Date(s)* _____

Consider the following progression, and note when certain features are observed in students' spelling and writing. When a feature is always present check Yes. The last place where you check *"Often"* is the stage of spelling development to report. The numbers refer to the scale on the Spelling-by-Stage Assessment.

How many words were spelled correctly? Report as a percentage of total correct to total spelled:

THE NUMBERS BELOW REFER TO THE SPELLING-BY-STAGE SCALE (1–15)

Preliterate

1	Marks on the page. [ ]	Yes _____	Often _____	No _____
	Scribbling followed the conventional direction. [——————→]	Yes _____	Often _____	No _____
	Symbols or known letters represented in pretend writing. [bybcl]	Yes _____	Often _____	No _____

Early Letter Name

2	Syllabic Writing. Key sounds are spelled. [P for *stop*]	Yes _____	Often _____	No _____
3	Beginning. Check Yes if ending sounds are included.	Yes _____	Often _____	No _____

Letter Name

4	A vowel in each word.	Yes _____	Often _____	No _____
5	Consonant blends and digraphs in *SH*IP, *DR*IVE and *WH*EN, *TR*AIN, *CH*ASE and *FL*OAT.	Yes _____	Often _____	No _____
6	Short vowels spelled correctly. [B**E**D, SH**I**P, WH**E**N] Includes preconsonantal nasals. [B**U**MP]	Yes _____	Often _____	No _____

Within Word Pattern

7	Uses but confuses long vowels [DRIEV, TRAIN, FLOTE, BEECHS]	Yes _____	Often _____	No _____
8	Spells many single syllable long vowels spelled correctly [DR**IVE**, TR**AIN**, FL**OAT**, B**EA**CHES]	Yes _____	Often _____	No _____
	Still experiments with long vowel patterns [DR**IE**V, TR**AI**N, FL**OTE**, B**EE**CHS]			
	Spells most consonant blends and digraphs correctly [*SH*IP, *DR*IVE and *WH*EN, *TR*AIN, *CH*ASE and *FL*OAT]			
9	Spells long vowels, consonant blends and digraphs, and low frequency consonant blends and digraphs [CAU**GH**T]	Yes _____	Often _____	No _____

Syllable Juncture

10	Consonant doubling [PO**PP**ING, CA**TT**LE, SQUI**RR**EL, CE**LL**AR]	Yes _____	Often _____	No _____
11	Plurals and other endings. [BEACH**ES**, POPP**ING**, PREPAR**ING**]	Yes _____	Often _____	No _____
12	Less frequent affixes.	Yes _____	Often _____	No _____
	suffixes [PUNC**TURE**, CEL**LAR**, PLEA**SURE**, FORTU**NATE**, CONFID**ENT**, CIVI**LIZE**, FLEX**IBLE**]			
	prefixes [**PREP**ARING, **CON**FIDENT, **OP**POSITION]			

Derivational Constancy

13	Knowledge of derived spellings [**PLEASURE**, **FORTUNA**TE]	Yes _____	Often _____	No _____
14	Knowledge of derived spellings [CON**FIDE**, **CIVIL**IZE]	Yes _____	Often _____	No _____
15	Knowledge of derived spellings [OP**POSITI**ON, **EMPHA**SIZE]	Yes _____	Often _____	No _____

Look at Figure 3–6 and circle the errors. If an error is not present in this table, write the error into the chart closest to the errors listed. Find the spelling stage where most of the errors are circled. What stage of spelling would you say the student is in? Is he or she in the beginning, middle, or end of this stage? Circle and date below.

Adapted from Bear (1988)

ing all vestiges of the previous stage. Therefore, it is helpful to think of the boundaries between stages of development as fuzzy. Because of this fuzziness, there are students who spell *ship* as SIP and spell *float* correctly. However, there are not many students who spell *ship* as SEP and still spell *float* correctly.

Counting the number of words spelled correctly is easy, and a starting point, but more qualitative information than the number of errors is needed to determine a stage of spelling development or to plan word study activities. Therefore, to obtain a qualitative analysis, a few other guides are used to determine a stage of orthographic knowledge.

Qualitative Spelling Checklist

In some ways, spelling knowledge is additive. Students learn some sight words and with that information they make phonic generalizations, and with those new generalizations, it is easier to learn more sight words. It follows that with more exposure to words through reading and writing, the larger the sight vocabularies become, and the deeper the students' knowledge of how words are spelled and recognized.

The checklist is good for first-time raters—it specifies spelling features.

The checklist presented in Figure 3–5 is also additive: start with question one and work through until "No's" start to be checked. With the assumption that this checklist describes a progression, it is apparent when a student's knowledge fades or gives out. For example, a student should get all "Yes" responses and gradually collect some "Often" responses and then two or three "No's" in a row. The responses should not go from Yes to No and back to Yes more than perhaps once. That is, when students start to miss items, they should continue to miss. For example, one does not usually learn to spell words like *fortunate* correctly before *bump,* nor do students stabilize on consonant doubling before mastering short vowel patterns.

Error Guide

The errors presented in Figure 3–6 are the most common ones observed for each word. The errors are arranged in terms of sophistication, and they are classified under the stage they represent. Note the progression for each word. For example, the growth in errors for *beaches* can be seen from B, BS, BCS, BCHS, to BEECHES.

The error guide is very efficient.

Refer now to Figure 3–7 for an example of a student's work. By circling the student's errors, and then matching the errors with the stages they represent, it was determined that this student was in the Middle Letter Name stage of development, Letter Name 4.

Circle errors and match to spelling stages.

The spelling sample in Figure 3–7 is an interesting one. This spelling sample was collected by the classroom teacher of a second grader in March. It is clear that the student, J.M., included a vowel in each major syllable, and that he was experimenting with short vowels. While he spelled *bed* correctly, he spelled *when* as WAN. As is discussed in detail in Chapter Six, it is natural for students to experiment with short vowels. In addition, J.M. had learned to spell a few consonant blends and digraphs, but probably not most of them. To plan word study instruction for this student, refer to the sequence of word study activities presented at the end of this chapter.

15-Point Scale Spelling-By-Stage Assessment

Each stage is divided into substages of Early, Middle, and Late, or Beginning, Middle, or High. With the help of the error guide and the checklist, it is evident what features students have mastered and which ones they are still working to master. The question then is this: Where does each student fit along the developmental continuum? If it appears that a student has worked through most of the features relevant to a stage, then she is probably in a high point of the

FIGURE 3–6 Elementary Inventory Error Guide

Stages	Early Letter Name	Letter Name	Within Word Pattern	Syllable Juncture	Derivational Constancy
1. bed	b bd	bad	bed		
2. ship	s sp shp	sep shep	sip ship		
3. drive	jrv drv	griv driv	drieve draive drive		
4. bump	b bp bmp	bop bomp bup	bump		
5. when	w yn wn	wan wen	wen when		
6. train	j t trn	jran chran tan tran	teran traen trane train		
7. closet	k cs kt clst	clast clost clozt	clozit closit		
8. chase	j jass cs	tas cas chass	case chais chase		
9. float	f vt ft flt	fot flot flott	flowt floaut flote float		
10. beaches	b bs bcs	bechs becis behis	bechise beches beeches beaches		

Stages	Within Word Pattern	Syllable Juncture	Derivational Constancy
11. preparing	preparng preypering	praparing prepairing preparing	
12. popping	popin poping	popping	
13. cattle	catl cadol	catel catle cattel cattle	
14. caught	cot cote cought caught		
15. inspection	inspshr inspechin	inspecshum inspecsion inspection	
16. puncture	pucshr pungchr puncker	punksher puncture puncture	
17. cellar	salr selr celr seler	seller sellar celler cellar	
18. pleasure	plasr plager plejer pleser plesher	plesour pleasure	pleasure
19. squirrel	scrl skwel skwerl	scqoril sqrarel squirle squirrel	
20. fortunate	forhnat frehnit foohinit	forchenut fochininte fortunet	fortunate

Stages	Within Word Pattern	Syllable Juncture	Derivational Constancy
21. confident		confedint confedent confodent confident confedent confident confodent confident	conphident confident
22. civilize		sivils sevelies sivilicse cifillazas sivelize sivalize civalise civilise civilize	
23. flexible		flecksibl flexobil fleckuble flecible flexeble flexibel flexable flexibal flexable flexible	flexible
24. opposition	opasion opasishan opozcison opishien opasitian	opasition oppasishion oppisition oposision oppasishion opposition	
25. emphasize		infaside infacize emfesize emfisize imfasize ephacise empasize emphasise	emphisize emphasize

Adapted from Bear & Barone (1989)
Note: The Preliterate Stage is not presented here.

FIGURE 3–7 Sample of a Marked Error Guide for J.M.*

Stages	Early Letter Name	Letter Name	Within Word Pattern
1. bed	b bd	bad	(bed)
2. ship	s sp shp	(sep) shep	sip ship
3. drive	jrv drv	griv (driv)	drieve draive drive
4. bump	b bp bmp	(bob) bomp bup	bump
5. when	w yn wn	(wan) whan	wen when
6. train	j t trn	jran chran tan (tran)	teran traen trane train
7. closet	k cs kt clst	clast clost (clozt)	clozit closit
8. chase	j jass cs	tas (cas) chas chass	case chais chase
9. float	f vt ft flt	fot (flot) flott	flowt floaut flote float
10. beaches	b bs bcs	bechs (becis) behis	bechise beches beeches beaches

Testing was discontinued after ten words—1/10, 10%
J.M. was considered to be in the Middle to Late Letter Name stage of development. See text for a complete discussion.
*Circled spellings are J.M.'s responses.

stage. Conversely, if a student is beginning to use the key elements of a stage, but still has some remnants from the previous stage, it can be said that the student is in an early point in that new stage.

Some teachers take the 15-point discrimination as a weighty decision. The exact placement of a student on the scale is not such an important decision. We are going to be safe about this when it comes to planning instruction, for we take a step backwards when we begin instruction, choosing word study activities at a slightly easier level than the stage determination would have indicated. Teachers take this step backwards because students need to learn how to sort words and to play the word study games, and clearly, it is easier to teach students how to sort when they can read the words easily. It is a golden rule to take a step backwards when beginning word study instruction, and so the determination of a stage for students is tempered by this practice.

> Be conservative in your rating so students have success.

Between raters, there are rarely differences greater than two points. In some cases, two teachers may disagree as to what stage a student is in. The gradations of High, Middle, and Low remind us of our relative differences. For example, one teacher may say that a student is in the Late Letter Name stage, and another teacher may say that the same student is in the Early Within Word Pattern stage: What is the difference between a student late in the Letter Name stage (Late Letter Name–6) and a student who is determined to be early in the Within Word Pattern stage (Early Within Word Pattern–7)? Both students are likely to be placed in the same word study groups.

The 15-point scale in Figure 3–8 is most useful to teachers when they start to group students for directed word study. Grouping for instruction is discussed in the section on organizing instruction.

Spelling Inventories In Other Languages

Teachers also develop spelling inventories for students who speak other languages. In developing a list for another language, words are used that are sensitive to some of the same orthographic features that we have discussed in the various English lists. Include words that contain features that may elicit substitutions based on place of articulation.

Two of Ed Henderson's students developed spelling inventories for other languages as part of their doctoral dissertations. Charlie Temple developed a

Box 3–3
Check Your Assessment With Ours

If you do not have a class to work with, or you want to see a broad spectrum of responses, please take a look at the nine cases presented in Figures 3–9 and 3–10.

What is particularly interesting about 3–9 is that these are samples from *adult* beginning readers. The qualitative spelling inventories have been used with adults for many years, and while there are more deviant or unclassifiable misspellings among adults who are in the first four stages of development, most adults demonstrate through invented spelling what they know about the orthography (Bear, 1988).

Our spelling analyses have been printed at the bottom of the chart. Were you close to our assessments? Was there an agreement of stages? If you are off on more than one or two cases, try again. One mental anchor is that Within Word Pattern students have mastered simple short vowel patterns, and they experiment with different long vowel spellings. If you use the 15-point scale, a point or two difference for several students is not exceptional. Chapters Five through Eight include many samples to consider.

FIGURE 3–8 15-Point Scale/Spelling-by-Stage Assessment

Spelling-by-Stage Assessment Scale

Late Derivational Constancy	15
Middle Derivational Constancy	14
Beginning Derivational Constancy	13
Late Syllable Juncture	12
Middle Syllable Juncture	11
Beginning Syllable Juncture	10
Late Within Word Pattern	9
Middle Within Word Pattern	8
Beginning Within Word Pattern	7
Late Letter Name	6
Middle Letter Name	5
Beginning Letter Name	4
Early Letter Name	3
Early Letter Name	2
Preliterate	1

Adapted from Bear (1988)

> Spanish and French inventories are used in bilingual and foreign language classes.

Spanish list for his dissertation, and it is presented in Figure 3–11 (Temple, 1978). Charlene Gill developed a list for French speaking Canadians which is presented in Figure 3–12 (Gill, 1980). These inventories are administered to students who speak Spanish or French as their first or primary language.

We also use the English lists with second language learners who have fair proficiency in English. Their spelling is analyzed to include an assessment of the impact of the primary language. For example, in Figure 3–11, the impact of Spanish on Martha's invented spellings are evident. Her invented spellings make a good deal of sense in relation to the vowels in Spanish. For example, the long *e,* which is represented with an *i* in Spanish (*si*), is used to spell the long *e* in *beaches* (BICHES) and *preparing* (PIBERING). Her spelling of *drive* follows from this similarity between *i* and *y* in Spanish. In Spanish, the *y* also makes a long *e* sound. In DRUAYV, Martha may have used the *y* as a long vowel marker for the long *i.* A similar confusion has occurred with *e.* In Spanish, the letter *e*

FIGURE 3–9 Four Students' Spelling and Spelling-by-Stage Assessment

Words	Jed	Robert	Mina	Jean
bed	BD	BAD	bed	bed
ship	S	SHOP	ship	ship
drive	JR	DRIVIE	DRIEV	drive
bump	BP	BUP	bump	bump
when	YB	WAN	when	when
train		TRAN	TRANE	train
closet		CALLET	closet	closet
chase		CHAS	CHAISE	chase
float		FALT	FLOTE	float
beaches		BEHES	BECHIS	beaches
preparing		REPEREN	PREPAIRING	preparing
popping		PIPEN	POPING	popping
cattle		CATEL	CATTELL	CATTEL
caught		CAT	COUT	cattle
inspection		NESA	INSPION	inspection
puncture		PANHER	POCHRER	PUNTURE
cellar		SELER	SILLER	CELLER
pleasure		PLESER	PLASHER	PLESURE
squirrel		SARL	SQULER	SQUIRLE
fortunate		FORERT	FORGENTE	fortunate

Adapted from Bear (1988)
Note: Ages and Level of Reading:
   Student 1: 34-year-old in a beginning stage of reading; Early Letter Name–3
   Student 2: 55-year-old Beginning Reader; Middle Letter Name–5
   Student 3: 27-year-old Transitional Reader; Within Word Pattern–8
   Student 4: 43-year-old Specialized Reader; Derivational Constancy–12

has a long *a* sound, and she has used an *e* for the long *a* in *train* (TRUEN), *chase* (CHEIS), and *preparing* (PREPERUEN). There are also substitutions of a short *o* with an *a*. In Spanish the vowels in *hot, father,* and perhaps *bump* are said the same way as the *a* in *gracias,* and this explains why she spelled *caught* as CAT. As these examples illustrate, students' invented spelling in other languages are not wrong, but are logical and "interestingly correct."

Upper Level and Content-Specific Spelling Inventories

The upper level spelling inventory (Figure 3–13) is used in middle school through postsecondary classrooms. The words in this list were chosen because they help identify, more specifically than the elementary inventory, what students in the Syllable Juncture and Derivational Constancy stages are doing in their spelling. As noted above, these words are arranged in order of difficulty, and the directions presented with the inventory suggest that the teacher stop giving the inventory to students who have missed five out of the first eight words. Students who score at this level are usually in the Within Word Pattern stage. On a subsequent day, pick up with the test in small groups. For the students who missed so many of the first words, move to the elementary list.

    Students' spelling on this upper level list shows how they make "the meaning connection" with the orthography (Templeton, 1983). Students in these final stages of spelling learn to preserve meaning in spite of changes in

FIGURE 3–10 Examples of Students' Spelling–September

	Sarah	Michael	Lucas	Anna	Amanda
Grade Words	1st	1st	2nd	3rd	3rd
bed	BD	bed	bed	bed	bed
ship	SP	SEP	ship	ship	ship
drive	JRV	DRIV	drive	drive	drive
bump	B	BOP	BUNP	bump	bump
when	WN	WHAN	when	when	when
train		TRAN	TRANE	train	train
closet		CLAST	CLOZIT	CLOSIT	closet
chase		CAS	chase	chase	chase
float		FLOT	FLOTE	FLOTE	float
beaches		BECIS	BECHES	BEACHS	beaches
preparing			PREPRING	PREPEARING	preparing
popping			POPING	popping	popping
cattle			CATOL	CATTEL	cattle
caught			COUT	COT	COUGHT
inspection			INSPECSIN	INSPECSHIN	inspection
puncture			PUCSHR	PUNKSHER	PUNCHER
cellar			SELR	SELLER	CELLER
pleasure			PLESER	PLEJER	PRESHER
squirrel			SKWEL	SKWREL	SQURRIEL
fortunate			FREHNIT	FOOHINIT	FORCHENT
Spelling-by-Stage Assessment	Early Letter Name-3	Middle Letter Name-5	Within Word Pattern-8	Syllable Juncture-10	Syllable Juncture-12

Adapted from Bear & Barone (1989)

sound. For example, in pronunciation, the second vowel in *reside* changes from a long i to a schwa sound in *resident*. In spite of this sound change, the spelling remains the same and is a cue to meaning.

This upper level inventory has been used in studies to relate spelling development and reading development in seventh and eighth graders and high school students. In addition, this list has been used to help screen students at the university level who are having reading difficulties as well as to screen students for GED programs to obtain a high school diploma.

| The meaning connection links vocabulary and spelling. |

The content specific spelling inventories in Figures 3–15 and 3–16 have been developed with high school biology and geometry teachers who want to assess students' general orthographic knowledge as well as their knowledge of the content specific vocabulary. Students who score well on these content specific inventories tend to do better in these classes than students who are unable to spell many of these content words correctly. The information provided in these content specific spelling inventories helps to assess students' literacy proficiency as well as their conceptual background knowledge.

Upper Level Spelling Inventory

The error guide in Figure 3–14 lists errors from students in the Within Word Pattern, Syllable Juncture, and Derivational Constancy stages. The errors found in students' spelling are probably listed here. As teachers circle the errors,

FIGURE 3–11a Spelling Inventory in Spanish

The Spelling List

1.	*Casa.*	Él no está en la casa.
2.	*Util.*	El perro es util al hombre.
3.	*Choque.*	El choque de los carros fue horrible.
4.	*Baño.*	Juan está tomando un baño.
5.	*Verdad.*	Díganme la verdad.
6.	*Cuero.*	Mi correa es de cuero.
7.	*Cara.*	Límpiate bien la cara.
8.	*Pecho.*	El niño tiene un hermoso pecho.
9.	*Puesto.*	Yo tengo puesto mi traje de baño.
10.	*Triste.*	La película fue muy triste.
11.	*Libertad.*	Los dominicanos aman la libertad.
12.	*Hinchado.*	El pie está hinchado.
13.	*Ayudan.*	Los alumnos ayudan a la profesora.
14.	*Cheque.*	El viajero quiere cambiar un cheque.
15.	*Callado.*	¿Qué tiene Juan? Está tan callado.
16.	*Traigo.*	Yo traigo mi pelota.
17.	*Invierno.*	En el invierno hace frio.
18.	*Bombón.*	El niño está comiendo un bombón.
19.	*Cerrar.*	Hay que cerrar la puerta.
20.	*Tienen.*	Los estudiantes tienen sus libros.

From Temple (1978)

FIGURE 3–11b Spelling by a Spanish-speaking ESL Student

Word to Spell	Marta's Invented Spelling
bed	bed
ship	ship
drive	DRUAYV
bump	BAMP
when	WEN
train	TRUEN
closet	closet
chase	CHEIS
float	FLOT
beaches	BECHES
preparing	PREPERUEN
popping	PAPEN
cattle	CATOL
caught	CAT
inspection	INPESCHEN
puncture	PANCHERT
cellar	SALER

they find that the errors fall fairly evenly in a column down the page. Errors that are not listed on this page are written beside the closest invented spelling.

Students in the Within Word Pattern stage and even in the Syllable Juncture stage omit syllables in the middle of words. It seems that for these students there can occasionally be an overload, and the middle syllables are forgotten.

The Within Word Pattern and early Syllable Juncture invented spellings often are misspellings of the suffixes with a phonetic rendering uncommon in English (e.g., SHUN for -*tion*). Students in the Within Word Pattern stage also

FIGURE 3–12 French Spelling Inventory

<u>Directives à l'intention du professeur:</u>

Ce test fait partie d'une étude sur les dispositions que les élèves ont pour orthographier les mots. Le but de ce test est de mettre à jour des <u>erreurs</u> en vue d'une analyse ultérieure. Donc, les mots peuvent sembler difficiles. Afin que tous les élèves fassent la même chose et que nous puissions ainsi comparer les résultats pouvez-vous s'il vous plait:

1. Expliquer aux élèves que ceci est un test qui permettra de voir comment d'après eux les mots doivent être orthographies. Il y aura beaucoup de mots qu'ils ne connaitront pas mais ils devront essayer de les orthographier, et ce, de la façon qu'ils jugeront la plus adéquate.
   N'ayez pas peur de deviner!
2. Lire les mots d'une facon normale, lire immédiatement la phrase, puis répéter le mot. Vous pouvez répéter le mot si les élèves le demandent.
3. Veuillez, s'il vous plait, ne donner aucune indication quant à l'orthographe.

Merci beaucoup!

LE TEST

1.	**soif**	J'ai chaud et j'ai soif.
2.	**magasins**	Tous les magasins sont fermés le dimanche.
3.	**humble**	Marie était très humble parce-qu'elle n'était pas riche.
4.	**regardent**	Les garçons regardent le cinéma.
5.	**feuilles**	En automne les feuilles sont belles.
6.	**bonhomme**	Le bonhomme de neige aime l'hiver.
7.	**nombre**	Donnez-moi le nombre d'élèves dans votre classe.
8.	oiseaux	Les oiseaux volent très haut.
9.	chaise	Le chien est sur la chaise.
10.	démarrent	Jean et Paul démarrent leurs voitures.
11.	conduit	Mon père me conduit à l'école.
12.	changeant	Le temps au printemps est changeant.
13.	pommier	Le pommier est chargé de pommes.
14.	sautent	Trois lapins sautent dans le forêt.
15.	collier	Le collier de Mme. Thibaut est couvert de diamants.
16.	pinceaux	Les peintres utilisent des pinceaux dans leur travail.
17.	œuvres	J'aime les œuvres du musée du Louvre.
18.	**bouteille**	La bouteille est pleine de lait.
19.	**enfants**	J'aime les enfants de Collège Marie de France.

From Gill (1980)

tend to overuse long vowel patterns (i.e., DECORATORE for *decorator,* and ENDIGHTMENT for *indictment.*

Students in the Syllable Juncture stage begin to spell common suffixes correctly, and towards the end of this stage they begin to also spell less common word endings correctly (i.e., the *-ate* in *fortunate,* the *-or* in *decorator,* and the *-ious* in *hilarious*). These students also become more accurate in spelling words in which the consonants are doubled (i.e., *commotion* and *propellant*).

During the Derivational Constancy stage, students make the meaning connection with classical roots and stems, and they spell the less common words correctly. This upper level spelling inventory includes several difficult and infrequent orthographic patterns that are spelled accurately by students who have developed quite a mature spoken and written vocabulary. For example, students who spell *indictment, adjourn,* and *camouflage* correctly demonstrate quite a sophisticated knowledge of English orthography.

Content Area Spelling Inventories

Several content specific spelling inventories have been developed (McIntosh & Bear, 1993). These content area inventories give teachers an indication as to

FIGURE 3–13 Upper Level Qualitative Spelling Inventory

CLL QUALITATIVE SPELLING INVENTORY
SPELLING-BY-STAGE ASSESSMENT   UPPER LEVELS

Instructions: Let the students know that you are administering this inventory to learn about how they spell. Let them know that this it not a test, but that they will be helping you by doing their best. Some of the words will be easy to spell; some will be more difficult. When they do not know how to spell a word, ask them to spell the best they can.

Possible script: "I am going to ask you to spell some words. Try to spell them the best you can. Some of the words will be easy to spell; some will be more difficult. When you do not know how to spell a word, spell it the best you can; write down all the sounds you feel and hear."

Say the word once, use the word in a sentence and then say the word a second time. Consider their work on the first eight words before continuing. You may want to stop testing when students miss 5 out of 8 words. See the text for further instructions on administration and interpretation.

Have students check their papers for their names and the date.

1. **confusion**   There was confusion when there was a power failure.   *confusion*
2. **pleasure**   It was our pleasure to have you come over.   *pleasure*
3. **resident**   Mr. Squires has been a resident of this town for over forty years.   *resident*
4. **puncture**   Joan saw the puncture in her bicycle tire.   *puncture*
5. **confidence** I have confidence in Donna.   *confidence*
6. **fortunate**   We were fortunate to have gotten back safely.   *fortunate*
7. **decorator**   The decorator helped me choose furniture for my living room.   *decorator*
8. **opposition** The coach said the opposition would give us a tough game.   *opposition*

If you wish, stop here, check papers, discontinue, or go to one of the elementary qualitative inventories if a student misspells 5 out of the first 8 words.

9. **prosperity**   During this period of prosperity, our income increased dramatically.   *prosperity*
10. **succession**   He fired several shots in rapid succession.   *succession*
11. **emphasize**   In conclusion, I want to emphasize the most important points.   *emphasize*
12. **correspond**   President Bush must correspond with many people each day.   *correspond*
13. **commotion**   The audience heard the commotion backstage.   *commotion*
14. **propellant**   The booster rocket is fueled by a liquid propellant.   *propellant*
15. **hilarious**   John thought the comedian was absolutely hilarious.   *hilarious*
16. **criticize**   The boss will criticize you for your work.   *criticize*
17. **indictment**   The attorney general made the indictment based on the grand jury's findings.   *indictment*
18. **reversible**   Terry wears a reversible coat in the winter.   *reversible*
19. **category**   I will put the bottles in one category and the cans in another.   *category*
20. **adjourn**   The meeting will adjourn at five o'clock.   *adjourn*
21. **excerpt**   I am going to read one excerpt from this chapter.   *excerpt*
22. **camouflage**   The soldier wore camouflage to avoid detection.   *camouflage*

how well students will be able to read printed materials related to the content areas.

The relationship between students' orthographic knowledge (as evidenced in word recognition and invented spelling) and reading achievement has been observed throughout the developmental sequence from Emergent through Specialized stages of reading and writing (Templeton & Bear, 1992).

The premise underlying the content area spelling assessments is that when students' orthographic knowledge is strong, their reading is easier and more fluent. Isn't it possible that the students who spell *oxygen* correctly are more capable readers than students who spell it as OXIGIN? Their ideas are no brighter, but their verbal proficiencies allow them to read with greater ease than the student who has a difficult time spelling and reading the key vocabulary.

The words teachers select for content area inventories are often the key vocabulary words for the course. The words in the content spelling inventories can also function as a prompt in the same way that a structured overview, a No

FIGURE 3–14 Upper Level Spelling Inventory Error Guide

STAGES:	WITHIN WORD PATTERN		SYLLABLE JUNCTURE			DERIVATIONAL CONSTANCY		
	Middle	*Late*	*Beginning*	*Middle*	*Late*	*Beginning*	*Middle*	*Late*
1. **confusion**	confushon	confusion confustion	conffusion	confussetion confussion	confusion			
2. **pleasure**	plasr plager	plejer	pleser	plesher	plesour plesure	pleasure		
3. **resident**	resatin		reserdent resudint	resadent resedint	reseadent resident			
4. **puncture**	pucshr pungchr	puncur	puncker	punksher	punchure puncture puncsure puncture			
5. **confidence**	confadence	confadents	confedense	confedence		confidense confidence convidence confidince confidence		
6. **fortunate**		forhnat frehnit	foohinit forchenut	fochininte fortunet fortunate				
7. **decorator**	dector	decrater	decorator		decorater decoratore decorator			
8. **opposition**	opasion	opasishan opozcison opishien	opasitian	oppasishion oppisition opposition oposision		opposition oposision		
9. **prosperity**		proparty properity	prosparaty prospearaty propserity	prosperity				
10. **succession**	sucksession	sucession	sucesion sucession	succession succession				
11. **emphasize**	infaside infacize	emfesize	emfisize	ephacise	empasise emphasise	emphisize emphasize		
12. **correspond**	corspond	corrospond	corispond	correspond	corespond correspond			
13. **commotion**	comoushown	comoshion camotion cumotion	comocion comosion	comoution comotion commotion		commossion commotion		
14. **propellant**	porpelent proplent	porpelont proppellent	propelent propellant	propelant	propellant	propellant		
15. **hilarious**	halaris hollarries	hallarious helariuse heleriaus halareous halarace	halaryous hollarous halaries	hularius	hilarious hilerious helarious			
16. **criticize**	critise crisize critize	critasise	criticise critasise	criticize critize critasize	critasize criticize critisize			
17. **indictment**	enditment inditment	enditement inditement	endightment	indightment	indicment			
18. **reversible**	reversbell reversabul	reversobol reversabel	reverseable reversabel	reversabile reversible	revercible reversable reversible			
19. **category**	cadagoure kadacorey	cadacory cadigore catagore	catagery catiguory catigorie	catagory categores	catorgory catagory category			
20. **adjourn**	ajurn agern	ajurn ajorne ajurne	adgurn adjurn	adjourne adjorn	adjurn adjourn			
21. **excerpt**	exherpt exhert	exherpt exsort exerp	ecsert exsert	exerpt	excert exsurpt exserpt			
22. **camouflage**	camoflosh camaphlauge	camaflauge camaflage camoufloge	camoflodge camagflag	comoflodge camaflague	camofloge camoufloge camouflage			

STAGES:	WITHIN WORD PATTERN		SYLLABLE JUNCTURE			DERIVATIONAL CONSTANCY		

**FIGURE 3–15 Qualitative Content Specific
Spelling Inventory: Biology**

1. allergy
2. antibiotic
3. antibody
4. antigen
5. benign
6. cancer
7. carcinogen
8. immune system
9. immunity
10. infection
11. inflammation
12. interferon
13. malignant
14. toxin
15. tumor
16. vaccine

Thanks to Lyn Girindo for help developing this list.

Book Directed Reading-Thinking Activity (DRTA) (Gill & Bear, 1988), a web, or a cluster help students to think about the topic they are studying. Teaching students these words in isolation, in rote vocabulary exercises, is *not* the direction to take. Instead, teachers can help students make *meaning connections* between what they know and what they are trying to learn (Templeton, 1992).

Teachers start to examine this meaning connection with students by asking them to star the words on the list that are familiar. Students who spell accurately, star more words. This record of familiarity with the topic can be a diagnostic reference for tracking students' vocabulary growth in the particular content area.

Finally, before collecting students' papers, some teachers use an overhead of the words and ask students to think about how the words are related to the content area. Together, the teacher and the students brainstorm a list of related words. For example, if *geology* were a word on an inventory, students could work together to find other words that have *geo* in them. The meaning relations are at the heart of word study in the content areas, and the spelling and meaning connection is discussed in more detail in Chapter Eight. As papers are collected, teachers may reiterate that students' work will help them determine what to teach and will not be a part of their grade.

Two content inventories, one for biology and one for geometry, are presented in Figures 3–15 and 3–16, respectively. In preliminary studies, the number of content words spelled correctly at the beginning of the year have been related to term grades. There are fewer exceptions than expected, and on average, in a given content class, the good readers and spellers usually have higher grade-point averages than students who are not as capable.

In part, the relationship between literacy achievement and achievement in content classes is strong because the ways in which students are tested are dependent upon their literacy proficiency. Because many teachers rely so heavily on literacy to communicate ideas, and because so much of content instruction is textbook oriented, students who have difficulty with these spelling tests often have problems earning good grades. Because they cannot read well, they are denied access to ideas: Every teacher needs to help students find materials to read which can be read with fair ease. Content area spelling inventories are

Can students read the texts with ease? A content spelling inventory gives some indication.

FIGURE 3–16 Qualitative Content Specific Spelling Inventory: Geometry

Instructions: Let students know that you are administering this inventory to learn about how students spell. Let them know that this is not a test, but that they will be helping you by doing their best. Some of the words will be easy to spell; some will be more difficult. When they do not know how to spell a word, ask them to *spell the best they can.*

Possible script. "I am going to ask you to spell some words that are related to geometry. Try to spell them the best you can. Some of the words will be easy to spell; some will be more difficult. If you do not know how to spell a word, spell it the best you can; write down all the sounds you feel and hear when you say the word."

Say the word clearly once; if you wish, read the sentence; and then say the word a second time. Make sure that their names, date, and class are at the top of the papers.

1. **perpendicular**   One tetherball pole has fallen down, but the other is still perpendicular. *perpendicular*
2. **adjacent**   I'm going to the sporting goods store that is adjacent to the 7–11. *adjacent*
3. **equilateral**   Equilateral triangles have three identical sides. *equilateral*
4. **hypotenuse**   Knowing the hypotenuse of a triangle can tell you a lot about the rest of the triangle. *hypotenuse*
5. **isosceles**   An isosceles triangle is a very even triangle. *isosceles*
6. **parallel**   The railroad runs parallel to Main Street. *parallel*
7. **vertex**   Look for the vertex of the last triangle. *vertex*
8. **altitude**   Tonight, Sirius, the Dog Star, is at an altitude of 18°. *altitude*
9. **obtuse**   This triangle is obtuse. *obtuse*
10. **polygon**   A polygon is a complicated shape. *polygon*
11. **triangle**   Go to where the three paths form a triangle. *triangle*
12. **vertical**   He's over there, under the tree that leans slightly from the vertical. *vertical*
13. **acute**   An acute angle is sometimes very small. *acute*
14. **bisector**   A bisector is a line that cuts an angle in half. *bisector*
15. **congruent**   Two of these angles are congruent. *congruent*
16. **quadrilateral**   Which of these two polygons is a quadrilateral? *quadrilateral*
17. **scalene**   Scalene triangles look somewhat lopsided. *scalene*
18. **tangent**   On the board you can see that Line B is tangent to Circle A. *tangent*
19. **trapezoid**   A trapezoid is an interesting shape. *trapezoid*
20. **collinear**   The two lines are not the same length, but they are collinear. *collinear*
21. **complementary**   Complementary angles fit together to form 90°. *complementary*
22. **intersect**   The two roads intersect somewhere by the river. *intersect*
23. **theorem**   A theorem can never be proved absolutely. *theorem*
24. **diameter**   The diameter is one measure of a circle. *diameter*
25. **radius**   The radius of a circle depends on the size of the circle. *radius*
26. **supplementary**   None of these pairs of angles are supplementary. *supplementary*
27. **degree**   A degree is a very small measure of a circle. *diameter*
28. **angle**   How large is that angle? *angle*
29. **geometry**   Geometry is the study of shapes. *geometry*
30. **cylinder**   Most cans are in the shape of a cylinder. *cylinder*

Thanks to Meggin McIntosh, Mark Zimmerman, Connie Merrill, and several Washoe County teachers for help developing this list.

used to find important mismatches between literacy achievement and academic achievement in a content area both in terms of students who read well, but do not complete assignments, versus students who work to exhaustion for the grades because they have a hard time reading the text. By studying the meaning connection in directed word study, teachers help students grow in both their conceptual and orthographic development.

In summary, the content spelling inventory is used to assess literacy achievement *and* the vocabulary knowledge students bring to their content studies. Students who are way off in their invented spellings of these content words are likely to have trouble reading the textbook.

Word Study Groups

Once it is clear what stages of development students are in, teachers begin to think about organizing instruction. In this section, we discuss grouping students for word study instruction through the **Developmental Classroom Profiles.** These profiles are pictures of students' orthographic knowledge and provide a starting point. First, the issue of grouping is considered, and then the discussion turns to the classroom profiles.

Why Group?

Word study groups are developed.

Those of us who have studied Henderson and Stauffer have learned to develop groups for some elementary instruction for directed word study and directed reading and writing activities (Henderson, 1990; Stauffer, 1980). Usually, teachers who use this approach conduct directed work in three and sometimes four small groups. Developmental Classroom Profiles like those below, help teachers think of literacy groups. Many teachers now divide classroom activity into three types of work:

1. *Circle* work with the teacher; i.e., directed word study groups
2. *Seat* work, in which students work in groups, pairs, or individually on activities and projects
3. *Center* work, in which students work individually or with a partner in centers or stations set up around the room

Roughly a third of the students work in centers, another third works at tables or at their seats, and the final third has time with the teacher in circle. This format is discussed at length in Chapter Four.

The point here is that directed instruction with the teacher is a special time for discussion and word study at a table or on the floor (Henderson, 1981; Templeton, 1991a). Teachers keep coming back to this configuration; it seems that it is easier to manage three groups than two, four, or five.

Recent trends in literacy instruction have discouraged many teachers from developing word study groups based on development. Indeed, there are many reasons to be suspicious of homogeneous or ability grouping because, often, the low groups receive inferior instruction (Stanovich, 1986). However, it

Word study with partners and individually.

can also be argued that students benefit from developmentally appropriate instruction, and that this type of instruction is difficult to achieve when students are heterogeneously grouped for word study.

Clearly, it is a mistake to use developmental grouping as the sole way to group students. Throughout the day, there must be a broad mixing of students across ability groups so that talents and ideas can be shared. Experience tells us that when students study a particular orthographic feature, it is best if students are in groups with others who are ready to benefit from directed word study; these groups create proximal learning partners for word study. For example, it is difficult to study long vowel patterns when some of the students in the group are in the Letter Name stage. As the developmental model has shown, students in the Within Word Pattern stage use but confuse long vowel patterns, and they benefit most from examination of this feature.

In addition to the homogeneous groups that work with the teacher in circle or small group sessions, and the word sorting partners in word study centers, there are times when students work together in word study workshops or even whole class word study sessions. While students work on different sorts and with different words, they can work side-by-side during word study sessions. This is a good time for teachers to observe students sorting, and it is a good way for students to show each other how they sort. After students sort, they are asked to explain their sorts to someone else before putting them away.

Developmental Classroom Profiles

It is a simple matter to fill in the developmental charts. As students' papers are reviewed, a record of their names are made underneath the 15-point scale. These charts are a good place to see the class at-a-glance. Figures 3–17 through 3–20 are templates that can be used. Templates for lower, middle, and upper elementary grades have also been included. These different forms give more record-keeping space underneath the stages which are most prominent at different grade levels. A generic template is included for multi-graded classes or where there is a large spread in stages of development.

Examples of three class profiles are presented in Figures 3–21, 3–22 and 3–23. Figures 3–21 and 3–22 are from the same class in September and May. To compare over time, it can be seen that the groups have stayed remarkably the same except that everyone is further up the scale; graphically, everyone has shifted to the left.

Once students' names are entered onto the template, teachers begin to look for groupings by thirds. Is there a natural break? The vertical lines in Figures 3–21 and 3–22 indicate the groups we developed for directed reading and word study instruction (Bear & Barone, 1989).

You will notice that the groups do not follow stages strictly. Figure 3–21 shows some Within Word Pattern students working with Syllable Juncture students. Especially in September, teachers are careful to take a step backwards, so that this group would begin with long vowel pattern study. Similarly, in the next group, someone in the middle of the Within Word Pattern is working with someone in the middle of the Letter Name stage. Some of the word study group placement decisions are based on social and psychological factors related to self-esteem, leadership, and behavior dynamics.

There was a fair amount of spread in the first through third grade class in Figure 3–21. Beginning in the third grade, in some schools, there is less of a spread in students' development. Such was the case for the third grade class in November profiled in Figure 3–23. The bulk of the students were centered around the beginning of the Syllable Juncture stage–9. In part, to make for a manageable setting, as noted by the arrows in the figure, three children were moved into the first group and one child worked in the third group. There were three groups:

8 students for Syllable Juncture word study:
Zac, Jaime, Daniel, Eric, Melanie, Sara, Paula, Cliff

8 students for late Within Word Pattern word study:
Elizabeth, Craig, Melissa, Josh, Josh C., Joshua, Sarah, Camille

7 students for Within Word Pattern word study:
Dominic, Josh B., Ian, Dustin, Emily, Brennen, Erik

There will be times when the same activity is used with two groups. This is fine; smaller groups of 8 to 10 students make it easier for students to listen to each other. Groups are also fluid, and if a student is challenged to frustration, or if a student is not challenged by the activities, then groups are reorganized. In closing this section, it should be reiterated that there are many literacy activities in which students are not grouped by developmental level, as in partner reading, and in the project work related to units of study.

The profiles are part of assessment.

FIGURE 3–17 Template for Lower Elementary Classroom Organization

Spelling-by-Stage Assessment
Lower Elementary Classrooms

Teacher _____   Date _____

Preliterate		Early Letter Name		Letter Name		Within Word Pattern			Syllable Juncture			Derivational Constancy
1	2	3	4	5	6	7	8	9	10	11	12	13	14	15

FIGURE 3–18 Template for Middle Elementary Classroom Organization

Spelling-by-Stage Assessment
Middle Elementary Classrooms

Teacher _____ Date _____

Derivational Constancy			*Syllable Juncture*			*Within Word Pattern*			*Letter Name*			*Early Letter Name*		*& Preliterate*
15	14	13	12	11	10	9	8	7	6	5	4	3	2	1

FIGURE 3–19 Template for Upper Elementary Classroom Organization

Spelling-by-Stage Assessment
Upper Elementary Classrooms

Teacher _____

Date _____

Early Letter Name & Preliterate			Letter Name			Within Word Pattern			Syllable Juncture			Derivational Constancy		
1	2	3	4	5	6	7	8	9	10	11	12	13	14	15

FIGURE 3-20 Template for Classroom Organization

Spelling-by-Stage Assessment

Teacher _____   Date _____

Derivational Constancy		Syllable Juncture		Within Word Pattern		Letter Name		Early Letter Name		Preliterate
15	14	13	12	11	10	9	8	7	6	5	4	3	2	1

FIGURE 3‑21 Example of First to Third, Multiaged Grouping in September

A First–Third, Multiaged Classroom—September

Derivational Constancy		Syllable Juncture	Within Word Pattern			Letter Name				Early Letter Name			Preliterate
13	12	11	10	9	8	7	6	5	4	3	2	1	
	Amanda	Matthew	Jess	Sam	Lucas	Nicole	Jesse	Michael	Mary	Sarah	Casey	Jed	
		Ryan	Imran	J.R.		Elder	Eldon		Gerald		Jamie		
		Jacob	Anna	Lyn					Loren				
		Amir	Chris										

FIGURE 3‑22 Example of First to Third, Multiaged Grouping in May

A First–Third, Multiaged Classroom—May

Derivational Constancy	Syllable Juncture		Within Word Pattern				Letter Name			Early Letter Name & Preliterate		
13	12	11	10	9	8	7	6	5	4	3	2	1
Jacob	Amanda	Ryan	Jesse	Sam	Lyn	Sarah	Loren	Jamie				
	Matthew	Jess	Eldon		Nicole			Casey				
	Imran	Chris			Michael							
	Anna	Elder			Lucas							
		Mary			Gerald							
					Jed							

Adapted from Bear & Barone (1989)

63

FIGURE 3–23 Example of Third Grade Grouping in Late November

Spelling-by-Stage Assessment—Late November
A Third Grade Classroom

Early Letter Name & Preliterate			Letter Name			Within Word Pattern			Syllable Juncture			Derivational Constancy		
1	2	3	4	5	6	7	8	9	10	11	12	13	14	15
						Josh B.	Dom.	Eliz.	Jamie	Zac				
						Dustin	Ian	Craig	Daniel					
							—Melanie · Emily	Eric						
							Brennen	Melissa	Sara					
								Josh						
								—Paula						
								Erik—						
								Josh C.						
								Joshua						
								Sarah						
								—Cliff						
								Camille						

Group III Within Word Pattern 7 Students	Group II Late Within Word Pattern 8 Students	Group I Syllable Juncture 8 Students

Stage:
Total:

Conclusion: From Assessment to Planning Word Study

Three word study groups cover the developmental ranges in most classes.

Assessments must be useful and help teachers plan instruction. Now that a stage of orthographic development has been determined for each student, and groups have been created for directed word study, it is the right time to consider how you will organize word study in your classroom.

Thus far, the foundation of word study has been presented. Chapters One and Two set the foundation for understanding orthographic development and its role in literacy development. This chapter has shown how to assess students' development, including how to use the assessments to group for instruction. Through these discussions, the characteristics of each stage of development have been presented. How students learn words, a developmental model, and ways to assess development have been explored in some detail. The rest of this book focuses on word study instruction. The next chapter shows what word study is and presents in some detail the specific steps for running the word study activities in Chapters Five through Eight.

4

What is Word Study?

Word study is a method for examining words, and this is the subject of Chapter Four. Based on the results of the spelling-by-stage assessment, teachers plan word study activities to help students learn about words.

Word sorts and picture sorts are integral to planning a word study program. **Word study** is an active process in which students categorize words and pictures. Through these sorts, students learn a good deal about words; this knowledge, in turn, improves students' reading and writing.

In this chapter several basic types of word sorts are introduced. As a method of instruction, 10 principles of word study are presented to help teachers gauge the development of their word study programs.

Some word study activities are easier than others, and as teachers plan activities, they find a balance in the difficulty of the activities they present. A progression for choosing activities is outlined in this chapter. Also, through several examples and general scheduling outlines, ways to organize word study classrooms at several age levels are presented. Through the course of this chapter, you will meet several of our favorite teachers and how they organize word study instruction.

Eight Types of Sorts

The sorts discussed here are spelling, vocabulary, or phonics activities that use categorization to reveal essential differences and similarities among words. In these sorts, students match words or pictures to specific **key words.** These key words or pictures designate the basic categorizations students examine during their sorting.

Word sorting activities provide opportunities for students to make logical decisions about the ways they think about word elements including sound, pattern, meaning, and use.

Repeated practice categorizing words by particular features helps students identify and understand **invariances** or commonalities of the orthography. Students' perception of the invariances in the orthography develops as they observe consistent patterns which remain the same. In English, the CVVC is an example of an invariant orthographic pattern; it is a consistent pattern associated with the long vowel sound. Progress in the students' understanding of the invariances is related to reading, writing, vocabulary, and spelling development. This is why we say that there is a synchrony among reading, writing, and spelling development (Bear, 1991b).

By categorizing words according to contrasting features, in a word study approach to spelling and vocabulary, students learn about the orthography for themselves. For example, at a certain point in development, students who misspell words that end with *ck* and *ke* should sort words like *tack, snake, quack, drake, lake, sack, rack* into two groups by vowel sound, as shown in Figure 4–1. Through this word study students discover the invariant pattern which goes with each sound.

Students are involved in a variety of word study activities that draw their attention to the patterns in English orthography. After only a few months of school, students become familiar with most of the sorts that we cover here. The different types of activities that we describe fall into the following categories.

Picture sorts
Word sorts
Word hunts
Closed sorts
Open sorts
Blind sorts
Writing sorts
Speed sorts

FIGURE 4–1 Sorting Words by Vowel Sounds

Picture Sorts

| Picture Sorts |

Picture sorting is a basic categorization task for grouping together pictures with similar sound features in their names (e.g., initial consonant sounds: bat/boy; man/moon; sun/sock, ring/rock). At different points in development, pictures are sorted by initial consonant sounds, consonant blends or digraphs, rhyming families, or vowel sounds. Picture sorting is particularly suited for students in the Preliterate, Letter Name, and Early Within Word Pattern stages of spelling development. These are the students who are focused on the alphabetic principle or the basic single-syllable patterns of English orthography.

Word study is a process of comparing and contrasting.

The basic premise of all sorting tasks in a word study approach to spelling instruction is to compare and contrast word elements, separating or categorizing the examples that go together from those that don't. Picture sorts, such as the one shown in Figure 4–2, are first modeled by teachers as they work with students who share similar word study needs. Working as a group, children are given several picture cards to sort into contrasting categories. They say the names of the pictures' words as they place them in the correct groups. They are guided to correct placement as necessary. At the end of this guided activity, students often work in buddy groups to independently sort larger stacks of pictures into the same categories.

Picture sorts work from the known to the unknown.

Picture sorting differs from traditional phonics activities from workbooks in four important ways. First, picture sorting works from the known to the unknown; the names of the pictures can already be pronounced. As children sort through a stack of picture cards, they pronounce the name of each picture, and they concentrate on analyzing the sounds within each word. This is not possible if students cannot read the words on the worksheet in the first place. Unfortunately, this is too often the case with unknown words in a workbook program.

FIGURE 4-2 Picture Sort by Initial Consonant Sounds

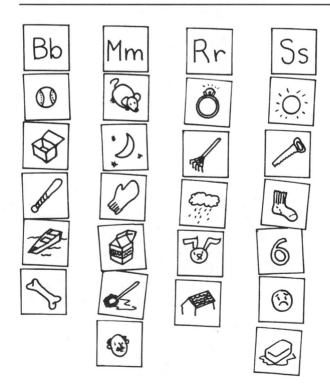

Picture sorts are analytic.

A second way in which picture sorting differs from a traditional workbook phonics format is that picture sorting is **analytic,** while most workbook phonics programs are **synthetic.** Rather than building up from the **phoneme** to the word, as workbook programs do in their synthetic approach, picture sorting begins with the whole, then examines its parts. In learning about vowel sounds, for example, the whole word is first pronounced—"cat." Only then is the initial consonant peeled off from the *at.* Through this analytic approach, picture sorting tasks work with **onsets** (beginning consonant elements) and **rimes** (the vowel and what follows), and not with individual phonemes. Research in phonemic awareness suggests that individual phonemes are more abstract and that analysis of onsets and rimes are more naturalistic and more understandable elements to examine (Goswami, 1990; Treiman, 1991).

Picture sorts require application.

A third way in which picture sorts differ from most phonics workbooks is that picture sorting does not involve drill or memorization, isolated sound drills or reliance on poorly understood rules. Picture sorting requires the application of higher-level critical thinking skills to make categorical judgments. Sorting tasks are conducted so that students determine similarities and differences among target features. When students make categorical decisions about whether the **medial,** or middle, vowel sound in "cat" sounds more like the medial vowel sound in "map" or "top," independent analysis and judgment are required. Students make decisions for themselves.

Students make decisions in picture sorts.

Picture sorts are efficient.

Efficiency is a fourth reason why picture sorts are more effective than worksheets. Picture sorting doubles the number of examples children study, and they study them in a short amount of time. Worksheets may have only three to five examples per page, and most of these exercises ask children to fill-in-the-blank or color their choices from the answers provided. It takes an average first grader 10 to 20 minutes to complete such a workbook activity, time which could be better spent reading. In contrast, sorting a stack of 20 to 30 picture cards takes just a few minutes, and the answers are not provided. Compare the number of examples in Figure 4–3 to see the differences!

Word Sorts

Word Sorts

Word sorting is like picture sorting except that printed word cards are used. Since learning to spell involves making associations between the spelling of words and their pronunciations, it is important that children know and can already pronounce most of the words to be sorted. Children who learn to read and spell well relate sound and spelling patterns of new words to the sound and spelling patterns of words they already know. Because students are sorting known words, their sorts help them discover the orthographic patterns which represent certain sounds and meanings.

Word sorting is useful for all students who have a functional sight word vocabulary. Students in the Letter Name stage sort their words into groups that share the same beginning sounds, by rhyming families, and by meaning. Students in the Within Word Pattern stage sort their words into groups by vowel patterns: dr*ai*n, tr*ai*n, Sp*ai*n vs. pl*a*te, t*a*ke or bl*a*me, for example. Within Word Pattern spellers hear the sounds and see the consistency in the way vowel sounds are spelled. Students in the Syllable Juncture stage benefit from sorting words into groups by syllable stress or syllable structure. Derivational Constancy spellers sort words by similarities in **alternation patterns** such as that in *sign* to *signal, denounce* to *denunciation, pronounce* to *pronunciation,* or *define* to *definition.*

Like the picture sorting routine, the word sort is first modeled by the teacher. Following the demonstration, children are guided in sorting written

FIGURE 4–3 Picture Sorting Offers More Sorting Opportunities Than Traditional Worksheets

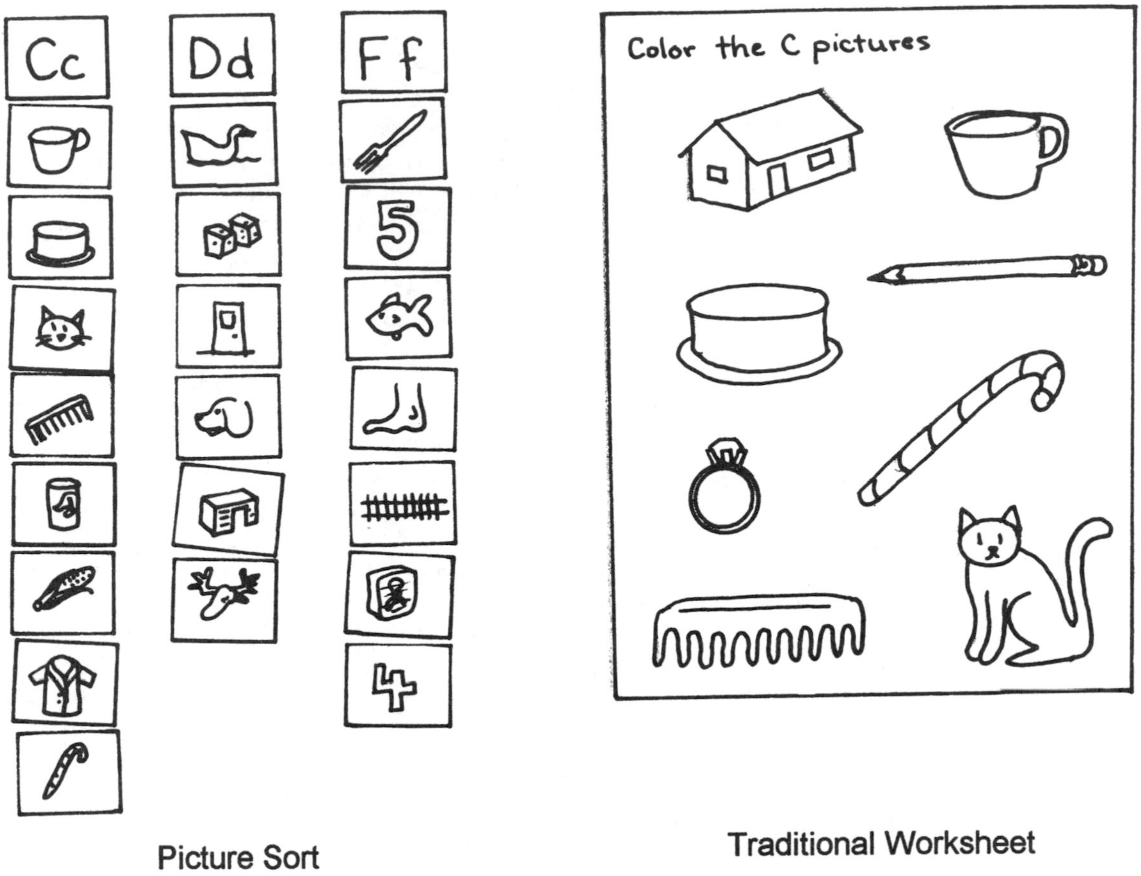

Picture Sort

Traditional Worksheet

words in contrasting categories and are directed towards correctness as necessary. After this guided practice, children team up in buddy pairs to practice independent sorting. These sorts might later be written into columns in word study notebooks, such as the one shown in Figure 4–4.

Let's walk through a series of word sorts which would be appropriate for a group of Within Word Pattern spellers. This series of word sorts would take place over a period of days or weeks, depending on the needs and progress of the group. By condensing it here, however, the concept of word sorting will come to light. These students sort to examine long vowels, and, in this example, they are studying long ē patterns.

The sorts begin when the students sort a deck of word cards into two piles by sound: long vowel sounds and short vowel sounds. This first sort is relatively easy. For "e" words, the categories may look like this:

men	cheap
sped	priest
head	clean
deaf	niece
thread	need
spent	thief
bent	creep

FIGURE 4-4 Word Study Notebook

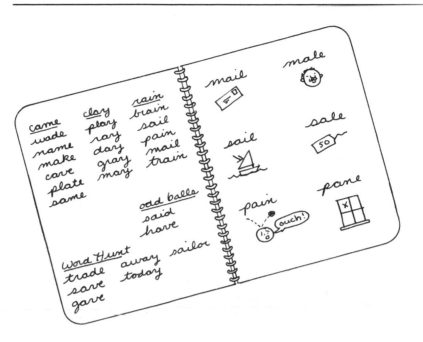

Take time to reflect on sound and pattern.

In the second step, students sort each column of words by orthographic patterns. There are three columns within the long vowel:

ea	*ie*	*ee*
cheap	priest	need
clean	niece	creep
thief		

The short vowels are sorted and studied in a similar way:

CVC	*CVCC*	*CVVC*
men	spent	head
sped	bent	thread

It is not surprising that these sorting tasks are not easy for children who, in the past, have looked at words by sound or isolated rule alone. For these students, there is a tendency to fixate on one category, sorting exclusively by either sound, pattern, or blind faith. Learning to consider both sound **and** pattern simultaneously requires reflection and continued practice. The goal is for students to sort sound and pattern automatically and without deliberation.

Word Hunts

Word Hunts

Word hunts are a bridge between word study and the students' reading and writing. In word hunts, students hunt through their reading and writing for words that are further examples of the pattern they are studying.

Teachers model word hunting with some text copied onto chart paper. In this demonstration, working line-by-line, students locate words that fit the categories under study. Finally, students return to texts they are reading and writing, and they hunt for other words which contain the same features. These words are then added to the columns in the word study notebook under the corresponding key word.

Here is an example of a word hunt by a small group of students in Mrs. Fitzgerald's third grade class. After reading folk tales, such as the one in Figure 4–5, and in word study, examining long ō and short ŏ patterns, they found and charted these lists from *The Three Billy Goats Gruff* (Galdone, 1973):

long	short	?
oh	not	voice
goat	gobble	who
go	cross	too
meadow	got	roared
so	on	
over		
troll		
don't		

After this sound sort, students sorted these words by orthographic patterns and organized them in their word study notebooks:

Groaned and *goat* were added to the *oa* column

Home was added to the *o consonant e* column

Troll and *told* were added to the *o consonant consonant* column

Meadow was added to the *ow* column

A new pattern of open, single, long "o" spellings was discovered with *so, going* and *over*

These word hunts add more examples for students to consider.

Closed Sorts

| Closed Sorts |

Most of the word sort tasks described in this book are **closed sorts.** In closed sorts, teachers define the categories and model the sorting procedure before the

FIGURE 4-5 Word Hunt with Story Retelling

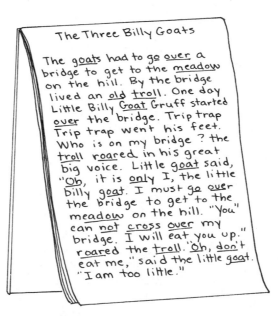

students sort (Gillet & Kita, 1978). Students are carefully guided to go through the same sorting task. As they work in small groups, teachers and students discuss the characteristics of each sort. Students gradually take control of the sorts, and there are many opportunities for students to practice sorting independently. In closed sorts, the categories are selected by the teacher according to the stage-by-spelling assessments described above. The particular sequences of activities are designed to meet the needs of particular groups of spellers.

Open Sorts

| Open Sorts |

In **open sorts** students create the categories with the packs of known words. These sorts are more diagnostic in nature because we get to see what categories students establish on their own. Open sorts show what students know about examining the orthography when they work on their own. Students often show us ways to organize words that we had not imagined. For example, sorting the same words, one student saw action words and "things," while another made three piles: one for long vowels, one for short, and words that did not fit in either group. Some of the most productive discussions about the orthography come when students explain the way they sorted in an open sort.

Blind Sorts and Writing Sorts

| Blind Sorts |

In addition to closed sorts and open sorts, there are **blind sorts** and **writing sorts.** A blind sort is a variation of a closed sort. The categories are determined by the teacher. The teacher or a classmate calls out words and students in the group point to the key word it would follow. Blind sorts are particularly useful for students who could use some time attending less to the visual patterns and more to the sounds. Blind sorts are best done in buddy pairs, with one buddy calling out the word for another.

| Writing Sorts |

Writing sorts are a variation of both closed sorts and blind sorts. In writing sorts, a word is called out by the teacher, and students write the word in the proper category using the column header (key word) as a model for spelling.

Speed Sorts

| Speed Sorts |

Speed sorts are attempted once students have become good at open and closed picture and word sorts. Speed sorting is no different than ordinary word or picture sorting except that students try to complete the task quickly. Speed sorting is appropriate only when accuracy is guaranteed. Thereafter, sorting for speed helps to arouse attention. The students try to beat their previous times, and this helps them build automaticity in the categorization of particular orthographic features. Students are paired for this activity, and they learn to chart their progress.

In these eight types of sorts, you can see that word sorting differs from traditional spelling instruction. In word sorting, students attend to sounds and patterns of words simultaneously. Word sort activities give students plenty of practice and experience manipulating and categorizing words by sound, pattern and meaning until they can sort quickly and accurately.

Ten Principles of Word Study Instruction

We know that we cannot teach students things they do not know something about. This is the underlying principle of Vygotsky's zone of proximal development and the motivating force behind the spelling-by-stage assessment described in Chapter Three. By classifying invented spellings developmentally, a zone of proximal development may be identified. By identifying spelling features students are experimenting with, we can plan word study activities which can help (Invernizzi, Abouzeid & Gill, 1994).

Don't feel as though you have to be an authority on English spelling before you begin. The spirit of inquiry is alive and well in classrooms where teachers say, "I don't know! How can we find out?" Here are the ten guiding principles, followed by detailed discussions, to lead you along the way:

1. Look for what students use but confuse.
2. A step backward is a step forward.
3. Use words students can read.
4. Compare words "that do" with words "that don't".
5. Sort by sight and sound.
6. Begin with obvious contrasts first.
7. Don't hide exceptions.
8. Avoid rules.
9. Work for automaticity.
10. Return to meaningful texts.

1) *Look for what students use but confuse.*

Work with features children "use but confuse" as opposed to those they totally neglect (see Figure 4–6). The teachable moment comes when students experiment with orthographic features. For example, students who spell *boat* as BOTE are ready to examine long vowel patterns. Students who spell *boat* as BOT are not experimenting with long vowel patterns, and they are not ready for any focused study of these patterns. As was discussed in Chapter Two, "using but confusing" is our signal that students are close to learning something new about the orthography. Take your cue from the students, not the curriculum. Examine misspellings on the spelling-by-stage assessment in Chapter Three to determine what

| "Use but confuse" |

FIGURE 4–6 Writing Samples With Examples of "Using But Confusing"

My Accident

Last year I scrapped my chian. I was shacking and my mom was too. My Dad met us at the docters offises. And I had to have stiches. Then my Dad bout me an ice crem cone. And we went home. I didn't go to school the nexs day. I was to tird.

students know and what they are trying to figure out. Teachers look to see what features are consistently present and correct, to determine what aspects of English orthography they already know. By looking for features which are used inconsistently, teachers determine those aspects of the orthography currently under negotiation. These are the features to target.

2) *A step backward is a step forward.*

> **Take a step backwards.**

Once you have identified students' stages of developmental word knowledge and the orthographic features under negotiation, take a step backward and build a scaffold of support. In setting up your categories, contrast something new with something that is already known. If, for example, you are beginning to introduce a new sound or pattern, be sure to present it in contrast to an old sound or pattern. We begin word study activities where the students will experience success. For example, students in the Letter Name stage begin by sorting words by initial consonant elements first; then they move quickly to short vowels. A step backwards is the first step forward in word study instruction.

3) *Use words students can read.*

Where should the words come from? From any and all sources that the children can read. Words come from language experience stories, from recent readings, words from poems, and even from words in old spelling books collecting dust on the shelf. Choose words to sort that students can read immediately and out of context.

> **Word sorts use words students can read.**

Since learning to spell involves achieving a match between the spoken language and the orthography, we want children to examine words which they can readily pronounce. Dialect does not alter the importance of this basic principle of word study. Whether one says /hog/ or /hôg/, it is still spelled *hog*. The consistency is in the orthography, and it is our job to make those consistencies explicit. It is easier to look across words for consistency of pattern when the words are easy for students to pronounce.

4) *Compare words "that do" with words "that don't".*

> **Compare words That Do and Words That Don't**

In order to learn what a Chesapeake Bay retriever looks like, you have to see a poodle or a bull dog, not another Chesapeake Bay retriever. What something *is* is also defined by what it *is not*; contrasts are essential to students building categories. For example, short vowels are contrasted with long vowels—*cat* to *cape*—and words that double consonants are contrasted with those that don't—*hopping* to *hoping* (see Figure 4–7).

5) *Sort by sight and sound.*

Students examine words by how they are spelled and how they sound. Both sight and sound are integrated into students' orthographic knowledge. Too often, students focus on visual patterns at the expense of how words are alike in sound.

Figure 4–8 illustrates the way students move from a sound sort to a sort by visual patterns. First, students sorted by the differences in sound between long a and short a. Then students subdivided the sound sort by orthographic patterns.

> **Sort by sight and sound.**

To establish categories, select a key word or picture which will label the category clearly. Students read both the key word (or picture) and the new word (or picture) each time a new example is categorized.

6) *Begin with obvious contrasts first.*

> **Begin with easy sorts.**

Whenever students begin the study of a new feature, teachers choose key words or pictures which are distinctive. For example, when students examine initial consonants, teachers do not begin with M with N . . . they share too many features to be distinct to the novice. They are both

FIGURE 4-7 Doubling Sort: Comparing Words "That Do" with Words "That Don't"

FIGURE 4-8 Word Sort by Sound Can Move to Word Sort by Pattern

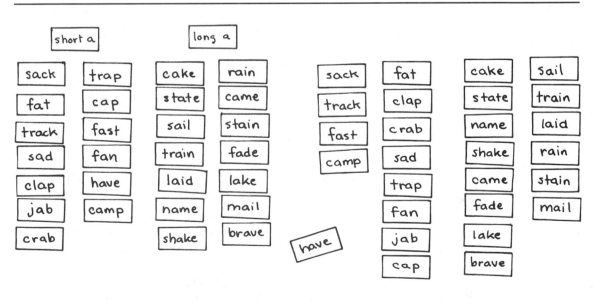

nasals, and they share three-fourths of the visual features as well. Better to begin contrasting M with something totally different at first—S for example—then work towards finer distinctions as these categorizations become quite automatic. Move from general, gross discriminations to more specific ones.

Likewise, be wary of two syllable words for beginners—even if only picture cards are used. *Banana* may start with a *b*, but the first *n* is pronounced the loudest, and some beginners are confused.

7) *Don't hide exceptions.*

Don't hide exceptions.

Exceptions arise when students make generalizations. We don't hide exceptions. By placing so called "irregular" words in a miscellaneous category, new categories of consistency frequently emerge. For example, in looking at long vowel patterns, students find these exceptions: *give, have,* and *love;* yet, it is no coincidence that they all have a *v,* and they form a consistent pattern. True exceptions do occur and become memorable as such.

8) *Avoid rules.*

In word sorts, students discover rules.

Avoid telling students spelling "rules." Students discover patterns and make generalizations for themselves. The teacher's job is to stack the deck so that these generalizations become explicit through the process of sorting words into categories of similarity. Instill in students the habit of looking at words and asking questions.

9) *Work for automaticity.*

See how fluently students sort.

Accuracy in sorting is not the ultimate indication of mastery, fluency in sorting is. Acquiring fluency in sorting and examining orthographic patterns leads to the fluency necessary for proficiency in reading and writing. Your students will move from hesitancy to fluency in their sorting.

10) *Return to meaningful texts.*

Word hunts connect word study to reading.

After sorting, students need to return to meaningful texts to hunt for other examples to add to the sorts. These hunts extend the analysis to a more difficult vocabulary. For example, after sorting one syllable words into categories labeled **cat, drain, snake,** a student added **tad**pole, ex**plain** and es**cape.** Through a simple word hunt, this child extended the categories to two-syllable words.

Teaching is not telling.

These ten principles of word study boil down to one golden rule of word study instruction: *Teaching is not telling.* In word study, students examine, manipulate, and categorize words. Teachers stack the deck, so to speak, to focus students on a particular contrast and to create a task which forces them to do so. Stacking the deck for a discovery approach to word study is not the absence of directed instruction. To the contrary, a systematic program of word study, guided by an informed interpretation of spelling errors and other literacy behaviors, is a teacher-directed, child-centered approach to vocabulary growth and spelling development.

The Organization of Word Study Instruction

There are many ways to organize word study. Some teachers conduct word study sessions with reading groups, and other teachers use a conference approach with separate word study groups. In both settings, teachers use interactive and cooperative group formats for brief periods of directed word study instruction.

There are some fundamentals to consider in setting up a word study program. First, we'll discuss the classroom, and then we'll turn to schedules for word study. Three schedules for word study are discussed in some detail:

Betty Lee presents a word study schedule ideal for first and second grades.

Our illustrator, Francine Johnston, builds word study into her meetings with reading groups.

Kathy Ganske works in separate word study groups in her fourth grade classroom.

Getting Ready For Word Study Instruction

What does a word study classroom look like? How is word study organized in the classroom? These questions are answered in two parts: physical and scheduling needs.

Physical Needs

Starting with the physical space and the number of students, you can plan for a portion of your classroom space to be dedicated to word study. First, a storage area is used for storing sorts. Many teachers use file cabinet or storage boxes to file the sorts in folders. In these folders are the materials needed for an activity—the word cards in a plastic sandwich bag, clipped to a folder; sometimes a gameboard or a list of words to write onto a blank gameboard; and special pieces to put on a game board.

In addition, teachers need a place to store picture sorts and word sorts. If students are beginning readers, a place to store word banks is needed. Finally, for students writing in word study notebooks, teachers need space for plastic baskets where students turn in their word study notebooks.

Find places for students to sort.

Hopefully, students' desks are large enough to provide a surface for word sorting. Floor space is also needed for sorting and some small group work. In addition, a center or station is designated as a word study area. As is apparent in Betty Lee's and Francine Johnston's classrooms, students rotate to the word study station where they work individually or with a partner to sort or play a game. A stopwatch is a part of some word study activities and is placed in the word study center. Many teachers also post chart size sound boards in this area.

There are fairly simple materials you will need for word study. Not much is needed, and some of the special materials are presented in this book.

From the materials store.   Chart paper, index cards to cut into word cards, scissors, crayons, markers, paper for word study notebooks and word study sheets, manila folders to store activities, game board materials (board, spinners, dice), containers for storing sorts.

From the bookstore.   Dictionaries for students, word books of all sorts from root books and etymological dictionaries to rhyme books. Books are listed in the activities in Chapters Five through Eight by developmental level.

From printing.   *Pictures for sorting*—take the pictures you need from this book, have them printed on card stock, and color them a bit (lamination is a personal choice). *Words for sorting*—use the lists you need in this book and write the words on word cards made from index cards.

Print pictures on card stock.

Sound boards—reproduce the sound boards in Chapter 6 for students as they need them. These sound boards use pictures to key students to sound-letter correspondences. These sound boards can be stapled inside students' writing notebooks for reference. The initial consonant and consonant blend and digraph boards are for the Preliterate and Early Letter Name stage learners. The vowel boards are for students in the Letter Name and Within

Word Pattern stages. Find a way to make poster-sized sound boards for display. You can use the pictures at the end of Chapters 5, 6, and 7 to make your own sound board posters. If you can find a chart maker, you can enlarge the actual sound boards we have provided. The paper is thin, so we also laminate the charts for increased durability.

Schedules for Word Study

The second step to organize word study instruction is to set up a schedule and to develop a weekly routine. Schedules vary greatly. Some teachers choose a conference approach or a workshop routine, and others build word study into their language arts block in which students rotate in groups from circle time with the teacher, to seat work and centers (Henderson, 1990; Templeton, 1992).

There are three features to consider in scheduling word study in your classroom:

Components of Directed Word Sorts:
♦ Conducted in small group
♦ Short in duration
♦ Follow up with independent practice

1. *Schedule time for small group work.*
   Students at the same developmental level work with a teacher for directed word study. During this time, teachers show students new ways to sort, and guide them through practice sorts using these new features.

2. *These directed lessons are short in duration.*
   There is a balance of activities. Over a week, approximately 15 minutes are dedicated each day to word study activities. This 15 minutes is an average; one day, students sort and discuss in a small group for 20 minutes. The following day, students may hunt for words in a story for eight minutes.

3. *Plan time for students to sort independently and with partners.*
   Students need time *to sort* through words on their own, and they need time *to search* for the orthographic features they are studying. Teachers build this independent work into center activities and games that students play together.

Progressive Skill Development

In the previous discussion, the *where* and *when* of word study have been discussed. Now is a good time to consider choosing activities over the course of a week. Ed Henderson, and Betty Lee, a renowned first grade teacher of thirty years, discussed a general progression in the types of word study activities we choose. In this progression students **recognize, recall, judge,** and **apply.**

Recognize

Students are presented a particular feature to consider. With key pictures and key words, teachers guide the students as they compare words. For example, when students analyze initial consonants, they compare the picture of a "man" with the key picture of a "mouse". Students compare pictures for sound, and written words for sounds and patterns. They recognize that two words share similar features. In this case, both words begin the same way. Students may also say that they are both animals. Both are right. Teachers guide students in a discussion of the features that students are ready to consider. To recognize is to be aware of a new orthographic feature.

Students recognize patterns.

When teachers work with students in small groups they use chart paper to make lists of the words they study. These charts often contain interesting lists of words and ideas, and they are posted around the room. *Display student generated word lists around the room.* Words listed on the walls call attention to the richness and power of a versatile vocabulary (Cunningham, 1991). Sometimes these charts chronicle discussions of content studies, and sometimes, these lists focus on the specific study of words: happy words, sad words, holiday or seasonal words, homophones, homographs, synonyms and antonyms—all provide a ready reference for writing. All the students have to do is glance up.

Recall

In this second step in the progression, students recall examples of the features they have studied in directed instruction. A key word or key picture is provided to remind students of the types of words they are looking for, and they hunt for examples. They are encouraged to look around the room for examples.

Students remember examples.

Students list the words that fit the category signified by the key word. Younger children draw their ideas. Students in a later stage of orthographic development generate rhyming words that follow a specific orthographic pattern. Individually, with partners, or in small groups, students recall words that follow patterns they had recorded in their word study notebooks the day before. These may be written down in lists as a "brainstorm" of words that match the key word or picture.

At the beginning of a recall exercise, students are given a few strategies to recall words. For example, if the key word is *beat*, students are shown that they can find other words by dropping the initial consonant and adding another to obtain *seat, neat, meat*.

Judge

In judgment activities, students look through words or pictures for words that match the features they are studying. In closed sorts, students make judgments as to which words fit in the categories established in the previous recognize and recall lessons. Word hunts in familiar readings encourage judgment. Students judge which words apply and which words do not. Students work with partners in word study centers, and they work in small groups to sort 20 words or pictures that fit particular patterns.

In closed sorts, students make judgments.

Apply

There are many application-type activities. Students apply what they have learned to create something new. Open sorts are application activities because students find and proclaim their own categories. For example, students who have studied the various patterns for long *e* can apply this information to sort long *o* words. When Beginning Readers reorganize their word bank cards according to the categories of contrast, they apply what they know to other words or pictures. Many teachers have children return to their writing folders to look for words they may have written earlier which follow the same sound or pattern.

One first grade teacher, Susan Smith, has her children "teach a word" at the end of each week. One child, who chose the word *floor* stood up with an illustrated picture of a house with floors on one side, and the words *floor* and *door* on the other. As he taught the word, he held up his picture and said "first floor, second floor." Then he flipped the card and held up word cards and said "*floor*, rhymes with *door*." Clearly this student made a creative application of his new found word knowledge!

Board games and card games, such as the one shown in Figure 4–9, which match and categorize word features, also provide opportunities for application in an enjoyable context.

As students become wordsmiths, you'll be surprised by the lists of words they create themselves. One class created an illustrated homophone dictionary in a "Big Book" format which expanded across an entire year (see Figure 4–10). By the end of the year, 250 homophone pairs had been collected from their

FIGURE 4-9 Board Game for Initial Consonant Sounds

FIGURE 4-10 Class Homophone Book

FIGURE 4–11 Betty Lee's Schedule of Word Study Activities

Betty Lee's Schedule				
Monday	*Tuesday*	*Wednesday*	*Thursday*	*Friday*
Picture sorting	Drawing and labeling	Cutting and pasting	Word Hunts Word Bank	Games

collective reading, illustrated, and arranged in alphabetical order. The words they learn in activities like this facilitate their growth as readers and writers.

Three Word Study Schedules

Many teachers plan their weekly word study routine around these progressive skills. In the following three examples, the teachers begin with a directed word study session in which they introduce the categories.

Betty Lee's Circle-Seat-Center

In her first grade classes, Betty Lee organizes her word study program around a rotation of these progressive skills over the course of a week. Using a circle-seat-center format, Betty Lee introduces her spelling concepts with *picture sorts* at circle time. Typically, Betty Lee is in circle working with a third of the class. A second third of the class is at their seats drawing pictures of words they recalled from a previous lesson. The final third of the class is stationed at different centers where some students were sorting in word study activities for their developmental levels.

♦ Circle for small groups.
♦ Seats for independent activities.
♦ Centers for partners and individual activities.

As the schedule in Figure 4–11 shows, on Monday, the teacher models the categorization routine and helps students recognize the sound and letters they were studying.

On Tuesday, students recall the feature introduced on Monday in *drawing and labeling* activities. The examples in Figure 4–12 show a student's recalling of initial consonants.

Wednesday is devoted to children judging other examples through *cutting and pasting* tasks. Students find their own pictures of words which begin with a particular consonant, and they cut the picture out and label it.

FIGURE 4-12 Draw and Label Activity

Thursday targets application of the concepts under study through word hunts, word bank activities, and other tasks in which children apply what they learned to other words.

Friday is game day, and the children delight in the opportunity to play board games, card games and other games in which the recognition, recall, and judgment of spelling features are applied.

Francine Johnston's Primary Schedule

The illustrator of this book, Francine Johnston, also works with word study groups in a circle-seat-center configuration. She suggests the following organizational plan. As you will see, students are assessed on Friday; there are some fine changes from the traditional whole class weekly spelling test.

Monday–Introduce the Sort. In reading groups, children receive a word study sheet with words for the week printed in boxes. Each group has different words, depending on their stage of development designated in the spelling-by-stage assessment.

| Teacher models a sort. |
Students read the words, and the teacher checks to be sure that the words are known by sight. Words that students cannot read are discarded. The teacher then models the word sort for the children using her own larger cards so that everyone can see. The children return to their seats to cut their words apart and practice the sort assigned in the group.

Tuesday–Practice the Sort and Write It. On Tuesday, students bring their words to the group and sort under the teacher's supervision. The teacher watches to see that the sorts are done correctly. Troublesome words may be discussed, and eliminated if necessary, and practice is scheduled.

Children are assigned to do a writing sort in a word study notebook. The words in the sort are to be written in the appropriate categories under the proper key word.

Wednesday–Blind Sorts and Writing Sorts. On Wednesday, students work in buddy pairs to do blind sorts. Key words or pictures are placed in front of the pair. The first child holds all the words and calls them out one at a time. The second child, without looking at the word, indicates the correct category. The roles are then reversed. After doing the blind sort, the teams do a blind writing sort. They take turns calling out the words to each other. On a page in their word study notebooks, students write the key words at the top. Words are written underneath the key words by categories.

| Do blind sorts in pairs. |

Thursday–Word Hunts. Word hunts are conducted in group, in buddy pairs, or individually. Students search through current reading material to find additional words that fit the categories for the week. New words are recorded in the word study notebooks, on the board, or on a chart.

| Students hunt for other words. |

Friday–Assessment. A traditional spelling test format is used, or students call out words to each other in buddy pairs. In either case, it is unnecessary to call out every word on the list. Teachers even call out some words that were not among the original list to see if students can generalize the principles. At other times, teachers have their students write the words in categories. Some credit may be given for writing the word in the correct category even if the word itself is misspelled.

Kathy Ganske's Fourth Grade Classroom

This schedule is representative of intermediate schedules for word study. There is a good deal of small group work, and word study notebooks become an important part of the word study scene.

Kathy works in a fourth grade class of 25 children who exhibit a wide range of instructional levels in reading and spelling. By administering her own spelling-by-stage assessment during the first few days of school, she grouped her multi-leveled pupils into three stages of developmental word knowledge (Ganske, 1994). One group was so large, however, that it was divided in two, and there are a total of four word study groups that she schedules for regular small group meetings.

On Monday morning, every child finds a word study sheet on his or her desk. This page is divided into rectangles, and in each rectangle, a word is written. Students in the same word study group have the same words. These rectangles are cut out by the children, and these words become the word cards they sort throughout the week.

| Students write words in categories.

In Kathy's classroom, children sort the words before school even begins in anticipation of the categories they might be sorting later on. For assessment, these spontaneous, before-school, open sorts are interesting for Mrs. Ganske to observe. They tell her what students already know.

Word study notebooks are central to Kathy's program. Like response journals, work in the notebooks is ongoing. Word study notebooks are used in five basic activities:

1. Write word sorts in their notebooks
2. Draw and label words that match the key words
3. Drop and add letters to make new words
4. Write sentences (and later, paragraphs and stories) using the words they are studying
5. Do word hunts in trade books and literature response journals and categorize by the key words

Teacher-directed Word Study. On Monday, while the rest of the class gets started on drawing and labeling in the notebooks, Mrs. Ganske works with students for a teacher-directed lesson on the week's feature. Everyone brings their cut-out word cards with them. The very first thing Mrs. Ganske does is go through her own stack of words one at a time, pronouncing each one, and talking about meaning. Students also give examples of each word's meaning and share their knowledge of where they have heard or seen the word before.

The next thing Mrs. Ganske does is establish the key words that guide the sorts. She asks students what they think the categories might be and why they think so. In many cases, students have already seen the consistencies in sound and/or pattern as they cut out the words, and they have anticipated the sort. Nevertheless, Mrs. Ganske carefully models the sorting of each word into each category; for each match, she returns to the key word to establish an analogy.

Though all of Mrs. Ganske's students are readers, the same approach is taken using picture cards. Picture sorts are particularly appropriate to focus on sound before looking at pattern. In either case, careful modeling is essential to the success of initiating a closed sort.

| Match new words to the key words.

As Mrs. Ganske models the sorting procedure, she allows plenty of opportunity for students to make an analogy themselves. In each case, the word on the card is pronounced, placed under a key word, and compared to the pronunciation of the key word (see Figure 4–13). In order for the word to be placed in a column, it must match the key word by sound and/or pattern. Teachers are sensitive to dialectical differences in pronunciation which effect students' sorting. One student in Wise County, Virginia, for example, pronounced the word *vein* as "vine" and was correct in placing *vein* in the miscellaneous column as opposed to the long-*a* group; to her, the word *vein* was a long-*i*. Word study allows students to find their own categories.

**FIGURE 4-13 Students Gather with Weekly Word Lists for
Introductory Sort**

Go from word
sorts to word
study notebooks.

Once the word sort has been demonstrated and discussed, students sort their own word cards right there on the floor in front of Mrs. Ganske. Working individually, students hold their cards, say the words, and then say the key word that heads each columns. Students read through the words in each column to see if there are any changes they would like to make. Mrs. Ganske checks the sorts and asks students to explain why they grouped the words the way they did. Misconceptions are corrected, and the sorting is remodeled if needed. Afterwards, students return to their desks to begin work in their word study notebooks.

After all students from the first group have been guided in their first sort of the week, Mrs. Ganske calls the second group to her place on the floor and begins the teacher-directed group sort with a different batch of words. This procedure is continued until all groups have met with Mrs. Ganske. At their desks, students work in their word study notebooks, and then return to their novels and response logs.

Buddy Pairs.　On Tuesday and Wednesday, there is no teacher-directed word study. Instead, students team into buddy pairs, and a schedule for going back to the "sorting table" is put on the board (see Figure 4–14).

Buddies sort for
accuracy and
speed.

Throughout the day, buddy pairs go back to the sorting table at 10-minute intervals to sort their word cards for accuracy and speed. The same word cards are used from the day before, as are the same key words for categories. One buddy times the other with a stop watch kept at the table, and then checks for correctness against the answer sheet. Partners work together to solve any discrepancies between their sort and the answer, and they write their categories in their word study notebooks. The partners return to their seats and pick up where they left off with their reading or writing.

Cooperative Groups.   On Wednesday all four word study groups convene at the same time in their respective groups. Students bring the books they are currently reading, and they gather around a large piece of chart or butcher paper spread on the floor. A leader is appointed and the same key words used on Monday and Tuesday are written across the top of the large sheet of paper. Students skim and scan pages in their books that they have already read, looking for words that match the key words according to the feature under study. As examples are found, students share their words.

The leader writes words that match the key words.

Much discussion may ensue as to whether or not a word contains the spelling feature in question. Often the dictionary is consulted, particularly to resolve questions of stress, syllabication, or meaning. Once a consensus is reached, the leader writes the word on the paper under the proper key word. The word hunt continues for a specified amount of time, and usually several examples are found for each column (see Figure 4–15).

Meanwhile, Mrs. Ganske circulates from group to group and comments on the frequency of one pattern over another. Some patterns are found in virtually every text again and again, while others are harder to find. Mrs. Ganske also

FIGURE 4-14 Speed Sort Schedule

Speed Sort Schedule

9:00   Caroline and Hannah
9:10   Ellie and Elizabeth
9:20   Peter and Lee
9:30   Colin and Trevor
9:40   Medgar and Daniel

FIGURE 4-15 Cooperative Group Word Sort

asks group members to provide reasons for the agreed-upon groupings. After this activity, the word hunt is recorded in each member's word study notebook.

For homework that night students find additional examples to add to their notebooks from the books they are reading at home. It is important, however, that students not confuse skimming for word patterns with reading for meaning. Only material previously read is used for word hunts.

Individual Practice.   Thursday is Mrs. Ganske's students' favorite day. If they wish, students can race Mrs. Ganske in sorting their word cards. Students who are interested in beating Mrs. Ganske, practice the night before. Students meet in their word study groups to practice sorting for speed and accuracy. Mrs. Ganske circulates from group to group and sorts the word cards while being timed. For the next few minutes, group members try to beat her time. Those who succeed get to put their name on the blackboard, and some special prize or privilege is awarded at the end of the day.

Evaluation and Monitoring Progress.   Friday completes the cycle for the week. Each group is "tested" on the spelling features they have examined through their hunting and sorting tasks all week. Not every word is tested, however; only a random sample of words that have been categorized under each key word are tested. In this way, the discriminating orthographic feature is emphasized, as opposed to rote memorization of a given list of words.

Knowledge of particular orthographic patterns can be checked once again in the form of nonsense words on Monday. Students may spell the word *remblete,* for example, and then Mrs. Ganske asks what key word they thought of to guide their spelling (*complete*). In this way, Mrs. Ganske gauges the degree that the categorical distinctions studied generalize to unknown words.

The following Monday starts another cycle of word study with another set of words for each group. (See Figure 4–16 for Mrs. Ganske's schedule.) Some features from the week before continue to be examined, but new ones are added, depending on the results from the spelling test on Friday. Group membership may also change depending on a given child's pace and progress, as Kathy continues to use developmental stages of spelling for grouping.

Students' word study notebooks are graded regularly as outlined by the criteria presented in Figure 4–17 where you can see the rules in Mrs. Ganske's classroom.

Mrs. Ganske's word study program is just one example of how to integrate spelling instruction into a reading-writing, process-oriented classroom. What is remarkable about Mrs. Ganske's routine is its centrality to both reading and writing in the classroom. Students return again and again to trade books they have already read to analyze the vocabulary.

It is wonderful to see how word study is integrated into other studies. Poetry lessons begin with reference to a word study lesson on syllable stress. And in discussions of reading response, dialogue journals, students have also

FIGURE 4–16 Mrs. Ganske's Weekly Word Study Schedule

Kathy Ganske's Schedule

Monday	*Tuesday*	*Wednesday*	*Thursday*	*Friday*
Group sort with teacher	Buddy sorts	Word hunt in trade books	Speed sort	Test

Word Study notebook assignments (Monday through Friday) ⟶

FIGURE 4-17 Word Study Notebook Rules

Word Study Notebook

Activities for this notebook include: write and draw, word sorts, and word hunts. You will be required to:
1. use color and details in your pictures
2. use the correct spelling of this week's words
3. use complete sentences
4. make good use of time during group word sorts and hunts

You will be evaluated in this manner:

* excellent work

✓ good work but you made a few mistakes and left out detail

R you need to redo this assignment

discussed descriptive words and a previous word study lesson on descriptive and comparative adjectives. An organized, systematic approach to word study instruction is integrated into the reading and writing of process oriented classrooms. Whatever routine you choose, your sequence of activities must fit comfortably within your reading/writing/language arts block of instruction. By incorporating a word study notebook as an ongoing activity, you will have a built-in record of activities and record of progress.

Matching Activities to Development

Activities are arranged in developmental order.

All that is left to set up a word study program is to target activities for your students based on the assessments in Chapter Three. The chart in Figure 4–18 outlines the basic word study activities for each stage of spelling. The chart also lists the characteristics of each stage of development in some detail. This chart will help you to focus on the developmental needs of your students.

FIGURE 4-18 Sequence of Development and Instruction

Each of the spelling stages is outlined below following this organization:

First, the Stage and corresponding Chapter is noted. The stages are discussed in terms of

A. Characteristics
B. Reading and Writing Activities
C. Word Study Focus

I. Preliterate Stage / Chapter Five
A. Characteristics
1. Scribbles letters and numbers

    2. No Concept of Word (Morris, 1992)

    3. No letter-sound correspondences between oral and written language

    4. Pretend reading and writing

B. Reading and Writing Activities

    1. Read to students, DLTAs, Creative Dramatics

    2. Plenty of oral language use

    3. Tracking one or two sentence dictations, group experience charts, and rhymes and ditties

    4. Pretend reading and writing, drawing, storytelling, and dramatics

C. Word Study Focus

    1. Concept sorts

    2. Learn to recognize alphabet

II. Letter Name Stage / Chapter Six

Early Letter Name

A. Characteristics

    1. Represent beginning and ending sounds

    2. Rudimentary/Functional Concept of Word

    3. Beginning Readers

    4. Disfluent and unexpressive oral reading

    5. Disfluent writing, word-by-word

B. Reading and Writing Activities

    1. Read to students

    2. Secure Concept of Word by plenty of reading in pattern books and simple rhymes

    3. Collect and reread individual dictations one paragraph long

    4. Begin to write in journals regularly

C. Word Study Focus

    1. Sort pictures and words by initial consonants

    2. Collect known words for word bank

    3. For most students, final consonants are learned without direct attention unless they are unspoken in dialect

    4. Introduce initial consonant blends (*blend*) and digraphs (*ship*). Have students see blends and digraphs as a unit (*bl, st, sp,* etc.). Students spell consonant blends and digraphs correctly during the next stage.

Middle to End of Letter Name Stage

A. Characteristics

    1. Correctly spells initial and final consonants and some blends and digraphs

    2. Uses letter names to spell vowels

    3. One-to-one correspondences between sounds and letters

    4. Short vowels are used in nearly all stressed syllables, and short vowels are spelled based on point of articulation

    5. Omits preconsonantal nasals in spelling (BOP or BUP for *bump*)

    6. Beginning Readers who fingerpoint, read aloud to themselves, are disfluent and slow readers and writers

    7. Functional Concept of Word

B. Reading and Writing Activities

    1. Read to students

    2. Encourage invented spellings

    3. Collect two to three paragraph-long dictations which are reread regularly

    4. Encourage more expansive writing and consider some of the revision steps of process writing

C. Word Study Focus
  1. Sort pictures and words by families (*-at, -ed*)
  2. Sort pictures and words by short vowels and CVC
  3. Continue to examine consonant blends and digraphs
  4. Collect known words for word bank
  5. Open and closed sorts and games on short vowels

III. Within Word Pattern Stage / Chapter Seven
  A. Characteristics
    1. Spells regular short vowel words correctly
    2. Uses long vowel markers (NALE for nail)
    3. Spells most single syllable words correctly
    4. Reads silently
    5. Fingerpointing fades, and some expression comes into oral reading
    6. Transitional stage of literacy development
    7. Writing approaches fluency
    8. Can write in extended fashion, can work on revision and editing
  B. Reading and Writing Activities
    1. Discontinue dictations when student can write half a page and read many books at independent, easy-reading level
    2. Begin earnest reading of simple chapter books
    3. Write each day, writer's workshops, conferencing, and publication
    4. Read to students
  C. Word Study Focus
    1. Discontinue word banks and begin a word study notebook which chronicles sorts; the first records can come from sorts from the previous stage.
    2. Continue with sorts and record sorts and groups in a word study notebook
    3. Replace sorts with word bank words with teacher-made sorts; emphasize that the students work with known words in sorts and discard unknown words
    4. Examine differences between long and short vowels; i.e., CVC versus CVVC or CVCe
    5. Through closed and open sorts and word study games examine long vowel patterns. Begin with one long vowel and then choose a second long vowel, study it, and compare to the previous long vowel
    6. Examine homographs and homophones (*plain* and *plane*), low frequency short vowel patterns (*caught*) with consonant digraphs, and r-influenced short vowels (burst, spark)

IV. Syllable Juncture Stage / Chapter Eight
  A. Characteristics
    1. Short and long vowel spelling is stable (1 syllable)
    2. Begin to experiment with combining syllables
    3. Reads with good fluency and expression
    4. Silent reading rate is faster than oral reading rate
    5. Written response is sophisticated and critical
  B. Generic Reading and Writing Activities
    1. Begin chapter books which may be 200 pages long
    2. Begin simple outlining skills and work with adjusting reading rates with purpose
    3. Continue to explore reading and writing styles and genre
    4. Read to students
  C. Word Study Focus
    1. Continue with open and closed sorts, word study notebooks, some word study games

    2. Begin this stage by examining consonant doubling and simple suffixes as in plurals

    3. Focus on words that students bring to word study from their reading and writing

    4. Join spelling and vocabulary studies; link meaning and spelling

    5. Word study can be engaged as part of grammar

    6. Sort and study affixes (prefixes and suffixes)

    7. Study stress and accent in two-syllable words

    8. Study polysyllabic words and their stressed or unstressed syllables

    9. Examine increasingly complex affixes and consonant doublings (*occasion*)

V. Derivational Constancy Stage / Chapter Eight

  A. Characteristics

    1. High frequency words mastered

    2. Errors on low frequency words

  B. Generic Reading and Writing Activities

    1. Plenty of reading and writing, exploring various genre as interests arise

    2. Develop secondary and postsecondary area study skills including textbook reading, notetaking, reading rates, test taking, report writing, and reference work

    3. Continue to focus on recreational reading

  C. Word Study Focus

    1. Continue with open and closed sorts, word study notebooks, some word study games

    2. Focus on words that students bring to word study from their reading and writing

    3. Join spelling and vocabulary studies; link meaning and spelling

    4. Introduce structural consistencies

    5. Examine vowel alternations

    6. Use word study books to examine classical vocabulary, Greek and Latin forms

    7. Develop an interest in etymology in the content areas

    8. Examine content related foreign borrowings

As you can see, this chart guides you to specific chapters where you will find an abundance of word study activities arranged by stage of spelling. In most classrooms, it is necessary to use activities from two or three of the four chapters to follow.

Word Study for Emergent Learners in the Preliterate Stage

This chapter will present an overview of the literacy development which occurs between the Preliterate and Early Letter Name stages of orthographic knowledge. This period is known as the **emergent** period of literacy development, a period during which imitation and experimentation with the form and function of print occurs. Preliterate children are busy orchestrating the many notes and movements essential to literacy; directionality, the distinctive features of print, the predictability of text, and how all of this correlates with oral language. The chief means of experimentation and growth during this critical stage is imitation and play. As we have seen in Figure 2–1, the Preliterate stage lies at the beginning of a lifetime of learning about written language.

To show how word study activities can be incorporated into literacy play, this chapter will highlight games and playful activities which focus on the following areas:

1. Concept and vocabulary growth
2. Playing with sounds
3. Concept of word development
4. Alphabet knowledge

All activities are arranged from easiest to hardest to accommodate a developmental, emergent progression.

This is a period of active exploration in the world of books and print. Through word study, Preliterate children are encouraged to categorize various aspects of language, both oral and written, and in doing so, expand their repertoire of literate behaviors. Let's look at the characteristics of emergent literacy and instruction that might facilitate its development.

Literacy Development of the Preliterate Child

The Preliterate stage of spelling development coincides with the evolution of emergent literacy behaviors. Preliterate spelling development is matched with emergent reading and writing in Figure 5–1. Children move into literacy gradually as they coordinate their oral language with various aspects of books and print.

Preliterate spellers cannot match words in speech to corresponding words on the page, and they have incomplete knowledge of the alphabet. The writing of a Preliterate child may look like scribble or the linear "pretend" writing in

Preliterate writing may look like hieroglyphics.

FIGURE 5–1 Synchrony of Reading, Writing, and Spelling Development

Stage I: Preliterate

Reading

1) Pretend Reading ⟶
   Directionality   Concept of Word
   (Ages 1-7)

Writing

2) Pretend Writing ⟶
   Mock Linear   Syllabic

Spelling

3) Preliterate ⟶ Early Letter Name

(bed)	2ry&	bd
(ship)	$@69	sp
(chase)	*6te	hc
(float)	&7%v	ft
(cattle)	@bn^	ktl

Based on Henderson (1990); adapted from Bear (1991b)

Figure 5–2. Later Preliterate writing may include some known letters, num bers, and hieroglyphics all mixed up in a sort of "symbol salad." Some Preliterate children are able to use the few letters they know to represent a salient sound in speech, but such youngsters would be quite advanced and at the tail-end of this Preliterate stage of word knowledge.

Some Preliterate children may have well developed language skills and express a great deal about stories and books; others may not. It is not necessary for children who have difficulty expressing themselves to learn to do that first before learning the alphabet or seeing printed words tracked in correspondence to speech. To withhold these essential components of the learning-to-read process would hold them in double jeopardy. Not only would they be behind in language and story development, but they would also be behind in acquiring the alphabetic principle as well. Of course all children need to be read to and immersed in the language and literature of their lives. But we can learn about stories AND learn about words and alphabet at the same time.

> Emergent readers learn about language, literature, and the alphabet simultaneously.

Preliterate Reading

The reading of the preliterate child is really pretend reading, or "reading" from memory. Pretend reading and reading from memory are both essential practices for movement into literacy. These forms of literacy play serve crucial purposes. Pretend reading is basically a paraphrase or spontaneous retelling which children produce while turning the pages of a familiar book. In pretend reading children rehearse the predictability of the text and pace their retelling to match the sequence of pictures. Through pretend reading children orchestrate many other concepts about books and print through an oral rendering: Directionality, sequence, dialogue, and the voice and cadence of written language (Sulzby, 1986).

Reading from memory is more exacting than pretend reading and serves another important purpose during this Preliterate stage. Reading from memory is a recitation of the text accompanied by fingerpointing behaviors which correspond

FIGURE 5–2 An Evolution of a Preliterate Child's Writing

in some fashion to this oral recitation. Reading from memory helps children coordinate spoken language with its counterpart in print. This phenomenon, called **concept of word,** is a watershed event which separates the Preliterate, emergent reader, from the Letter Name, beginning reader (Morris, 1981).

Preliterate children's attempts to touch individual words while reading from memory are initially quite inconsistent and vague. Such children may realize that they should end up on the last word on the page, but the units that come in between are a blur. Their fingerpointing is likewise nebulous and "squishy." This strategy for "reading" is mirrored in their writing, in which word boundaries and print distinctions are also obscured (see Figure 5–3).

Other children are aware that there are units to be reckoned with while reading, though they are not exactly sure what these units are. Such children may attempt to touch the print in correspondence to stressed beats in speech. Syllables may even be treated as separate words in print. This strategy is revealed in their fingerpoint reading as well as in their writing. In fingerpoint reading, a child might point to the word "the" in the line "Sam, Sam the baker man," while saying "the baker," then point to the word "baker" while saying "man." Figure 5–4 illustrates the phenomenon of getting off-track on two-syllable words.

Words gradually begin to evolve as distinct entities with their boundaries defined by beginning and ending sounds. Children's Early Letter Name spelling also provides evidence of this understanding. Early Letter Name spelling is illustrated in Figure 5–5 and will be described in the next chapter.

> Preliterate spellers can not match speech to print.

FIGURE 5–3 Preliterate Writing Without Word Boundaries

"I like housekeeping"

Preliterate Writing

Like preliterate reading, preliterate writing is largely pretend. Regardless of most children's culture and where they live, this pretend writing occurs spontaneously wherever writing is encouraged, modeled, and incorporated into play (Ferreiro & Teberosky, 1982). It begins with pictorial representations, then advances to labeling these pictures with creative representations of speech. Children first approximate the most global contours of our writing system: top-to-bottom and **linearity.** Later, smaller segments such as numbers, letters, and words are also imitated. Not until the end of this stage does writing achieve a direct relation to speech, and when it does, conventional literacy will soon follow.

The ability to write emerges in children in much the same way that it first emerged in humankind. Pictures, initially used for decorative purposes, came to be used intentionally as mnemonic devices. Later, a picture of a king and a picture of wood were combined to cue the name *Kingwood.* A rebus system of this sort led to the invention of the **syllabary** in which speech sounds were directly represented with hieroglyphs. It was this direct link to speech which heralded the emergence of literacy on the face of the earth. It was preceded, however, by a period of 40,000 years of prewriting—with pictorial representations (Gelb, 1963).

FIGURE 5–4 Trying to Match Voice to Print

FIGURE 5–5 Early Letter Name Spelling with Word Boundaries

Like our prehistoric ancestors, the child's first task is to discover that scribbling can represent something and, thereafter, to differentiate drawing from writing and representation from communication. The child must come to realize that when she draws what she conceives to be a fairy, her representation does not *say* "fairy"—*writing* is necessary to communicate the complete message. Figure 5–2 presents a progression of drawings and their accompanying utterances which culminate in a clear differentiation between picture and writing.

There are many similarities between infant talk and Preliterate writing. When babies learn to talk, they do not begin by speaking in phonemes first, then syllables, words, and finally phrases. In fact, it is quite the other way around. They begin by cooing in phrasal contours, approximating the music of their mother tongue. Likewise, children begin to write by approximating the broader contours of our writing system; they begin with the linear arrangement of print. This kind of pretend writing has been called **mock linear** (Clay, 1975). Later, as some letters and numbers are learned, these are interchanged along with creative hieroglyphics or "symbol salad" as children experiment with the distinctive features of print. (Mock linear writing and symbol salad writing are both shown in Figure 5–2.)

> Consonants may stand for syllables.

When babies move into what we conventionally recognize as baby talk, they give up their melodious cooing to concentrate on smaller segments, usually stressed syllables. "Dat!" is hardly as fluid as "Aheaheaheah," but these awkward exclamations will be smoothed out in time. Likewise, global knowledge of writing and letter forms is temporarily abandoned as children concentrate their attention on the specifics of letter formation and the representation of the most salient sounds of speech. Such attention often leads children to spit out parts of words on paper, often using single consonants to stand for entire syllables. As Figure 5–6 illustrates, the message is often indecipherable because children do not understand the purpose or need for spaces and tend to run their syllables and words together on paper.

Here is where the similarity between spoken and written language breaks down. As discussed in Chapter One, we don't really talk in words, and there is really no such thing as an isolated phoneme. Both words and phonemes are artifacts of print and do not naturally coincide with acoustic realities such as syllables. The *concept* of word and the *concept* of a phoneme must be taught; both will emerge as children gradually acquire the alphabetic principle and coordinate the units of speech with the printed units on the page.

Preliterate Spelling

Preliterate spelling doesn't occur until the end of the emergent stage of literacy development. Why? Because children need to be able to do four things in order

FIGURE 5–6 Syllabic, Consonant Frame Writing

HejKO+B

"She jumped up and caught the ball "

To invent a
spelling:
✦ Know a few
letters
✦ Write a few
letters
✦ Know a few
letter-sound
relationships
✦ Have
phonemic
awareness

to invent a spelling, and learning to do these four things is what development in the Preliterate stage is all about. By the time a child can do all four, she is well on her way to literacy.

First, in order to invent a spelling, a child will need to know some letters. She won't have to know ALL of the letters, but she'll need to know enough to get started. Second, she'll need to know how to *write* the letters that she knows, maybe not ALL of the letters that she knows, but certainly enough to put something down. Third, she'll need to know that letters represent sounds. Again, she won't have to know ALL of the letter sounds; indeed, if she knows the NAMES of the letters, she might use those as substitutes. (More on this is covered later in Chapter Six where we discuss Letter Name spelling.) Fourth, she will need to listen for sounds in speech and match the sounds to letters. This ability to divide speech into smaller units of sound is called **phonemic awareness.** In order to invent a spelling, a child must have some degree of phonemic awareness. By the time a child has control over all four of these aspects she is at the end of the Preliterate Stage.

When literacy development has occurred in a balanced environment, phonemic awareness and the ability to invent a spelling go hand in hand. That is, if children are able to discern only the most salient sound, then they usually will put down only one letter: for example, S for *mouse* or D for *and* or T for *mitten.* Later, as children begin to achieve a concept of word, they may be able to discern one or two sounds which correspond to the beginning and/or the end of word units. Such children will usually put down one or two letters, as in D for *dog* or KT for *cat.* If children know how to write their letters, their invented spelling will reflect their degree of phonemic awareness.

Invented
spellings reflect
phonemic
awareness.

When a child can match letter names with phonemes in her speech, she is well on her way to true literacy attainment. As the spelling samples in Figure 5–7 depict, the phonemes represented are always the most salient, but the most salient are not always at the beginning of what we call a "word." Notice also that word boundaries are confused with syllables, suffixes, and articles. When letter names are coordinated with word boundaries in a consistent fashion, a child is no longer a Preliterate speller. Spelling which honors word boundaries is Early Letter Name.

Teaching children the names of the alphabet letters and the sounds they represent is enormously helpful to children during this Preliterate stage of spelling development. But children don't have to get them all straight before they begin. As with oral language learning, written language learning involves forming and testing hypotheses as new bits of knowledge are perceived and internalized. And like the incessant chatter of the growing

FIGURE 5–7 Preliterate Spelling Sample

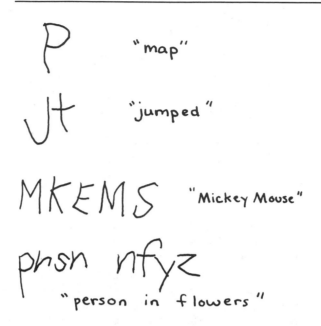

<table>
<tr><td>P</td><td>"map"</td></tr>
<tr><td>Jt</td><td>"jumped"</td></tr>
<tr><td>MKEMS</td><td>"Mickey Mouse"</td></tr>
<tr><td>phsn nfyz</td><td>"person in flowers"</td></tr>
</table>

| In pretend writing, learners test hypotheses. |

child, it is the extensive practice in approximating our writing system which extends the child's reach. Pretend writing and pretend reading must come first, and as they evolve, real reading and real writing naturally follow (Chomsky, 1971).

| Encourage pretend writing. |

Early Literacy Learning and Instruction

To emerge from the Preliterate stage to the Letter Name stages of beginning reading, students must have many opportunities to experiment with written language. They must see their own spoken language transcribed into print, and they must be supported in making the speech-to-print match by choral recitation and fingerpoint memory reading. They must be allowed to exercise their growing knowledge by being encouraged to write, even if this writing is little more than scribble. The most important condition for emergent literacy to blossom is the opportunity to practice, no matter how closely the child may approximate the standard.

Preliterate children will write, or pretend to write, well before they learn to read, provided they are encouraged to do so (Chomsky, 1971). The trick in developmental literacy instruction is how to give that encouragement. The mere act of leaving one's mark on paper (or elsewhere) has been called the *fundamental graphic act* (Gibson & Yonas, 1968)—an irresistible act of self-fulfillment. One has to do little more than provide immediate and ready access to implements of writing (markers, crayons, pencils, chalk) and provide a visible role model by drawing and writing yourself. Creating a conducive environment for writing also helps: a grocery store play area where grocery lists are drawn and labeled; a restaurant where menus are offered and orders are written; a writing center with a variety of paper, alphabet stamps and markers. Outfitted and supported accordingly, writing will happen spontaneously without formal instruction and well before children can spell or properly compose (Strickland & Morrow, 1989).

Model the reading process for Emergent readers.

Emergent reading instruction for Preliterate children consists of modeling the reading process. Teachers record children's experiences in picture captions and dictated accounts, then model how to read by fingerpointing to each word as it is spoken. Early literacy instruction also consists of talk about where one begins to read and where one goes after that. Teachers demonstrate the left-to-right directionality and the return sweep at the end of each line. Of course, all the talk and demonstration in the world won't get very far without hands-on practice. Early literacy instruction includes lots of guided practice on fingerpointing to familiar texts in a left-to-right progression.

Connect speech to print by:
✦ Choral reading
✦ Finger point reading
✦ Picture captions
✦ Sentence strips

The materials best suited for Preliterate, emergent readers are familiar nursery rhymes and other poems, songs, jump rope jingles, and children's own talk written down. Familiarity with songs and other rhymes helps bridge the gap between speech and print and helps cultivate the sense that what can be sung or recited can be written or read. Recording children's own language in the form of picture captions and dictated experience stories also nurtures the notion that print is talk written down. The ownership which comes with having one's own experiences recorded in one's own language is a powerful incentive to explore the world of print.

Techniques which are useful for fostering literacy development include choral recitation and fingerpoint memory reading. Extensive work rebuilding familiar rhymes and jingles with sentence strips in pocket charts is also quite helpful. Matching word cards to individual words on the sentence strips is an explicit way to direct attention to words in print. Reading and re-reading is the technique of choice. As is true with all of the stages of word knowledge described in this book, the best way to create a reader is to make reading happen, even if it's just pretend.

Four goals for Emergent readers:
✦ Vocabulary and concepts
✦ Concept of word
✦ Awareness of sounds
✦ Alphabet knowledge

The instructional plan for the emergent reader must aim toward the development of four main components of the learning-to-read process:

1. Concept development and vocabulary growth
2. Concept of word
3. Awareness of sounds
4. Alphabet knowledge and writing

If these four components are addressed on a daily basis, no matter how far along the emergent continuum a child may be, reading should inevitably follow.

The next section looks at the characteristics of Preliterate, emergent readers relative to these four components of developmental word knowledge.

Characteristics of Vocabulary Growth and Orthographic Development

Preliterate children do not spell conventionally because they have not made the letter-sound connection. On the 15-point scale described in Chapter 3, the Preliterate stage corresponds to scores of 0–1. They have very tenuous understandings of how units of speech and units of print are related. Nevertheless, they can and do analyze speech and apply their knowledge of the orthography. In this section, the remarkable ways in which Preliterate spellers analyze speech and apply it to what they *do* know about print will be examined. Bear in mind, however, that Preliterate understandings of how units of speech correspond to units of print operates within a larger context of concept, language, and vocabulary growth (Snow, 1983). For this reason, we will first take a look at the characteristics of Preliterate concept development and vocabulary growth.

FIGURE 5–8 15-Point Scale for Spelling-by-Stage Assessment

Late Derivational Constancy	15
Middle Derivational Constancy	14
Beginning Derivational Constancy	13
Late Syllable Juncture	12
Middle Syllable Juncture	11
Beginning Syllable Juncture	10
Late Within Word Pattern	9
Middle Within Word Pattern	8
Beginning Within Word Pattern	7
Late Letter Name	6
Middle Letter Name	5
Beginning Letter Name	4
Early Letter Name	3
Early Letter Name	2
Preliterate	**1**

Vocabulary Growth and Concept Development

Four-and five-year-olds know 5,000 words.

By the time a flourishing child is four or five years old, she has acquired a working oral vocabulary of over 5,000 words. She has mastered the basic subject-verb-object word order of the English language, and may take great delight in the silliness of word sounds and meanings. Many children have learned to recite the days of the week, and some, the months of the year. But to assume that these same children need no further experience with the vocabulary of time, is to stunt their conceptual understanding of the larger framework of time—how days, weeks, months, and years relate to one another. Ask some precocious five-year-olds to name the four seasons of the year, and nine out of ten of them will recite the names of the months instead. Ask kindergartners to tell you what season of the year December falls in, and many will no doubt tell you "Christmas." These are the answers from children who know the *names* of the days, the months, and the seasons, but don't really understand the *relationships* among them.

Vocabulary and concepts continue to expand.

Young children use many words whose meanings they do not fully comprehend. Their knowledge of words is only partially formed by the information gleaned from their few years of life. In order to extend the partial understandings of words they already have, and to acquire new word meanings as well, children must be given experiences which allow them to add new features to their existing store of word knowledge. Basic concept-development tasks are a surprisingly simple way to provide such experiences, and we describe these in the word study activities section in the second half of this chapter.

Concept sorts build vocabulary.

Awareness of Sounds

Preliterate children already know their sounds. We know this because they can talk. What they don't know is which sound to pay attention to. Terms such as "beginning sound" assume that a child knows where the beginning is, and until a child achieves the speech-to-print match, "beginning" is a relative concept.

Preliterate children rely on the feel of their mouths as they analyze the speech stream. In the phrase "onceuponatime," for example, the tongue touches another part of the mouth only for the /s/ sound of "once," the /n/ sound of "upon," and the /t/ sound of "time." The lips touch each other twice: for the /p/ sound in the middle of "upon" and for the "m" sound at the end of "time." Preliterate children pay attention only to those points of an utterance where one part of the mouth touches another. In the phrase "onceuponatime," one part of the mouth touches another for the /s/, /p/, /n/, /t/, and /m/ sounds, and these same sounds also correspond to syllable boundaries. Of all the points of contact felt in a phrase such as "onceuponatime," only the most tangible, most fully felt articulations are likely to be heeded. In most cases, the most forcefully articulated sounds are those which receive the most stress in the rhythm of the phrase as a whole. To Preliterate children, this translates as "the loudest," and it is this loudest or most prominent sound of stressed syllables which Preliterate children choose to segment in their analysis of speech. If some letters are known, these will be matched accordingly. Figure 5–9 presents a few examples of Lee's analysis of phrases in her elephant story relative to her knowledge of the alphabet.

| Picture sorts are for concept and sound classification. |

The goal of word study instruction for emergent readers is not to teach them their sounds, but to help them classify the sounds they already know into categories which coincide with printed word boundaries. These categories include beginnings and ends. Linguistically, the category which corresponds to beginning consonant sounds is termed **alliteration,** and the category that stands for ending sounds is termed **rhyme.** To classify these sound units, students must also achieve a concept of word. The characteristics of this critical phenomenon are described below.

Concept of Word

Preliterate children do not have a concept of word in print. What they point to as they recite may not coincide with printed word units at all. Like the babbling infant imitating the intonation contours of speech, the preliterate child points

FIGURE 5–9 Lee's Elephant Story

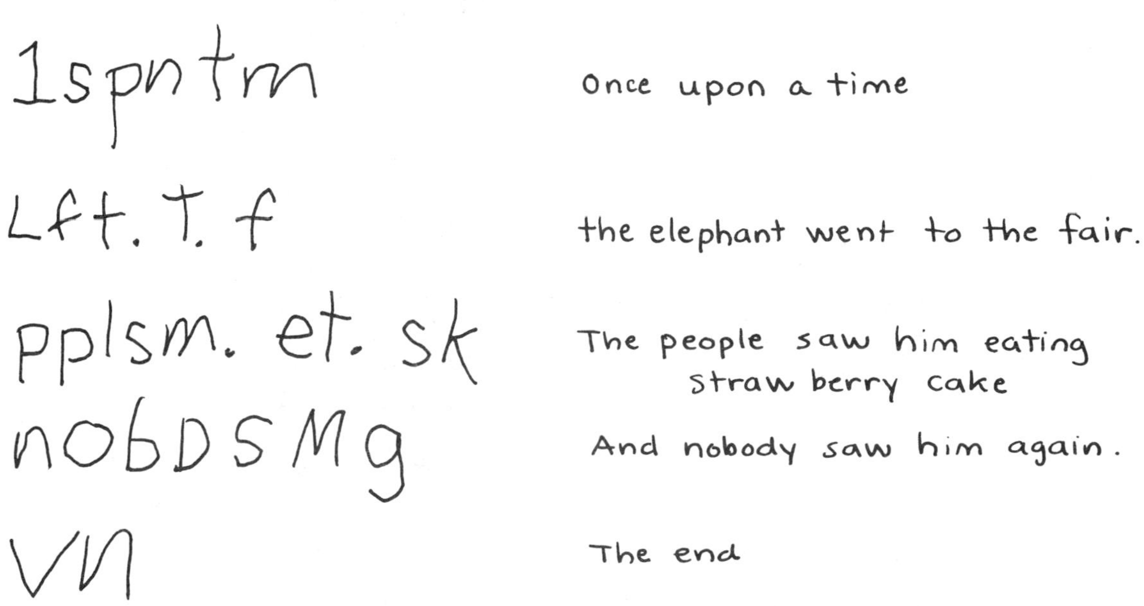

1spntrm   Once upon a time

Lft. T. f   the elephant went to the fair.

pplsm. et. sk   The people saw him eating
                                straw berry cake

nobDSMg   And nobody saw him again.

VN   The end

Self-correcting in finger point reading signals the onset of concept of word.

in a rhythmic approximation of the memorized text with little attention to word boundaries or even, perhaps, direction on the page.

Through the teacher's demonstrations, children's fingerpointing behaviors change. Left-to-right movement becomes habitualized, though children may not routinely use letter or word units to guide their tracking. As white spaces are noted and much talk about words is introduced, children begin to track rhythmically across the text, pointing to words for each stressed beat in the recitation. As children become aware that print has something to do with sound, their fingerpointing becomes more precise and changes from a gross rhythm to a closer match with syllables. This works well for one-syllable words, but not so well for words of two or more syllables. For example, in the traditional ditty "Sam, Sam the Baker Man," children may pronounce "ker," the second syllable of "baker," but point to the next word, *man*. Later, as children learn the alphabet and the sounds associated with the letters, beginning sounds will anchor the children's fingerpointing more directly to the memorized recitation: They realize that when they say the word *man*, they need to have their finger on a word beginning with an *m*. If they don't, they must start again—and these self-corrections herald the onset of a concept of word in print. Figure 5–10 shows the

FIGURE 5–10 Voice-To-Print Match in Relation to Orthographic Development

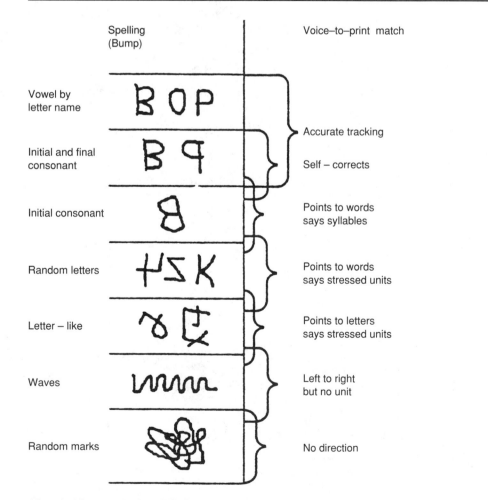

Adapted with permission from Gill (1992).

progression of fingerpointing accuracy in relation to the orthographic development during this Preliterate to Early Letter Name stage of word knowledge.

Achieving a concept of word is necessary for movement forward in orthographic development. Without the stable frame of analysis that the concept of word provides, the process of dividing the speech stream is determined by syllables and stress. English, however, is written with an alphabet rather than a syllabary; because of this, learning about letters and individual letter sounds is critical. Children come to coordinate printed word units with spoken units by virtue of the beginning sounds of words, and this boundary helps to keep words separate (Morris, 1993; Roberts, 1992). Prior to achieving a concept of word, Preliterate children, as well as adults who are Preliterate, have great difficulty identifying individual phonemes within words (Morais et al., 1979). There is an interaction between alphabetic knowledge, the ability to match speech to print, and phonemic awareness (Tunmer, 1991). Below, we will describe the details involved in acquiring the alphabetic principle.

Alphabet Knowledge

Alphabet knowledge is a critical ingredient for advancement into literacy. Letters must be differentiated from numbers and from each other. Letters have names and shapes, and they must be formed in particular ways. Unlike other aspects of life, directional orientation is vital for letters. In the three-dimensional world, a chair is a chair whether you approach it from the front or from the back, whether you approach it from the left or from the right. Not so with letters. A *b* is a *b* and a *d* is a *d*. Print is one of the few things in life where direction makes a difference. Figure 5–2 shows Preliterate writing in the early stages of alphabet acquisition. Note the mixture of numbers and letters and backwards formations in the child's efforts to spell "macaroni."

| Letters share features in sight, sound, and how they are written. |

The alphabet takes time to learn. Many letter names share similar sounds. The letter-name *B*, for example, shares the sound of the letter name *E*, as do *P, D, T, C, G, V,* and *Z*. There are visual similarities as well. There are verticals with circles in *p, q, d* and *b*. Verticals and horizontals intersect in *T, L, H, F, E,* and *I*. Intersecting diagonals are shared by *K, A* (which also share parts of letter name sounds), *M, N, V, W, X,* and *Z*. Even movements overlap in the formation of letters: the up-down-up-down motion is basic to *M, N, W,* and *V;* a circular movement is required of *B, C, D, G, O, P, Q, R, U,* and *S;* and the direction of these movements hinges critically on where one begins on the page (see Clay, 1975, for a detailed discussion of the acquisition of these distinctive features of letters).

Preliterate, emergent writers appear to practice these distinctive features on their own, provided they are given a model. Whole pages of circular symbols may supplant months of vertical intersections (see Figure 5–11). Meanwhile, letters which share distinctive visual features will continue to be confused for some time; *b*'s may be mistaken for *d*'s, *n*'s for *u*'s and so forth. Provided with the incentive to practice and the means to do so, Preliterate children will rehearse letter names, practice letter writing, and match upper case to lower case with delight.

| Use a game-like format to teach the alphabet. |

Most mainstream, middle-class children take a good five years to acquire all this alphabet knowledge at home and in preschool. Magnetic letters on the refrigerator door, alphabetic puzzles, and commercial alphabet games are staples in many middle-class homes (Adams, 1990). Truly advantaged youngsters also have an attentive mother or father at the kitchen table modeling speech segmentation as they encourage their child to write a grocery list using invented spelling. Yet many of these children also require directed experiences provided by formal schooling to fully understand the complexity of the alphabet.

FIGURE 5–11 Connie and Ellie's Preliterate Writing

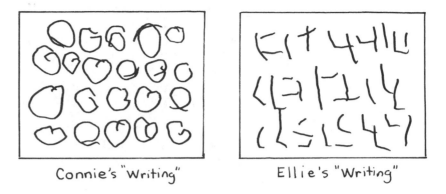

Connie's "Writing"　　　　Ellie's "Writing"

The best way to share five years of accumulated alphabet knowledge with those who have not been privy to this information is to teach it directly, in as naturalistic, fun, and game-like a manner as possible (Delpit, 1988). The word study activities described below are designed to do just that.

Word Study Instruction for Preliterate Learners

Word study instruction for the Preliterate, emergent reader is designed to foster the four areas of word knowledge presented in this chapter:

1. Development of concepts and vocabulary
2. Awareness of speech sounds
3. Concept of word
4. Knowledge of the alphabet

There is no set sequence to word study instruction for the Preliterate, emergent reader. Rather, all four areas of word knowledge must be nurtured simultaneously. It is not the case that concept sorts must precede sound awareness activities which in turn must precede concept of word and alphabet endeavors. Following the lead of the child, all of these activities can and should happen simultaneously.

Concept Sorts

> Children learn by comparing and contrasting.

The human mind appears to work by using a compare-and-contrast categorization system to develop concepts and attributes. The sorting activities appropriate for Preliterate, emergent readers build on and reinforce this natural tendency. By stacking the deck with familiar objects, ideas, animals, and things, teachers can devise sorting tasks which will help children differentiate and expand existing concepts and labels for those concepts. Fruits can be grouped separately from vegetables, and interesting concepts can be developed along the way. Pictures of farm animals can be sorted out and distinguished from zoo animals. Extinct animals can be categorized separately from the living. Sorting tasks such as these provide opportunities for concept formation which underlies vocabulary growth.

Words relating to weather and the seasons provide a particularly rich arena for concept and vocabulary development. Sorting pictures of people dressed in a seasonal variety of clothing can direct attention to the importance of weather in differentiating the seasons. Bathing suits, shorts, tank tops, and sunglasses can all go under the hot sun of summer. Scarves, mittens, snowsuits, and leggings may be placed under the cold snowflake of winter. Light jackets, sweaters, long trousers, and long-sleeved shirts must be sorted out between spring and fall on the basis of some other discriminating variable—color perhaps (light flowering prints vs. the darker hues of autumn) or the texture of fabric. Seasonal classifications may be derived using pictures of trees, flowers, garden fruits, or vegetables. School events, holiday pageants, and birthdays are also familiar landmarks to be associated with the label of the season as they help to personalize and make relevant the passing of time. In this way, children may build from a simple conceptual understanding of time and weather to a more clearly delineated understanding of the attributes of season. Figure 5–12 illustrates a concept sort for seasons.

| Concept sorts are for categorization.

Read-alouds can also provide background knowledge which some children may not have experienced. For example, books about seasons, weather, transportation, and how seeds grow provide basic vocabulary and information about the world which are essential to comprehending written texts. After listening to Ruth Heller's book *Chickens Aren't The Only Ones,* children might be provided picture cards to sort into groups—for example birds, mammals, and reptiles. In this way children may build upon a simple conceptual understanding of where eggs come from to include other attributes of the animal kingdom. Concept sorts based on daily life experiences and information gleaned from books develop and expand children's understandings of their world and their language to talk about it.

There are many other objects and events in our daily life which, for the child, remain unclassified in a sea of unrelated variety. Take "furniture," for example. One five-year-old child knew about tables, chairs, sofas, and beds, and she knew about ovens, refrigerators, and blenders. But, in her mind these were all an undifferentiated collection of "things in a house." Simply by sorting these items into two different categories—tables, chairs, sofas, and beds on the one

FIGURE 5–12 Concept Sort for Seasons

hand and refrigerators, ovens, microwaves, and blenders on the other—she was able to differentiate the attributes of furniture from those of appliances. In this way the concept of "furniture" and the concept of "appliance" began to emerge, and the words followed shortly thereafter.

Language is concept driven.

Since language is concept-based, children of diverse cultures may have different conceptual foundations. As teachers, we must be particularly sensitive to ethnic and cultural diversity in the classroom. We cannot expect children to learn words which label notions unconnected to their experience. We should provide opportunities for children to categorize familiar objects from their surroundings and familiar experiences from their daily lives according to similarity and difference. Our first charge is to find out what those experiences are.

The concept sorts described in the Activities section (page 112) are all variations on the theme of categorization tasks. In addition to basic sorting, concept development activities are generally followed by *draw and label,* then *cut and paste* procedures as discussed in Chapter Four. As always, we recommend having children *write* at every possible opportunity during or following the concept sorts. Categories and examples can be labeled with pretend writing or invented spellings. We offer several examples of the basic concept sorting task beginning with children's books as the catalyst. Further ideas for sorting pictures and objects into conceptual groupings are in the activities section at the end of this chapter.

Playing with Sounds

Preliterate children must become aware that speech can be divided into smaller segments of sound before they will advance in literacy. The ability to attend to and categorize these sounds in various ways is necessary to become an Early Letter Name speller. Awareness of sounds, however, does not have to precede or follow alphabet knowledge or reading instruction. Awareness of sounds is heightened by print, and because of this, is a reciprocal, on-going byproduct of the learning-to-read process.

Rhyme and alliteration focus on sounds.

Sound awareness activities for Preliterate, emergent readers focus on the concepts of *alliteration* (beginning sounds) and *rhyme* (ending sounds). Sound awareness activities differ from alphabet activities in that they are mostly oral-language games. Many will follow the singing of songs or the reading aloud of a rhyming book and involve word play in imitation of the rhyming or alliteration pattern presented.

Word play should be part of every young child's day. Learning the words to songs as well as the simple recitation of jingles, nursery rhymes, and poems will fill children's ears with the sounds of language. From such activities many children will readily develop concepts of rhyme and alliteration, and they soon will be able to identify and create rhymes of their own. Other children will need more structured activities that draw their attention specifically to rhyming words.

Children's books encourage sound and word play.

The easiest activity involving rhyming books and poems is simply to pause and let the children supply the second rhyming word in a couplet. When picture books are used, children will have the support of the illustration to help them out. *I Can't Said the Ant* by Polly Cameron is an old favorite. The illustrations and repetitive pattern will have children joining in to supply many of the rhyming words. *Each Peach Pear Plum* by Janet and Alan Ahlberg is a current favorite; many others are listed in the Activities section below.

Rhyming book read alouds can be followed by picture sorts for rhymes. For example, Barbara Straus and Helen Friedland's *See You Later Alligator* features simple rhymes such as "See you eating honey, bunny." Children can create their own "See you later" rhymes by laying out pictures of assorted animals and rhyming foods or objects (see Figure 5–13). To make it easier for beginners, we recommend laying out just two pictures that rhyme and one that does not. This odd-one-out set-up enables children to identify more readily the two rhyming pictures. They have only to pick up an animal and a rhyming picture. As children grow in their ability to listen for rhymes, the number of possibilities can be increased from three to four sets of pictures at a time.

Songs are naturally full of rhythm and rhyme and hold great appeal for children. Several songs recorded by Raffi, a popular singer and songwriter for children, are particularly well suited for language play. Alliteration and rhyme are featured in the song "Willaby Wallaby Woo" from the collection *Singable Songs for the Very Young* (Raffi, 1976). It goes like this:

> Willaby Wallaby Wee, an elephant sat on me.
> Willaby Wallaby Woo, an elephant sat on you.
> Willaby Wallaby Wustin, an elephant sat on Justin.
> Willaby Wallaby Wanya, an elephant sat on Tanya.

The song continues, creating a rhyme starting with "W" for everyone's name. After hearing the song played several times, the children can begin to sing it using the names of their classmates around the circle, perhaps passing along a stuffed elephant to add to the fun. The song can be changed to focus on alliteration by holding up a particular letter to insert in front of every word. A *B,* for example, would result in "Billaby Ballaby Boo," while an *F* would produce "Fillaby Fallaby Foo."

Of course, not all sound awareness activities have to be embedded in song or verse. Many games which focus on particular sound segments take the form of guessing games such as "I Spy" or "I'm thinking of . . ." In these games the beginning sound is exaggerated and other clues are provided as well. For example, "I'm thinking of something you are reading right now that begins with a /buh/-/buh/-/buh/-/buh/-/buh/ sound. Did you guess "book"? This game is particularly appealing to preschoolers and kindergartners when their own names are used.

As children become more adept at listening for rhymes and alliteration, it becomes possible to play a variety of categorization and matching games. Traditional games such as Bingo and Concentration are always winners. Picture cards can be matched to other picture cards which begin with the same

FIGURE 5–13 "See You Later Alligator" Odd-Man-Out

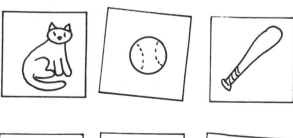

sound or which rhyme. As letters are learned, picture cards can be grouped together under the letter which corresponds to the beginning sound. Of course, in order to know where the beginning is, a child must also develop a concept of word. Word study activities for the development of a concept of word are described in the Activities section (page 122).

Concept of Word Development

The best way for children to achieve a concept of word is to have them point to the words of a familiar text. These texts might be picture captions, dictated experience stories, poems, songs, or simple rhythmic or patterned storybooks. Once these texts become familiar, children can be encouraged to memory-read them, pointing to each word as it is spoken.

> Children must point to words to develop concept of word.

The easiest way to help children make connections between speech and print is to write captions beneath the pictures they draw. First have the children draw a picture of their favorite toy or Halloween costume, for example, and encourage them to include as much detail as possible. While they are finishing their drawings, walk around and ask each child to tell something about his or her picture. Choose a simple phrase or sentence that the child speaks, and write it verbatim beneath the picture (see Figure 5–14). Say each word as you write it, then read the caption by pointing to each word. Later, the child may attempt to reread the caption to a buddy.

Many such experiences will be necessary before most children achieve a solid match between speech and print. Nevertheless, simple picture captions are a great place to start. The writing and the drawing come from the powerful combination of the child's language and experience. The picture clues will serve as a useful mnemonic whenever children attempt to reread the caption.

> Dictated experience stories link speech to print.

Like picture captions, spoken or dictated accounts of children's experiences also help them link speech to print. This approach has traditionally been referred to as **Language Experience** (Nessel & Jones, 1981; Hall, 1980; Stauffer, 1980). Field trips, cooking activities, playground episodes, and class pets all provide opportunities for shared experiences in which the children's own language abounds. Their observations and comments can then be written down next to each child's name (Daniel says, "The pumpkins were rotten."). In this format, attention to words and to their boundaries will be highlighted in a meaningful context. For example, children may be asked to locate their own

FIGURE 5–14 Drawing with Caption

This is a firetruck
going to the house.

name in the dictated account, or to find a word that starts with the same letter as their own name (see Figure 5–15). Each line can be illustrated to remind children of the content of that particular sentence as they attempt to re-read it at a later date.

Rhythmic texts are particularly appealing to young children, and like picture captions and dictated accounts, lend themselves to anticipation and memory support. Children enjoy playing with rhythmic structures at the phrasal level, and the interplay of rhythm and stress on words of one and two syllables facilitates awareness of how speech and print are coordinated. Eventually, knowledge of initial consonant sounds will provide the necessary anchor to track accurately, even in the face of two-syllable words. At such times, though, rhythmic texts may throw children off in their tracking, and a move to less rhythmic, less predictable texts may be in order (Cathey, 1992). Cultivating a child's concept of word in text is like playing a fish on the line. Both require reeling in and letting go in a responsive interplay of tension.

No matter what the medium, the important thing from a word study point of view is to focus on individual words within the text, whether that text be picture captions, dictated accounts, poems, songs or predictable, rhythmic pattern books.

All of these formats call attention to words and their features. There are additional ways in which children can manipulate these texts such that words can be highlighted. For example, children may rebuild the text on sentence strips in a pocket chart, then match individual word cards to the same words in

Rhythmic texts facilitate a speech-to-print match.

FIGURE 5–15 Dictated Account on Chart Paper

The Fire Station
Amanda said, "We went to the
      fire station yesterday."
Jason said, "We rode on a
      big orange bus.
Clint said, "I liked the
      ladder truck. It was huge!"
D.J. said, "The firemen told
      us how to be safe."
Beth said, "Firemen wear
      big boots and a mask."

each sentence strip. Sentence strips may be cut into individual words, and children can reassemble the words in the correct order. The text can be reproduced; in every line a content word can be left out, cued only by an initial consonant with a line after it. This format calls attention to word boundaries by cuing the beginning sound. One teacher we know writes dictated accounts using carbon paper, then later has her children cut out individual words from the carbon copy to paste right on top of the original. Other activities for focusing on words and word boundaries are described in the Activities section (page 122). Of course all the word work in the world won't achieve a concept of word without knowledge of the alphabet, so word study focusing on the ABC's is described below.

Alphabet Games and Matching Activities

How is the alphabet learned? The same way that concepts and words for concepts are learned—through active exploration of the relationships between letter names, the sounds of the letter names, their visual characteristics and the motor movement involved in their formation. By noting the salient, stable characteristics of *B* in many contexts and across many different fonts, sizes, shapes and textures, a rudimentary concept of *B* is formed (see Figure 5–16). Every new encounter with *B* adds new attributes to the concept of *B,* and a hierarchy of identifying attributes begins to form. As the concept of *B* develops in detail, the name for these concepts ("B") becomes more readily and reliably available. A letter, after all, is a name, and a name is a word attached to a concept. And like concepts, the distinctive features entailed in a letter's name, look, feel, and formation must be actively manipulated to be identified and grouped.

The alphabet games and activities described at the end of this chapter also build on the basic theme of compare-and-contrast categorization routines. Letters will be matched and sorted according to similarities and differences. The activities are designed to develop all aspects of alphabet knowledge including letter recognition, letter naming, letter writing, and letter sound.

Begin alphabet study with children's names.

Many alphabet activities begin with the child's name; building it with letter tiles, cutting it out of play dough, or matching it letter-for-letter with a second set. Few children can resist the temptation to write their own name, even if they have to copy it. Encouraging children to write or copy their own name,

FIGURE 5–16 Different Print Styles

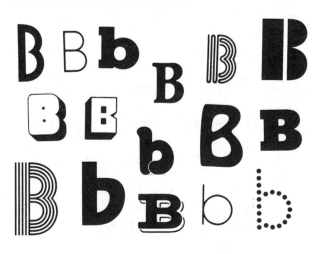

and the names of other family members or friends, is a great introduction to the alphabet as well as to writing. Even writing the letters they know—Katie's letter (K), Mommy's letter (M), or any other letter that they know or would like to know—is alluring to the emergent writer. *Happy Birthday, Grandma,* and *love* are frequently requested and point to the compelling need for personalization, ownership, and purpose (Ashton-Warner, 1963).

For alphabet acquisition: sort, match, name and write letters.

To develop letter recognition skill, letters must be matched, one to another. Again, Bingo and Concentration are excellent for this. At the end of this chapter, you will see variations of many of these traditional games; matching upper case to upper case, lower case to lower case, and finally upper case to lower case. We have added a writing component to many of these matching games to incorporate letter formation. Sorting tasks, matching games, picture labeling, and writing are as important to acquiring the alphabetic principle as seeing letters in meaningful print.

Towards the end of this Preliterate stage of word knowledge, children will have made the connection that letters can represent sound segments in speech. As this connection is developing, we have children sort picture cards into groups under letters which correspond to the beginning sound. This basic initial consonant picture sorting routine will be described in detail in Chapter Six, where we discuss the Letter Name speller.

Activities for Preliterate, Emergent Readers

The activities for Preliterate, emergent readers are grouped according to the following categories:

1. Concept sorts
2. Playing with sounds
3. Concept of word devlopment
4. Alphabet games and matching activities

In each section, the activities have been arranged in increasing order of difficulty. To emphasize the centrality of reading, we have placed the activities which spin off of books at the very front of each section. As noted earlier in this chapter, it is *not* the case that concept sorts must precede sound awareness, which in turn must precede concept of word development or alphabet. In reality, all of these activities could happen simultaneously.

The format of many of these sorting activities are generic to all stages of developmental word knowledge, board games, sorting folders, and the like. Generic games and activities may be found by looking for the generic symbol throughout the book: **GA**

Concept Sorts

Sort; draw and label; cut and paste; write

The activities for concept sorts are all variations on the theme of categorization tasks. In addition to the basic sorting tasks, activities are generally followed by **draw and label,** then **cut and paste** procedures as discussed in Chapter Four. As always, we recommend having children write at every possible opportunity during or following the concept sorts. Categories and examples can be labeled with invented spellings.

A Beginning With Children's Books 5–1

Materials

Preliterate; Concept Sort

Gregory the Terrible Eater, by Marjorie Sharmat, tells the story of a young goat who wants to eat real food while his parents constantly urge him to eat "junk food." In this case the goats' favorite foods really are junk from the local dump: tires, tin cans, old rags, etc. Collect real objects or pictures of items suggested by the story. They might include fruits, vegetables, newspaper, shoe laces, spaghetti, pieces of clothing, etc.

Procedures

1. After enjoying this story together the children can be introduced to a **group concept sort** categorized by "Real Food" and "Junk Food." Gather the children on the rug, around a large table or before a pocket chart, and challenge them to group the items by the things Gregory liked and the things he didn't like.

2. After deciding where everything should go, ask the students to describe how the things in that category are alike. Decide on a keyword or descriptive phrase that will **label each category.** "Real Food" and "Junk Food" seems an obvious possibility, but your children might be more inventive. As you print the selected keywords on cards, model writing for the children. Say each word slowly and talk about the sounds you hear in the words and the letters you need to spell them. Each child in the group might also be given a card and asked to label one of the individual items using invented spelling.

3. Plan time for **individual sorting.** Keep the items and keyword cards available so that children will be free to redo the sort on their own or with a partner at another time, perhaps during free time or center time.

4. **Draw and Label** or **Cut-and-Paste** activities should follow-up the sorting. This may be done as a group activity, in which case a section of a bulletin board or a large sheet of paper is divided into two sections and labeled with the keywords. If children do it individually, each child can be given a sheet of construction paper folded into two sections. The children might be asked to draw items or they might be given a collection of magazines or catalogs to look through for pictures which they cut out and paste into the correct category (seed catalogs are great for fruits and vegetables). Again, they can be encouraged to use invented spelling to label not only the keywords, but also each item in the category.

Variations

Other books will also serve as the starting point for concept sorts of many kinds. Here are just a few suggestions:

Noisy Nora by Rosemary Wells—sort pictures that suggest noisy activities or objects with pictures that suggest quiet activities.*

The Country Mouse and the City Mouse, a traditional tale included in a collection by John Wallner—sort pictures of things you would see in the country and things you would see in the city.

Alexander and the Wind-Up Mouse by Leo Lionni—sort pictures of real animals and toy animals or imaginary animals.

Amos and Boris by William Steig—sort pictures of things that Amos would see on the land and things that Boris would see in the ocean.

Is it Red? Is it Yellow? Is it Blue? by Tana Hoban—one of many books that suggests sorting objects and pictures by color.

My Very First Book of Shapes by Eric Carle—one of many book that leads into sorting activity based upon shapes.

---

*Thanks to Elizabeth Shuett for this idea.

Paste the Pasta 5–2

Preliterate;
Concept Sort

This classic sorting task was first shown to us by Ann Fordham in the McGuffey Reading Center. Categorizing pasta by size, shape, and color is a good hands-on activity that introduces the idea of sorting to young children. Many early childhood curricula include the study of pattern, but being able to categorize by particular attributes must come first. It is difficult for young children to stay focused upon a single attribute of interest. They may begin sorting by color and then switch to shape in midstream. They will need many activities such as this one, sorting real, concrete objects that have different features.

Materials

You will need three to six types of pasta that vary in size and shape. You may find pasta of various colors or you can dye your own by shaking the pasta in a jar with a tablespoon of alcohol and a few drops of food coloring. Lay it out on newspaper to dry. If you dye your own, make sure that any one color has a variety of shapes and sizes. Two or three colors is enough.

Procedures

1. Prepare a mixture of all the dried pasta and give each child a handful. Each child or small group will also need a sheet of paper divided into columns on which to sort their pasta.
2. Begin with an **open sort** in which you invite the students to come up with their own way of grouping. This will give you an opportunity to evaluate which of the children understand attribute sorting and who will need more guidance. Ask the children to share their ideas and show their groups. Discuss the different features or attributes by which they can sort.
3. Ask them to re-sort using a category different from their first one. You might end up this activity by letting the students glue the pasta onto their paper by categories and labeling their chosen sorts (see Figure 5–17).

FIGURE 5–17 Paste the Pasta

Variations

There is no end to the objects you can find to sort with your students as you explore the different features that define your categories. Here are some suggestions:

Shoes—girls/boys, right/left, tie/velcro/slip-on
Handcovers—mittens/gloves, knit/woven, right/left
Coats—short/long, button/zip, hood/no hood
Buttons—two holes/four holes/no holes, shapes, colors, size
Lunch Containers—boxes/bags, plastic/metal/nylon
Legos®—color, shape, number of "dots," length
Blocks—shape, color, size

GA Guess My Category 5–3

*Preliterate;
Concept Sort*

When children are comfortable with the idea of concept sorts, you can introduce any new collection of objects or pictures with an activity called "Guess My Category." Pictures for this and other sorts can be found in the back of this chapter; additional pictures can be cut from magazines and mounted on cardstock for easier handling. An easy beginning example might be pictures of clothing and pictures of food. And, remember that real objects are always an option.*

Procedure

1. Do not tell in advance what the categories are. It will be the job of the group to decide how the things in each category are alike. Begin by sorting two or three pictures into each group. When you pick up the next picture invite someone to guess where it will go. Continue doing this until all the pictures have been sorted. Try to keep the children who have caught on to the attributes of interest from telling the others until the end.
2. Now give small groups of children sets of pictures that might be grouped in a variety of ways. Ask each small group to come up with their own categories working together. Allow them to have a miscellaneous group for those things which do not fit the categories they establish.
3. After the groups are finished working, let them visit each others' sorts and try to guess the categories that were used. Or, Guess My Category items can later be placed in centers where students may work together to form different groupings. They can dictate to an aide, parent volunteer, or older student their reason for putting together the objects as they did, or they can compose their reason using invented spelling.

A All My Friends Photograph Sort 5–4

*Preliterate;
Concept Sort*

This is another example of an open-ended sort that involves guessing each other's categories. Pat Love passed this one along to us from Hollymead Elementary School in Charlottesville, Virginia.

---

*Thanks to Pat Brummett for this idea.

Materials

You will need copies of the children's school photographs made into a composite sheet. These can usually be copied quite successfully on a xerox machine so that you can have a complete set for each child or small group. The students will also need a sheet of construction paper which they can divide into columns for sorting.

Procedures

1. Brainstorm with the children some of the ways that the pictures might be grouped (by hair length, hair color, clothing, boys/girls, facial expressions).
2. Let them work in groups to sort by these or other categories they discover. After pasting their pictures into the columns on their paper, each group can hold up their effort and ask the others in the class to guess their categories. The category labels or keywords should then be written on the papers.
3. Students could be asked to bring in extra photographs from home. These may be sorted according to places (inside/outside, home/vacation, holidays, and so forth); number of people in the photograph (adults, sisters, brothers); number of animals in the photograph; seasons (by clothing, outside trees/plants); age, and so forth.
4. As children learn to recognize their classmates' names, have them match the names to the pictures. Later, these names may be sorted by beginning letter, then placed under the corresponding letter of an ABC wall strip. Names beginning with certain letters may be graphed.

Thematic Units as a Starting Point for Concept Sorts

Teachers of young children often organize their curriculum into thematic units of study. Such units frequently lend themselves to concept sorts which will review and extend the understandings central to the goals of the unit. Here are some examples.

 Food Group Unit 5–5

Preliterate; Concept Sort

Gregory the Terrible Eater serves as an excellent introduction to the study of healthy eating. The same pictures which the children have drawn or cut out can serve as the beginning pictures for categories such as "meats," "grains," "fruits and vegetables," and "dairy products." After categorizing the foods in a group sorting activity, the students should be asked to **draw** or **cut out** pictures of additional foods for a wall chart or individual sheet which is then labeled with invented spellings.

 Animal Unit 5–6

Preliterate; Concept Sort

The study of animals particularly lends itself to concept sorts and can be used as a way of introducing a unit. Lay out a collection of pictures of animals and ask the students to think of ways that they can be grouped together. Such an open sort will result in many different categories based on attributes such as

FIGURE 5–18 Farm Animals/Zoo Animals

what color they are, how many legs they have, whether they have fur or feathers, and so on. A lively discussion will arise as students discover that some animals will go in different categories.

The direction you eventually want this activity to go will depend upon the goal of your unit. Many simple preschool books feature farm animals and zoo animals. After much reading of books, observations of live animals, filmstrips, and discussion, more inclusive categories will begin to determine the sorting. If you are studying animal habitats, then you will eventually guide the children to sorting the animals by the places they live (see Figure 5–18). If you are studying classes of animals, then the students must eventually learn to sort them into mammals, fish, amphibians, and birds. If you are focusing on the food chain, your categories may be carnivores, herbivores, and omnivores.

A | Transportation Unit 5–7

Preliterate;
Concept Sort

Here is another open sort to start off a unit on transportation. A collection of toy vehicles (planes, boats, cars, and trucks) can be laid on the floor or table and the children invited to think of which ones might go together. Encourage them to think up a variety of possibilities that will divide everything into only two or three categories. After each suggestion, sort the vehicles by the identified attributes, and write the keywords down on a chart or chalkboard. Some possibilities include plastic/metal, big/little, old/new, one color/many colors, windows/no windows, wheels/no wheels, land/air/water.

After exploring this open sort thoroughly, have the children select the suggestion they liked the best. They can then be given a sheet of construction paper, and after labeling their categories **draw** or **cut out** pictures for each. As always, they should be encouraged to **label** the pictures with invented spelling.

Variations

Other concept sorts might be developed along the same lines. The following list of categories represents some that are frequently confused by preschool, kindergarten and first grade children.

real, imaginary
wet, dry, damp
natural, man-made
plastic, wood, metal
reptiles, mammals
farm animals, zoo animals, wild
mother animals, baby animals, daddy
smooth, rough
hard, soft, rough, bumpy
play vehicles, work vehicles
water, land, or air transportation
kitchen tools, office tools, shop tools
holidays and seasons
sweet, sour, bitter
thick, thin, narrow, wide

Playing With Sounds

Emergent readers need to develop the insight that speech is made up of smaller segments of sound. The ability to attend to and categorize these sounds in various ways is necessary in order to develop satisfactorily as readers, writers, and spellers. As discussed earlier in this chapter, awareness of sounds does *not* have to precede formal reading instruction. Awareness of sounds is heightened by knowledge of print.

A | Beginning With Children's Books   5–8

Preliterate;
Sound Sort

Oh, A-Hunting We Will Go, by John Langstaff, is a book that lends itself to a number of rhyming activities. As the children in the story hunt for different animals, they chant a patterned rhyme:

Oh, a-hunting we will go
A-hunting we will go
We'll catch a goat
And put him in a boat
And then we'll let him go.

Procedures

1. As the teacher reads the story aloud, she can pause before the name of the place the animal will be put to allow the children to guess the rhyming word. Soon the children can chime in and read along in a choral fashion, using the pictures to cue the different animals and places.
2. After enjoying the story together several times the teacher can put out a collection of animal pictures from the story (fox, mouse, goat, whale, and so forth) and pictures of the places they were put (box, house, boat, pail) for the children to match by rhyme. The book and the pictures may be put in a center for children to reread on their own and play the matching game.
3. Children can also be involved in creating their own rhymes to fit the pattern presented in the book. Brainstorm some animals that did not show up in the book, and try to think of rhyming places. Where would you put a cat? (in a hat), a moose? (in a caboose), an alligator? (in an

elevator), a sheep? (in a jeep), or a kangaroo? (in a zoo). The class-created ideas can then be written on chart paper for group reading.

Variations

After reading some rhyming books aloud, you can follow up with an activity that has the children sorting or matching rhyming pictures. *The Missing Tarts* by B.G. Hennessy, for example, features Mother Goose characters and a rhyming object or place. Pictures of the characters and their rhyming object can be laid out or put in a pocket chart for the children to match. (Look for rhyming pictures among the picture cards in the chapters that follow.) To make it easier for beginners, just put out the two pictures that rhyme and one that does not. As children grow in their understanding of listening for rhymes, the number of possibilities can be increased to three or four sets at a time. Will Little Bo Peep or Ol' King Cole go with the sheep or the bowl? The rhyming pattern in Donald Crew's *Ten Black Dots* can be extended to eleven, twelve, and so on. "Twelve dots can make an ice cream *cone* or the buttons to dial a _____." Here are some other rhyming books to get you started:

Barchas, S.E. (1975). *I Was Walking Down the Road.* Illustrated by Jack Kent. New York: Scholastic.
Benjamin, A. (1987). *Rat-a-tat, Pitter Pat.* Photographs by Margaret Miller. New York: Crowell.
Cherry, L. (1988). *Who Is Sick Today?* New York: Dutton.
Hoffman, P. (1990). *We Play.* Ilustrated by Sara Wilson. New York: Scholastic.
McLenighan, V. (1982). *Stop-Go, Fast-Slow.* Chicago, IL: Children's Press.
Slepian, J. & Seidler, A. (1967). *The Hungry Thing.* Illustrated by Richard E. Martin. New York: Follet.
Yektai, N. (1987). *Bears in Pairs.* New York: Macmillan.

Some rhyming books are so repetitive and simple that children can easily memorize them and enjoy them on their own before they are real readers. Douglas Florian has a series of books that feature only two or three words on a page: *A Beach Day, A Winter Day, City Street,* and *Nature Walk.* These books can also be used to introduce concept sorts in which summer/winter and city/country can be contrasted. *Play Day* and *One Sun,* by Bruce Macmillan, are some of the simplest rhyming books available. They feature "hinkpink" rhymes such as "white kite" or "bear chair" with a vivid photograph to cue the child's response. After hearing these books read aloud two or three times, young children may be able to recite the words or track the print successfully for themselves and will get great satisfaction from the feeling that they can read. *Mitten Kitten* and *Carrot Parrot,* two other very simple rhyming books by Jerome Martin, feature lift-the-flap pages to reveal a rhyming word that shares not only the same letters but a picture part as well.

 Inventing Rhymes   5–9

Preliterate;
Sound Sort

Making up one's own rhymes is likely to come after the ability to identify rhymes. Thinking up rhyming words to make sense in a poem is quite an accomplishment without a good sense of rhyme and an extensive vocabulary. Children need supported efforts to create rhymes, and a good place to start is pure nonsense. No one was a greater master of this than Dr. Suess. *There's a*

Wocket in My Pocket takes us on a tour of a young boy's home in which all manner of odd creatures have taken up residence. There is a "woset" in his closet, a "zlock" behind the clock, and a "nink" in the sink. After reading this to a group, ask children to imagine what animal would live in their cubby, under the rug, or in the lunchroom. Their efforts should rhyme, to be sure, but anything will do: a rubby, snubby, or frubby might all live in a cubby.

Nonsense rhymes are a delightful way to cultivate awareness of sounds. Word play directs children's attention to the sounds of our language while meaning is willingly suspended. Reading books like Slepian and Seidler's *The Hungry Thing* not only exposes children to lots of rhyme but also to lots of word play that can stimulate children to invent their own. Here is more language play that you can introduce to your children through poetry and song.

A Using Songs for Rhyme and Alliteration 5–10

Preliterate;
Sound Sort

Earlier we mentioned how appropriate the singer/songwriter Raffi is for young children. Other songs by Raffi that can lead to inventive fun with rhymes and sounds are:

"Apples and Bananas" (from *One Light, One Sun*)
"Spider on the Floor" (from *Singable Songs for the Very Young*)
"Down By the Bay" (Also available as a book, from *Singable Songs for the Very Young*)

Another song which features names, rhyme, and alliteration is the "The Name Game," originally sung by Shirley Ellis. It has apparently passed into the oral tradition of neighborhood kids and may be known by some children in your class. Sing the song over and over, substituting the name of a different child on every round. It goes like this:

"Sam Sam Bo Bam, Bannana Fanna Bo Fam, Fee Fi Mo Mam, Sam!"

Shirley becomes:

"Shirley Shirley Bo Birley, Bannana Fanna Bo Firly, Fee Fi Mo Mirly, Shirley!"

Marcia becomes:

"Marcia Marcia Bo Barcia, Bannana Fanna Bo Farcia, Fee Fi Mo Marcia, Marcia!"

You may also hold up the first letter or letters on the first sound of each name used.

Lend an ear to the playground chants your children already know and encourage them to share them with you. Generations of children have made up variations of "Miss Mary Mack Mack Mack . . ." and a new generation with a taste for Rap is creating a whole new repertoire. You can take an active role in teaching these jingles to your students. Here are some printed sources:

Cole, J. (1989). *101 Jump-Rope Rhymes*. New York: Scholastic.
Cole, J. & Calmenson, S. (1990). *Miss Mary Mack and Other Children's Street Rhymes*. Illustrated by Alan Tiegreen. New York: Morrouno.
Schwartz, A. (1989). *I Saw You in the Bathtub*. New York: Harper Collins.
Withers, C. (1948). *Rocket In My Pocket*. New York: Holt, Rinehart.

Rhyming Games

There are many commercially-made games which feature rhyming words and pictures. These should be made available for the children to use on a regular basis—especially after they have explored the notion of rhyme through lots of books, poems, and group activities such as those above. We will describe two games here which are based on familiar formats. Many of the pictures needed to create rhyming activities such as these can be found in the picture sets in the back of the chapters, especially in the short and long vowel sets in Chapters 6 and 7.

GA Rhyming Bingo 5–11

Materials

Preliterate; Sound Sort

Prepare enough Bingo gameboards for the number of children who will participate (small groups of three to five are probably ideal). An appropriate gameboard size for young children is a 9" x 9" board divided into nine 3" x 3" squares; for older students, the gameboard can be expanded up to a 4" x 4" or 5" x 5" array. Xerox two or three sets of pictures from the appendices and form rhyming groups such as *cat/hat/mat/bat* from the Short A collection or *snake/cake/rake* from the Long A collection. Randomly paste all but one of each rhyming group in the spaces on the gameboards, then laminate them for durability. Each gameboard must be different.

Prepare a complementary set of cards on which you paste the remaining picture from each rhyming group. These will become the deck from which rhyming words are called aloud during the game.

You will need some kind of marker to cover the squares on the gameboard. These may be as simple as 2" squares of construction paper, plastic chips, bottle caps, or pennies.

Procedures

1. Each child receives a game board and markers to cover spaces.
2. The teacher or a designated child is the caller who turns over cards from the deck and calls out the name of the picture.
3. Each player searches his or her gameboard for a picture that rhymes with the one that has been called out. Players can cover a match with a marker to claim the space.
4. The winner is the first player to cover a row in any direction, or the first player to fill his or her entire board.

A Rhyming Concentration 5–12

Materials

Preliterate; Sound Sort

Assemble a collection of six to ten rhyming *pairs* from the pictures in the back of Chapters Six and Seven (such as **goat/boat** and **rope/soap** from the Long O pictures). Paste the pictures on cards and laminate for durability. Be sure the pictures do not show through from the backside.

Procedures

This is a game for two or three children which is played like the traditional Concentration or the more current Memory game.
1. Shuffle the pictures and then lay them face down in rows.
2. Players take turns flipping over two pictures at a time. If the two pictures rhyme, the player keeps the cards to hold to the end of the game. The player who makes a match gets another turn.

3. The winner is the child who has the most matches at the end of the game.

Variation

When children are able to read, this game can be played with word cards instead of picture cards.

Concept of Word Development

Fingerpoint reading to memorized rhymes and pattern books is the best way to achieve a concept of word. Emergent readers need a lot of support in learning how to track print in correspondence with their speech. The following activities provide a few ways to go about getting kids connected to the words on the page.

 Rhyming for Reading 5–13

Preliterate;
Concept of Word

After playing with the sounds in rhyming songs and jump rope jingles, an important further step is to let the children see and interact with the printed form. From such experiences children will begin to develop the concept of a printed word. Here is one example.

There Was A Little Turtle

This classic poem is one of many that can be used to foster a concept of word.

Materials

Record the words on a sheet of 24" wide chart paper—big enough for all to see. Some teachers have special pointers (variations we have heard of include the rib bone of a cow and the beam of a flashlight), but a finger will do fine when the chart is at eye level.

Procedures

1. Teach the children the words to the song "There Was a Little Turtle" and show them how to do the finger play if you know it. Sing it over and over until everyone knows it well (see Figure 5–19).
2. Model for the children how to point to the words as they are said. Invite children to take their own turn at tracking the words as they or their classmates chant the words. From repeated opportunities, teachers can easily monitor the children's developing concept of word, from vague sweeps from left to right, to self-corrected, careful matching of speech to print.
3. Smaller copies of class songs and poems can be sent home with the children and/or kept in a class book.

 Cut-Up Sentences 5–14

Preliterate;
Concept of Word

Discussed earlier, this activity deserves mention again here. Children will rebuild familiar sentences from cut-up sentence strips. Write a familiar sen-

FIGURE 5–19 Rhymes for Reading

tence or a dictated sentence on a sentence strip. Sentences might come from a book or a poem the group has read together such as the turtle rhyme in the previous activity. Ask the students to cut apart the words in the sentence and demonstrate how to do this. Ask the students to reconstruct the sentence. (You may want to provide a model for children to match below.) Demonstrate how to find the words. "What letter would you expect to see at the beginning of swam?" Leave the word cards and model sentence strips with a pocket chart in a center for children to practice in their spare time. Put individual words into an envelope with the sentence written on the outside (see Figure 5–20). These can be sent home with the children to reassemble with their parents.

A **Be The Sentence** 5–15

Preliterate;
Concept of Word

Children can also rebuild familiar sentences by pretending to be the words themselves. Write a familiar sentence on a chart or on the board. Start with short sentences such as "Today is Monday" or "I love you." Then write each word from the sentence on a large card. Give each word to a child, naming it for them. "Stephanie, you are the word 'Monday'; Lorenzo, you are the word 'is'." Ask the children to work together to arrange themselves into the sentence. Have another child read the sentence to check the direction and order. Try this again with another group of children, then leave the words out for children to work with on their own.

FIGURE 5–20 Cut-up Sentences

| **A** | **Using the Morning Message to Develop a Concept of Word** | **5–16** |

Preliterate;
Concept of Word

Each morning teachers talk with the entire group to discover bits of classroom news which can be part of the morning message. In preschools or early kindergarten, this may be only one sentence, but over time, it can grow to be as long as the teacher and children desire. When a sentence has been selected for the morning message, you may recite it together with the children to decide how many words it contains, holding up a finger for each word. Then, draw a line for each word on the board or chart (see Figure 5–21).

> "Boys and girls, let's say our sentence, 'We hope it will snow.' How many words did we say? I'll draw a line here for every word we will need to write. . . "

——— ——— ——— ——— ———.

Repeat each word, emphasizing the sounds and getting the children's ideas about what letters are needed.

> "The first word we need to write is we'-Wwwwww-eeeeee." What letter do we need for the first sound in wwweee'?"
> A child might suggest the letter Y.
> "The name of the letter Y does start with that sound. Does anyone have another idea?"

Every letter in every word need not be discussed at length. Focus on what is appropriate for the developmental level of your students. Model and talk about concepts of print such as left to right, return sweep, capitalization, punctuation, as well as letter formation. Clap the syllables in longer words, spelling one syllable at a time.

After the morning message is complete, read it aloud to the group, touching each word. If your sentence contains a two- or three-syllable word, touch it for every syllable, helping children see how it works. Read the sentence chorally and let individual children come up and touch the words as they read it. The morning message should be left up all day. Some children may want to copy it. You might want to use it for the cut-up sentence or a "be-the-sentence" activities described earlier.

FIGURE 5–21 Morning Messages

Alphabet Games and Matching Activities

The activities presented in this section are designed to develop all aspects of alphabet knowledge, including letter recognition (both upper and lower case), letter naming, letter writing, and letter sounds. No child is too young to begin learning the alphabet (some lucky infants actually teethe on a teething toy in the shape of the letter that starts their own name!). As in the other sections, alphabet activities which spin off of children's picture books are presented first. Thereafter, the games and activities have been arranged from easiest to hardest, from front to back. You may notice that these activities address more than one letter at a time: For children who *haven't* cut their teeth on alphabet letters and picture books, one letter per week is a mere drop in the bucket against the 1,000-to 1,700-hour advantage of their peers (Adams, 1990). Besides, learning the alphabet proceeds in much the same way as learning anything else—by categorizing features that are the same and contrasting those with other features that are different. In order to follow this basic process of concept attainment, we must deal with more than one letter at a time.

| **A** | **Beginning with Alphabet Books** | **5–17** |

Preliterate;
Alphabet

On a regular basis, share alphabet books with children of all ages. Some books are suitable for toddlers and merely require the naming of the letter and a single accompanying picture, such as in Dick Bruna's *B is for Bear*. Others, such as Graeme Base's *Animalia,* will keep even upper elementary children engaged as they try to name all the things which are hidden away in the illustrations. Many ABC books can be incorporated into thematic units, such as Jerry Pallota's *The Yucky Reptile Book* or Mary Azarian's *A Farmer's Alphabet*. Some alphabet books present special puzzles such as Jan Garten's *The Alphabet Tale*. Children are invited to predict the upcoming animal by showing just the tip of its tail on the preceding page.

Merely setting alphabet books out for children to stumble across is not enough. Share them with a group as you would other good literature, and plan follow-up activities when appropriate. Following is a list of some outstanding ABC books and a few follow-up suggestions.

Anglund, Joan Walsh. (1960). *In a pumpkin shell.* (Alphabet Mother Goose). San Diego, CA: Harcourt Brace, Jovanovich.

Anno, Mitsumasa. (1975). *Anno's alphabet.* New York: Crowell.

Aylesworth, J. (1992). *Old black fly.* Illustrated by Stephen Gammell. New York: Scholastic.

Azarian, M. (1981). *A farmer's alphabet.* Boston: David Godine.

Base, Graeme. (1986). *Animalia.* New York: Harry Abrams.

Baskin, Leonard. (1972). *Hosie's alphabet.* New York: Viking Press.

Bayor, J. (1984). *A: My name is Alice.* Illustrated by Steven Kellogg. New York: Dial.

Blake, Q. (1989). *Quinton Blake's ABC.* New York: Knoff.

Chess, V. (1979). *Alfred's alphabet walk.* New York: Greenwillow.

Falls, C.B. (1923). *ABC book.* New York: Doubleday.

Gág, W. (1933). *The ABC bunny.* Hand Lettered by Howard Gág. New York: Coward-McCann.

Geisert, Arthur. (1986). *Pigs from A to Z.* Boston: Houghton Mifflin.

Hague, K. (1984). *Alphabears: An ABC book.* Illustrated by Michael Hague. New York: Holt, Rinehart & Winston.

McPhail, D. (1989). *David McPhail's animals A to Z.* New York: Scholastic.

Musgrove, M. (1976). *Ashanti to Zulu: African traditions.* Illustrated by Leo and Diane Dillon. New York: Dial.

Owens, Mary Beth. (1988). *A caribou alphabet.* Brunswick, ME: Dog Ear Press.

Pallotta, J. (1989). *The yucky reptile alphabet book.* Illustrated by Ralph Masiello. New York: Trumpet Club.

Thornhill, J. (1988). *The wildlife A-B-C: A nature alphabet book.* New York: Simon & Schuster.

A **Alphabet Book Follow-Ups** 5–18

Procedures

| Preliterate; Alphabet |

1. Discuss the pattern of the books, solve the puzzle, talk about the words that begin with each letter as you go back through the books a second time.
2. Pick one or two letters to work on, and list the words for just those letters. Brainstorm other words that begin with that letter, and write them under the letter on chart paper.
3. Make individual or class alphabet books. You might decide on a theme or pattern for the book. Refer back to the alphabet books you have read

for ideas. One idea might be a noun-verb format, for example, ants/attack, bees/buzz, cats/cry, dogs/doze, etc.

4. Look up a particular letter you are studying in several alphabet books or a picture dictionary to find other things that begin with that sound. This is an excellent introduction to using resource books.*

A A *Chicka Chicka Boom Boom* Sort   5–19

Preliterate;
Alphabet

Chicka Chicka Boom Boom is a great way to move from children's books to alphabet recognition and letter sound activities. After reading this delightful book to and with her children, Pat Love demonstrates how to match foam "Laurie Letters," one at a time, to the letters printed in the book. Figure 5–22 show Pat's working "boom boards" for letter sorting. As Figure 5–22 shows, there is one letter on each side of the coconut tree. Picture cards can be sorted according to beginning sounds under the corresponding letter.

A Starting With Children's Names   5–20

Preliterate;
Alphabet

Children are naturally interested in their own names and their friends'. Names are an ideal point from which to begin the study of alphabet letters. We like the idea of a "name of the day" so much better than a "letter of the week." Many more letters are covered in a much shorter time!

FIGURE 5–22 *Chicka Chicka Boom Boom* **Board**

*Thanks to Jennifer Sudduth for these ideas.

Materials

Prepare a card for each child on which his or her name is written in neatly executed block letters. You might want to put the name in all capitals on one side and in lower case on the other (except for the first letter, of course). Put all the names in a box or can. Have additional blank cards ready to be cut apart as described below.*

Procedures

1. Each day, with great fanfare, a name is drawn from the box or can and becomes the "name of the day." Children chant or echo the letters in the name as the teacher points to each one. A cheer led by the teacher, such as the one below, is lots of fun:

   Teacher: "Give me a *T*."

   Children: "*T*!"

   Teacher: "Give me an *O*"

   Children: "*O*!"

   Teacher: "Give me an *M*."

   Children: "*M*!"

   Teacher: "What have we got?"

   Children: "Tom!"

2. On the additional card, the teacher writes the name of the child as the children recite the letters needed. Then she cuts the letters apart and hands out the letters to children in the group. The children are then challenged to put the letters back in order to spell the name correctly. This can be done in a pocket chart or on a chalkboard ledge and repeated many times. The featured child can be given all the letters to arrange.

3. All the children in the group should attempt to spell the featured name. This might be done on individual chalkboards or on pieces of paper. This is an opportunity to offer some handwriting instruction as the teacher models for the children. Discuss the details of direction and movement of letter formation as the children imitate your motions.

4. Each day the featured name is added to a display of all the names that have come before. By displaying them in a pocket chart or on magnetized cards that stick to a metal chalkboard, they can be used for sorting activities such as these:

   Sort the names by the number of letters
   Sort the names by the number of syllables
   Sort the names that share particular letters
   Sort the names that belong to boys and girls
   Sort the names by alphabetical order

5. Create a permanent display of the names and encourage children to practice writing their own and their friends' names. If you have a writing center, you might put all the names on index cards in a box for reference. Children can be encouraged to reproduce names not only by copying the names with pencils, chalk, and markers, but also with rubber stamps, foam cutout letters, linkletters, or letter tiles.

---

*(For more information on using student's names to develop alphabet knowledge, see *Phonics They Use: Words for Reading and Writing* by Pat Cunningham.)

FIGURE 5–23 One Child's Name

| **A** | **One Child's Name** | **5–21** |

Preliterate;
Alphabet

Individual children may need additional help learning the letters in their names. For them, the following activity is valuable:

1. Spell out a child's name with letter cards, tiles, foam, or plastic letters.
2. Spell it with upper case letters in the first row and ask the child to match lower case letters in the row below, as shown in Figure 5–23.
3. Mix up the top row and have the child unscramble the letters to form the name once again. Have the child name the letters as this is done.
4. Mix up the bottom row and repeat.
5. Rematch the upper and lower case tiles, letter for letter, naming each letter again as they are touched.
6. Next take blank cards and place one blank card beneath each letter. Write each letter on each blank card, discussing the details of direction and movement in letter formation as you do. Give the child a piece of paper to imitate your letter formations. Alternate this activity for upper and lower case.
7. Play Concentration or Memory with the set of capitals and lower case letters needed to spell a child's name. (See further directions for Concentration below.)*

| **A** | **Alphabet Scrapbook** | **5–22** |

Preliterate;
Alphabet

Materials

Prepare a blank dictionary for each child by stapling together sheets of paper. (Seven sheets of paper folded and stapled in the middle is enough for one letter per page).

Procedures

1. An alphabet book can be used in a variety of ways. Children can practice writing upper case and lower case forms of the letter on each page.
2. Children can cut out letters in different fonts or styles from magazines and newspapers and paste them into their scrapbooks.

---

*Darrell Morris presents this activity in the context of a tutoring session for an emergent reader in his excellent book, *Case Studies in Teaching Beginning Readers: The Howard Street Tutoring Manual.*

FIGURE 5-24 Alphabet Scrap Book

3. Children can **draw** pictures and other things which begin with that letter sound. These pictures can be **labeled** with its beginning letter (see Figure 5–24).
4. Magazine pictures can be **cut and pasted** onto the corresponding letter page. These pictures, too, can be **labeled** with the beginning letter-sound.
5. As children begin to acquire sight words from repeated readings, they can be added to the alphabet to create a dictionary of known words.

A The Alphabet Song and Tracking Activities 5–23

Preliterate; Alphabet

Every early childhood classroom should have an alphabet strip or chart at eye level. Too often these strips are put up way out of the children's reach. We believe that the best location for the strips is to be posted on desk tops or tabletops for easy reference. Here is an activity that makes active use of these charts.

Procedures

1. Learn the ABC song to the tune of "Twinkle Twinkle Little Star."
2. Model pointing to each letter, as the song is sung or the letters are chanted. Then ask the children to fingerpoint to the letters as they sing or chant.
3. When students know about half of the alphabet, they can work on putting a set of letter cards, tiles, or link letters in ABC order from A to Z. Use capital letters or lower case, or match the two (see Figure 5–25). Keep an ABC strip or chart nearby as a ready reference.

A Alphabet Eggs 5–24

Materials

Preliterate; Alphabet

Create a simple set of puzzles designed to practice the pairing of capital and lower case letters. On poster board, draw and cut out 26 4-inch egg shapes. Write an upper case letter on the left half and the matching lower case letter

FIGURE 5–25 Alphabet Link Letters

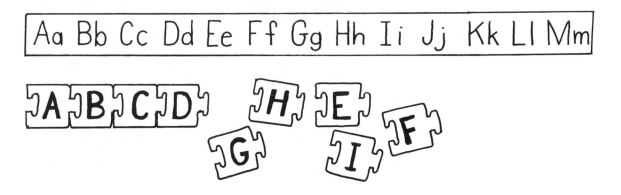

on the right portion. Cut the eggs in half using a zigzag line (see Figure 5–26). Make each zigzag slightly different so the activity is self-checking. Students should say the letters to themselves and put the eggs back together by matching the upper and lower case form.*

Variations

There are many other matching activities that can further the recognition of upper case/lower case pairs. In October, for example, pumpkin shapes can be cut into two parts with a zigzag. In February, heart shapes can be cut apart the same way. There is no end to the matching possibilities. Acorn caps can be matched to bottoms, balls to baseball gloves, frogs to lily pads, and so on.

 Alphabet Concentraion   5–25

Materials

Preliterate;
Alphabet

Create a set of cards with capitals and lower case forms of the letters written on one side. Be sure they cannot be seen from the backside. Use some letters the child may need to work on as well as some he or she knows quite well. You might use the letters in a child's name. Do not try this with all 26 letters at once; eight to ten pairs is probably enough.

FIGURE 5–26 Alphabet Eggs

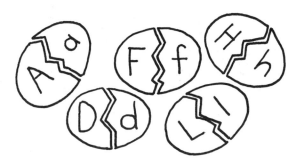

*Thanks to Elizabeth Schuett for this idea.

Procedures

1. To play Concentration or Memory, begin by turning all the cards face down in a square array.
2. Each player in turn flips over two cards. If the two make a match, the player may keep the cards in his or her own pile and take another turn.
3. The game is over when all the cards have been matched, and the winner is the player with the most cards.

Variations

You can also play the game using upper case to upper case matching or lower case to lower case matching. As letter sounds are learned, this game can be played by matching consonant letters to pictures that begin with that letter sound.

 Letter Spin 5–26

Materials

Preliterate;
Alphabet

Make a spinner with 6 to 8 spaces, and label each space with a capital letter. If you laminate the spinner before labeling, it you can reuse it with other letters. Just write in the letters with a grease pencil or non-permanent overhead transparency pen. Create a set of small cards, three or four for each letter, with the lower case forms matching the letters on the spinner (see Figure 5–27).*

FIGURE 5–27 Letter Spin

---

*Thanks to Alison Dwier-Selden for this idea.

Procedures

1. Lay out all the lower case cards face up.
2. Each player in turn spins and lands on an upper case letter. He or she then picks up *one* card that has the corresponding lower case form, orally identifying the letter.
3. Play continues until all the letter cards have been picked up.
4. The winner is the player with the most cards when the game ends.

Variation

Students can be asked to write the upper and lower case forms of the letter after each turn.

A   Alpha-Bit Sort   5–27

Materials

Preliterate;
Alphabet

For this sorting activity, you will need a box of alphabet cereal—enough to give each child a handful. Prepare a sorting board for each child by dividing a paper into 26 squares. Label each square with an upper or lower case letter.

Procedures

1. Allow the children to work individually or in teams to sort their own cereal onto their papers (see Figure 5–28). Discard (or eat) broken or deformed letters.
2. After the children are done sorting they can count the number of letters in each category (e.g., A-8, B-4).
3. Eat the cereal! (Or glue it down.)*

FIGURE 5–28 Alpha–Bit Sort

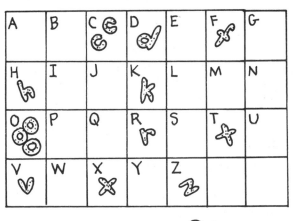

---

*Thanks to Janet Brown Watts for this idea.

Variation

Have the children write their names using the cereal.

A | Sorting Letters with Different Print Styles 5–28

Children need to see a variety of print styles before they will be able readily to identify their ABC's in different contexts.

Materials

Preliterate; Alphabet

Get a collection of different print styles by cutting letters from newspapers, catalogs, magazines, and other print sources. A good source for styles is a how-to lettering book from a library. Xerox the different alphabets, cut the letters apart, mount them on small cards, and laminate for durability. Use both capitals and lower case, but avoid cursive styles for now. You may want to set up a sorting board with labeled categories as shown in the illustration in Figure 5–29, or simply have the children sort on any surface.

Procedures

1. After modeling the sort with a group of children, place the materials in a center where they can work independently.
2. Don't put out too many different letters at any one time—four or five is probably enough, with eight to twelve variations for each.

Extensions

Draw children's attention to different letter forms wherever you encounter them. Environmental print is especially rich in creative lettering styles. Encourage the children to bring in samples from home—like the big letters on a bag of dog food or cereal—and create a display on a bulletin board or in a big book. If you have created Alphabet Scrapbooks (described above), children can paste in samples of different lettering styles.

GA | Soundline 5–29

This classic activity can be used to focus on letter matching or letter-sound correspondences.

Materials

Preliterate; Alphabet

Rope, clothespins, markers, tagboard, glue, pictures, scissors, and laminating film.

Procedures

1. Mark upper and lower case letters on the top of the clothespins.
2. Find pictures for each sound letter and attach these to a square of tagboard.
3. Write the name of the picture on the back of the square, underline the first letter, and then laminate it.

FIGURE 5–29 Sort Letters with Different Fonts

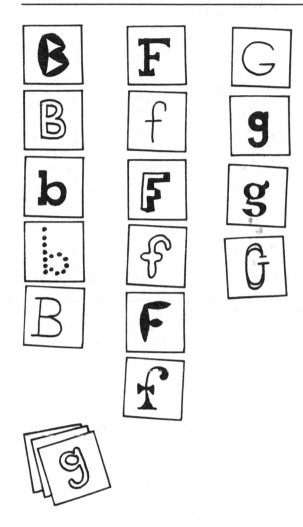

4. Students can match the picture card to the clothespin and hang it on the rope (see Figure 5–30).*

Variation

Focus on letter matching or letter sounds. Children's names can also be used. Hang a string from a clothesline to attach other pictures.

A | Initial Consonant Picture Sorts   5–30

Preliterate;
Alphabet

This is the most rudimentary of all the sorting tasks having to do with letter sounds or patterns. It is the primary means of categorizing beginning sounds and associating them with the letters that represent them. We know that this activity is getting results when children begin to spell initial and final consonant sounds correctly in their writing. Children who represent begin-

*Leslie Robertson contributed this activity.

FIGURE 5–30 Clothes Line "Soundline"

ning and ending consonant sounds are at the tail-end of the Preliterate, Emergent stage of developmental word knowledge. This doesn't mean that such children no longer need practice. Children need continued practice in categorizing beginning sounds until these are totally automatic. Only then can they focus their attention on the middle of the word. More on this in Chapter Six!

Materials

Consonant picture cards, consonant letters

Procedures

1. Begin with two sounds which are distinctly different and which can be said slowly without distorting their identity. We recommend starting with *B, S, M,* or *R.*
2. Choose a picture to correspond to each sound, such as bed, man, ring, and sun.
3. Lay these key pictures down under their corresponding letter.
4. Shuffle the rest of the picture cards and say to the child: "Now we're going to listen for the sound at the beginning of these words. We'll decide if it begins like "man" or "sun."
5. Model the categorization of the beginning sound of the first picture card yourself.
6. If the next picture is of a sail, for example, say "sail, *sssss*ail, *ssss*ail begins like *ssss*un, so I'll put it under the picture of the sun."
7. After placing the picture card of sail under sun, say, "Sun, sail; they both begin with *s.*" Then point to the letter *S.*
8. Model in the same way for the next picture card drawn, a mop (see Figure 5–31).
9. After modeling several picture cards in this manner, let the child have a turn.
10. Continue taking turns categorizing *S* and *M* pictures accordingly.
11. If a child makes a mistake, correct it immediately. Just say, "*Mat* would go under *man.*"

FIGURE 5–31 Initial Consonant Picture Sort

12. After all the pictures have been sorted, name all the pictures in each category from the top down. A comment like, "All these pictures start with *M*, so get your mouth ready" is very helpful.
13. Have the child repeat this sort immediately without taking turns.

Variations

After children sort *M* and *S* quickly and with understanding, add a third category—for example, *R*. And after that, add a fourth category like *B*. Four categories is about the maximum for initial consonant picture sorting, which must be built up gradually. After four categories, initiate a new set of two different contrasts and build up gradually to three, then four, categories to sort.

GA **Spin-A-Letter, Pick-A-Sound** 5–31

| Preliterate; Alphabet |

This game is quite advanced and should be played only after children have had lots of experience with basic initial consonant picture sorts.

Materials

You will need a spinner divided into 3 to 6 sections and labeled with the letter to be practiced (e.g., C, H, D, F); a collection of picture cards; individual playing boards divided like a tic-tac-toe board (optional). 9" x 9" is a good size for small pictures, each box measuring 3" x 3".

Procedures

1. To begin play, children (2 to 4 players) take turns drawing cards and turning them face up on their boards or in a three-by-three array until all the spaces are filled.

2. The first player spins and can remove all those pictures that begin with the sound indicated by the spinner. The pictures go into his/her "point pile."

3. That same player draws enough pictures from the pile to replace the gaps in his or her board before play moves to the next child.

4. Play continues until one child has removed all pictures and there are no more to be drawn as replacements. The winner is the player who has the most pictures in his/her point pile.

Variations

(1) A large cube could be used like a die instead of a spinner.
(2) Tic-tac-toe game:
 Players prepare boards as described above, but when they spin, they can turn one picture that has that feature face down. The winner is the one who turns down three in a row.*

[A] Alphabet Zoo 5–32

Materials

Preliterate; Alphabet | Tag board, markers, ruler, and small plastic zoo animals.

Procedures

1. Rule off tag board into 27 squares.
2. Label each with the letters of the alphabet. The extra box is labeled for unknowns.
3. Have children place each animal figurine into the proper square, according to its beginning sound.

Variations

This can also be done with small objects (for example, matchbox cars, cereals, and candies).**

[GA] Initial Consonant Follow-The-Path Game 5–33

Preliterate; Alphabet | This classic game has been adapted to word study instruction for children in all stages of developmental word knowledge. It can be used to develop basic letter recognition or letter-sound correspondence. Follow-the-Path games can be used to review initial consonant sounds after children have already practiced categorizing targeted sounds in basic picture sorting activities. You'll see this game adapted for many other word study purposes in Chapters Six and Seven.

Materials

You will need a follow-the-path model on pages 239–244 to xerox and reproduce a set of picture cards; and two pawns to move around the board.

---

*Thanks to Francine Johnston for inventing this great game.
**Thanks to Jennifer Lovelace for this idea.

FIGURE 5–32 Follow the Path Game

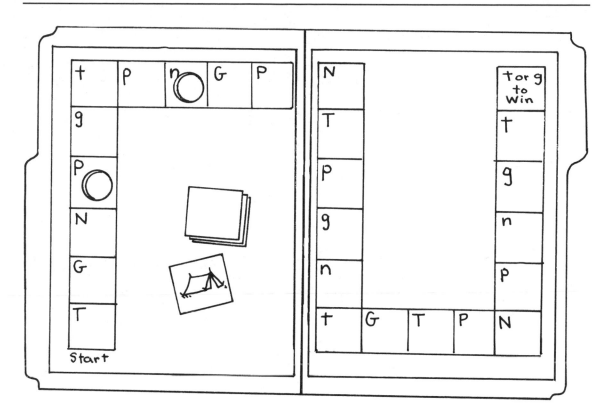

Procedure

1. Turn the picture cards face down.
2. Each player draws a picture in turn and moves their pawn to the space on the path which is marked by the corresponding beginning consonant (see Figure 5–32).
3. The winner is the first to arrive at the destination.

Variations

Using the format, match drawn letter cards to the corresponding letter on the racetrack. Match upper case to upper case, lower case to lower case, or upper to lower case.

The word study activities for Preliterate spellers, Emergent readers promote concept and vocabulary development, awareness of sounds, concept of word, and the alphabetic principle. These activities spring from and return to children's books and are extended through writing.

Once children achieve a concept of word in print and can segment speech and represent beginning and ending consonant sounds in their spelling, they are no longer Emergent, but Beginning readers. This is also when they move into the next stage of spelling, the Letter Name stage. Word study for the Letter Name speller, Beginning reader is described in Chapter 6.

6

Word Study for Beginners in the Letter Name Stage

Beginning reading is a time for support.

This stage of literacy development is a period of beginnings: Students begin to read and write in a conventional way. In word study, students begin to add words to their picture and letter sorts. This is also a period of support. The reading materials and activities provide rich contextual support and in word study, the words students sort are words they know at sight. In the following discussion of reading and writing development and instruction, we will look closely at the support teachers provide and the way literacy develops during this stage. The discussion of the instructional practices suggests ways for students to categorize words in sorts as well as ways for teachers to develop word study programs for beginners.

Literacy Development and Instruction of Letter Name Students

This stage is called the Letter Name stage because students use the names of the letters of the alphabet in their analyses of the orthography in reading and writing. Letter Name spellers have the ability to segment words into sounds. With their knowledge of the alphabet, they begin this stage with syllabic writing in which they spell the most salient or prominent sounds in words. As students fingerpoint read more accurately and fluently, they also show a clearer understanding of word boundaries. In addition to writing the most prominent sounds, students spell the beginnings and endings of words. In the middle of this stage, students include a vowel in each stressed syllable, and they spell short vowels by matching the way they articulate the letter names of the vowels. By the end of the Letter Name stage, students have learned how to spell words with short vowels, and they can read most single syllable words in their reading.

Letter Name spelling develops in synchrony with the Beginning stages of reading and writing. As can be seen in Figure 6–1, spelling development is matched with the reading and writing behaviors.

Reading

Students who are in the early part of the Letter Name stage of spelling have recently acquired a Concept of Word. In Chapter Two, Concept of Word was defined as the ability to fingerpoint read a memorized text accurately. **Tracking** is a term we use to describe students' ability to point accurately to the words in

FIGURE 6–1 Synchrony Among Reading, Writing, and Spelling Development

Stage II: Letter Name

Reading

1) Beginning ——————————————————————→
   Rudimentary Concept of Word ———→ Functional Concept of Word
                    Reads many single syllable words correctly
                    Rereads pattern books and dictations
                    Reading is disfluent
                    Reads aloud
                    Fingerpoints
   (Ages 5 - 9)

Writing

2) Beginning ——————————————————————→
            Can reread what was written
            Summarizes events and provides retellings in writing
            Volume increases from a few words to several sentences or more
            Writes disfluently

Orthographic knowledge and spelling ————————————————→

3) **Early Letter Name** ———→   **Middle and Late Letter Name** →
   Spells predominant sounds and   Spells the consonants and vowel
   then first and last consonants   sounds in each syllable

Examples of Invented Spellings:

	Early Letter Name		Middle and Late Letter Name
(bed)	d	b,bd	bad
(ship)	p	s,sp	sep, shep
(chase)	a	c, cs	cas, chas
(float)	t	f, ft	fot, flot
(cattle)	t	c, kd, ctl	catl, cadol
(cellar)	s	s, slr	salr, celr
(pleasure)	s	p, pjr, plgr	plasr, plager

the texts that they read. Practically, this means that students who can track, students who have a Concept of Word, can read familiar rhymes, familiar passages from pattern books, and their own dictations.

Beginning Readers read slowly, except when they read well memorized texts. And they read aloud to themselves. They have not acquired a sight vocabulary that facilitates a steady flow across the page. Their reading is described as disfluent and unexpressive. Beginning Readers read aloud when they read to themselves, and silent reading is rarely evidenced. We know that this is so when we visit most first grade classrooms during SSR (Sustained Silent Reading) and DEAR (Drop Everything and Read) and hear a steady hum of voices. Beginning Readers also tend to point to the words as they read. Disfluency, reading aloud to oneself, and fingerpointing are natural reading behaviors to look for in Beginning Readers.

Three behaviors of Beginning Readers:
✦ Read aloud
✦ Disfluent
✦ Fingerpoint

Writing

In the previous stage of development, Emergent readers in the Preliterate stage were unable to read what they had written for there were no clear letter-sound correspondences in what they wrote. Students in the early Letter Name stage can reread most of what they write. However, because so many vowels are omitted by early Letter Name spellers, there are times when they will have difficulty rereading what they have written. This is especially true during the early part of this stage when they spell only one or two sounds of each word.

There are two prerequisites for students to move to the beginning writing stage and to write down most any word that comes to mind:

1. Students must be able to isolate the sounds within a word, and this is developed as students acquire a stable Concept of Word. This ability to isolate sounds is often called phonemic segmentation.
2. Students need to know the letter names of most of the letters of the alphabet.

Reading and Writing Fluency

50 words per minute can be a good reading rate for a Beginning reader.

Students in the early Letter Name stage are often described as word-by-word readers (Bear, 1991b). Students' fluency in reading and writing is constrained by their orthographic knowledge. They do not know enough sight words, nor do they know enough about the orthography to read words quickly enough to permit fluent reading or writing. Because they spend so much time reading the words, they have little time to read unfamiliar materials with fluency and expression. Often, Beginning readers' reading rates are painfully slow. For example, a Beginning reader may reread a familiar text, either a dictation or a pattern book at 50 words per minute compared to mature readers who average 250 words per minute. (During the next stage students begin to read and write with greater fluency.)

To help themselves keep their places while they read, most Beginning readers fingerpoint to the words when they read. The third behavior which is common for beginners is that they read aloud when they read to themselves. The act of reading aloud buys processing time. While they hold the words they have just read in memory, they read the next word. Reading the word aloud gives them time to try to fit the words together into a phrase.

Beginning writers write slowly.

There is a similar pattern of disfluency in beginning writing, for students usually write slowly, and they often work through spelling words letter-by-letter (Bear, 1991a). As in reading, orthographic knowledge makes writing easier and more fluent. The more students know about how words are spelled, the more easily and fluently they can write, and consequently, the more time they can give to working with and expressing ideas. Beginning writers benefit from support writing activities in which they use patterns from their reading—predictable books, for example, in their writing.

Literacy Learning and Instruction

Support Materials:
✦ Pattern stories
✦ Rhymes
✦ Student dictations

To exercise and grow as readers and writers, these students need plenty of support. Reading materials include pattern books, rhymes, group experience charts and individual dictations. Students may not memorize these texts verbatim, but there are enough cues from the few written words they recognize, and they remember enough of the phrases to be able to reread these materials accurately and with increased fluency as they practice reading these familiar texts.

Students use their orthographic knowledge to read the words in these familiar texts. At this developmental level, their orthographic knowledge of initial consonant letter names and sounds is stable. Together with their Concept of Word, Beginning readers use their orthographic knowledge to track their way through the words.

For example, in a pattern book like *Brown Bear, Brown Bear* (Martin, 1983), students may use their knowledge of the letter name "b" when they read the first line. Also in this story, Concept of Word helps students keep at the word level when reading sentences like:

I see a yellow duck

Looking at me.

The two-syllable words would confuse students who do not have a Concept of Word.

The reading materials best suited for Beginning readers are highly predictable and familiar. Familiarity with the subject and the language supports students as they read, and in the course of this support reading, the words students read become known sight words—they begin to stand in recognition on their own. As is emphasized throughout this text, students learn to read words by doing plenty of reading.

Support Reading
Techniques:
✦ Choral
✦ Echo
✦ Repeated

Support reading techniques like choral, repeated, and partner reading, play an important role in the instruction of beginners. Language experience charts, and individual dictations are particularly successful in providing support and opportunities for beginners to read as fluently as they can, and still read each word. To encourage fluency, we make Personal Readers for students. These Personal Readers are collections of their familiar rhymes, pattern stories, group experience charts, and individual dictations (see Figure 6–7). The entries are usually reproductions of the texts from a pattern book, or a copy of their group or individual dictations. The stories in the Personal Readers are numbered, and the date they are introduced is noted. Students are enormously proud of their Personal Readers, and the materials in them are used to harvest known words which are later used in word study activities.

Beginners have
Personal Readers
that contain the
materials they
can read
successfully.

Most of the word study activities in this chapter require students to work with **known** words. This chapter provides detailed instructions on using these support materials and activities. In addition, the process for collecting sight words and managing word banks is also discussed. Students collect sight words as they reread these familiar materials. Their knowledge of known words provides a base for word study activities. As teachers practice these activities with students, they see that word study activities help beginners read and spell single syllable words.

Specific instructions for working with known words are presented in the following discussion as well as in the first several word study activities of this chapter. We emphasize the use of known words because we know how difficult it is for students to study the orthography when they have to work hard at simply reading the words. Students enjoy manipulating these known words when they are written on word cards. Please take the time to develop a management system for these sight words. This is the only stage when students will need personal word banks, and it is worth the investment of time to help students examine the orthographic patterns of these known words.

Support writing
by imitating
patterns from
books.

In writing, support activities give beginners the opportunity to write with greater fluency. Sometimes students write for a bit, and then dictate the rest of their stories to a teacher or student. Teachers also provide patterns in writing to help beginners use words in their writing. For example, many students make up their own words to pattern stories: "Pink Panther, Pink Panther, What do you see." A more complex pattern like Kenneth Koch's "I used to be, but now I am" poems (Koch, 1970) give students support by reducing the number of words they need to recall.

Characteristics of Orthographic Development

The Letter Name stage begins with syllabic writing in which each letter stands for a syllable. During the early part of the Letter Name stage students spell the most prominent sounds of a syllable. Slightly after this syllabic writing, students honor word boundaries by spelling the first and last sounds in a word. On the 15-point scale, early Letter Name spelling corresponds to 1 and 2.

The diagnostic assessment techniques discussed in Chapter Three help teachers place a students' spelling along the 15-point scale (see Figure 6–2.) The next point of orthographic development is evident when students begin to place a vowel in each stressed syllable. They use their phonemic awareness and knowledge of the orthography to spell the vowels. The following discussion of the way students spell the short vowels demonstrates what fine linguists children can be, and what fine distinctions they can make in the way words are formed in their mouths. This part of the Letter Name stage corresponds to points 3–5 on the Spelling-by-Stage Assessment.

In this section, the wondrous way students analyze English orthography and speech are examined. This discussion helps explain why students spell words the way they do. It is evident that children are our finest linguists who, without a mature vocabulary, exercise their knowledge of the sound system more vigorously than we do as adults.

> At a tacit level, children are natural linguists.

The Alphabet and the Name of the Letters: The "Letter Name"

Letter Name students use the sound of the letter name to spell. Students in the early part of this stage and the students in the middle and later part of Letter Name are quite different from each other in one obvious way. In the early Letter Name stage, students spell mostly with consonants and a few vowels. They enter the Letter Name stage when initial consonants are represented at the beginning and ends of words. In the middle and latter parts of this stage, students place a vowel in each stressed syllable. In the word study activities that follow, activities are included in which students sort known words to be-

> Letter Name spellers study the alphabetic principle in consonants and short vowel patterns.

FIGURE 6–2 15-Point Scale for Spelling-by-Stage Assessment

Late Derivational Constancy	15
Middle Derivational Constancy	14
Beginning Derivational Constancy	13
Late Syllable Juncture	12
Middle Syllable Juncture	11
Beginning Syllable Juncture	10
Late Within Word Pattern	9
Middle Within Word Pattern	8
Beginning Within Word Pattern	7
Late Letter Name	**6**
Middle Letter Name	**5**
Beginning Letter Name	**4**
Early Letter Name	**3**
Early Letter Name	**2**
Preliterate	1

come more facile with the alphabetic principle, and then in the middle to end of the Letter Name stage, the activities focus their examinations of the alphabetic principle in the short vowel patterns.

The Letter Name stage describes students who use their knowledge of the actual names of the letters of the alphabet to spell. For example, the match between the letter names and the letter sounds for *t* in "tee" and *d* in "dee" are clear. In spelling the word *like,* students who know that the letter l is said "el" have a clear clue from the letter name. In spelling the second consonant sound, a student may have to choose between a *c* or a *k*. A child named Corey may spell *like* as LC, using familiar letters.

Sometimes students include vowels in their spelling, especially when they spell some long vowels. For example, students in the early part of this stage spell *like* as LIC. Using a strategy of beginning and ending, and syllabic writing, students can luck out. We tend to think of early Letter Name stage spelling as largely consonantal.

Some letter names do not cue students in to the sound they represent. The letter name for w is such a letter. The letter name w sounds more like "double u," and not "wuh". Consequently when early Letter Name spellers spell *when,* they may spell it YN. Why do students use a *y*? When you say the letter name y, you can feel your lips moving to make the shape of the "wuh" sound. The letter *y* is the closest letter name to the sound at the beginning of *when*.

Where Beginning Letter Name–4 spellers spell *bake* as BK, students in the Late Letter Name–6 stage include vowels in stressed long vowel syllables (i.e., they spell *bake* as BAK) and they begin to include a vowel in short vowel syllables. In the early Letter Name stage, *sit* will be spelled ST; now students spell *sit* SET. In polysyllabic words, students often omit vowels, as in VAC-SHUN for *vacation*.

> The letter name for *y* says the *w* sound:
> YN for *when*

How Sounds Are Articulated in the Mouth

> *jr* and *dr* are similar in articulation:
> JR for *dr*

Early Letter Name and Letter Name students rely not only on what they hear in the letter names, but also on how the letters are made in the mouth when they spell unknown words. An example to work with to demonstrate this point is the way students spell *dr* in *drive*. In the Early Letter Name stage, students are misled in their spelling by the similarity between the way that "jr" and "dr" are made, and they may spell *drive* as JRV. Test how sounds are made in similar ways by contrasting how you say these words for yourself:

Say "drive," and then say "jrive."

Don't they sound alike? Phonetically, "dr" and "jr" are quite similar, with one distinguishing feature: the placement of the tongue—the tongue in saying "dr" is usually said with the tip of the tongue on the roof of the mouth, touching the palate. Don't the sounds *dr* and *jr* feel alike? Linguists call these sounds *affricates,* and they are made by a closure of sound followed by a slow release of sound.

There are several other affricates to consider: *ch, dr, tr*. In their writing, students use the consonant blends and digraphs they know best. For example, children who are familiar with words that begin with *ch* may spell *train* as CHRAN. The affricates are a fine example of the way Letter Name spellers match the letter names with how they say or articulate the sounds they are trying to spell. During the Letter Name stage, students rely heavily on information about the way words and sounds are articulated, how the sounds feel as they say the words, as well as how the words sound. One implication for instruction is that students in the Letter Name stage benefit from saying the words they are sorting so that they can feel the shape of their mouths as they say the words.

There are several other ways in which students relate sounds to the ways the sounds are made. There are the glides, as in the "w" sound as well as in "v" and "f". Basing a decision on the way a sound feels, students may spell *love* as LF, or oven as OFN.

As noted above, early Letter Name spellers omit most vowels in their spelling, and they focus on writing the consonants. The musical quality of the vowel may have something to do with why students in the early Letter Name do not include vowels. In speech, the vowel is the music and glue of the syllable. The quality of the vowel is determined by the shape of the mouth and jaw, the opening of the vocal tract, the force of air from the lungs, and the vibration of the vocal cords. What is perhaps most distinctive about the vowel is that there is no audible friction; this is left to the consonant.

Studies in acoustical phonetics have demonstrated that when vowels are separated from consonants, vowels are like musical tones. On the other hand, when consonants are separated from vowels they sound like noise, a click, or a snap of the fingers, and nothing like speech. The centrality of the vowel to the syllable can be seen when we try to say a consonant without a vowel. Say the letter B. What vowels did you attach to the B? If you said the letter name, then you would have said the long vowel ē, as in "bee." Now say "buh". The vowel this time is the schwa, ə, a vowel made in the middle of the mouth. Now try to say a "b" sound without a vowel. Try to whisper B and cut your breath short in a whisper. The whisper is as close as we come to separating a vowel from a consonant. Without the music of the vowel, the consonant would just be noise. For beginning writers in the early Letter Name stage of spelling, it is as if the consonant were the proverbial squeaky wheel; at first, the consonant seems to demand more attention than the vowel.

Consonants exert quite an influence on vowels. The principle of coarticulation in speech also demonstrates the impact a consonant can have on a vowel. For example, the vowel in *bat* is different than the "a" sound in bad as well as the "a" in bar. In the first case, did you notice that the "a" in *bad* was longer than the "a" in *bat?* As a matter of fact, in many dictionaries you can find bad written ba:d where the : means that the "a" has a longer duration than expected.

It is easier to tell that the vowel in *bar* is quite different than the "a" in *bat*. This is because the consonant "r" sound has the qualities of what are known in linguistics as **liquids,** and in the case of the "r" sound. The "r" influences the pronunciation of the vowel. Another liquid is the sound of the "l". Again, you can see that the "a" in *ball* is not quite the same as the "a" in *bat*. Students in the Letter Name stage study the glides "r" and "l" when they study short vowels.

There are patterns of substitutions connected to students' articulation. We observe these substitutions in students' spelling. These patterns are useful to understand students' development, but *instruction* in articulation is an altogether different issue. Sometimes we move too quickly from observation to instruction. Just because students substitute a *f* for a *v* does not mean that teachers present sorts to "teach" this difference. These initial consonants deserve some attention, but no more than any other consonants. We do not advocate asking students to reflect on how they articulate sounds. Their perception of sounds should be fine. In word study the attention is more on orthographic patterns than it is to sounds and articulation. While some sounding out is necessary, and something that students do, students do not reflect at a conscious level on how sounds are articulated, though they do have an enormous amount of information about articulation which they use at a tacit level.

---

f and *v* are also articulated alike: OFN for *oven*

Consonants are noise; vowels are music.

L and r sounds color the pronunciation of vowels. Compare the vowels in *bar*, *bat*, and *ball*.

Tacit knowledge is our unconscious knowledge.

Letter Name Spelling and the Vowel

Consider the ways vowels are made in the mouth. Linguists describe the vowels in terms of where they are located in the mouth and by the positioning of the tongue. The production of the vowel can be traced as air passes through the vocal cords into the mouth where it is further shaped by the position of the tongue and the way air passes around it.

In modern literacy instruction, teachers have taught students the differences between long and short vowels, for a total of 10 vowels. This distinction between five short and five long vowels may be derived from the 10 central long and short vowels of classical Latin (a, e, i, o, and u). The five long and five short vowels may be contrasted, in part, by their duration—supposedly, longer vowels sound longer than short vowels (Fromkin & Rodman, 1993).

What terms do teachers use with students to talk about the vowels? In many cases, students come to teachers with terms already. For example, some students know what consonants and vowels are, and others don't. Find a common base of terms to use in discussions. The simplest language to talk about vowels is probably the best. For example, we talk about the beginning and middle sounds in words: "Find a picture of a word that sounds like ball at the beginning." or "Bet and bend—Do they sound alike in the middle?" Descriptions like "in the middle" seem to suffice to draw students' attention to the vowels. Teachers can teach students the vowels and show them the differences between long and short vowels. The vowel sound boards and picture sorts are designed to help teachers examine the vowels with students.

Students may be taught to use terms to describe sounds, but the important thing to look for is students' ability to be able to read words and write words quickly and easily enough to be able to create meaning in their reading and writing. We want orthographic knowledge to come forward easily, and tacitly. Over time, we have seen that the long-short distinction has provided an adequate description for initial discussions with students about vowels.

During the Letter Name stage, students use the alphabetic principle to spell so that each letter represents a sound. Letter Name spellers have no difficulty using a letter name to spell long vowels. As examples, students spell *line* as LIN, *rain* as RAN, and *boat* as BOT. Letter Name spellers include a vowel in each stressed syllable. For example, the Letter Name student may spell *blanket* BLAKT. In this case the first vowel is stressed, and the schwa (ə) in the second, unstressed syllable is omitted.

Perhaps what is most interesting about the invented spelling in the Letter Name stage is the way students spell the short vowels. To spell short vowels, students rely on the Letter Names of the alphabet. The problem with short vowels is that there is not a letter of the alphabet that stands for short vowels; for example, there is no letter name that says the "eh" in *bet*. How do students choose a letter name for a short vowel? The answer is straightforward: They use their knowledge of the letter names to find the letter of the alphabet which is closest in terms of point of articulation to the short vowel they are trying to spell. This is a strategy that students use without conscious reflection.

However, it has been some time since most adults have analyzed sounds at this level; therefore, let's take a moment to consider the vowels and where they are made. The position of the words in Figure 6–3, illustrates some of the basic contrasts among vowels in English. The vowels are drawn in this space to mimic the general area where speakers can feel the articulation of the vowel. To talk about articulation is to describe the shape of the mouth and tongue while the word is being said. Compare the vowels in this figure by feeling the air pass through the mouth as the following words are said in a sequence from BEET to BOOT:

Find out what terms students know. It helps for them to know the terms consonant *and* vowel.

Letter Name spellers use letter names to spell short vowels. Long a is close to the short e.

beet bit bait bet bat bye bah bought boat put boot

Try saying this string several times. Feel how the production of the vowels moves from the top front, down the front, back and up. As you read the words in Figure 6–3, feel how the rounded vowels are made. Feel how the tongue is raised in the back, and how the lips are pursed as they are pronounced.

There are many other words that sound and feel the same way as these words. Here is a list of words for each of the vowels in Figure 6–3.

beet beat receive key believe amoeba people Caesar Vaseline serene
bit consist injury bin
bait ray great eight gauge reign they
bet serenity says guest dead said
bat pan act laugh comrade
bye bite sight by die Stein aisle choir liar island height sign
bah fought cot father palm sergeant honor hospital melodic
bought bore caught stalk core saw ball awe
boat go beau grow though toe own over
put foot butcher could
boot mule lute who sewer through to too two move Lou
(Adapted from Fromkin and Rodman, 1993, p. 209)

Feel where the vowel is made in your mouth.

Given the teacher's and students' dialects, the way a word is pronounced may not match these examples. For example, many people say *caught* and *cot* the same way. Some native speakers of English pronounce *bought, bore, caught,* and *stalk* with different vowels. This demonstrates that teachers need to be aware of dialectical differences when students sort and talk about words. It should be noted that these differences do not interfere with word study. An awareness of these differences enhances word study and brings greater accuracy to students' studies.

Listen for how students pronounce words as they sort. Dialects influence the way we sort.

Several vowels in English are really a combination of sounds, and when these vowels are created, the tongue moves two or three times to combine sounds. In Figure 6–3, the words in italics are described as vowel **glides** in which there are audible changes as the vowels are said (B**YE**, B**OAT**, B**AI**T, c**ow**, and b**oy**) (Crystal, 1987). For example, the long i in *bye* is a combination of "ah" as in *father* and "ee" as in *fee*. Some diphthongs not presented in Figure 6–3 are more complex, and involve two discreet movements of the tongue (e.g., "fire", "power" and "sure").

FIGURE 6–3 Vowels in the Mouth

Tongue Height	Front ◄――――――――――――――――――► Back

Adapted from Fromkin and Rodman (1993, p. 202)

The air stream for some of the vowels in Figure 6–3 is felt in the middle of the mouth with the tongue raised at this midpoint. There are the reduced vowels (vowels made right towards the middle of the mouth: *but* and *the*) as well as other middle vowels such as the following:

c**ow** ab**ou**t br**ow**n d**ou**bt c**ow**ard
b**oy** d**oi**ly
b**u**t c**u**t t**ou**gh am**o**ng **o**ven d**oe**s c**o**ver fl**oo**d
th**e** sof**a** **a**lone symph**o**ny s**u**ppose mel**o**dy tedi**ou**s **A**merica

After feeling the various areas of the mouth, next say two words and compare their locations. There are vowels made in the front and high part of the mouth, there are vowels that are said in the back and low part of the mouth, and there are words made in the middle of the mouth. By saying these words and contrasting them, you can feel the difference among the vowels, and, in particular, the comparisons among short and long vowels. For example, it is easy to feel that both BEET and BOOT are made at the top of the mouth, but that the articulatory configuration for pronouncing BEET passes through the front and top of the mouth, where in BOOT the air passes at the top, but further back in the mouth.

Compare the vowels in these words. First there is the long and then the short vowel.

BEET	bit	($\bar{e}$ – $\breve{i}$)
BAIT	bet	($\bar{a}$ – $\breve{e}$)
BOAT	but	($\bar{o}$ – $\breve{u}$)

They are close to each other. In this analysis, feel how air is shaped as it moves through the mouth.

Spelling Short Vowels

Now let's return to the question of how students choose a letter name to represent a short vowel. Without being consciously aware that they are doing this, Letter Name spellers spell short vowels with the closest letter name to that short vowel. There are five letter names to choose from: a, e, i, o, and u. What letter name is closest to "eh" in *bet*? In this case, the answer is the letter name "a". The wondrous aspect of this substitution is that students rely on the place of articulation to find the closest letter name (Read, 1975).

Place of articulation refers to the way the vowel is made in the mouth and with the tongue. We can feel where the vowels are made in the mouth as was done with the contrasts in Figure 6–3. The following contrasts are like the ones above. As the words are pronounced, pay attention to where the tongue is in the mouth, and how the tongue is shaped.

To feel how sounds are made in the mouth, try saying the following word pairs:

bed – bait
bed – beet

Short vowels are matched to the letter name of long vowels.

These pairs can be said so as to isolate the vowel to sense the place of articulation. Which was most like *bed: bait* or *beet*? Repeat the pairs several times to **feel** the way the short e sound is closer to the letter name a, the long $\bar{a}$ in *bait,* than it is to the long $\bar{e}$ in *beet.*

Students in the Letter Name stage use this information about articulation to spell *bet* as BAT. Students choose a letter name of the vowel to match with the short vowel based on how similar the words feel in the mouth. These letter name substitutions for short vowels are predictable. The following chart will help you remember how the letter names of vowels are substituted for the short vowel sounds:

Invented Spelling				Word		
BAT	for	bet	A	→		e
BET	for	*bit*	E	→		i
PIT	for	*pot*	I	→		o
POT	for	put	O	→		u

Consonant-Vowel-Consonant (CVC) is the basic short vowel pattern.

Over the course of the Letter Name stage, students learn to spell short vowel words and they see that short vowels follow a specific pattern, a **Consonant-Vowel-Consonant (CVC) pattern.** This CVC pattern is the common pattern that stretches across all short vowels from the short a in *pat* to the short u in *fun*.

In their study of short vowels, students learn to contrast vowels, and they begin to see orthographic patterns more clearly. The sight words, their known words, provide a base for studying the CVC pattern. In reading and directed word study, these known words provide the tension between what is and what they think about the orthography. This CVC pattern provides a basis for learning about short vowels.

As they mature and learn more sight words, students face the ambiguities of the **homographs** in their invented spellings. For example, students in the Letter Name stage will spell *bent, bet, bat, bait* the same way: BAT. There are too many homographs for efficiency in word recognition, and this is not the way we spell most of these words. The burden of so many homographs is a catalyst for change—a good problem. When students are proficient spellers of basic short vowel patterns, the disequilibrium begins: When students are certain that *bat* is spelled *bat,* they catch themselves when they try to spell long vowel patterns. There is dissonance when they realize, in this example, that "bat" is spelled bat. Shortly, this will force them to find other ways to spell a word like *bait.* When students are able to spell these basic short vowel patterns, and they begin to experiment with long vowel patterns, they have entered the next spelling stage—Within Word Pattern.

Other Orthographic Features

There are three other features we see students working through during this stage. It is good to know something about these features:

1. Influences on the vowel
2. Consonant blends and digraphs
3. Preconsonantal nasals

We tend to study these features towards the end of this stage, but we can study the features whenever students have enough examples in their word banks or whenever they show an interest in these features. For example, the influence of the letter r on the short vowel patterns is profound and may become a topic of study when students say that they wanted to separate out a word like *bar* from the other short vowels.

Influences on the Vowel

w, l, and *r* influence the pronunciation of vowels.

The w and l sounds have their own influences on vowels. For example, the vowel in words like *ball* and *saw* contrast with more common short vowels, as in *bat* and *sand*. And yet, all of these words are CVC pattern words.

The influence of the r creates other patterns for students to examine. In words like *car, fur,* and *bird* the r colors the pronunciation of the vowel. Compare these words with other CVC without the r:

car	cat
fur	full
bird	bid

Notice that for many speakers, when they say the "r" in these words, the tongue is "retracted and raised in such a way as to partially close the oral passage" (Southworth & Chander, 1974). Are these short vowels, and if so, how are the vowels in *cat* and *car* the same? R-influenced vowels are difficult to discern by sound alone. For example, *fur* and *sir* are said the same way, and so sound does not cue students to the correct spelling.

R-influenced vowels which follow a CVC pattern are examined during the Letter Name stage as word families. R-influenced vowels are studied across short vowels (e.g., *fur–her, for–war*). In the Within Word Pattern stage, students study homophones and homographs which are influenced by the "r," (e.g., four and for). Also students contrast consonant blends and R-influenced vowels (e.g., *from–farm, crush–curl, price–purse, bruise–burn, dark–draw, tarp–trap*).

Consonant Blends and Digraphs

Blends are 2 or 3 letters blended together. *bl, st* Digraphs are 2 or 3 letters that make one sound: *ch, wh*

Consider now the way Letter Name spellers use and examine consonant blends and digraphs. Blends are composed of two or three consonants. They form a spelling pattern, but the letter sounds remain distinct. The word *blend* itself contains two blends *bl-* and *-nd*, and when the blend is said, the individual sounds can be heard. A consonant digraph is nearly the same. A consonant digraph is thought of as two or three letters that make a new sound. Here are some common consonant blends and digraphs. Notice that there are blends and digraphs at the beginning and end of words.

black, bright, brought, spin, splash, spleen,

spindle, church, cheese, bunch, ranch

Throughout the Letter Name stage, students refine their understanding of consonants. Students become more consistent in the frequency with which they use consonant blends and digraphs in their spelling, and in their reading, they recognize words with consonant blends and digraphs with greater accuracy and fluency (Bear, 1992). Students' tacit understanding of consonant blends and digraphs grows along with their sight vocabularies and their understanding of the basic CVC patterns which contain consonant blends and digraphs.

Preconsonantal Nasals

N and m are nasals.

Some letter-sound combinations are more subtle than others. The **preconsonantal nasals** are sounds that are mostly omitted during the Letter Name stage (*bump* may be spelled BOP and *stamp* may be spelled STAP). The nasal sounds are made by air passing through the nasal cavity in the mouth. And in pronunciation, the nasal sound can be highly integrated into the following consonants (observe this in words like *stand* and *stamp*). It is as if the consonant dominates and absorbs the nasal. When students begin to spell words with pre-consonantal nasals correctly they are also at the end of the Letter Name stage (*bump, stand, bring, stump* and *stamp*).

Word Study Instruction

The focus for word study during this stage begins with initial consonants and works through the short vowels. Word study during this stage makes use of students' word banks and the pattern books, rhymes, and individual dictations students read. In this section, the sequence of word study throughout this stage is discussed, and ways to use word banks are presented. A number of important ways to organize word study instruction are outlined in the context of a discussion of several generic activities.

Sequence of Word Study

The sequence of word study is based on the sound, pattern, and meaning principles we have observed students working with; and during this stage of development, students focus primarily on sound and then pattern principles. In referring to Figure 6–1, consider the invented spellings and what they tell us about how students experiment with the orthography. There is an order to their experimentation, and in this developmental sense, then, students take the lead in word study. The sequence of word study activities is designed to complement their learning.

Students focus on sound *and* pattern.

The sequence of word study for Letter Name spellers spans the study of initial consonants, consonant blends and digraphs, and short vowels. What in students' development guides us in choosing word study activities? Initially, they use beginning consonants in their writing, so this is what we examine in word study. After students have learned to use most of the consonants, they use vowels in each stressed syllable. When they start placing a vowel in each syllable, we begin short vowel word study. At the end of this stage, students begin to use long vowel patterns in their spelling, and this is when we begin to examine long vowel word patterns and move on to the focus for word study in the next stage.

What is the exact sequence to study the consonants, and then the short vowels? We would like to be exact here, but the exact sequence will not be the same for each student. The exact sequence for word study of consonants and vowels is not the same for each student, and throughout this stage, teachers look through students' word banks for the examples students have to work with. There are three factors which impact the sequence and the pace of the word study:

1) Utmost is the students' development. Consider the pace of the students' learning. While the general sequence will be the same, the pace varies and we need to vary the length of time we spend on word study activities with different students. For this reason, membership in our word study groups is fluid.

2) Because word study always works with known words, word study during this stage is constrained by students' sight vocabularies. The size of their individual banks of known words varies, and during the beginning and middle parts of this stage, students' word banks may be between 20 and 50 words. An initial consonant sort with words can be limited: How many words does a student have for the 20 consonants and 6 vowels? In a bank of 20 words, a student may have

only three words that sound like "cat" at the beginning. This is why we use pictures. Word banks seldom have enough words for initial consonant study.

Teachers can help create a common base of sight words by using pattern books with alliteration, and plenty of repetition, as well as plenty of shared experiences that are described in Group Experience Charts and Individual Dictations. For example, in a patterned dictation based on eating fruits, it is likely that several children will acquire the names of fruits as sight words. Thus when they want to find words that sound like "bed" at the beginning, several children will have the word *banana*.

Factors which impact sequence:
♦ Pace of students' learning
♦ Known words students can sort
♦ Curriculum you need to cover

3) The third factor is the curriculum. Some school districts and schools specify through their curriculum guides what orthographic features should be studied. The developmental outline presented in this book provides clear guidelines for what features to study in what order. Teachers use the sequence presented here and still cover the features specified in their districts' curriculum.

The sequence that we use proceeds as follows:

Beginning consonants
Introduce consonant blends and digraphs
Short vowel families
CVC patterns for each vowel
Consonant blends and digraphs
Preconsonantal nasals

We begin now with an in-depth study of each of these areas of word study instruction. First we will present a thorough discussion of how to develop word banks and how to organize instruction.

Sequence of Instruction During the Early Letter Name Stage

Begin with picture sorts on how the pictures sound alike at the beginning.

Word study begins with the beginning consonants for the student in the early Letter Name stage. We begin with simple picture sorts in which students compare pictures based on how they "sound at the beginning." Beginning consonant pictures are contrasted in a particular order, starting with frequently occurring initial consonants where the contrasts or differences are clear both visually and by sound. There are five sets of initial consonants we study. The first four letters are *b*, *m*, *r*, and *s*. These consonants occur frequently in written English, and they are visually distinct and also distinct in articulation. Figure 6–4 is an example of a sort that started with pictures and then included sight words from the students' word bank of sight words. Students in the early Letter Name stage sorted pictures and then found words from their word banks that fit under the categories set out by the teacher.

The five sets of initial consonants are presented in Activity 6–3 below. The initial consonants are grouped roughly by frequency. Students' orthographic knowledge increases as they compare beginning consonants. As we have noted above, be sure to look at the words students have in their word banks. If the class has just studied hats, the teacher may want to study *h* instead of *g*. Here are the groupings we suggest:

There are five sets of initial consonants.

b	m	r	s
t	g	n	p
c	h	f	d
l	k	j	w
y	z	v	q^u

FIGURE 6–4 Initial Consonant Picture and Word Sort

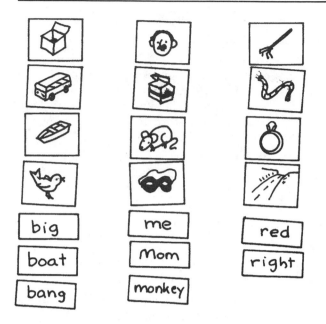

These consonants are arranged so that letters within groups are visually and phonetically distinct, and the order is based also in part on how frequently they occur. Look in the dictionary; there are more words that start with *b* than with *n*, etc.

A few final consonants are introduced and studied, but like many of the initial consonants, once students have learned the frequently occurring initial consonants, they can easily use them to spell final consonants. Not much time is devoted to the study of final consonants. The study of final consonants is covered when the students examine word families. When students consistently omit final consonants in their writing, we may draw their attention to them through word study activities that are similar to the initial consonant sorts. For example, we may hunt for words and pictures of words that end like *bat*.

In all of the studies of initial and final consonants, students start with sound contrasts through picture sorts and contrast games, and then they go to their bank of known words, their word banks, to find words that begin or end in the same or a similar way.

After students study initial consonants, we turn to the study of initial consonant digraphs and blends. The goal of word study of consonant blends and digraphs is to have students ready to look at the "vowel and what follows" (Henderson, 1990). The following beginning digraphs are the first to be studied:

ch
sh
th
wh

In a few of the word study activities below, there will be sound boards that include these digraphs and blends.

The study of initial consonant blends begins with the easiest contrasts of the single initial consonants with its blend. For example, pictures that begin with a *b* may be contrasted with pictures that begin with the *bl* blend. The letter *b* is one of the most frequently occurring initial consonants, and it has two frequently occurring consonant blends: *bl* and *br*. Similarly, in previous word study, *speak* would be placed under a picture of a **sun**; now, *speak* would be sorted underneath a picture of a **spoon**. ·

Starting with picture and sound sorts, students sort pictures of words that begin with a b, with the same sound that they hear and feel at the beginning of words like "ball" and "bat" and the sound that they hear and feel at the beginning when they say "*bl*anket" and "*bl*ue". Over one or two months, more contrasts are added as students become proficient with the easier sorts. A progression in the study of initial consonants might involve these comparisons:

> compare *b* to other consonants, like *m, r,* and *s*
> compare *b* to *bl*
> compare *b* to *br*
> compare *b, br, bl*

Several weeks can be dedicated to sorting for consonant blends and digraphs. Most of the consonant blend and digraph study is done with pictures, primarily because students do not have many sight words to bring to the sorts. When they look through their word banks of known words, they do not have many exemplars to work from. How many sight words does a student at this point know that begin with *ch* or *sp*? Probably just a few of each.

For this reason, and unlike initial consonants, students in the early part of the Letter Name stage are not expected to acquire great fluency or accuracy in spelling and sorting consonant blends and digraphs. Students become proficient in using consonant blends and digraphs in their spelling towards the end of the Letter Name stage, and during the next stage, the Within Word Pattern stage, after they have collected enough sight words that contain these orthographic features. At this time, the focus is on the blends and digraphs as consonantal units that precede or follow a vowel as in the CVC patterns (e.g., *plan, sick, spot*).

The word study activities involving blends and digraphs help students see blends and digraphs as one consonant unit. This knowledge of digraphs and blends will help them when they study short vowels in detail. For example, students begin to see *tr* as one consonant unit and later, they consider *trap* as three sounds, and a CVC pattern. Similarly, they see that even a word like *black* is a CVC pattern where *bl* is one unit, the vowel a is another, and the third is the final consonant blend *ck*. The students also work through sorts in which they consider features like the *ll* in *ball,* and the *nd* in *blend* or *stand*.

Sequence of Instruction During the Middle and End of the Letter Name Stage

Developmentally, the middle of the Letter Name stage is noted for the appearance of a vowel in each stressed syllable. Brian's spelling in the following example is a good reminder of students who are solidly in the middle of the Letter Name stage:

BED	(bed)
SEP	(ship)
JRIV	(drive)
BUP	(bump)
WAN	(when)

MIDDLE LETTER NAME–5

Brian is eight-years-six-months old and in third grade. He makes predictable letter substitutions, and it is clear that he is experimenting with short vowels and is now ready to study them in word study activities.

(margin note) Compare initial consonants with related blends and digraphs: *b, bl, br*

(margin note) Consonant digraphs and blends are seen as one consonant unit in the CVC pattern.

Word families are a first look at short vowel patterns.

Beginning with word families, students begin a systematic study of short vowels. From the middle of Letter Name spelling to the beginning of the next stage students study the family resemblances within and across short vowels. The discussion begins with the study of **word families** when we examine phonograms like -*at, -in,* or -*ot.*

What should be the order of short vowel word study? The constraints were discussed earlier. Assuming that students are ready to examine short vowels, teachers choose the short vowel which best suits their students. Looking through their word banks, teachers see if there is a predominance of one short vowel. If so, teachers may begin with that vowel. In moving from one short vowel to another, compare and contrast short vowels that are fairly distinct from each other. If there is no predominance of a particular short vowel in students' word banks, we recommend that teachers move from short a to short i or short o, and that they try not to move directly from a short a to a short e or a short e to a short i.

Conduct picture sorts to contrast vowel sounds.

For each vowel, begin with the basic categories for that vowel and be sure to conduct several sound sorts with that vowel. Conduct picture sorts which contrast that short vowel with its corresponding long vowel (*cat* and *cake*) and create picture sorts in which two short vowels are contrasted. For example, short a can be compared to short i, as seen in Figure 6–5.

The study of the orthographic patterns for a short vowel begins with the word families and then moves to the students' word banks to find examples of the categories that were established in the picture and family sorts. Activities involving sound wheels and flip books are presented at this time and are included in the Letter Name stage activities to follow. Students use teacher-made sorts to look at similarities and differences among short vowel patterns. For example, while studying the short i word families, students may sort the words into the following columns:

FIGURE 6–5 Picture Sort by Short a and Short i

(Short a)   (Short i)

Sort word families of known words.

pig	bit	bin	bill
dig	hit	fin	fill
fig	sit	tin	hill
big	kit	chin	

In conducting these family sorts, students need not be able to read all the words, but should know at least one word from each column. In this phonogram sort—*-ig -it -in -ill*—students reread their sorts. In reflecting on what these words have in common, we look for them to declare that they all sound alike in the middle, that they have three basic sounds. Some students observe that *bill, fill,* and *till* have four letters. This is a good time to think about the differences between sounds and the numbers of letters. A word like *chin* can extend the discussion to consonant blends and digraphs. If students agree that the words sound pretty much alike in the middle, then the teacher can begin to expand the features of the short i to include consonant blends and digraphs in words like *chip* and *sick*.

All along, students refer to their individual word banks for examples of the word families they are studying. They bring a variety of other words that sound like *pig* in the middle, and then together in small groups they add their words to this sort. These individual examples are central to word study during this stage, and so teachers want to be sure to have a way for students to collect words for their word banks. The first activities are used to teach students how to harvest known words from the stories and rhymes they read in their Personal Readers.

Words like *fill, stick,* and *bit* are all CVC pattern words.

In working with students to examine the various short vowel patterns for each vowel, their attention is drawn to the fact that these are CVC patterns. Over the course of studying the short vowels, students see that the CVC pattern is the basic pattern for all short vowels. Sometimes students get stuck on rhyming families, and they forget about the CVC pattern. Be sure that students can see that words like *bet, bell, Ben,* and *bed* are short e, CVC words.

The differences between the R-influenced and other short vowel CVC pattern words are profound and need to be examined so that students understand that R-influenced vowel words follow the CVC pattern, and also that they form a major sub-category of short vowels, in this case, short a. The basic R-influenced words like *car, far, tar,* and *fir, sir, stir* can be examined as families, and as part of the CVC category.

When students have examined one short vowel in detail, choose another vowel to study. Begin by comparing the rhyming families as in *cat—bit, can—bin, call—bill.* After these initial comparisons, study this second vowel in detail. As teachers finish studying the second vowel, compare the orthographic patterns across vowels as in the two sorts below:

cat	can	call		bit	bin	bill
bat	fan	fall		kit	fin	hill
rat	sand	ball		sit	win	fill

Students can see in sorts like these the similarities in patterns between two vowels.

Study the first short vowel for some time. The time spent will pay off when students study other vowels.

We recommend that teachers take some time to examine one short vowel and its many families and patterns. The time invested in the study of one short vowel will make the study of subsequent short vowels run smoothly. Consider the different examples of short e words that students might bring together from their word banks during small group word study:

Single Consonants	Doublet or Blend	Other
bed	fell	head
leg	chest	read
net	best	bread
ten	desk	bend
met	fence	send
net	dress	
men	left	
red	tell	
bet	bell	
fed		

Students continue with similar sorts for each short vowel. This short e sort and the following short o sort are similar:

Single Consonants	Blend	Other
hot	cost	log
got	frost	frog
Bob	sock	gone
not	lost	crawl
got	fox	saw
job	box	paw
chop	soft	
stop		won
top		son
shop		done
		from

The short o has a number of other categories including the short *u* sound in *won* and the rounded *o* as in *log* and *frog*.

At the end of the Letter Name stage students broaden their examination of the short vowels they studied earlier. They are able to sort their short a words into many categories, in part because they have many more sight words, and in part because their orthographic knowledge has expanded. They certainly have come a long way from the -*at* family.

Figure 6–6 is a sort by Jeff who was late in the Letter Name stage. This is an advanced sort of short a. First Jeff was asked to go through his word bank and find the word cards that had an *a* in them, and then to take out the words that sounded like *gate* in the middle. A picture of a *gate* was to used to remind him of this category. Going through his word bank and selecting these known words took three minutes. He was asked to take the remaining words and sort them into a number of piles.

Jeff completed this sort in five minutes. He explained his sort by saying that he sorted words into categories for short a. He also told the group that the first four columns fit the CVC pattern. He placed *what* and *again* in the **Miscellaneous** pile. He also created a column of words that started with an a. He was interested in the "uh" sound in about, and we discussed the **schwa** sound, the upside down and backwards e in the dictionary. The final column consisted of long a words that sounded like "gate" in the middle.

In some of the final sorts and games of this stage students reexamine consonant blends and digraphs. At this time, they have many more sight words that contain beginning and ending consonant blends and digraphs. Students see that there are many words like *match* and *check* that can be included in their studies of short vowels. As part of this study they also study preconso-

In advanced Letter Name sorts, students sort their words into several categories.

Study consonant blends and digraphs again at the end of the Letter Name stage.

FIGURE 6–6 Jeff's Late Letter Name Stage Open Sort

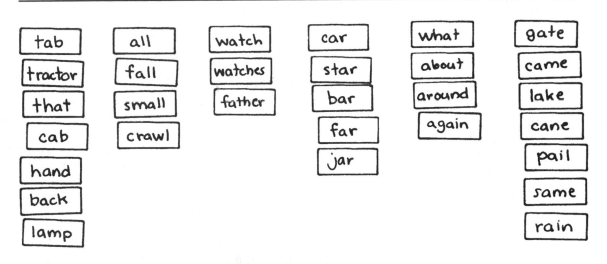

nantal nasals. Many of these activities with consonant digraphs can be continued when students are in the Within Word Pattern stage. Once students can spell and read most single-syllable short vowel words, they begin to experiment with the spelling patterns for long vowels. Introduce long vowel word study activities from the next chapter when they begin to experiment with long vowel spelling patterns.

This sequence of word study easily spans kindergarten through second grade. There will be a handful of students in third grade, and a few students in this stage in grades four through six. Now we turn to the activities that complement this stage and sequence of word study.

There are two aspects of the word study which are crucial to understand for this stage:

1. The development and use of individual word banks
2. The basic organization of word study activities for Letter Name spellers

Developing and Using Word Banks

It is crucial that students work with known words. During this Letter Name stage, the word banks are developed as they are collections of known words students use in word sorts and word study games. In this section, procedures to develop and manage word banks are presented. With the picture cards and individual collections or banks of known words, teachers are ready to conduct word study activities in small groups and in centers with students in the Letter Name stage.

Use Known Words

Both the words and pictures students use in word sorting activities must be known on sight. Words or pictures that are not read accurately should be discarded from the sort. Why put an obstacle in the way of students when they examine words? There is an added burden in word study if students must labor to pronounce words before analyzing their features and relationships to other words. Known words are always used because they make it easier for students to look across words for similarities and differences among words.

Where Do The Words Come From?

The words come from any source where a child can find known words. Usually, these words come from dictations, small group experience charts, rhymes, poems, and pattern books that they read. While words can come from students' names and labels (like Wendy's, BUM® Equipment), it is best if the words in the word banks can be traced back to meaningful and familiar text. By using words which come from familiar readings, by numbering the stories and rhymes and the word cards, students can go back to a primary source to find a word in their word banks which they temporarily have been unable to read.

Personal Readers, such as the one in Figure 6–7, are individual student collections of copies of group experience charts, rhymes and ditties, as well as individual dictations, and selected passages from pattern books which students can read independently or with some support from a teacher or partner. Teachers help students develop these readers for repeated and supported reading activities. Except for the individual dictations, many of the selections in personal readers are the same among many students. Personal readers are an ideal place for students to collect words from their word banks. The steps to follow to develop individual dictations and pattern stories and rhymes for these Personal Readers are presented in the third and fourth activities below.

Personal Readers are the best source of word bank words.

Students Harvest Known Words

Words are harvested from stories in students' Personal Readers. Students collect sight words from group experience charts, individual dictations, rhymes, and pattern stories. The steps to harvest sight words are presented in the first activity.

FIGURE 6–7 A Personal Reader—Short-Term and Long-Term Word Banks

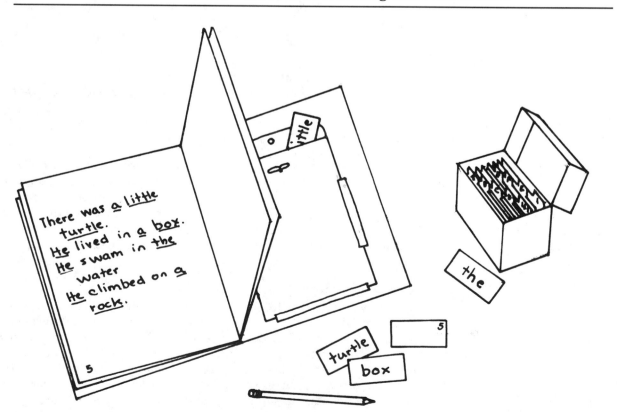

The short-term word bank is pasted to the back of the Personal Readers.

Students can also collect sight words from stories they have read. For some of the easiest books, the words from the book can be put on word cards which are stored in a library pocket in the back of the book. After reading an easy text, students are taught to read through the words in the pocket to see which words they know at sight. Students write the words they know onto their own word cards which are placed in their word banks.

We want to be sure that unknown words do not enter students' word banks. A short-term word bank can be developed as a holding spot for words students want to harvest into their permanent or long-term word banks. A short-term word bank can be made from a 6" x 8" envelope or small plastic bag taped to the inside back cover of students' Personal Readers. These envelopes are for words students recognize from the latest stories and dictations. Periodically, sometimes once a week or when new materials are added to students' personal readers, teachers work with students in small groups to have them read through the words in their short-term word banks. Words they know at sight go into the long-term or permanent word bank.

On the back of each word card, students write down the number of the story in their personal reader from which the word has come. In addition, if the words are going to be shared in word study games, students also write their initials on the back of the word cards.

The long-term word bank contains words students can read easily.

The long-term word bank is kept in a box, a small margarine container, a can, or a fast-food container. Plastic and metal index card file boxes are nice to have if they are available. When file boxes are at a premium, we have started with margarine containers for the first 50 words and then moved to a box. At any given time in either a first or second grade classroom, there are no more than a third of the students who need these smaller containers, and a third who need the larger boxes. In first grade, there may be as many as two-thirds of the class who use margarine containers for their long-term word banks.

How words are selected for the word bank can be seen in the following activities for working with individual dictations and other familiar texts, like pattern books or simple stories. The first sequence is for individual dictations, and the second is for patterned stories and rhymes.

We keep a supply of low tension rubber bands or library card envelopes to wrap or store selected sight words. In this way, word sorts can be started on one day and continued on the day following. For example, one day a teacher can ask students to look through their banks for all of the words that have a letter *a* in them. The students place these words in library card holders or wrap them in rubber bands. The next day, students sort these words by sound according to the vowels they hear in the middle.

We also keep a small container of blank word cards. The blank cards are used by students to make their word banks to take home and by teachers who want to have fairly neat word cards for each individual who is working with word banks. Visitors can help with the word banks by cutting word cards and writing down students' known words.

When Do Students Stop Using Word Banks?

There are three signs to look for to tell when to discontinue word banks:

1. The student is at the end of the Letter Name stage of spelling.
2. There are at least 200 words in the word bank.
3. It is possible to use teacher-made sorts in which students recognize nearly all of the words easily.

At this point, students no longer need individualized word banks.

Word banks grow to 150 to 250 words.

Students' word banks increase slowly and steadily. At first, students do not have enough words in their banks to use them much for sorting. This is an important time to show students how to collect words for their word banks. Gradually, word banks increase to 50 words, and then there are plenty of words for many sorts. Once the word banks grow to between 150 to 250 words, they become clumsy to manage. It takes students too long to hunt through their banks for examples of a particular short vowel; there are too many words to read through. At this time, it is likely that the teacher can introduce teacher-made word sorts.

Teacher-Made Sorts

Teacher-made sorts begin at the end of the Letter Name stage.

During most of the Letter Name stage, known words from students' word banks are used in sorting. Near the end of the Letter Name stage, teachers can often move to teacher-made sorts and away from individual word banks. This occurs when teachers can make a pack of word cards that students can read easily. If students can read at sight 18 out of 20 word cards in a teacher-made sort, then the words can be used in closed and open word sorts. As long as students weed out the unknown words before sorting, they will be able to use teacher-made sorts successfully. A variety of sorts are made to use in small groups, in centers, and in assessment.

Organizing Word Sorting Activities

In word study activities, students make decisions about words based on patterns they see, hear, and feel when they sort words and pictures (Barnes, 1989; Gillet & Kita, 1978; Morris, 1982). Word sorts are a part of language arts instruction, and teachers introduce sorts to their students in small groups. Once students understand how they are to sort, they become involved in sorting activities in small groups, with partners and individually. The word sorts help students progress in their overall reading, spelling, and vocabulary development.

Picture Sorts and Word Sorts

Color some of the pictures to make them easier to read.

Picture sorts use simple pictures of objects or actions that key students to a particular orthographic feature of a word; at this stage picture sorts focus on beginning consonants, beginning consonant blends and digraphs, and short and long vowels. The pictures do not have the words on them. With these pictures, students focus on the sound features of the words. Usually, after a picture sort, students go to their individual word banks to hunt for words that have similar sounds. The picture cards included in this book are just the right size for use in these sorts. They are the same size as the word cards, and the pictures are easily recognizable. Most of us color in some of the pictures slightly, using a yellow marker to highlight the action in the few pictures that show action (e.g., the drops of water dripping from the picture of the socks).

Show students categories for sorting picture and known words.

Many Letter Name stage sorts begin with pictures. The pictures compel students to analyze articulatory and sound patterns. Teachers show students how to sort, and they show students the basic categories. For example, students may be shown that a picture of a fish will head one column representing short i, and that another column would be headed with a picture of a kite, representing long i.

Students read through the pictures to be sure that they can recognize the pictures, and then they sort the pictures by the sound in the middle. At this point, if there is time, students are instructed to look through their word banks for words that sound like *fish* in the middle and words that sound like *kite* in the middle. These word cards are placed under the appropriate picture cards. Some teachers worry that older students will not want to sort pictures by sound. We have found that as long as the sorts are developmentally appropriate, students of all ages are receptive to sorting by pictures and words.

Open and Closed Sorts

Open sorts: Students define categories Closed sorts: Teacher defines categories

As was discussed in Chapter 4, teachers establish the categories in closed sorts before the students begin, and in open sorts, students establish the categories as they sort through the words and pictures. Before entering a new type of sort, it is good to demonstrate the sort in a small group, and then run a few closed sorts on that feature so that students become familiar with the particular categories. For example, when students begin to sort for short i, teachers present a few closed picture sorts in which students compare short i pictures headed with a picture of a fish with long i pictures headed with a picture of a kite. Generally, teachers demonstrate through closed sorts in small group any word sort that students are expected to sort independently. For management purposes, the sorts are organized in classification folders.

Classification Folders

Manila file folders are used in word study activities to hold materials and to help students sort their words or pictures into categories (see Figure 6–8). Classification folders are divided into three to five columns, and many teachers laminate them. For open sorts, the categories are undefined, but the manila folder provides a frame for the sort. Also, the folders provide storage for a sort with the

FIGURE 6–8 Classification Folders

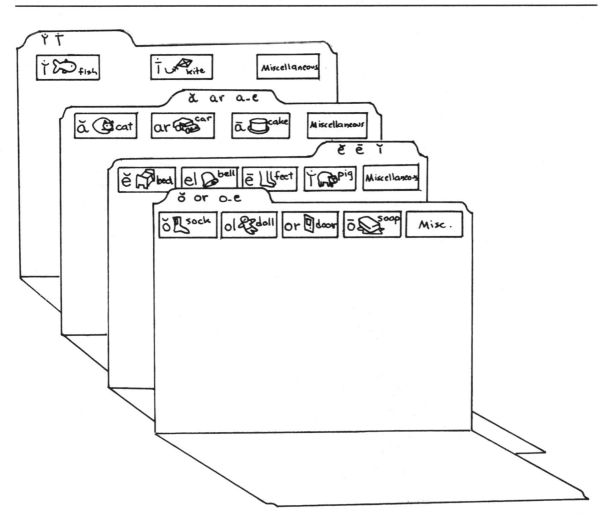

addition of a plastic bag to hold the pictures or words. Some teachers have hanging folders in which they place these sorts, ready for student use. Especially when there is no room in a class for centers, teachers use these hanging folders as a place to store the activities that students can take back to their tables.

Four headings of classification folders that we have used during this spelling stage are illustrated in Figure 6-8. In the activities to follow there are many pictures and word lists that students can use to sort with these classification folders.

Where Are Sorts Stored?

Teacher-made word sorts and picture sorts can be stored in small boxes, like bank check boxes, with wraps around the cards for identification. For storage, some teachers buy boxes with a dozen or so drawers (such as those used to store screws, nuts and bolts), and the drawers are labeled by feature.

> Word study centers contain individual and partner sorts.

Teachers also set up word study areas in their classrooms. Usually there are two centers available to students in this area so that during center periods, two students or two pairs can work in word study centers at one time. The sorts for particular groups of students can be color coded at these centers. For example, the Letter Name students may know to use the red folder for sorting when they work at a word study center. Word study centers also have sound boards available for easy reference, and there are sorting folders and plastic containers which students use in sorting.

When teachers are ready to replace the sorts in the centers, they can sit in the word study area, pull the sorts from the word and picture boxes, and put the old sorts back in the storage boxes. Many teachers have students keep their long term word banks in the word study area. In this way, while teachers plan word study activities, they can easily look through students' banks to see what examples they can draw on in the new sorts.

FIGURE 6–9 Students Can Complete Sorts Independently

Timers help students maintain a good pace.

Where do students sort? They can sort at their desks, in small groups, and individually or with a partner on the floor or in a word study center (see Figure 6–9). Sometimes teachers remind students that they need to work at a good pace. Small two-minute sand glasses that come with several games or stop watches are used to keep up the pace of the sorting.

The word study activities that follow have been divided into two sections:

Early Letter Name Sorts and Games
Letter Name Sorts and Games

There are five further divisions among the activities to indicate the focus for word study: Harvesting Words, Studying Consonants, Word Families, Short Vowels, and Other Features.

Activities for Letter Name Stage Students

The following activities are arranged in order of difficulty using the Spelling-by-Stage Assessment presented in Chapter 3. The first half of the activities are for students in the early part of this stage and is divided into three sections to match the sequence of instruction already described:

> Harvesting and Maintaining Word Banks
> Building Support Materials
> Studying Consonants

The second half of the activities in this chapter are for students from the middle to late part of the Letter Name Stage and are divided into these three headings:

> Word Families   Short Vowels   Other Features

Sorts which can be used with a variety of features are marked as generic activities and the symbol **GA** .

The word sorts presented at the end of this and other chapters can be used in these generic activities.

Early Letter Name/Letter Name; Word Bank Words

Harvesting and Maintaining Word Banks

Students need to have a stock of sight words that they can read with ease. The following activities help students develop and maintain a word bank. Through the use of familiar rhymes and small group and individual dictations, students begin to harvest sight words.

A Harvesting Known Words 6–1

Familiar stories, poems, group and individual dictations, and rhymes are the primary sources for harvesting known words.

Procedures

1. From Personal Readers, make copies of familiar reading materials for each child.
2. Students underline known words in a familiar text. The first few times students underline known words, it is likely that they will read the

text, a story, or dictation, underlining each word. Many of the words underlined in this sequential manner will not actually be known words that they recognize easily out of context. After they go through the next step a few times, they will realize that the underlined words have to be words they **really** know. (See the text for further discussion.)

3. A teacher, helper, or partner listens and checks as a student says the underlined words. Often, the helper points to the words in random order.

4. Known words are written on **word cards.** On the back of the cards, write the number of the story from the Personal Reader. Because word cards get mixed up in some sorts and word study games, students should also write their initials on the back of their cards.

A The Grand Sort for Beginning Readers 6–2

Early Letter
Name/Letter
Name;
Word Bank
Words

This is an important sort in which students read through their individual word banks. Students use words harvested from familiar stories and dictations. In this sort, students simply go through their word cards, and they say the words they know, putting them in one pile, and placing the unknown words to the side. Holding each card, the student says each word.

Known words are placed directly in front of the student. Unknown words are discarded either in a pile to the side or directly above the known words. The student tries to move quickly through the pile. The words that students put in the "I know" pile are used in subsequent sorts.

What do you do with the unknown words? The unknown words can be discarded. However, discarding words can be a touchy point for some students who are hesitant to throw away unknown words. Here, the teacher needs to monitor the activity. There is no harm in letting a few temporarily unknown words remain, but the big mistake is when a student proceeds to another word study activity with a number of unknown words. Working with so many unknown words makes students' work hesitant, and prone to errors.

Variations

Once the teacher has shown students how to do this sort, various partnerships can be established. Have students work in pairs. This is a good opportunity for heterogeneous groups.

Often students want to go back and try again on words. We show them how to figure out an unknown word. We show them how to go back to their Personal Readers. Referring to the number on the back of the card, a student returns to his or her Personal Reader and reads until the word is found. This is an important activity to promote students' use of context to figure out new words.

A Collecting Individual Dictations and Group Experience Charts 6–3

Early Letter
Name/Letter
Name;
Support
Materials

These activities are part of the Language Experience Approach (Stauffer, 1980) and are conducted in small groups up to ten, or individually.

The group experience charts are for children in the early part of this stage. Individual dictations can be collected from all children in this stage. For the group experience charts, the contributions should be one, or at most, two sentences long. Individual dictations range from a few sentences to three paragraphs.

This activity is divided into a four day sequence. It can be accomplished in fewer days in smaller groups.

Day I: Share an experience and collect dictations

Find a stimulus, or experience to share with students. It should be interesting and be a memorable experience that encourages students to talk. For some individual dictations, students can be prompted to tell a personal experience without a prop or special event.

If there is a common experience, share the experience and collect dictations. In a group experience, students need to do plenty of talking before they dictate. For an individual dictation, students work individually with a teacher while other members of the group draw pictures of the experience or stimulus.

When the student talk has been plentiful, collect individual dictations. Ask each student to tell you something to write down. Write down what the student says about the experience or stimulus; keep the dictation to a length that the student can reread.

Reread the story to the student and make any changes he or she requests. The students then provide a title for the dictation. Reread the dictation with the student.

Before Day II type a copy of the dictations

(Many teachers who have a computer in class use the word processor to take the dictation.) For students involved in the group experience chart, the students focus on their individual contributions. These dictations are placed in students' Personal Readers. The entries are numbered.

Day II: Reread dictations and underline known words

Choral read the dictations. Support the students' reading. (The students should reread these familiar materials two or three times each day.)

The second thing students do is underline known words. "Underline words you really know." You can point to the underlined words randomly to make sure they know the words they underline.

Day III: Choral read and make word cards of known words

Students can work together, or individually. Provide support and compare the amount of support the students need.

Make word cards for underlined words that are recognized accurately and quickly. On the back of the word cards, students write down the number of the story, as well as their initials. Put these words in the short-term word bank, which can be an envelope taped to the back of the Personal Reader. Harvest these words into long-term word banks when you begin a new story or rhyme.

Day IV and on: Choral read and review new word cards

Students continue to reread their dictations, review the words in their word banks, and complete their pictures. A new dictation or story cycle is begun when students can read their new readings with good accuracy and modest fluency.

 Sharing Rhymes and Pattern Stories in Groups 6–4

Early Letter
Name/Letter
Name;
Support
Materials

These support materials are essential in the primary classroom. Use rhymes and pattern stories to harvest known words.

Preparation

Find a rhyme, ditty, or pattern story which students will find memorable and readable. Consider the length and how much of the text is readable. You can focus on one major pattern or verse. Find a big book or make a chart of the text. Make copies of the rhymes and patterns for students' Personal Readers.

Day I: Introduce and read the text

Look at the pictures with the students for information about the rhyme or pattern story.

Read the rhyme or story to students, running a finger underneath the text. Read fluently, but not too fast; read with expression, and rhythmically. Stop periodically to discuss and enjoy the story.

For students in the early part of this stage, teachers focus on a small part of the text. Lead students to reflect on the story by asking general questions like: "What did you think of the story?" "What was your favorite part?" Ask students to help you return to a few favorite pages. Reread these parts of the text and point to a few words to see if some students are able to recognize words at sight.

Day II: Reread the rhyme or story

Reread as much of the text as students can read with ease. Again, check for length—passages can range from one line to several sentences. Choral read the story or rhyme with the students. Decide which parts of the text will be compiled for Personal Readers.

Students draw a picture to go with the rhyme or story.

Type the text onto a single page or two which can be duplicated and included in Personal Readers. Number and date this entry, and make copies of the text students are rereading.

Day III: Choral read and underline known words

Choral read the passage several times—read from the chart and from Personal Readers. The teacher provides as much support as is needed.

Students underline words they know and want to include in their word banks. Check students on the words they have underlined.

Students continue to draw their pictures and reread the text. Encourage students to write their own versions of the rhyme or pattern book, to read to each other. Work on reading fluency and expression and feeling. Encourage dramatic reading.

Day IV: Choral read and write known words on cards

Begin by choral reading. Check the words students have underlined. Write these words on word cards and put the cards into an envelope or bag in the short-term word bank.

Harvest these words into long term word banks when you begin a new story or rhyme.

Studying Consonants

These activities include picture and word sorts which focus on beginning consonants and consonant blends and digraphs.

 Sound Boards   6–5

Early Letter Name; Initial Consonants

Sound boards are physical aids students use to study initial consonants, initial consonant blends and digraphs, and vowels. These boards contain pictures of words that have the feature being studied. The first sound board is the initial consonant sound board which students use when they begin to examine the alphabetic principle. An 8" x 10" copy of the sound boards included in this chapter are placed at the front of students' writing books. These boards make it easy for students to find letters to stand for the sounds they want to use.

Teachers often make a poster by drawing their own pictures. Recently, the new technology of chart printers has made it possible to take the individual sound boards presented below and enlarge them to poster size. The sound board posters can be placed in a prominent place in primary classrooms, and this gives beginning writers the opportunity to refer to the enlarged sound boards for the letters of a word they want to write.

The consonant board begins with the letter b. Both the upper case and lower case letters start each line. Each letter is followed by a key picture which begins with a letter of the alphabet. Following the picture, there is a key word which has the orthographic feature.

Students are shown how to read these boards across from the top left and to the right. For example, we might say, "Here is an upper case and lower case b, and here is a picture of a ball. The word *ball* begins with a b." In addition, students are shown how the sound boards can be used when they are looking for a letter to stand for a sound they are trying to spell. Similar sound boards for consonant blends and digraphs as well as for short vowels are presented in the activities below. (Figures 6–23, 6–24, and 6–25 present samples of these sound boards.)

A · How to Use Initial Consonant and Blend and Digraph Sound Boards · 6–6

Early Letter Name; Initial Consonants

Sound boards are keys to remind students about initial consonant sounds. Sound boards can be made into posters. Students refer to the sound board when they are beginning to use the alphabet in their writing. Working with a sound board repeatedly helps the student internalize the sound which is represented by a particular letter.

Procedures

To introduce the letters to be examined, say something like, "Here's a b. Here's a picture of a bell; when we say "bell," the first sound we feel and hear is a b. And don't you know, the word bell, written here, begins with a b." Notice that the teacher never said that the word bell begins with the "buh" sound, or that the letter b sounds like "buh." The difference is a subtle but important one.

A student-size copy of the sound board is given to each student to be taped into the students' writing book for easy reference.

Once students use initial consonants accurately, they compare initial consonant blends and digraphs with the single consonants.

A · Picture Sorting for Initial Consonants · 6–7

Early Letter Name; Initial Consonants

The picture cards at the end of this chapter are arranged in alphabetical order. The pictures are easy to read. The sorts can be conducted as closed and open sorts.

Closed Sort

Use a classification folder with a picture of a bell and a mouse at the top, with a blank column for pictures that don't fit. "Sort through the picture cards for words that sound like ball at the beginning and pictures that sound like monkey at the beginning."

Open Sort

Ask students to use the pictures to sort them as they wish. Some students will sort by meaning, such as by the concept of animals. Others will look for initial consonants. You may suggest that you did a sound sort, and had two columns, and a miscellaneous column.

Beginning with b m r s, there are five sets of initial consonants. You need not sort each letter of every set. Many students move on to the next stage of development before they finish sorting all of the initial consonants.

Initial Consonants

b	m	r	s
t	g	n	p
c	h	f	d
l	k	j	w
y	z	v	qu

Beginning Digraphs

ch	sh	th	wh

Variations

1. Make a class book of initial consonant picture books.
2. Use cut-out pictures or draw pictures.

 ## Drawing Pictures of Initial Consonant Words 6–8

Early Letter Name; Initial Consonants

Following the sequence for the study of initial consonants presented above, students draw pictures of words that begin with the same sound. Students refer to the sound boards. Introduce a few other picture cards which represent that initial consonant which students can key in on.

"Draw pictures of words that sound like ball at the beginning. Underneath the picture, write the letter and then draw a line (b__). I will fill in the rest of the word when I come around to see how you are doing."

Before moving to a new activity, walk around to ask students to read their pictures to you. Fill in the rest of the word for them, and make notes for your records.

Variations

Students hunt for pictures in magazines and catalogs. Classroom visitors and helpers can fill in the rest of the words. Students can work in pairs.

 ## Sound-a-Like Concentraion 6–9

Early Letter Name; Initial Consonants

Continuing with the sequence of initial consonant study, use letter cards to play the game called Concentration. Use four pictures for each consonant, e.g., 4 B's, 4 M's, 4 R's, and 4 S's. 16 pictures is a good number for Concentration. Use the pictures at the end of this chapter.

Procedures

This is a game for one person, two people, or two pairs.

1. Do I know the name of these pictures? Students call out the pictures before beginning.
2. Picture cards are placed face down on the table. Students turn two cards up to find an initial sound match. The reason for the match must be declared.

Variations

1. Add more pictures as they progress through the sets of initial consonants.
2. Mix-in consonant digraph and blend pictures.

 Word Hunts 6–10

Early Letter Name; Initial Consonants

Students search for and circle or cut out words which contain the orthographic feature(s) under study. This is one of the most generic activities with five variations presented.

The words can be written on a piece of paper or cut out and pasted onto a sheet of paper. Word Hunts can be an independent activity, an activity with partners or triads, or small groups.

Students circle words by a particular feature: "Circle all of the words you can find which sound the same as ___ at the beginning." Students hunt through newspapers, magazines or copies of familiar texts found in Personal Readers.

Variations

1. In Letter Name stage, students hunt for words that begin with the particular initial consonant blends and digraphs they are studying.
   Students can also hunt for pictures. Pictures are pasted to a page and shared. Group and individual picture books can be collected (e.g., My B Book). When hunting for pictures, it helps if the teacher, aide or student helper rips out pages on which there are pictures which contain the feature being hunted.
2. In the Letter Name stage, students hunt for words that sound like the short vowel they are studying. For example, a student could be asked to find words that sound like "red" in the middle. These words can be added to word banks. Pictures are also hunted.
3. There can be a game format in which teams of two or three students hunt for words in a given time period. Students read the words to the teacher or group.
4. One to three students can walk around the room hunting for words they know. Students write down the words they find which are in their word banks.
5. Put together grab bags of objects. Students sort the objects into boxes, cans, or classification folders which are marked with a lead picture for objects that begin in the same way. A check sheet can be provided.

 Initial Sound Bingo 6–11

Early Letter Name; Initial Consonants

In this version of Bingo, students discriminate among the initial sounds. This is another generic acitivity that can be expanded to consonant blends and digraphs and vowels.

FIGURE 6–10 Blend Bingo Boards

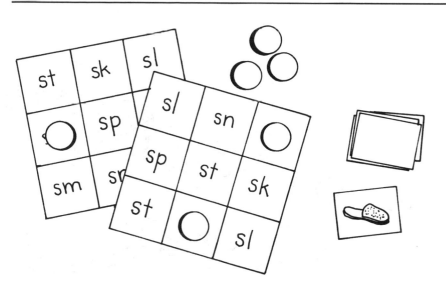

Make Bingo cards with nine squares that feature the sounds written on the squares (see Figure 6–10). You also need bingo markers, and picture cards to match sounds.

Procedures

Work in a center, or small group with two to four children. Students review the pictures for recognition. Picture cards are shuffled. Each student gets a bingo card and markers.

Students take turns drawing a card from the stack and calling out the picture name. Students place a marker on the corresponding square. Play continues until someone gets bingo. Then repeat the game.

 Match! 6–12

Early Letter Name; Initial Consonants

In this game, students make matches of the features they have recently studied. This game is played in pairs using pictures. Each student has a pack of pictures. At the same time, students turn up a picture card. The first person to recognize and say "Match!" gets the pair. Accuracy can be questioned and categories declared. There can be penalties for calling out Match carelessly.

Variations

Words from students' word banks can be included.

A Alphabetizing 6–13

Early Letter Name; Initial Consonants

Students put their word bank words in alphabetical order by initial consonants.

Large alphabet strips and word banks are used in this activity. Make a large alphabet strip up to six feet long (see Figure 6–11), and laminate it.

FIGURE 6–11 Alphabetizing with an Alphabet Strip

A student lays out the alphabet strip and takes his or her word bank, and places the words in alphabetical order.

Variations

1. Pictures can be included.
2. Students can alphabetize by second and third letters if they are in the Letter Name stage.

 Beginnings and Ends 6–14

This is a picture sort to match initial and final consonants (e.g., lam*p* matches *p*urple.

Procedures

Early Letter Name; Initial and Final Consonants

1. The teacher shows students how to match the pictures.
2. Students review pictures making sure they can identify the initial and final consonants.
3. Answer sheets with pictures can be provided.

These pictures can be found at the end of Chapters 5, 6, and 7. Wendy Brown put together a fine list of words.

Beginning/End Matches

book/tub	gate/leg	nurse/pin	teeth/goat
brick/sub	ghost/log	pencil/map	teeth/net
desk/red	ghost/mug	pig/mop	tent/nut
dishes/bed	goat/dog	pin/zip	tie/sit
dog/mad	hose/fish	rain/pear	toes/hit
doll/road	key/sick	seal/lips	two/boat
gas/bug	nest/sun	tail/belt	

Variations

Students make up some of their own matches with pictures, or on cards for a friend to try.

| **GA** | **Make A Record of Your Sorts** | **6–15** |

Early Letter
Name;
Initial
Consonants

Make notes of the word study activities. Write down some of the ways words or pictures were sorted.

Name _____   **Buddy** _____

Word Sort Activity: Date _____

Word Sort Activity: Date _____

Word Sort Activity: Date _____

Word Sort Activity: Date _____

Word Families

Word families are the easiest vowel patterns to study. See how quickly students can brainstorm words from these families: *-at, -et, -ed, -all, -ar, -un.* For students in the middle of the Letter Name stage, students who are using vowels in their invented spelling, words and pictures from these families are easy to find. Knowledge of these families increases the size of students' word banks substantially. Obviously, the words in the families rhyme, and too often, word study of short vowels stops at the rhyming. Be sure to move outside of rhyming and word families to compare short vowels that do not rhyme but have the same short vowel (i.e., *bet, red, felt,* etc.)

A mix of word sorts and games with word families is presented in the activities below. We emphasize the utility of the open and closed sorts. Word lists and pictures for further sorting are presented at the end of this chapter.

A | ## Short Vowel Wheels and Flip Charts | 6–16

Letter Name;
Word Families

Wheels and flip charts are fun for students to play with independently or with partners. The wheels and flip charts are used to reinforce the patterns. Prior to using the wheels and charts, students have worked in small groups to sort for pictures from the various families. They have also looked through their word banks for words from the family.

To make Word Family Wheels follow these three steps:

1. Cut two 6" circles from tagboard. Cut a wedge from one circle at the 9 o'clock spot and write the vowel and ending consonants to the right of it. Make a round hole in the middle.
2. On a second tagboard circle write beginning sounds that form words with that family. For example, the *-op* family can be formed with b, c, h, l, m, p, s, t, ch, sh, cl, and st.

   Space the letters evenly around the outside edge so that only one at a time will show though the "window" wedge. Cut a slit in the middle of the circle.
3. Put the circle with the wedge on top of the other circle. Push a brass fastener through the round hole and the slit. Flatten the fastener, making sure the top circle can turn (see Figure 6–12).

Variations

1. Flip books can be used the same way.
2. Students draw pictures of the words.
3. Students make their own flip books.

 A | ## 4-Square | 6–17

Letter Name;
Word Families

Four square is played in large or small groups. Students work in teams for five minutes to combine initial consonants and word families (e.g., *-at, -ap, -an, -ad*).

Procedures

1. Take a chart or shower curtain and divide it into large squares, and mark the squares off with masking tape. Write a word family in each square.

FIGURE 6–12 Short Vowel Wheels and Flip Chart

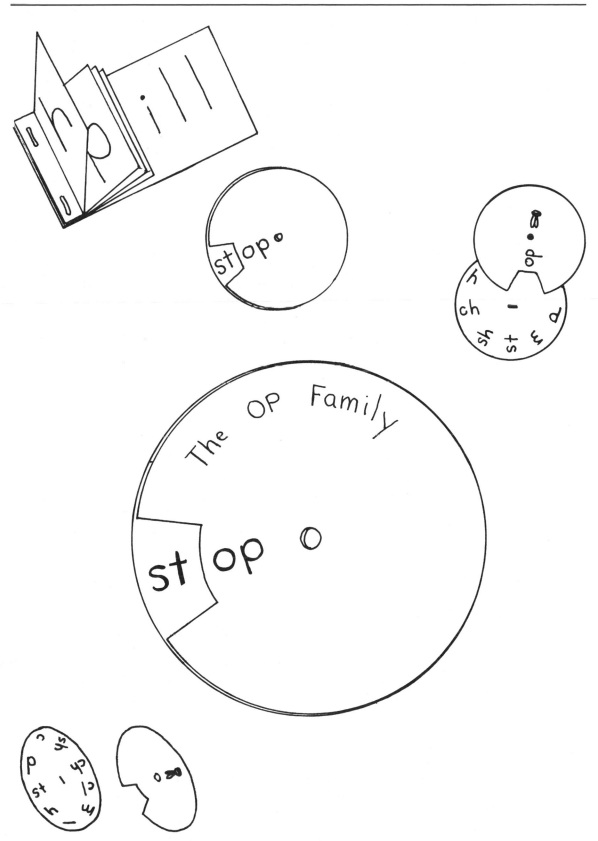

2. Review some families by reading and showing students a list of words by family. Also share pictures for each family and keep them in view for students to use.
3. Designate a recorder, a timer, and someone to throw the beach ball. Divide the rest of the group into fourths.
4. One student is picked as IT to throw the ball to the person standing in each square. The person in the square who catches the ball says a word from the word family and spells the word for the recorder to write the word on the chalkboard or chart paper.
5. Students take turns picking a square to stand in, racing against a set timer (5 minutes) to generate as many words as possible.

Variations

1. Students make their own lists of word families.
2. Groups or individuals make word study mini-books to illustrate.
3. Use 4-square as a whole class, tossing the ball out with examples on the tables.
4. Use the ball toss with any concept or vocabulary sort and set the timer to race against the clock for generating as many words into the sorts, e.g., vegetables versus fruit.

Marty Whitlow contributed this activity and suggested these word lists:

-*at*	cat	sat	bat	rat	mat
-*ap*	map	lap	rap	snap	cap
-*an*	pan	fan	man	can	ran
-*ad*	sad	rad	mad	had	pad

Fast Draw

6–18

Letter Name;
Word Families

This activity builds automaticity of word families, vowel patterns, initial consonants, or blends as two teams play this drawing and guessing game.

Students need a chalkboard or chart paper, word cards with the relevant patterns being studied, a stopwatch or watch with second hand.

Procedures

A person is chosen as drawer for each team. The drawer chooses a word card and writes down the word family at the top of the board. She or he then draws a picture of the word chosen. The team tries to guess the word. The team that guesses their picture in the least amount of time scores a point. The teacher or a designated student can be scorekeeper and timer. At the end of each round a new drawer is chosen.

Roll the Dice

6–19

Letter Name;
Word Families

This game is for 2 to 4 players. It reinforces word families, and builds automaticity.

Materials

The teacher uses a large dice with 4 contrasting word families; i.e. *-an,* *-ap, -ag,* and *-at.* A blank side is labeled "Lose A Turn," and another is labeled "Roll Again." You will also need a blackboard or paper for recording words (see Figure 6–13).

Procedures

Students roll the dice. If the dice lands on a word family space, the student must come up with a word for that family and record it on chalkboard or paper. Students keep their own lists and can use a word used by someone else. If a player is stumped or lands on "Lose A Turn," the dice is passed to the next person. If the student lands on "Roll," he or she rolls again. The person who records the most words at the end of the allotted time wins.

Variations

1. Can play with two dice and have two teams for a relay. Each team has a recorder. The first person of each team rolls the dice and quickly calls out an appropriate word. The recorder records the words on the board. The player hands the dice over to the next player and goes quickly to the end of the line. With this variation you would not need to lose a turn or roll again.
2. This game can also be used with vowel patterns, beginning consonants or blends.

A ## Home Mini-Charts 6–20

| Letter Name; Word Families | This is an activity that starts as a small group activity and reaches home.* |

Procedures

On a chart, paste a picture that reminds students of the word family they are studying. In a small group, students write down words to go with the vowel families they are studying.

Students make their own mini-charts which they take home. Students like to put these on the refrigerator at home to see how many words their families can add. They return in a few days to share these charts.

The charts can be collected into a word family notebook.

FIGURE 6–13 Die for Roll the Dice

---

*Patsy Stine contributed the ideas for this sort.

Variations

For students who have studied several families, the chart can be divided into thirds or quarters. A word family is in each section.

Short Vowels

Students know about vowel families. This is the time that students look more broadly at vowel patterns. Students learn about the basic short vowel, Consonant-Vowel-Consonant (CVC) pattern.

A Classic Closed Short i and Long i Sort   6–21

Letter Name; Short Vowels

Students look through their word banks and begin to contrast short and long vowel sounds. These can be conducted as individual or small group sorts.

This sort can be used with any short vowel, and is a fine sort for short vowel families.

Procedures

1. Students search through their word banks for words that have an I in them.
2. Introduce the pictures they are to sort by. For example, for the short i, we use a picture of a **fish** and a **kite.** A third column is for words that do not fit—the Miscellaneous pile.
3. When students are through, have them read through their columns to check their work. Students also explain why they sorted the ways they did.
4. Students look at other students' sorts.

Variations

1. Copy the sort onto a piece of paper, or a group chart.
2. Add a sand clock or a timer set to improve students' pace.
3. Compare the short i words with other short vowel sorts.
4. Students working in the Within Word Pattern stage can participate in this sort, but their focus is on the long vowel words and patterns (e.g. bike, tie, light).
5. Review word banks for other words that have either a short i or a long i sound (e.g., bye).

Here is an example of how one child sorted his I words:

Picture of a Fish	Picture of a Kite	Miscellaneous Pile
hit	night	dirt
sick	dime	sink
knit	giant	third
gills	light	
ring	find	
	bride	
	rhyme	
	sign	
	tie	

As an extension, the group focused on the short vowel words and developed these categories and columns for the short vowels:

hit	sick	gills	ring
bit	Rick	bills	sing
sit	lick	hills	finger
knit	(fix)	will	

GA **Teacher-Made Short Vowel Word Sorts**   **6–22**

Letter Name;	This is a real classic! This activity includes the basic directions to conduct open
Short Vowels	and closed word sorts with small groups.

Procedures

1. The teacher puts together a list of between 16 and 25 words she thinks students can read with ease (perhaps *bag, rag, Dan,* and *ran*). These words are written onto a blank word sheet and a copy is made for each student in the group. (Sometimes we photocopy our masters, sometimes the students fill in their own word sheets.) A blank word sheet for this activity is included at the end of this chapter.
2. Students read each word on the word sheet, and cross through words they can not read easily.
3. Students cut up their word sheets.
4. Students use classification folders to sort the words according to categories defined either by the teacher (Closed Sort) or defined by the student (Open Sort).
5. Students write their own exemplars on blank word cards.

Variations

1. The same procedures can be used for pictures.
2. Students work in pairs.
3. Students make their own lists of the same pattern.
4. Instead of cutting up the word sheets, students number the words by category (e.g., 1 for words like bag, a 2 by words that sound like *beg* in the middle, and a 3 by words which fit in the miscellaneous pile).

Here are some sample lists to use in teacher made sorts:

a) bad beg
   tan, rag, fan, let, bell, said, bag, rat
   lap, tall, net, yet, back, clan, sack, den
   sell, Ned, bad, Dan, ran, pen, send, pet
b) pit pot
   tin, pig, trick, drop, cot, rock, pit, win
   wig, sick, hop, dot, chin, dig, brick, pot
   shop, got, pin, fig, stick, chop, stop, not
c) wag wave (This sort would come late in the Letter Name stage.)
   pat, clam, bag, strange, wave, gnat, mat, jacks
   glad, plate, date, slam, pat, sad, race, paste
   stand, sat, wag, bat, ape, tape, pale

GA Show Me

Materials

This activity requires that students have individual pockets to hold letter cards. To make a pocket, cut paper into rectangles about 9" x 7". Fold up one inch along the nine-inch side, then fold into overlapping thirds. Staple at the edges and in the creases to make three pockets (see Figure 6–14).

Cut additional paper into cards 2" x 4" to make 14 for each student. Print letters on the top half of each card making sure the entire letter is visible when inserted in the pocket. A useful assortment of letters for this activity includes the five short vowels and b, d, f, g, m, n, p, r, t. Too many consonants can be hard to manage.

Procedures

Each student gets a pocket and an assortment of letter cards. When the teacher or designated caller names a word, the students put the necessary letters in the spaces and fold up their pockets. When "Show Me" is announced, everyone opens their pocket at once for the teacher to see. The emphasis is on practice, not competition, but points for accuracy could be kept if desired.

Start with words having the same short vowel such as *bad, pat* or *man,* where the students focus primarily on the consonants. Words could be called by families to help students see how the patterns work. Add another short vowel such as "o" to the set of letters to compare medial sounds and gradually work up to all five vowels.

Here are some words which can be spelled with the consonants:
- *a* bad, mad, pad, bag, tag, rat, dam, ram
  fan, man, pan, tan, ran, map, nap
  tap, rap, bat, fat, mat, pat, rat
- *o* mob, rob, nod, rod, bog, dog, fog
  mop, top, dot, got, not, pot, rot
- *i* fib, rib, big, pig, rig, dim, rim, fin, pin
  tin, dip, nip, tip, rip, bit, fit, pit
- *u* rub, tub, bud, mud, bug, dug, tug
  rug, bun, gun, run, but, nut, rut
- *e* bed, red, beg, peg, pen, bet, get, met, net, pet

FIGURE 6–14 Letter Holder for "Show Me"

Variations

1. The Show Me pockets are used just for beginning sounds and/or ending sounds.
2. Long vowel patterns are spelled using a four-pocket folder.*

 Hopping Frog Game 6–24

Letter Name;
Short Vowels

This is a fun game for two to four players. Students should be solidly in the Letter Name stage. This activity reinforces their understanding of short vowel patterns.**

Materials

Use a game board or use a manila folder to make your own course. Cut green circles for lily pads for each space. A few lists are given below.

You'll need four frog markers. The spinner is marked into five sections, with a vowel and illustrating picture in each (i.e., "a", apple; "e", ten; "i", fish; "o", frog; "u", sun). Figure 6–15 shows you a sample board for the game.

Procedures

Each child selects a frog marker. The first child then spins and must place her marker on the first word which matches the vowel sound she lands on (i.e., "e"–get). She then pronounces this word and must say another word with the same vowel sound to stay on that space. The second player then spins and plays. The first player who can finish the course and hop his frog off the board wins.

Variations

1. Students can write down the words they land on and organize them in columns by short vowel:

"a"	"e"	"i"	"o"	"u"
ran	get	did	got	cup
hat	step	big	fox	jump

2. The same game plan could be applied to other aspects of words—long vowel patterns and inflected endings.

Here is a broad based list for Letter Name. Select others which fit your needs.

"a"		"e"		"i"		"o"		"u"	
band	bad	step	get	wish	big	stop	dog	junk	but
fast	sat	yes	leg	did	hid	box	hop	cup	sun
can	cat	met	wet	fish	pig	not	got	jump	bug
ran	hat	pet	ten	in	spin	fox	on	run	up

*Francine Johnston learned this game from Marjory Beatty.
**This game was developed by Janet Bloodgood and has become a favorite.

FIGURE 6–15 Frog Marker and Game Board

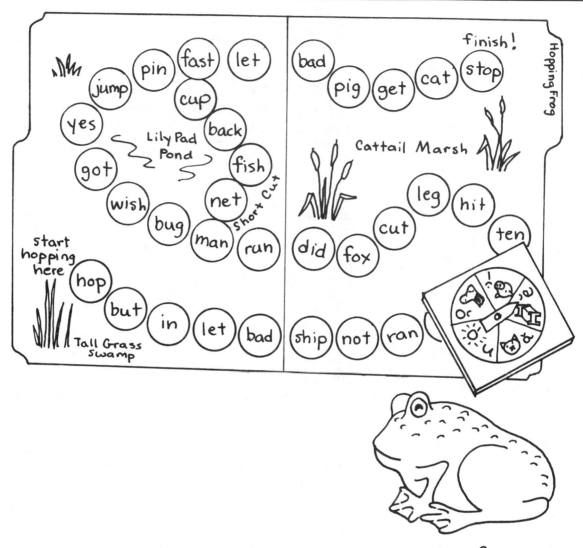

 frog marker

| GA | **Directions to Make a Game Spinner** | 6–25 |

Materials

Letter Name;
Short Vowels

Cut a pointer from soft plastic, such as milk jugs, and punch out hole in center. A small metal washer placed under the pointer helps (see Figure 6–16).*

Procedure

1. Glue circle onto heavy card board.
2. Cut narrow slot in center with point or sharp scissors.
3. Put paper fastener through pointer hole and tight slot in spinner base.
4. Flatten fastener "legs" leaving space for pointer to spin freely.

*Francine Johnston wrote this practical guide to making a spinner for word study games.

FIGURE 6–16 Directions for Making a Game Spinner

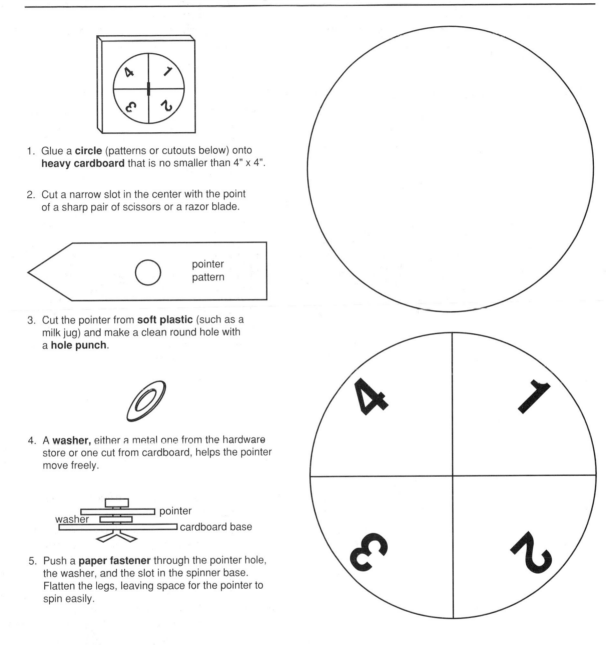

1. Glue a **circle** (patterns or cutouts below) onto **heavy cardboard** that is no smaller than 4" x 4".

2. Cut a narrow slot in the center with the point of a sharp pair of scissors or a razor blade.

3. Cut the pointer from **soft plastic** (such as a milk jug) and make a clean round hole with a **hole punch**.

4. A **washer**, either a metal one from the hardware store or one cut from cardboard, helps the pointer move freely.

5. Push a **paper fastener** through the pointer hole, the washer, and the slot in the spinner base. Flatten the legs, leaving space for the pointer to spin easily.

 Follow the Path   6–26

Letter Name;
Short Vowels

This game gives students practice distinguishing short vowels—a, i, and u. Students must know how to sort short vowels already.

Procedures

This game is for four to six players working independently, and requires playing pieces for each player, a spinner or die, paper, and pencils. The playing board has words written in the spaces (see Figure 6–17).*

---

*This variation of Scattergories was developed by Marilyn Edwards.

FIGURE 6–17 Follow the Path board

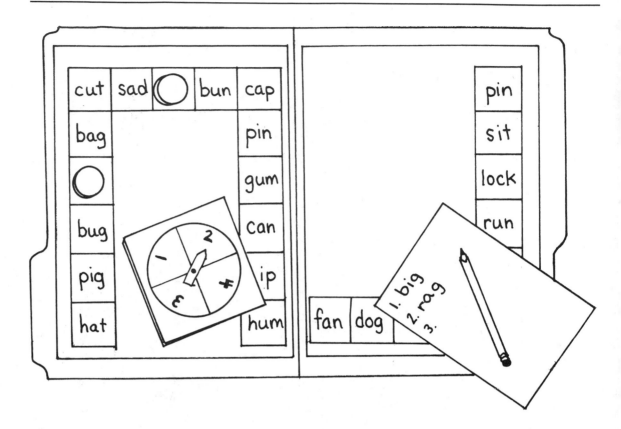

The object is to make new words to rhyme with words on the game board that do not match the other players'.

1. Spin to determine who goes first. Play proceeds clockwise.
2. First player spins and moves the number of places indicated on spinner.
3. Player says the word. All players write a word by changing initial letter/letters to make a rhyming word. Players number their words as they go. Play continues until someone reaches the end of the path.
4. Beginning with the player who reaches the end first, each player reads the first word on his or her list. Players who have a word that *does not match* the other players' words gets to circle their word; for example, players have *cat, bat, cat,* and *splat*. Players having the words *bat* and *splat* would circle their words. Continue until all words have been compared.
5. Each circle is worth 1 point, plus the player who reaches the end first receives 2 extra points.

These words could be used in the spaces on the board for studying short vowel patterns:

> hat, pig, bug, bag, sit, cup, sad, pick, bun, cap, pin, gum, can, dip, hut, back, pink, bump

Variations

For follow-up, students make lists of the words they have collected under appropriate headings (e.g., bat, pig, cup).

Word Study Go Fish   **6–27**

Letter Name;
Short Vowels

This classic game has been adapted to word study. The focus here is on short vowel patterns, but variations include fishing for long vowels and even initial consonant elements.*

Materials

Decks of blank cards which have matching pairs of one-syllable words written on them must be prepared and, preferably, laminated. Cards may be set up so that beginning consonants/blends, final consonants, vowels, and/or vowel and what follows (i.e., rhyming patterns) are featured.

Procedures

1. Students play fish. "Give me all your words that sound like *hen* in the middle." This game is usually played with two to four players.
2. A teacher's assistance is needed at first until students get the hang of playing and making categories.
3. Go Fish involves a deck of word cards, five of which are dealt to each player and the remainder placed in the middle as a pool from which to draw. The first player asks any other player for a match to a card in her hand. If she receives a matching card, she may put the pair down and ask for another card. If the other player does not have the card requested, he tells the first player to "Go Fish," which means that she must draw a card from the "fish pond." The first player's turn is over when she can no longer make a match. Play continues around the circle until one player has used up all the cards in his hand. Points can be won by the first person to go out and by the person who has the most matching cards.

Variations

More cards for a match can be required. There are four forms of Word Study Go Fish, listed here in order of increasing complexity:

    Beginning Sound Go Fish
    Ending Sound Go Fish
    Short Vowel Go Fish
    Rhyming Word Go Fish

Late in the Letter Name stage, these three lists could be used for Word Study Fish:

a) lad, leg, card, dig, hop, dot, bat, mad, fed
   slip, fig, mop, hot, cat, sad, sled, lip, pig
   top, stop, sat, peg, red, tip, big, chop, cot
b) brag, drag, flag, tag, bad, had, mad, sad, flap
   map, slap, trap, back, sack, track, fast, last, mast
   get, jet, bet, let, set, red, fed, shed, sled
c) chin, win, tin, dig, fig, pig, wig, brick, stick
   trick, chop, drop, hop, stop, cot, dot, cut, nut
   run, sun, just, must, trust, red, fed, shed, sled

---

*Janet W. Bloodgood took this word study game and put into words the familiar game of Fish.

| **GA** | **Make Words with Cubes Game** | **6–28** |

Letter Name;
Short Vowels

Students sort letter cubes to make words. This game is for students late in the Letter Name stage and can be used throughout the Within Word Pattern stage.

Materials

Letter cubes which can be found in many games (Boggle® and Perquackery®) are needed. The students need a sand clock or timer, paper and pencil, and a Record Sheet such as the one shown in Figure 6–18.

Procedures

1. In pairs, students take turns being the player or word maker and the scribe or secretary. The scribe uses a Record Sheet as shown in Figure 6–18.
2. Letters are shaken and spilled out onto the table. The person making the words gets to arrange the letter cubes in a row for easy reference before timing begins. The cubes can not be changed. (Blank cubes can be discarded and later used as wild cubes.) Start the sand clock.
3. The word maker makes words, calls them out as he or she arranges the cubes, and then spells it to the scribe. The letters can be moved around to make more words: If a student makes *ran* then *r* can be taken off, and the *c* is added for *can*. Errors should be ignored at this point. Write the words in columns by the number of letters in the words.
4. At the end of the sand clock (one turn or two), students review the words. The word maker reads the list to the scribe. The scribe checks for accuracy. Scoring: Count up the total number of letters used. Multiplication can be used, e.g., four 3-letter words = 12.
5. The teacher can demonstrate in small group the various ways words can be generated.

FIGURE 6–18 Record Sheet for Cube Game

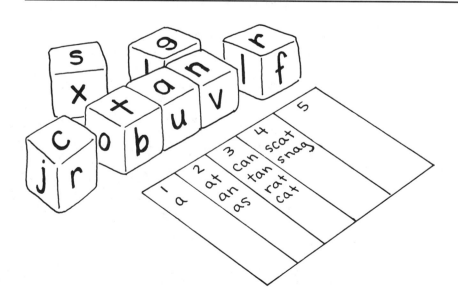

Variation

This is a wonderful diagnostic game. Students in this stage make many more 3-letter words. Students soon realize that the bigger the words they make, the greater their score. Students in the Within Word Pattern stage will make more 4-letter words.

| **GA** | Word Study Trivial Pursuit® | 6–29 |

Letter Name; Short Vowels

This game is designed for up to four players and one referee. After initial introduction by the teacher, students can play the game independently.

Materials

Posterboard, squares approximately 1½" in four different colors of construction paper, word cards with exemplars for the spelling concept being studied, envelopes made from the four colors of construction paper, die or spinner, and game piece markers.

How To Make It

1. To construct the game board, glue squares of colored construction paper onto the posterboard, alternating colors and making a trail from start to finish covering the entire board.
2. Make four envelopes to hold four different packets of word cards out of construction paper corresponding to the four colors on the game board (red squares and red envelope, orange squares and orange envelope, brown squares and brown envelope, green squares and green envelope). (See Figure 6–19.)

To Play

1. Players pick order by spinning or tossing die. Winner chooses what color to be. Each player in turn selects a color.
2. Players take the packet of word cards corresponding to their color and call these words out when another player lands on their respective color. If players land on their own color, they may take another turn.

   For example, suppose player "A" spins a five and lands on a green square. If "A" is not holding the green packet, the person with the green packet calls out a word. "A" spells the word correctly, and the card is placed face up on the table/floor next to the caller. Player "B" takes a turn and also lands on a green square. After successfully spelling her word, she must decide if it is to be placed on top of the first word (follows the same pattern) or beside it (is a different pattern).

   Players continue starting a new pile whenever necessary. In this way, they spell the words as well as sort them by pattern. Whichever color the player lands on is the packet from which the word is chosen for the player to spell and sort, unless it is the player's own color. If it is the player's own color, the player spins again.
3. If the player misspells the word, the player must go back one square and try a word from that color providing it is not her or his own color (in which case the player moves back two squares). If she is unable to spell that word, the player remains where she is and loses one turn. If the player is unable to sort the word properly, she must move back one space (again providing it is not her color and if so, two spaces), but does

FIGURE 6–19 Gameboard for Word Study Trivial Pursuit®

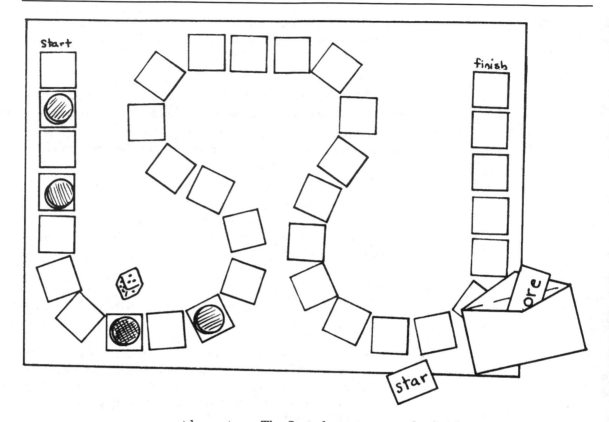

not lose a turn. The first player to get to the finish square is the winner and will be referee the next time. Since the students would have been previously exposed to the pattern in the pockets and were approaching automaticity, there should be few spelling or sorting mistakes.*

Variations

1. This game is used simply for word sorting (without the spelling practice). In this variation, players present the word instead of calling it out for another player, and the player reads the word and sorts it.
2. The game is played with four different categories of words, one for each envelope, or with three categories and the fourth color being the free space, or with two patterns divided up between the four envelopes.
3. Since neither the game board, nor the envelopes would be marked, the board can be used for any word patterns that are being studied.

Having several "sets" of the game allows different groups of 5 students to play the same game while practicing different patterns. Refer to the word sorting lists to develop sets.

Other Features

Towards the end of the Letter Name stage students examine blends and digraphs again. They can read many more words that include consonant blends and digraphs. This is also a good time to examine the preconsonantal nasals.

*This version of Trivial Pursuits was developed by Rita Loyacono.

FIGURE 6–20 Word Maker Cards

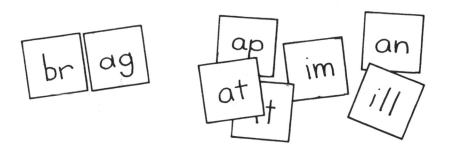

A

Word Maker with Initial Consonants Blends and Digraphs   6–30

Letter Name;
Consonant
Blends and
Digraphs

Students match blends and digraphs with word families to make words.*

Procedures

1. Begin blend work by sorting pictures of single consonant versus blends (e.g., *s* vs. *sl*). This should go quickly.
2. Begin with a few blends and study them thoroughly with a combination of activities that includes sorting picture cards, cutting out magazine pictures, and drawing and labeling pictures of words that begin with the consonant blends and digraphs students are studying.
3. Show students how to make words with the other blends and digraphs. Students are given cards with blends and consonant digraphs and several word endings (see Figure 6–20). Students write down all of the words they can make using the blends, digraphs and word endings. Continue to add blends and digraphs.

There are three groupings of these blends:

s- blends:	sc, sk, sm, sn, sp, st, sw	-l blends:	bl, cl, fl, gl, pl, sl
-r blends:	br, cr, dr, fr, gr, pr, tr	digraphs:	sh, ch, th, wh, ph

Here are some examples:

tr + ap	cr + ack	br + ing	st + ack
sl + ip	fl + ag	cl + ub	bl + ack
br + ag	cl + ap	sm + ell	sl + ing
cr + ash	cr + ib	sp + ot	tr + amp
tr + ack	sp + in	pl + ot	

Variations

1. Consonant bingo can be adapted to blend and digraph bingo.
2. These short vowel words with blends and digraphs can be incorporated into previous sorts like the following:

hat	big	top
man	fit	mom
bad	trip	pot
brat	rip	crop
nap	lick	job
grab	brick	lock

*Katherine Preston contributed to this activity.

A | Closed Sorts to Integrate Word Families With Digraphs and Blends

6–31

Letter Name;
Consonant
Blends and
Digraphs

Through closed sorts using classification folders, the digraphs and blends are integrated into the word families. Here is a sequence suggested by Francine Johnston to compare words.

Blends & Digraphs				Word Families			
1. sh	s	h		-at			
2. ch	c	h		-at	-an		
3. ch	sh	th		-ag	-ap	-ad	
4. st	s	t		-it	-ip		
5. sp	s	p		-in	-ig	-ill	
6. st	sp	sk	sm	-it	-at	-in	-an
7. sl	sn	sc	sw	-ot	-og	-op	
8. gl	pl	bl	cl	-et	-en	-ed	-ell
9. bl	br	gl	gr	-ell	-ill	-all	
10. cl	cr	fl	fr	-ut	-ug	-un	
11. gr	tr	dr	pr	-ug	-ag	-ig	-og
12. wh	qu	tw	k	-ash	-ish	-ush	
13.				-ack	-ick	-ock	-uck
14.				-ank	-ink	-unk	
15.				-ing	-ang	-ung	-ong
16.				-amp	-imp	-ump	

A | Gruff Drops Troll at Bridge Game

6–32

Letter Name;
Consonant
Blends and
Digraphs

This game is for two to four players and reinforces r-blends.*

Materials

Manila folder with a game course filled in with "consonant plus 'r'" blend letters (as shown in Figure 5–21), 4 button markers, and picture cards of the features being studied.

Procedures

1. Each player selects a button marker. Students turn over picture cards containing the "consonant-plus-r" blend pictures. Players move the marker to the correct space as turns are taken. Winner drops the troll from the bridge by drawing the "dr" (for "drop") picture card for the last space.
2. This game was developed after reading Paul Galdone's *The Three Billy Goats Gruff* book. This book was also part of a class study of "monster" books.
3. The study began with a big book reading of *The Monster* (Riverside Publications). Many of the "monster" books yielded a great crop of "consonant plus 'r'" word search activities.

---

*This board game was developed as a literature extension by Esther Heatley.

FIGURE 6–21 Gameboard for Gruff Drops Troll

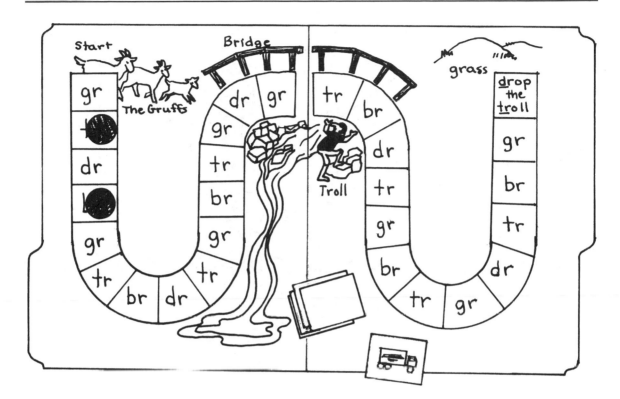

| A | **Sea World Diorama** | 6–33 |

Letter Name;
Consonant
Blends and
Digraphs

Students create a sea world diorama while they study the *sh* digraph.

Materials

Pictures and things that begin with "s" and "sh." To make a diorama students will need a shoe box, construction paper and colorful tissue paper, glue, scissors, markers, sand, tiny shells, or cut up natural sponges.

Procedures

1. Show students a simple picture sort between "s" and "sh" picture cards.
2. After the sort, have students think of animals and things in the sea that begin with "s" and "sh".
3. On a piece of paper, list the things found in the sea that begin with "s" and "sh".
4. Introduce students to how a diorama is constructed (see Figure 6–22).
5. Students draw and cut out pictures of things that belong in the sea and begin with "s" and "sh". With glue, have them place their sea creatures / items in their shoe boxes. Small shells or some natural sponges add decoration. Cover the bottom of the "sea" with sand.
6. Students fill their shoe boxes with as many sea creatures they can think of that begin with "s" and "sh". Here is an abbreviated list:

FIGURE 6–22 A Diorama for Sea World

Picture list:
Starfish, seals, sea horses, sunfish, sword fish, scuba divers, sunken ships, sea snakes, sharks, sea anemone, sea weed, sponges, shrimp, shells, etc. *

Variations

1. Have aides (parents, other students) look for these pictures. Students work in small groups to develop just one diorama.
2. Expand the sea diorama with sea blends (e.g., st-, sc-, sw-) or create other types of dioramas.
3. Similar books can be used. Elizabeth Schuett recommended *Sheep on a Ship* by Nancy Shaw.

Materials for Letter Name Stage Word Study

This section, and the pages that follow, contain the materials to copy onto card stock for use with students in the classroom. How to use these materials has been discussed at length throughout this chapter. You will also find that these materials can be used in activities presented in Chapter 5, as well as in the upcoming chapter on Within Word Pattern word study. Templates of gameboards are also included for your use.

Pictures

The first series of pictures to follow are sound boards: initial consonant, consonant blends and digraphs, and vowels (Figures 6–23, 6–24, and 6–25). These sound boards can be duplicated for students and made into a chart with a chart maker.

---

*This activity was developed by Cindy Booth.

FIGURE 6-23 Initial Consonant Sound Board

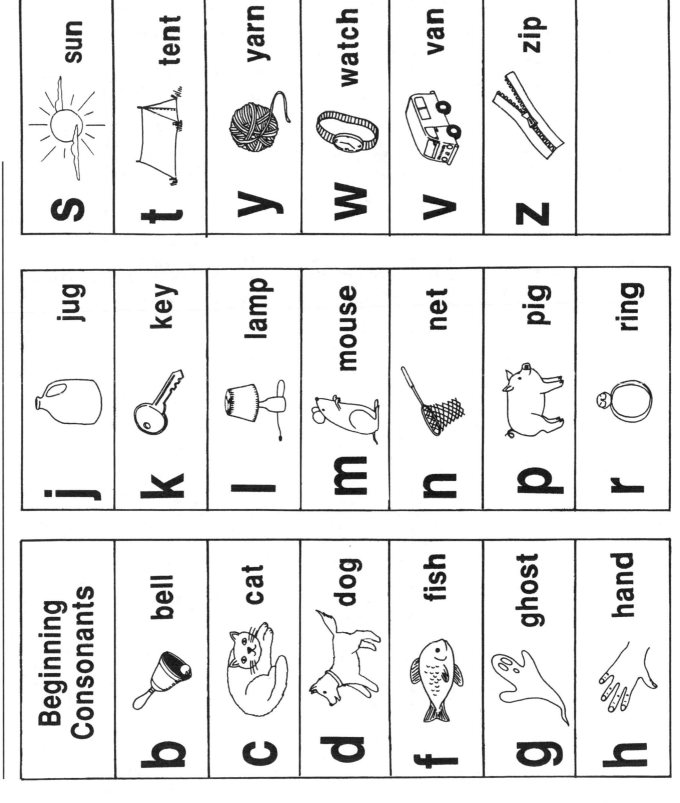

Beginning Consonants		
b bell	**j** jug	**s** sun
c cat	**k** key	**t** tent
d dog	**l** lamp	**y** yarn
f fish	**m** mouse	**w** watch
g ghost	**n** net	**v** van
h hand	**p** pig	**z** zip
	r ring	

FIGURE 6–24 Consonant Blend and Digraph Sound Board

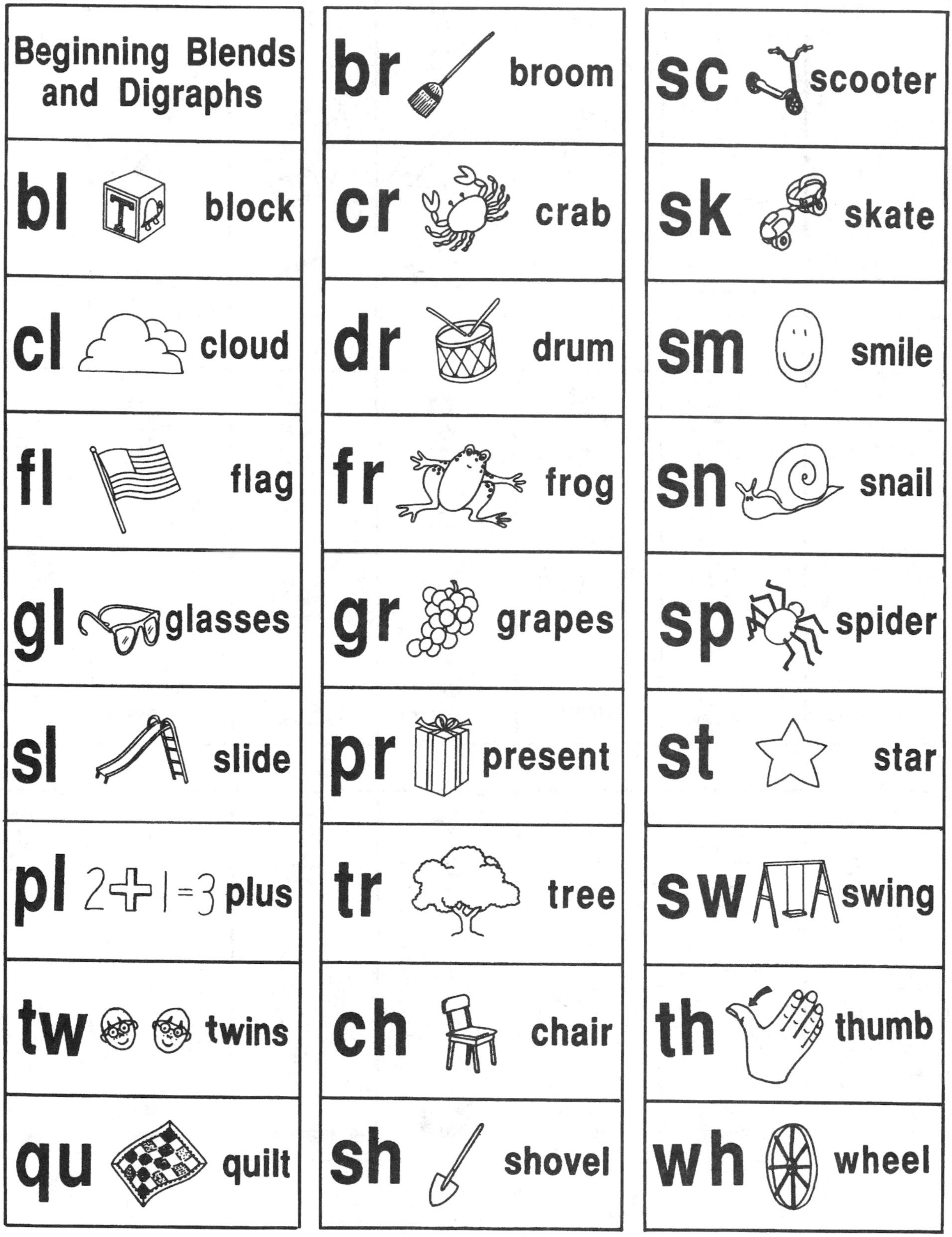

Beginning Blends and Digraphs		
bl block	**br** broom	**sc** scooter
cl cloud	**cr** crab	**sk** skate
fl flag	**dr** drum	**sm** smile
gl glasses	**fr** frog	**sn** snail
sl slide	**gr** grapes	**sp** spider
pl 2+1=3 plus	**pr** present	**st** star
tw twins	**tr** tree	**sw** swing
qu quilt	**ch** chair	**th** thumb
	sh shovel	**wh** wheel

FIGURE 6–25 Medial Vowels Sound Board

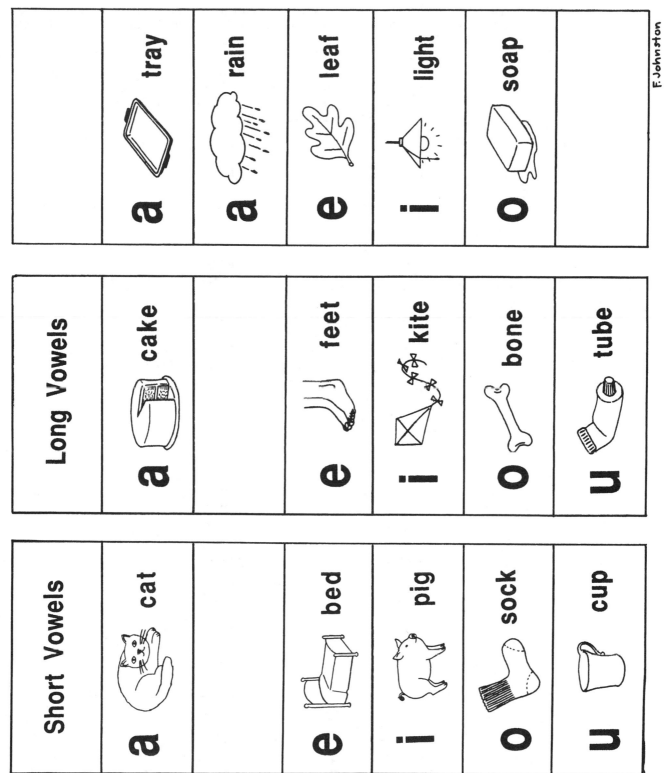

Short Vowels			Long Vowels				tray
a cat			a cake		a		rain
e bed			e feet		e		leaf
i pig			i kite		i		light
o sock			o bone		o		soap
u cup			u tube				

F. Johnston

The sound boards are followed by pages of individual pictures. These pictures are used in the sorts and games discussed throughout this book. Initial consonant picture sheets come first, followed by consonant blends and digraphs, and then short vowels. Although grouped in this way, the individual pictures can be used in many ways from concept sorts to long vowel sorts.

Following is a list of pictures from initial consonant picture sheets that can be used in vowel sorts. An extra copy of these pictures, reproduced on card stock, is good to have in reserve.

Short a:

bat	fan	gas	hand	hat	ham	lamp
man	mask	mat	pan	van	clap	glass
snap	quack	track	trap	grass	crab	crack

Short e:

bell	belt	nest	pen	ten	well	web
yell	shed	sled	smell	dress		

Short i:

dishes	king	pin	six	witch	ship	skip
chick	chin	whip	clip	switch	swim	stick
drill	drip	grill	brick	bridge	crib	

Short o:

dog	jog	log	shop	chop	block	stop
frog						

Short u:

cup	duck	gun	jump	nut	rug	tub
thumb	plus	plug	plum	stump	skull	skunk
drum	truck	trunk	brush			

Word Lists and Blank Word Study Sheet

Once students have completed some picture sorts, conduct open and closed sorts with known words. The following word lists are used to make a variety of sorts. To create open and closed sorts, combine 10 or so words from two or three lists. For example, you can choose two or three families and mix them together for an open sort. (See the previous activities for sorts and games that use these words.)

These words are arranged in lists of word families for short vowels. The short vowels are followed by lists of words with preconsonantals (*bump*). Finally, there is a list of features which follows the sequence for studying word families that is used in the Book Buddy program at the University of Virginia.

A blank word study sheet is included in Figure 6–62 on page 237. Known words for word study are written on the blank squares. Students cut the sheets into word cards for sorting. This is used as a template for teacher-made sorts for students in the Letter Name and Within Word Pattern stages.

Short a (and -all)

-AT: bat, cat, fat, hat, mat, pat, rat, sat, that, flat, brat, chat
-AN: can, fan, man, pan, ran, tan, van, plan, than

-ACK: back, pack, jack, rack, sack, tack, black, quack, crack, track, shack, smack, snack, stack, whack
-AB: cab, dab, jab, nab, lab, tab, blab, crab, scab, stab, grab
-AD: bad, dad, had, mad, pad, sad, rad, glad
-AG: bag, rag, sag, wag, nag, flag, brag, drag, shag, snag
-AM: am, dam, ham, ram, jam, clam, slam, cram, wham, swam
-AP: cap, lap, map, nap, rap, tap, zap, clap, flap, slap, trap, chap, snap
-ASH: bash, cash, dash, hash, mash, rash, sash, flash, trash, crash, smash
-AND: band, hand, land, sand, brand, grand, stand
-ANK: bank, sank, tank, yank, blank, plank, crank, drank, prank, spank, thank
-ALL: ball, call, fall, hall, mall, tall, wall, small, stall
-ANG: bang, fang, hang, sang, rang, clang

Short i

-IT: bit, kit, fit, hit, lit, pit, sit, quit, skit, spit
-IG: big, dig, fig, pig, rig, wig, zig
-ILL: bill, dill, fill, hill, kill, mill, pill, will, drill, grill, chill, skill, spill, still
-IN: bin, fin, pin, tin, win, grin, thin, twin, chin, shin, skin, spin
-ICK: lick, kick, pick, sick, tick, click, slick, quick, trick, chick, flick, brick, stick, thick
-ID: bid did, kid, hid, lid, slid, skid
-IP: dip, hip, lip, nip, rip, sip, tip, zip, whip, clip, flip, slip, skip, drip, trip, chip, ship, snip, grip
-INK: ink, link, mink, pink, sink, rink, wink, blink, drink, stink, think
-ING: king, sing, ring, wing, sling, bring, sting, swing, thing

Short o

-OT: cot, dot, got, hot, jot, lot, not, pot, rot, blot, slot, plot, shot, spot
-OG: dog, bog, fog, hog, jog, log, clog, frog
-OCK: dock, lock, rock, sock, tock, block, clock, flock, smock, shock
-OB: cob, job, rob, gob, mob, sob, snob, blob, glob
-OP: cop, hop, pop, mop, top, clop, flop, slop, chop, shop, stop

Short e

-ET: bet, get, jet, let, met, net, pet, set, wet, vet, fret
-EN: den, hen, men, ten, pen, then, when
-ED: bed, fed, led, red, wed, bled, fled, sled, shed
-ELL: bell, fell, jell, sell, tell, well, shell, smell, spell
-EG: beg, peg, leg, keg
-ECK: deck, neck, peck, wreck, speck, check

Short u

-UT: but, cut, gut, hut, nut, rut, shut
-UB: cub, hub, rub, tub, club, grub, snub, stub
-UG: bug, dug, hug, jug, mug, rug, tug, slug, plug, drug, snug
-UCK: buck, duck, luck, suck, tuck, yuck, pluck, cluck, truck, stuck
-UFF: buff, cuff, huff, muff, puff, fluff
-UM: bum, gum, hum, drum, plum, slum, glum, scum, chum
-UN: bun, fun, gun, run, sun, spun, stun
-UP: up, cup, pup

-USH: gush, hush, mush, rush, blush, flush, brush, crush
-UMP: bump, jump, dump, hump, lump, pump, rump, plump, stump, thump

Preconsonantal Nasals

-amp	-ump	-ink	-ank
cramp	rump	brink	crank
stamp	jump	pink	rank
lamp	plump	wink	frank
camp	dump	link	hank
ramp	stump	drink	tank
damp	lump	sink	stank

Reading Book Buddy Word Family Study Sequence

1. -at
2. -at   -an
3. -at   -ag   -ap
4. -an   -ad   -ap
5. -ack
6. -ad   -ag   -ack
7. Combine all short a families
8. -og   -ot
9. -og   -ot   -op   -ock
10. All short o families
11. -at   -ot
12. -ack   -ock
13. -ag   -og   -ap   -op
14. Compare a and o families
15. -ill   -ig   -ip
16. -ip   -ap   -op
17. -en   -et
18. -ut   -un   -ug
19. -at   -et   -ut   -ot
20. -ag   -og   -ig   -ug   -eg
21. Compare all families
22. -ack   -ock   -ick   -uck
23. -all   -ell   -ill
24. -ang   -ing   -ung   -ong
25. -ink   -ank   -unk
26. -amp   -ump   -and   -uff

Gameboards

Templates in Figures 6–63 through 6–69 can be copied and pasted into a manila folder for a gameboard. Several models are included for your use: racetrack, U-gameboard, S-gameboard, and rectangle gameboard. Determine a start and finish on the boards, and the words or pictures to sort can be written or placed on the gameboard.

FIGURE 6-26 Picture Cards for Sorts and Games

FIGURE 6–27 Picture Cards for Sorts and Games

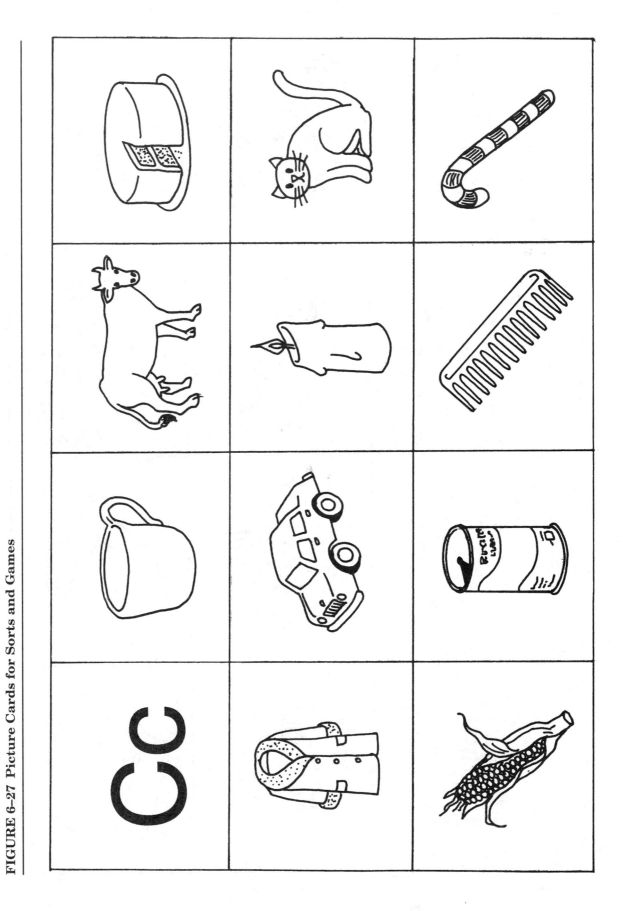

FIGURE 6–28 Picture Cards for Sorts and Games

FIGURE 6–29 Picture Cards for Sorts and Games

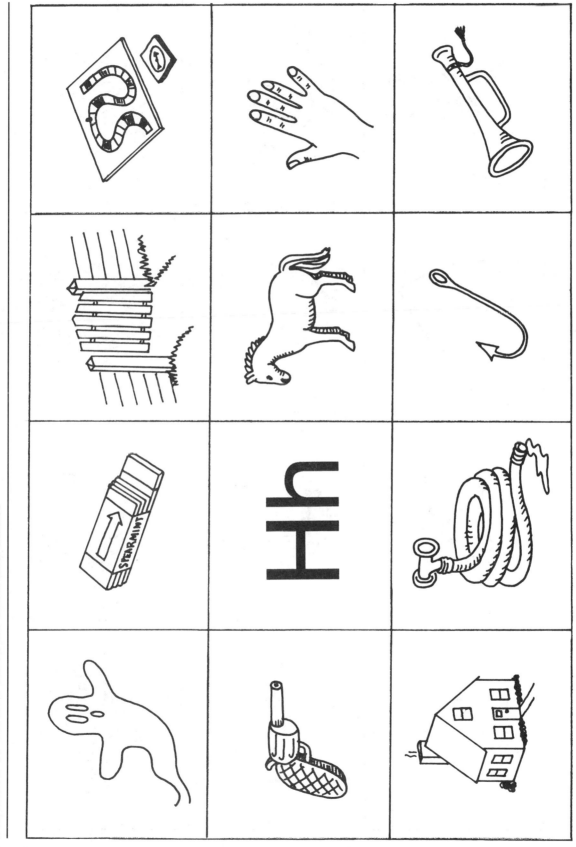

FIGURE 6–30 Picture Cards for Sorts and Games

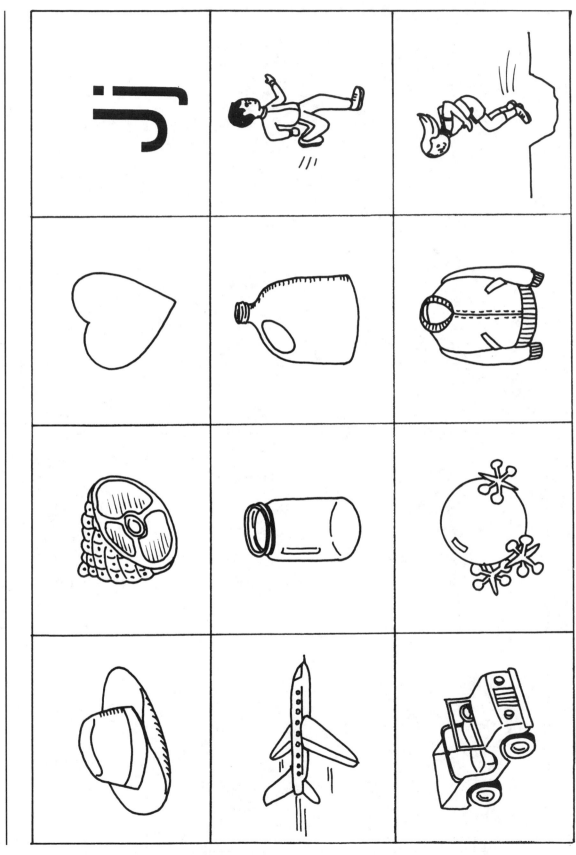

FIGURE 6–31 Picture Cards for Sorts and Games

206

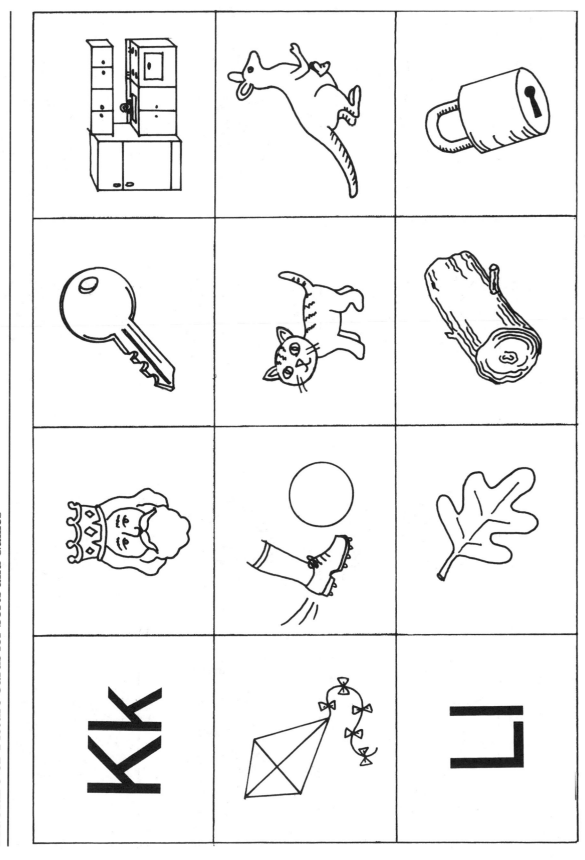

FIGURE 6-32 Picture Cards for Sorts and Games

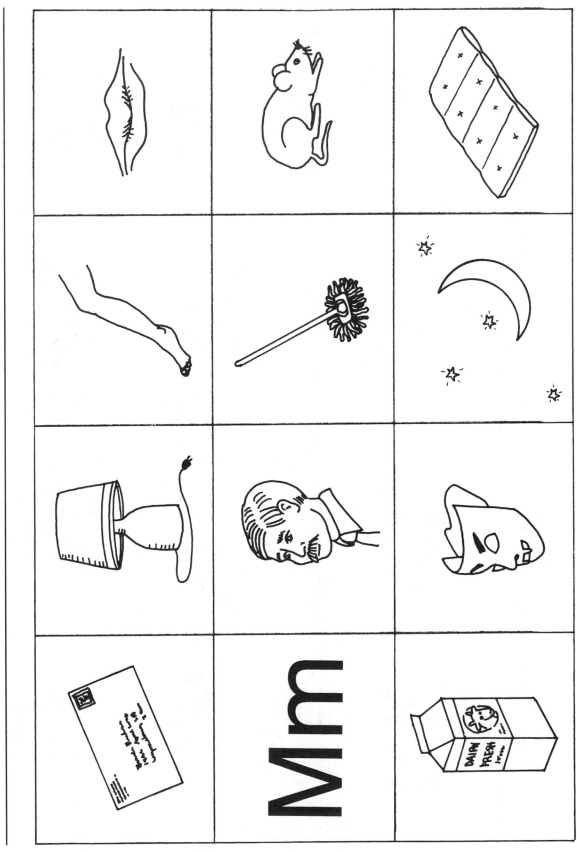

FIGURE 6-33 Picture Cards for Sorts and Games

FIGURE 6-34 Picture Cards for Sorts and Games

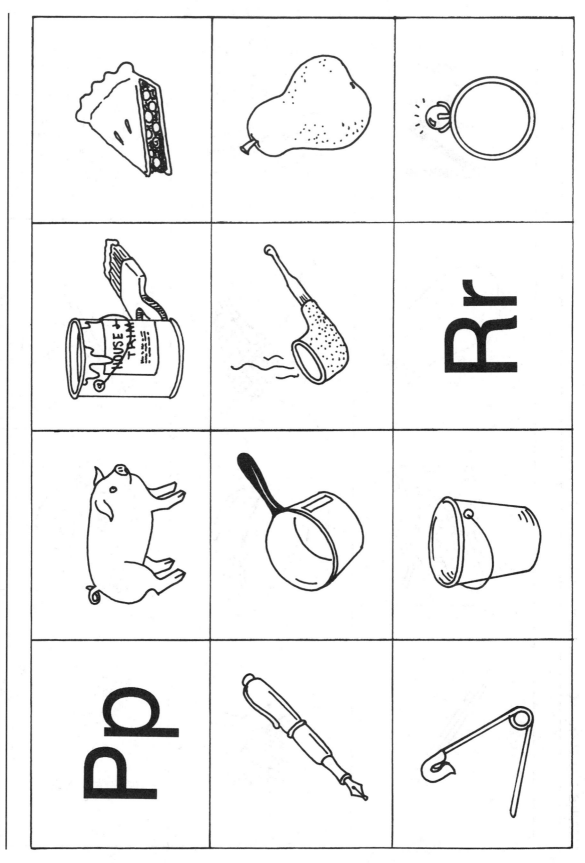

FIGURE 6-35 Picture Cards for Sorts and Games

FIGURE 6-36 Picture Cards for Sorts and Games

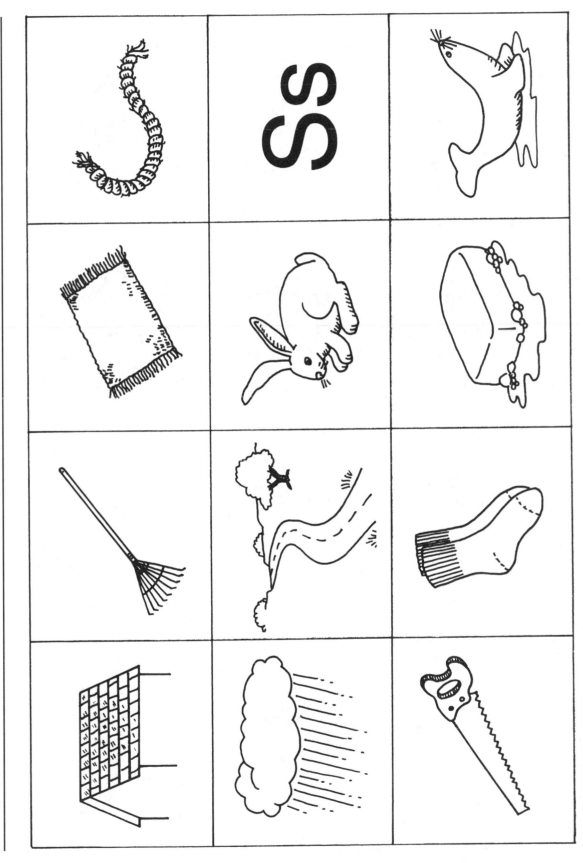

FIGURE 6-37 Picture Cards for Sorts and Games

FIGURE 6–38 Picture Cards for Sorts and Games

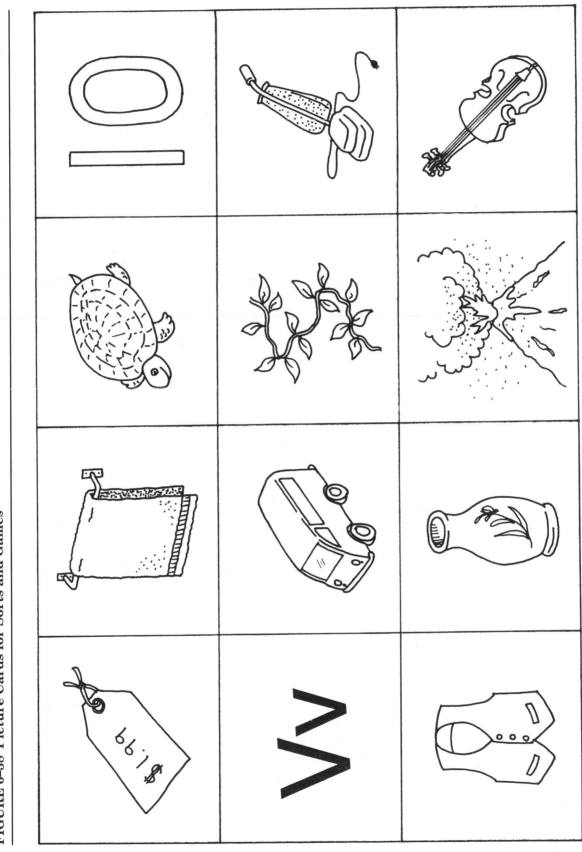

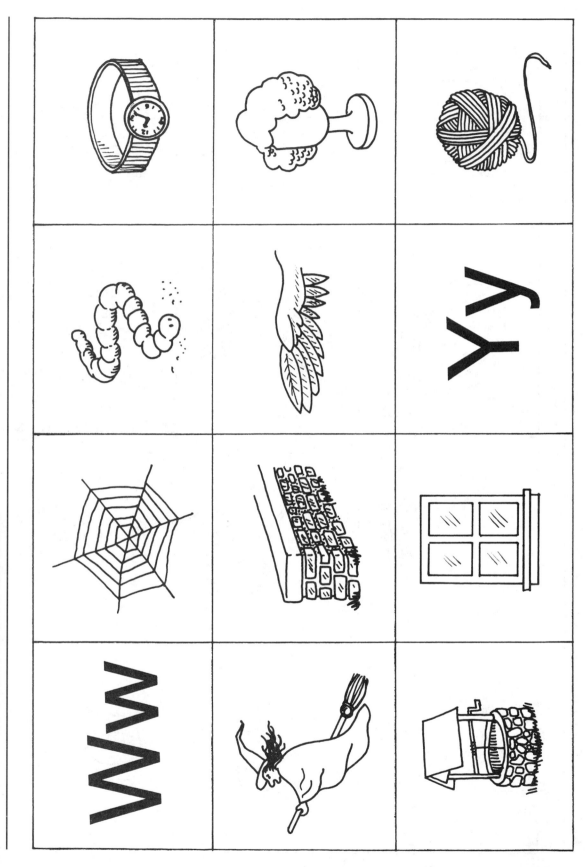

FIGURE 6–39 Picture Cards for Sorts and Games

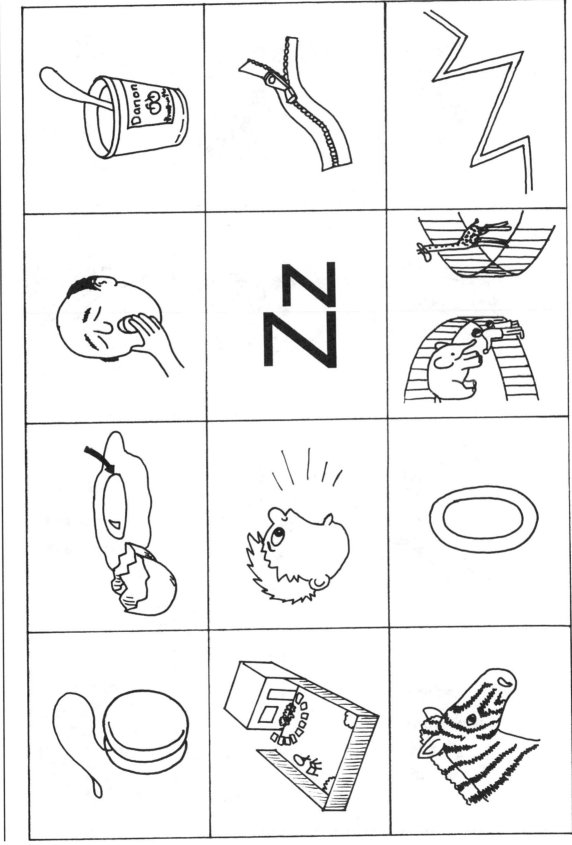

FIGURE 6-40 Picture Cards for Sorts and Games

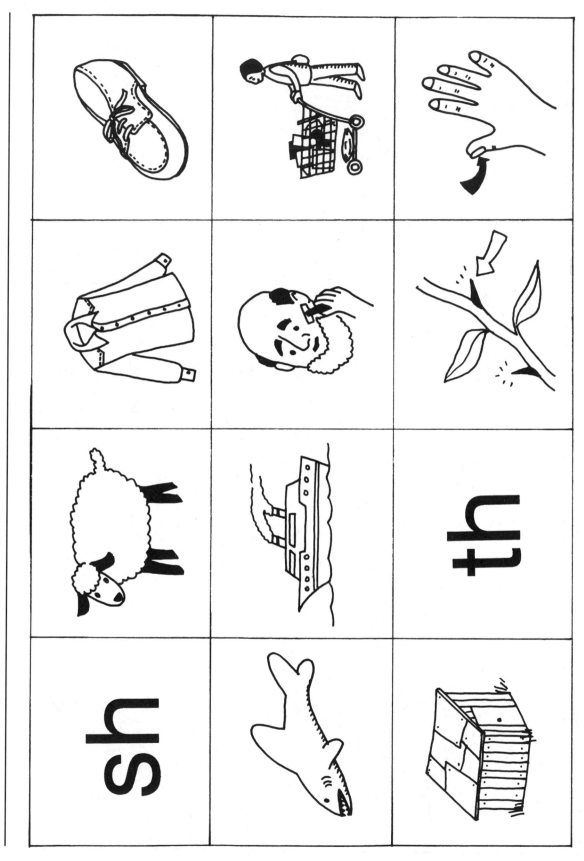

FIGURE 6-41 Picture Cards for Sorts and Games

FIGURE 6-42 Picture Cards for Sorts and Games

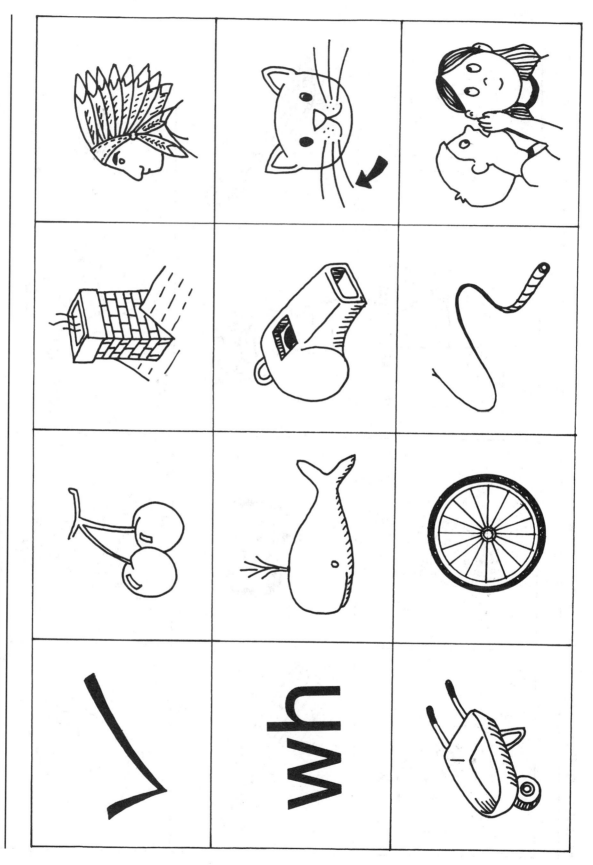

FIGURE 6-43 Picture Cards for Sorts and Games

FIGURE 6-44 Picture Cards for Sorts and Games

FIGURE 6-45 Picture Cards for Sorts and Games

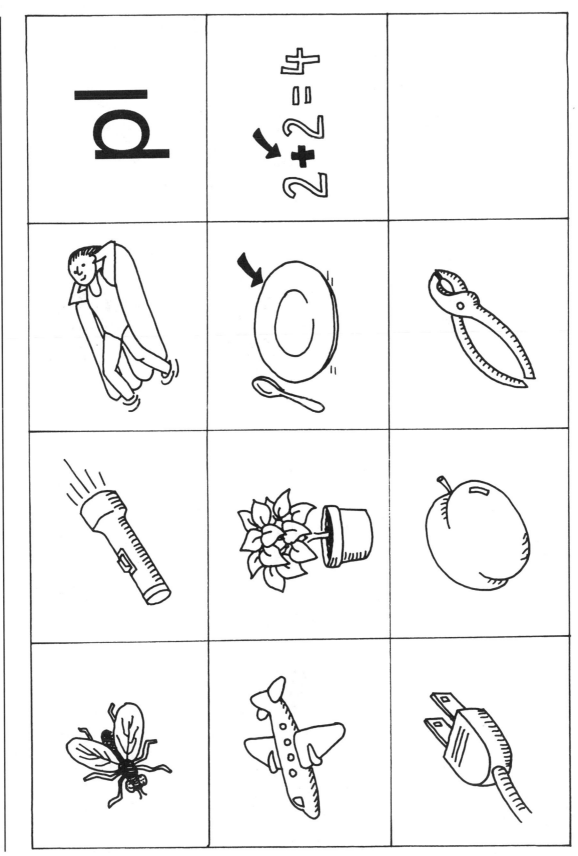

FIGURE 6-46 Picture Cards for Sorts and Games

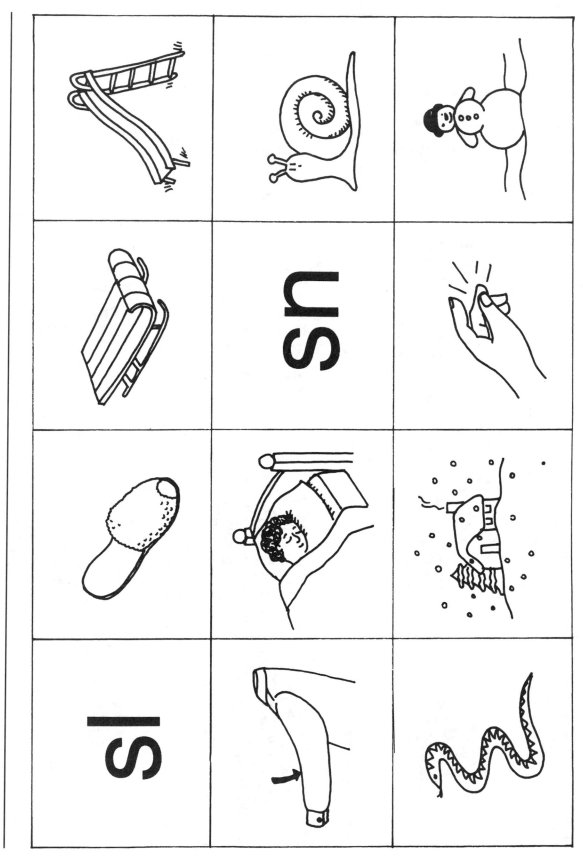

FIGURE 6–47 Picture Cards for Sorts and Games

FIGURE 6–48 Picture Cards for Sorts and Games

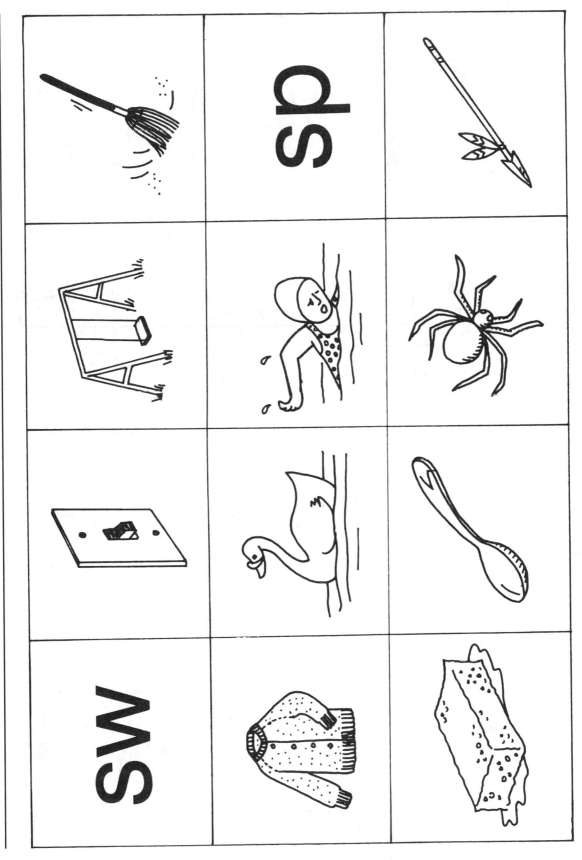

FIGURE 6–49 Picture Cards for Sorts and Games

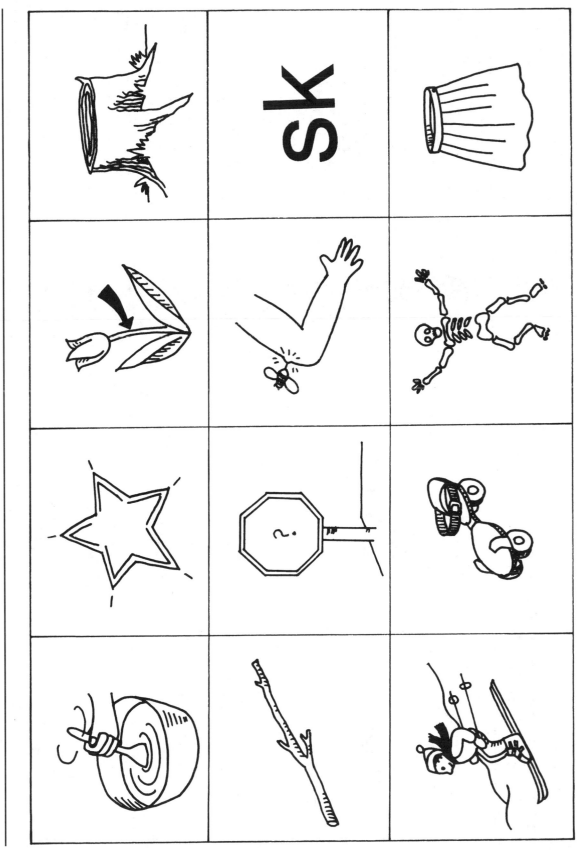

FIGURE 6-50 Picture Cards for Sorts and Games

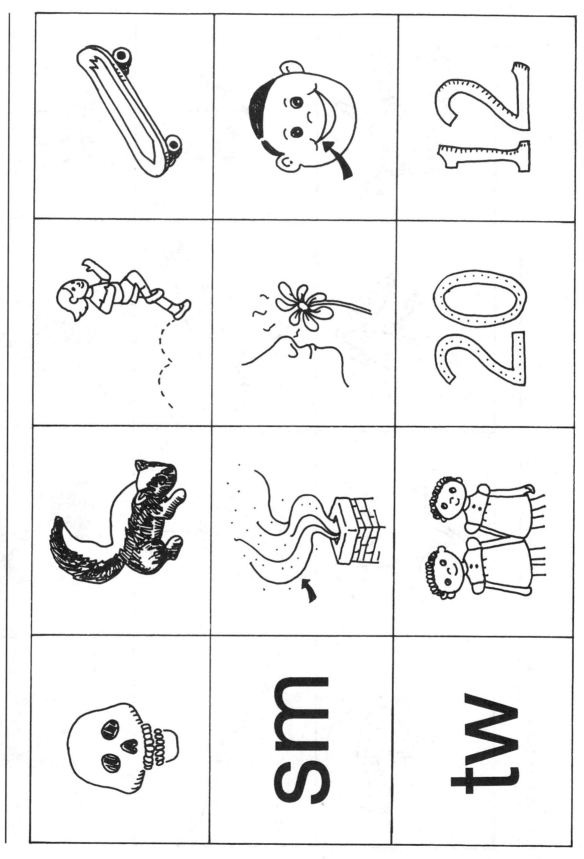

FIGURE 6-51 Picture Cards for Sorts and Games

FIGURE 6–52 Picture Cards for Sorts and Games

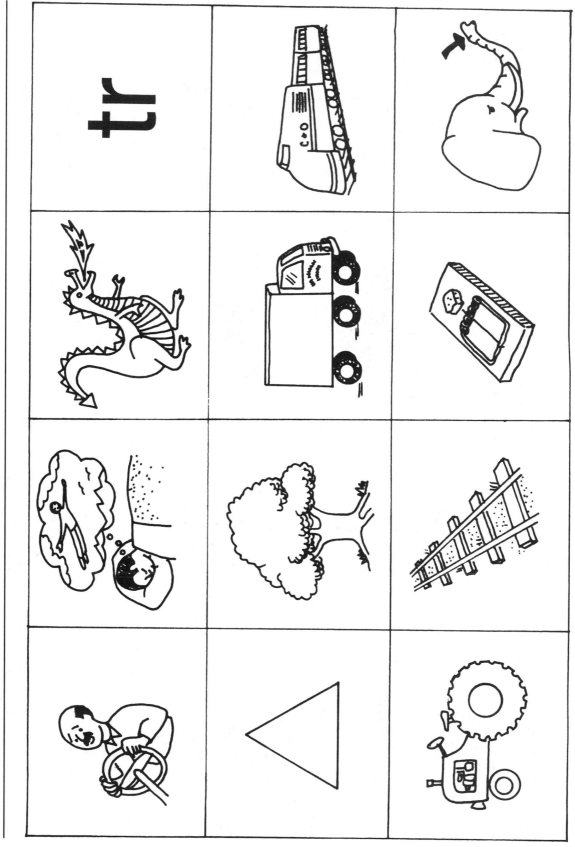

FIGURE 6–53 Picture Cards for Sorts and Games

FIGURE 6-54 Picture Cards for Sorts and Games

FIGURE 6-55 Picture Cards for Sorts and Games

FIGURE 6–56 Picture Cards for Sorts and Games

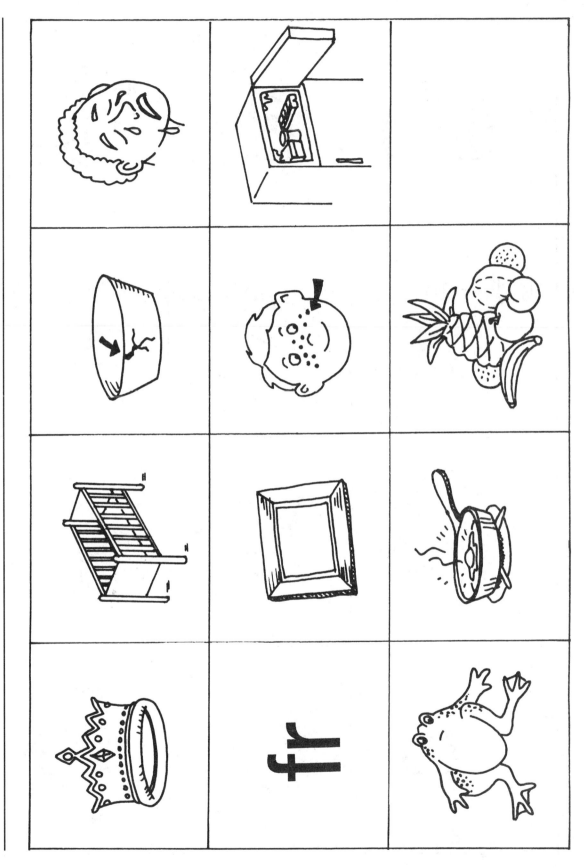

FIGURE 6-57 Picture Cards for Sorts and Games

FIGURE 6–58 Picture Cards for Sorts and Games

233

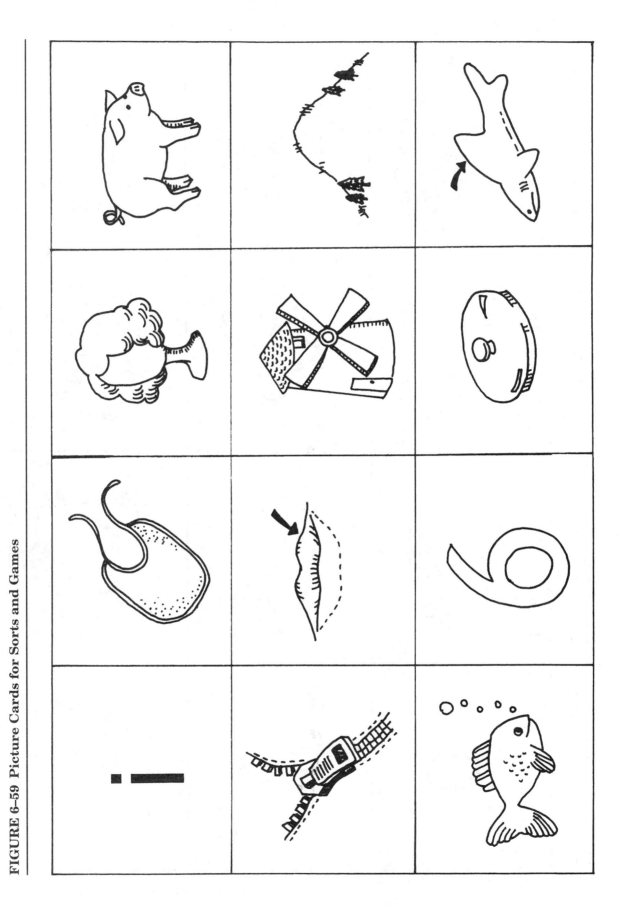

FIGURE 6-59 Picture Cards for Sorts and Games

FIGURE 6-60 Picture Cards for Sorts and Games

235

FIGURE 6-61 Picture Cards for Sorts and Games

FIGURE 5-62 Blank Field Study Sheet

FIGURE 6–63 Racetrack Gameboard (left and right)

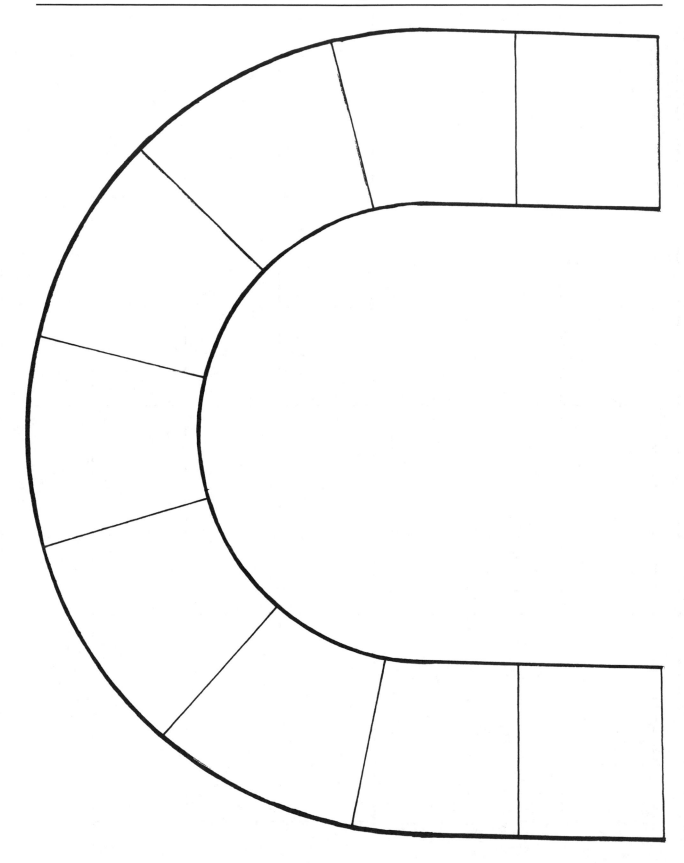

FIGURE 6–64 U-gameboard (left)

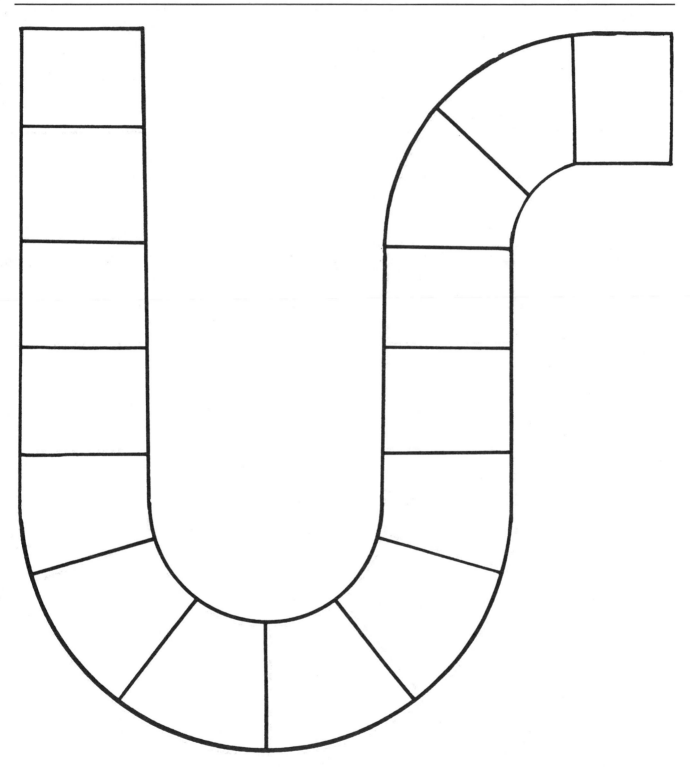

FIGURE 6–65 U-gameboard (right)

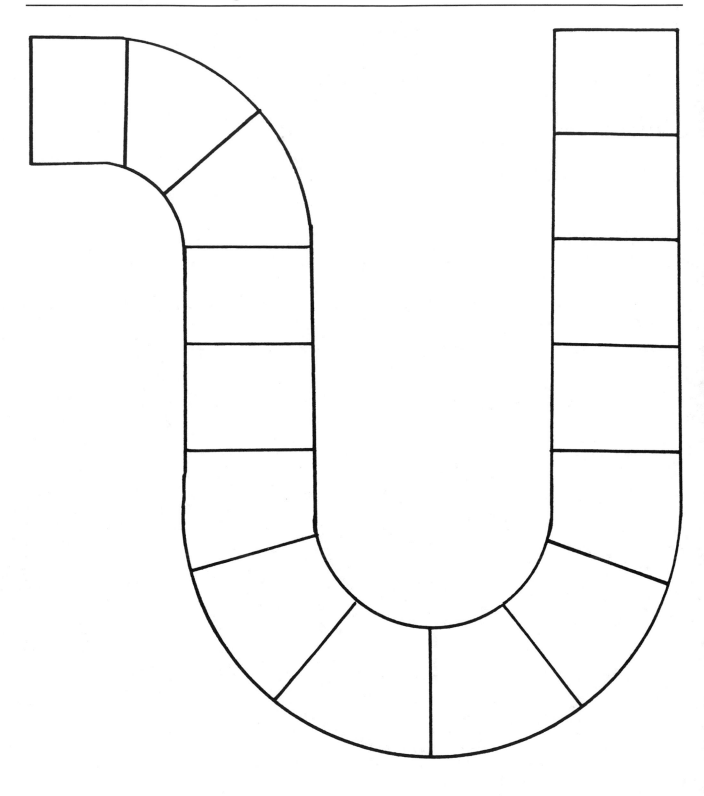

FIGURE 6–66 S-gameboard (left)

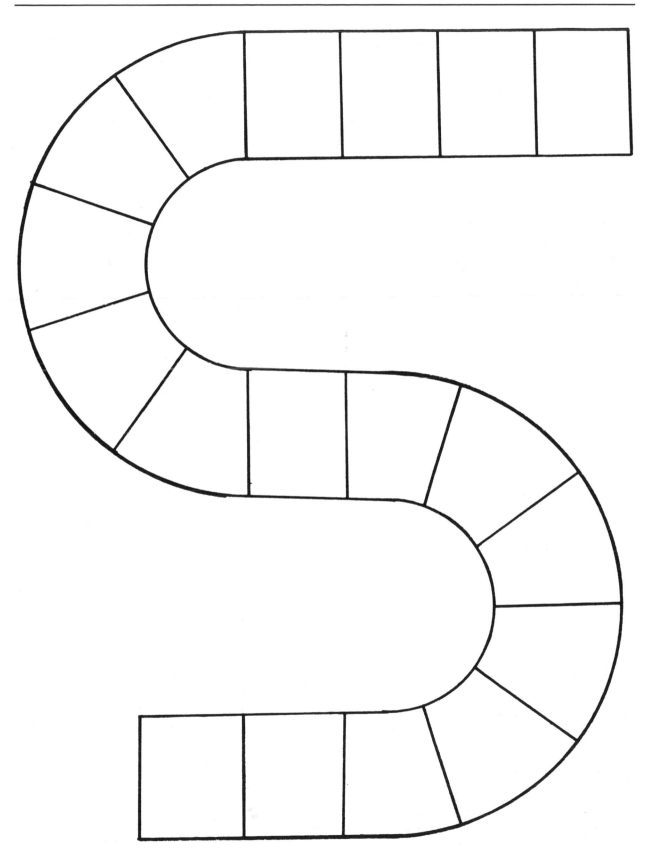

FIGURE 6–67 S-gameboard (right)

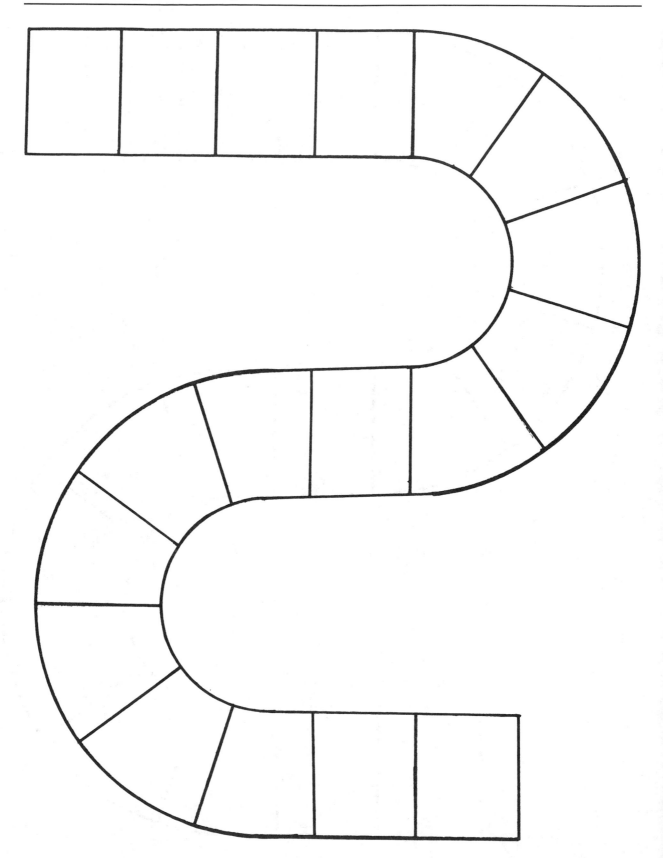

FIGURE 6–68 Rectangle Gameboard (left)

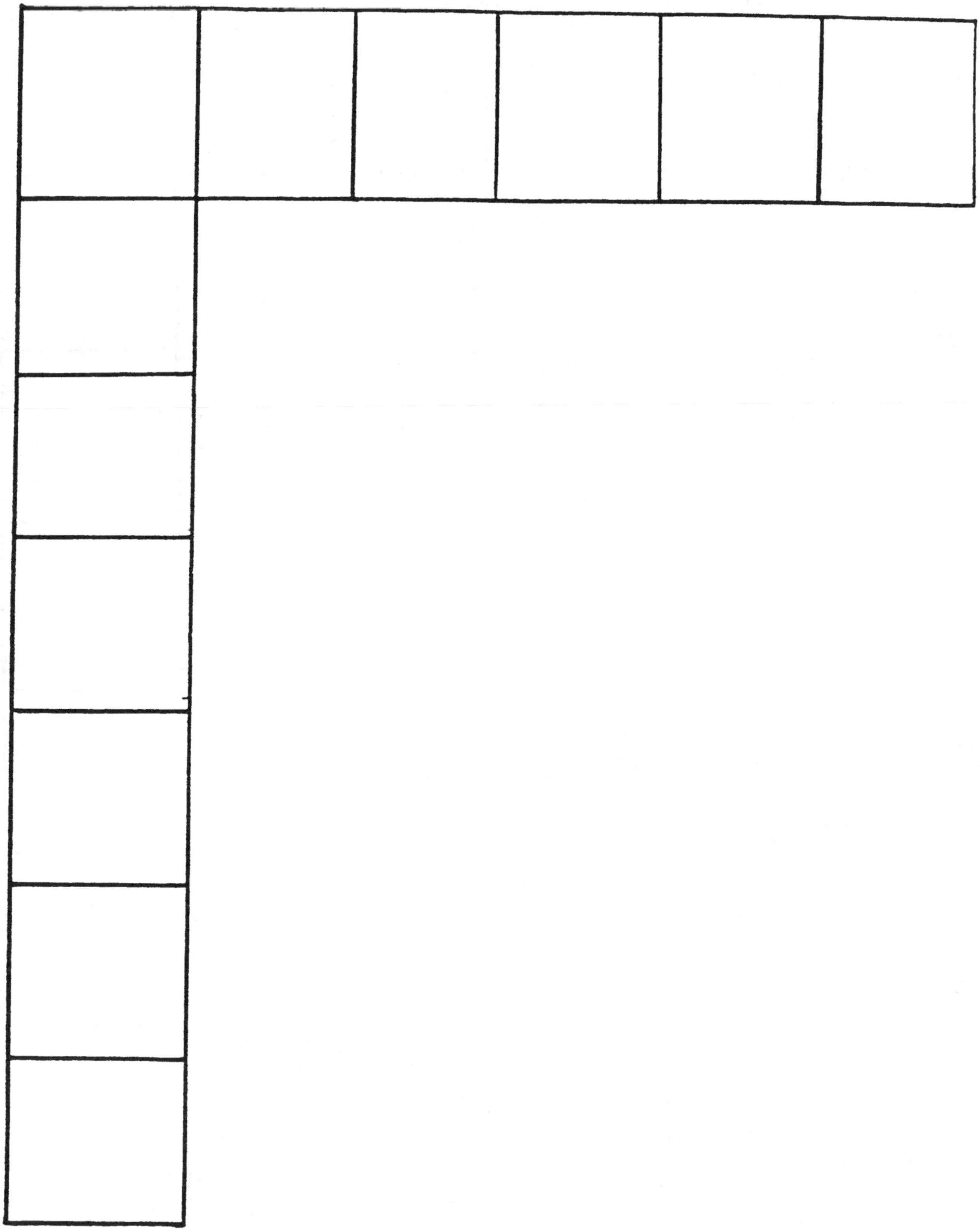

FIGURE 6–69 Rectangle Gameboard (right)

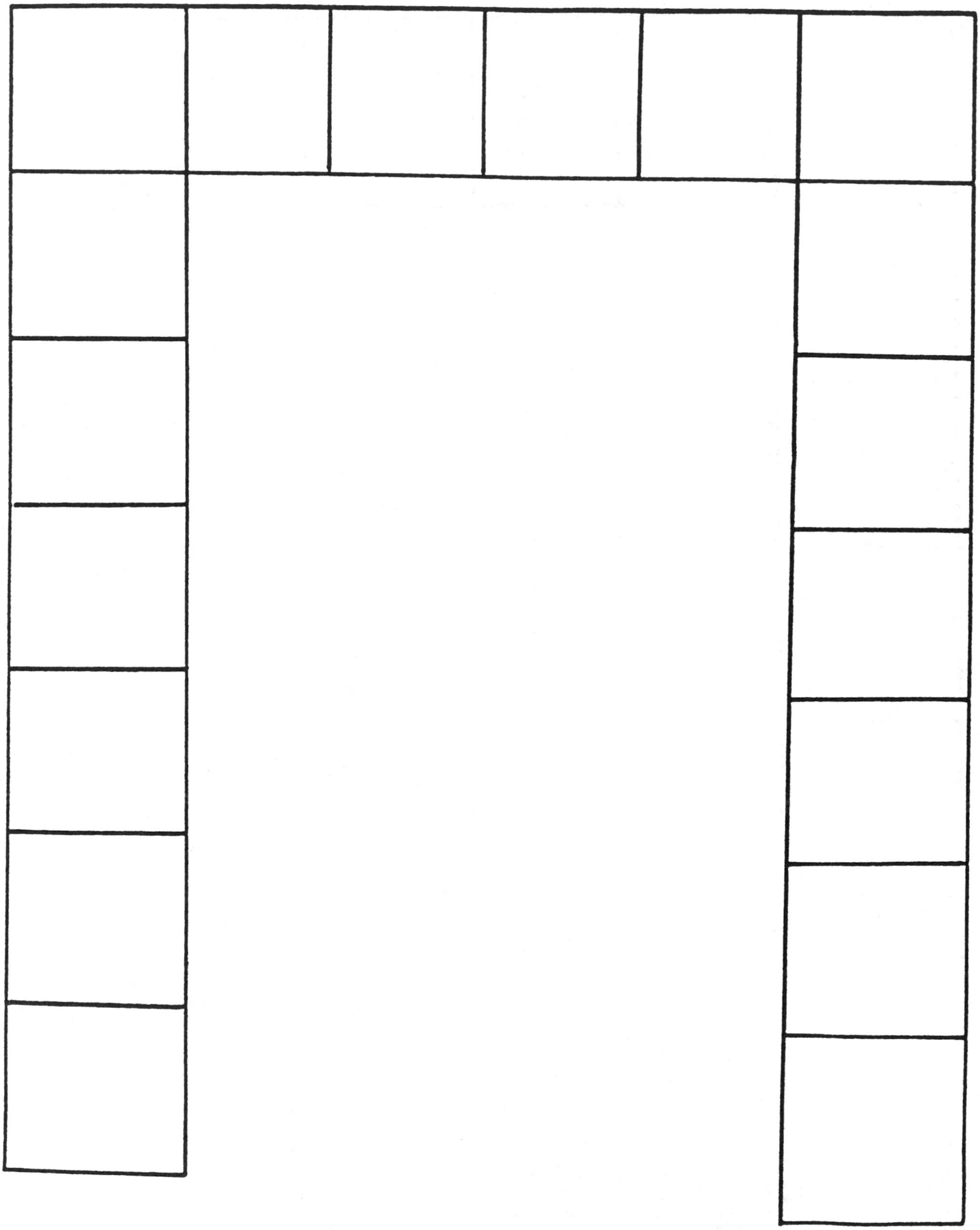

7

Word Study for Transitional Learners in the Within Word Pattern Stage

Orthographic development and word study instruction during Stage III is the subject of this chapter. We open with a discussion of the reading, writing, and spelling behaviors which are characteristic of the Transitional stage of literacy development. The activities, as in previous chapters, are arranged in order from the easiest to the most difficult activities. Guidelines to organize instruction appear after this discussion of development.

There is a growth in fluency in spelling and word study.

Transitional learners are in the Within Word Pattern stage of spelling. Students begin to examine long vowel patterns of single syllable words in detail, and then they study the infrequent vowel patterns and complex consonant patterns (Henderson, 1990). Word banks are no longer needed because students use teacher-made sorts. Just as there is an increasing fluency in reading and writing, there is a similar growth in fluency and flexibility evident in spelling and word study activities and games.

Literacy Development and Instruction for Students in the Within Word Pattern Stage

As noted in Figure 7–1, students in this Transitional stage read and write with tentative fluency and expression. This is a fragile period of development between the Beginning stage when students' reading and writing are quite labored and the Intermediate stage when students can read nearly all texts that come before them, including newspapers and nonspecialized magazines.

Orthographic development during this period is fresh and interesting, and students make rapid progress in their understanding of single-syllable orthographic patterns. During this stage of development, students learn to spell long vowel patterns, and in reading, most single-syllable words are read accurately and with increasing fluency. With basic contextual support from the text, Transitional readers can read many two-syllable words.

Reading

Longer pattern books are easy reading for Transitional readers.

Transitional readers approach fluency in their reading, and there are many books they can read with ease. Well-written readers, folk tales, and pattern books are good for students to read because they promote fluency. The longer

FIGURE 7–1   Synchrony Among Reading, Writing, and Spelling Development

STAGE III: Within Word Pattern

Reading

1) Transitional ———————→
    Silent reading
    Stop fingerpointing
    Approaching fluency and phrasal reading
    Greater expression
    (Ages 6 - 12)

Writing

2) Transitional ———————→
    Approaching fluency
    Greater planning time, more detail in organization

Orthographic Knowledge and Spelling

3) Within Word Pattern Stage of Spelling ———————→

(bed)	bed
(ship)	ship
(chase)	CHAIS, chase
(float)	FLOTE, float
(cattle)	CATEL, CATOL
(cellar)	SALER, CELER
(pleasure)	PLESER, PLESHER

The synchrony of the five stages of literacy development is presented in Figure 2–1, on page 14.

pattern books provide texts which are written at students' independent, functional level. Books in the *Toad and Frog* and the *I Can Read* series are instructional level materials for these Transitional readers.

Increasingly, throughout this stage, students read with greater fluency and expression compared to the disfluent reading of the Beginning readers (Bear, 1992; Bear & Cathey, 1989). This stage begins when students stop reading in the word-by-word and unexpressive fashion apparent in Stage II, Beginning Literacy. Because they can read many words quickly, they plan their reading in larger units. These larger units now approach a phrasal level which corresponds to the syntactic levels of the text. Transitional readers begin to read in phrases, pausing at the end of sentences, and they read with greater expression by emphasizing particular words as they read, and by saying some short phrases with a rise or fall in intonation.

Transitional readers also begin to read silently when they read to themselves. In the previous stage, students preferred to read orally. Transitional readers read in phrasal and syntactic units, and they stop reading aloud when they read to themselves. They no longer need the support that oral reading contributes; the phrases are read fast enough for students to bypass reading aloud. Students read silently to themselves during sustained silent reading (SSR) or Drop Everything and Read (DEAR).

Teachers observe that most of the fingerpointing characteristics of the Beginning stage drop away. In silent reading, Transitional readers approach rates of 100 words per minute in easy material.

While Transitional learners are no longer beginners, they are not sufficiently skilled to read most texts with ease. They can read and reread support materials like pattern books and lengthy individual dictations with good fluency and expression. However, in easy, but unfamiliar and less predictable texts,

Transitional learners read in phrases.

Transitional readers read silently.

Transitional readers are more hesitant and slow in their reading and writing. There is a certain bridled feeling that can be heard as they approach fluency.

Writing

Writing also becomes more fluent during this period of development. The physical act of writing is performed with greater speed and less conscious focus on the explicit act of writing (Bear, 1991a). This added fluency gives Transitional writers more time to concentrate on ideas, and this may account for the greater depth and complexity in their expression.

There is greater sophistication in the way Transitional writers express their ideas. They are better at putting their entire message into words, and generally, their writing is clearer as it offers more detail. Cognitively they compose with a better sense of the reader's background knowledge. In style, Transitional writers learn to do more than present sequences of events; their stories often have morals or themes which build from the central activities of the major characters. Transitional writers also use a greater variety of story devices to begin and end their stories, and they use capital letters and sentence punctuation correctly.

When Transitional learners write responses and reactions to what they read and do, they continue to retell and summarize their experiences and the events in a story, and they begin to include generalizations and analyses which show the reader the deeper processing of the writer (Barone, 1989).

Literacy Learning and Instruction

Transitional readers are good partners for Beginning readers during Readers' Workshops. Through their reading with Beginners, they model reading fluency and expression. Unlike more advanced readers who often grow impatient, Transitional readers enjoy following along as Beginning readers reread their pattern stories and individual dictations.

Transitional readers explore different genre, and for the first time, they read chapter books. By the end of this stage, they can read books like *Amelia Bedelia* with ease, and they can read simple chapter books like *Nate the Great*. Informational books become more accessible; for example, they read informational books from the *I Can Read* series as well as the easy texts in informational magazines like *Ranger Rick*. Because there are so many books Transitional readers can read with ease, the support provided by individual dictations and pattern books are no longer required. At an instructional level, there are many more difficult books that students can read with good understanding as well as moderate accuracy and fluency. Students can begin easy chapter books like the *Boxcar Series* and Beverly Cleary's work.

Students in the Transitional stage work in small groups for Readers' and Writers' Workshops. In these workshops and in conferences with teachers, students discuss their readings and writings in greater depth than they did as Beginners. In small groups, students discuss the stories they have read, and they look into their reading materials to share specific ideas and language they thought were interesting. Independently and with partners they can read books without a teacher's support. This independence makes it possible to use reading conference time to share and discuss ideas in more detail.

In writing conferences and directed lessons, teachers help Transitional writers through the steps of the writing process. Because they have often written more and written with greater clarity and detail than the Beginning writers, writing conferences and workshops include more of the revision and

---

Margin notes:

Writing is longer and more detailed.

Stories begin to focus on morals and central characters.

Students begin to read easy chapter and informational books.

Readers' and Writers' workshops become an integral part of instruction.

Revision and editing become more integral to the writing process.

editing parts of the writing process. Students also begin to use more punctuation conventions of writing, such as quotation marks for dialogue.

Teachers find Transitional stage students in the early part of first grade. The greatest number of Transitional students are in the second, third, and fourth grades. But you will certainly find corrective and remedial readers in the secondary grades who are in this stage of orthographic development. Many students stagnate at this point of literacy development. Perhaps twenty-five percent of the adult population in the United States is stunted at this point of literacy proficiency. Many students who progress no further than the Transitional stage revert back to Beginning behaviors as their knowledge atrophies.

> Many adults are Transitional readers and writers.

There are also a few postsecondary students who are poor spellers and adequate readers who need to return to this Transitional stage of orthographic development when they aim to improve their spelling ability and reading vocabulary. These are the adults who can read at sight the many words they see regularly, but may have difficulty reading fairly common polysyllabic words like *repetition,* and may spell some two syllable words incorrectly; i.e., double consonants (*betting* as BETING) or the schwa in the second syllable (*label* as LABLE). It is important to take a step back and conduct word study activities that help them cement their knowledge of vowel patterns in single-syllable words to get a running start as they study two-syllable words.

> For students who have trouble with polysyllabic words, return to Within Word Pattern study of vowel patterns in single syllable words.

Experience is crucial during this stage. Students must read for a full 25 to 30 minutes each day in instructional- and independent-level materials. They need this practice to propel them into the next stage; otherwise, they will stagnate and shrivel up as readers and writers. This puts word study into perspective for teachers. If students are not doing plenty of reading, all of the word study in the world will not help.

> 25-30 minutes of reading each day is a must.

Characteristics of Orthographic Development

> Within Word Pattern stage students study:
> ◆ Long vowel patterns
> ◆ Other abstract patterns
> ◆ R-influenced words
> ◆ Consonant blends and digraphs

In the Letter Name stage, students learned about short vowel patterns, starting with word families. Throughout this beginning stage students became competent reading single syllable short vowel words, and many long vowel words. In spelling, these beginners examined the orthography using their letter name knowledge and a linear strategy in which each letter represented one sound. In contrast, students in the Within Word Pattern stage move beyond a letter name strategy; they learn long vowel patterns and other abstract vowel patterns, and their knowledge in spelling r-influenced single-syllable words and consonant blends and digraphs is substantial. Each of these aspects of orthographic development are discussed in this section. The Spelling-by-Stage Assessment from Chapter Three placed these students in the range highlighted in Figure 7–2.

Studying the Abstract Nature of Long Vowels

> Long vowel patterns are not linear; they are more abstract.

Students in the Within Word Pattern stage demonstrate an awareness that there is not a simple letter-sound relationship in all English words. Unlike the three sounds in the CVC pattern of the short vowels studied in the Letter Name stage, students in the Within Word Pattern stage analyze the orthography with a greater interest and subsequent understanding of pattern (Templeton, 1992). A level of abstract thinking is evident in students' thinking about long vowel patterns (Bear, 1992). They demonstrate in their invented spelling and word study an understanding that the common long vowel patterns are not linear like the short vowel patterns they learned about in the previous stage. For example, students in the Within Word Pattern know that the

FIGURE 7–2 15-Point Scale Spelling-by-Stage Assessment

Late Derivational Constancy	15
Middle Derivational Constancy	14
Beginning Derivational Constancy	13
Late Syllable Juncture	12
Middle Syllable Juncture	11
Beginning Syllable Juncture	10
Late Within Word Pattern	**9**
Middle Within Word Pattern	**8**
Beginning Within Word Pattern	**7**
Late Letter Name	6
Middle Letter Name	5
Beginning Letter Name	4
Early Letter Name	3
Early Letter Name	2
Preliterate	1

Within Word Pattern learners experiment with long vowel patterns: FETE for feet; NALE for nail.

ea in *meat* makes the long ē sound. They may not know this in explicit terms, but on an intuitive level, they know that the *ea* acts as a vowel diagraph representing one sound. The awareness of how long vowels are represented, this ability to see the orthography abstractly, signifies most clearly the move into the Within Word Pattern stage.

Throughout this stage, students experiment with ("use but confuse") long vowel patterns. By the end of the Within Word Pattern stage, students have a good understanding of short *and* long vowel spelling patterns. This knowledge of long and short vowel patterns is prerequisite to the examination of the way syllables are joined during the next stage of development, the Syllable Juncture stage (Templeton & Bear, 1992a). For example, when students have immediate recognition of words like *bet* and *beat* they soon begin to see that *betting* has two *t*'s and *beating* has one *t*. The activities in this chapter will guide students as they finish their study of the fundamental single-syllable words and patterns.

Students begin to make the "meaning connection" (Templeton, 1983) during this stage of development as they observe the interface between the pronunciation and the spelling of vowels. They can begin to see the history of the English language in the orthography. As you may know, many of the silent letters were once pronounced, and a remnant of the previous patterns of pronunciation have remained in the spelling. For example, in Middle English, the *k* in *knife* and *knight* were once pronounced. Similarly, the silent *e* at the end of many words was once pronounced. For example, *wife* once was pronounced *wee-fuh*. Usually, we do not think about this meaning connection until the next stage. The history of words, their *etymology,* will be discussed in detail in the next chapter. However, some of this knowledge begins during the Within Word Pattern stage and can be broached in vocabulary studies of many of the single-syllable words. As you will see in some of the activities, students create semantic sorts that are collections of words on a particular topic (e.g., baseball words, space words, or government words).

Semantic sorts guide students to the meaning connection.

Students at this stage of development experiment with several other orthographic features including reexaminations of r-influenced vowels and consonant blends and digraphs.

R-Influenced Vowels

As our friend Neva Viise says, "R is a robber!" The presence of an *r* following a vowel robs the sound from the vowel before it. This causes some words with different short vowels to become homophones (*fir/fur*) and makes short vowel sounds spelled with "e," "i," and "u" indistinguishable in many cases (*herd, bird, curd*). Even long vowel sounds before the robber "r" are not as clear as the same vowels preceding other consonants (*pair* versus *pain*). These behaviors of r-influenced vowels cause spelling confusions. The activities on r-influenced vowels help students understand what happens when r influences vowels, and through this word study, students learn to spell these often troublesome words.

There are a number of word sorting activities for students to consider; these sorts make a nice bridge between the regular short vowel patterns and more abstract long vowel patterns.

The r-influenced vowel sorts draw students' attention to the location of the "r" and to the subtle difference in sound which location creates. The activities on r-influenced word study begin with the initial consonant blend as in **grill**. The second group of "r" activities are classic r-influenced vowels in which the "r" sound impacts the vowel. Words in the second column below are influenced by the "r". This point can be made by contrasting the r-influenced vowel with consonant blends and digraphs.

> Compare r-influenced words that sound alike but do not look alike: fir/turn, care/hair

grill	girl
crush	curl
fry	first
price	purse
bruise	burn
cream	tear
dry	dark
wrap	war

Consonant Patterns and Another Look at Consonant Blends and Digraphs

> Take another look at consonant blends and digraphs: -tch/catch; -ch/coach.

Without much directed word study during this stage of development, students demonstrate an understanding of consonant blends and digraphs at the beginning and ending of single-syllable words (i.e., *frost* and *bridge*). In their word study, students may work through some sorts in which initial consonants and consonant blends are contrasted (e.g., *b* to *bl*, to *br*). Students keep lists of the words they know that use specific patterns, and at this time, they study the final consonant patterns for short and long vowels. From Venezky (1970), Henderson called these complex consonant patterns (Henderson, 1990). For example, students in the Within Word Pattern stage will collect and examine words that end in *-tch* (catch), *-edge* (ledge), *-ch* (coach). By collecting plenty of examples of final consonant patterns, they see that some patterns are associated with short vowels and are contrasted with long vowel patterns:

coach vs. scotch	rage vs. badge
beach vs. fetch	huge vs. fudge

This word study is quite successful because students have many sight words to use as exemplars. As you may recall, this was one of the problems that Letter Name spellers had when they examined consonant digraphs and blends—they did not have enough exemplars to draw from.

Other Vowel Patterns

Look at less frequent vowel patterns: oi, ow, ou.

This is also a time to examine other vowel patterns. Most of these other patterns are short vowel patterns, but they include vowels which are neither long nor short. These vowel patterns are usually less frequent, and they are usually abstract in that more than one letter is used to represent one sound. This would include vowel diphthongs in words like *boil, brown,* and *cloud.* They are like the long vowels because there is more than one letter in the orthographic patterns. For example, consider *caught, sink, calf,* and *thought.* In these examples, the vowel patterns involve either a second vowel or the vowel is influenced by a letter that has some vowel-like qualities; (i.e., *bulk* and *crowd*). The word study notebooks and student-generated lists are used in small group sessions to examine these patterns.

Homophones and Homographs

Homophones are words that sound alike but look different: *hare* and *hair.*

Once students understand the basic differences between long and short vowels they also become aware of the numerous mismatches between pronunciation and spelling. These inconsistencies are in the spelling for various reasons. It is not helpful to throw up our arms when we talk to students to say that this is just the way English spelling is. In some words, as discussed above, the spelling pattern is a remnant of the way the word used to be pronounced. Students enjoy creating lists of homophones (*bear* and *bare*) and homographs (*read* [present tense], and *read* [past tense]).

Homographs are words that look alike but sound differently: *lead* (short e) and *lead* (long e); *tear* (long e) and *tear* (long a).

We think that there is a good reason why words that sound alike are spelled differently: a certain amount of redundancy in the orthography may actually make the meaning clearer. When two words which sound the same are spelled differently, the spelling may make the reading easier. Perhaps you can see the need for redundancy in the orthography in a sentence in which homophones are substituted for one another:

The weigh Peat cot the bare was knot fare.

(The way Pete caught the bear was not fair.)

In word recognition, students use their knowledge of various orthographic, syntactic, and semantic systems (Cutler, Mehler, Norris, & Segui, 1987). In fact, these various systems work as a team, but for different words in various contexts one system will reign over another.

You will find in discussions of homophones and homographs that you also talk about the meaning and grammatical function of words. The language of grammar and semantics is necessary to discuss these differences between homographs and homophones. For example, to talk about the homophones *read* and *red,* it makes sense to talk about the past tense of the verb "to read" and the color word "red." You will find these grammar studies are also part of the language arts curricular goals for many grades.

Word Study Instruction

Within the sequence of word study for students in this stage, and as a part of individual and small group activities, students are involved in word sorts and work in word study notebooks. These are the most generic of activities for this stage. They are discussed as they appear in the sequence of word study.

Sequence of Word Study

The sequence of word study during this stage is as follows:

1. Focus on one long vowel.
2. Contrast short vowels and long vowels with the picture cards (ă vs. ˘ āce). R-influenced vowels are included at this time.
3. Collect words students know that sound like the long vowel being studied.
4. Examine the various orthographic patterns for that vowel (*nail,* f**ace,** *ba**y***).
5. Collect numerous examples of each pattern, and sort the words according to their sound and spelling similarities.
6. Move to a second long vowel and follow the same sequence. Begin with an examination of the similarities between the two long vowel patterns (e.g., *bay* and *key*).
7. Explore each of the long vowels in the way that has been described here.
8. As students progress through the long vowels, include some word studies of consonant patterns (c**atch,** coa**ch**). Also, examine r-influenced vowels from *car* to *cure.*
9. Once students have completed an examination of the long vowel patterns, move to other vowel patterns like the diphthongs (*crow*n, ar**oun**d)
10. Finally, reexamine long vowel patterns again, and review the generalizations you can make about the differences among vowel patterns (e.g., ***ow*** in *throw* and *cow*).

    This sequence leads naturally to a discussion of two-syllable orthographic patterns (i.e., *hopping* from *hop* and *hoping* from *hope*). Students who are interested in these differences begin word studies grouped in the next chapter on Syllable Juncture word study.

Sequence of word study for Within Word Pattern.

Begin by focusing on one vowel.

Teacher-made Sorts

Because there are so many words that students can recognize with ease, you can stop using word banks with students; you may have noticed that the word banks are large and bulky, and difficult to manage. They can be replaced by word sorts that you make for the students. As you will see, in the activities that follow, there are literally dozens of sorts for you to write onto word cards for students' sorting.

There are three basic steps for traditional sorting lessons using teacher-made sorts.

Three steps in teacher made sorts:
♦ Introduce sort
♦ Students sort
♦ Share categories

1. **Introduce the sort.**

   The teacher introduces the sort and introduces the words that head the columns students are to sort by; for example, "Find all the words you can that sound like *fish* in the middle and which sound like *kite* in the middle."

   At other times, teachers may conduct these as open sorts in which students discover the categories for themselves.

2. **Students sort.**

   Students work independently to sort the words in the teacher-made word pack:

   a. Read through the words and discard unknowns.

   b. Use a classification folder, such as the one shown in Figure 7–3, and

FIGURE 7–3 Long Vowel Sorts: Students Sort by Sound

  place the key words at the top of each column.

 c. Sort the rest of the words by saying a word and then the word at the head of each column to find the correct column. Observe how fluently and accurately the student can sort the words.

3. **Whole group sharing.**

  The whole group comes back together to share. Often, students write their sorts into word study notebooks. Students work together with classification folders whose columns have been designated by the teacher.

  This sequence may take a total of twenty minutes. Word study can be a part of the language arts time when you meet with students. Sitting at a table or on the floor, students share their sorts, and they make lists of words that follow particular sound and spelling patterns. Word study notebooks are used to document the activity, and they serve as handy references that preserve continuity from one small group, word study session to another.

Word Study Notebooks

Word study notebooks replace word banks.

Like the charts with columns, word study notebooks are organized collections of words students examine for different purposes. The transition from word banks to word study notebooks and teacher-made sorts can begin by contrasting the short vowels studied in the previous stage with the long vowels. You may find that you begin word study notebooks with the whole class, and that while most students are in the Within Word Pattern stage or higher, there may be a few students who are in the Letter Name stage. These students record in notebooks the word sorts from their word banks.

Word study notebooks have a long instructional life in learning. They can be used for vocabulary and orthographic study all the way through college classes. Many of us still keep a word study notebook as a regular entry in our journals. Word study notebooks are used when students study vowel patterns in single syllable words, when students want to make a list of words from a science lesson, or when they discover collections of words that are related by their derivational histories. Many of these examinations are focused on the relationships among word meanings.

Toward the end of the Within Word Pattern stage, word study notebooks are valuable repositories for collecting words that are related through *meaning*. To begin this relational type of thinking about vocabulary, we conduct *semantic sorts* with greater vigor at this point. For example, we may start by asking students to collect on a page in their notebooks words that are related to food. As a small group, students categorize the words they have collected into subcategories, for example utensils, fruits, desserts, and fast food.

Activities for word study notebooks evolve out of the word sorts and small group brainstorming sessions. Follow the sequence of activities presented below, and use the generic word study activities presented at the beginning of this section.

> Word study notebooks are a place to collect and arrange words and concepts.

> Semantic sorts are meaning sorts.

Activities for Students in the Within Word Pattern Stage

Our activities include teacher-made word sorts and the development of word study notebooks. The sorts become more complex because the categories expand tremendously as the various long vowel patterns of each vowel are explored. With different word and picture lists, the games introduced in the previous chapter become Within Word Pattern stage activities.

In picture sorts, students look for similarities and differences among the vowel sounds in single-syllable words. Accuracy and fluency in sorting continue to be the criteria for success before moving to other sorts. After sorting, students discuss their sorts and explain their categories, and finally, they document their work in word study notebooks.

As in the previous chapters, the generic activities are marked with the generic logo. Pictures for long vowel sorts are included at the end of the chapter. While some lists of words for teacher-made sorts are presented throughout the activities, extensive word lists for teacher-made word sorts are also presented at the end of the chapter.

The activities are partitioned according to developmental sequence: Beginning, Middle, and End of the Within Word Pattern stage.

Beginning Within Word Pattern Sorts

This is quite an interesting period of change in word study for students. The teacher sorts provide a great deal more diversity in word sorting. The beginning sorts in this stage help make this transition from short vowels to long vowels. Several important generic activities are introduced in this section.

 A | **Long Vowel Sound Board** | **7–1**

Beginning Within Word Pattern; Long Vowels

The vowel sound boards are a reference for students about long vowel sounds. Directions for using a sound board are discussed in Chapter Six, and sound boards appear in Figures 6–23, 6–24, and 6–25.

Use pictures of long and short vowels to contrast these types of vowels. The key phrase to set up this contrast is, "Look at these two pictures and say their names. See if these names sound alike in the middle."

Teachers create large sound boards by using a chart maker if one is available, and by using pictures from this book and pasting them on poster boards. The sound board can be cut apart to use as headings for the sorts to follow.

GA Picture Sorts Contrasting Long and Short Vowels 7–2

Beginning Within Word Pattern; Long and Short Vowels

This is an excellent bridge activity for students in the early part of this stage. Students work individually and in small groups to examine the basic sound differences among short and long vowel patterns.

Materials

Focus on one vowel and choose 14 short vowel pictures and 14 long vowel pictures from the pictures of long vowels, at the end of the chapter, and the pictures of short vowels from the previous chapter. The pictures at the end of Chapters Six and Seven can be used for these picture sorts.

Procedures

1. Students say the names of the pictures, and discard pictures they do not recognize.
2. On a classification folder, the teacher places a picture at the top of the first two columns to fit the categories the students are to use in their sorting. A third column referred to as "Miscellaneous," "Crazy," or "Oddball" is established for words that for various reasons do not fit.
3. Students sort the pictures underneath the column heads.
4. Students read their completed sorts by column. As they read the words in each column, they make any changes they wish, and at the end of reading each column, students declare the reason why they sorted as they did.

Variations

This same activity can be conducted as an open sort with pictures.

A Word Bank Hunts 7–3

This open sort gives a clear picture of what students already see in the orthographic patterns in these words. It allows them to identify and sort known words for a long vowel.

Procedures

Beginning Within Word Pattern; One Long Vowel

1. Ask students to go through their word banks to find words that sound like one of the long vowel words from the vowel sound board: "Find all the words you can that sound like *cake* in the middle."
2. Students read the words aloud and are asked what words could be grouped together.

Variations

Use the long vowel pictures instead of words.

GA Word Study Notebooks 7–4

Within Word Pattern; Long Vowels

Word study notebooks are an important part of the word study program at this stage. They are discussed in some detail above. We often use spiral notebooks, but the notebook can also be a computer disk or two pieces of paper folded and stapled.

To note briefly here, the notebook is a diary and collection of words students have studied. Words are grouped by orthographic patterns and by meaning. The notebooks document students' word study and vocabulary program.

Procedures

In small groups, use the word study notebooks as a diary of word study. Ask students to bring their word study notebooks to small group meetings. Use shelving with baskets as a storage area for word study notebooks.

Variation

Word study lists can be reproduced for inclusion in notebooks.

GA Teacher-made Word Sorts of Long Vowels 7–5

Within Word Pattern; Long and Short Vowels

In small groups of between six to eight, students follow this sequence of lessons to examine long vowel patterns:

Procedures

1. **Choose one long vowel to study.**
   Students may spend up to a month studying that first vowel.
2. **Conduct picture sorts.**
   Contrast long and short vowel words for that vowel. Use the pictures at the end of this chapter and Chapter Six.
3. **Conduct word sorts.**
   a) Begin by contrasting short vowel patterns with long vowel patterns. For example, here are two sorts which contrast long and short vowels:

i.	<u>fan</u>	<u>lane</u>	<u>far</u>	
	CVC	CVCe	R-influenced	
ii.	<u>rain</u>	<u>may</u>	<u>call</u>	<u>have</u>
	CVVC	CVV	-all	Miscellaneous

   b) Focus on the various long vowel patterns. For example, here are the columns for the long a patterns:

<u>came</u>	<u>nail</u>	<u>pay</u>
CVCe	CVVC	CVV

   Words from students' word banks as well as the words in the lists at the end of this chapter are used. There are numerous sorts for each vowel contrast in the back of this chapter. Write these words on word cards for students to use in word sorts. Sorts should consist of between 16 and 30 words or pictures.

   Begin each teacher-made sort by the student reading the words for accuracy. Students set aside words they cannot read or pictures they do not recognize.
4. **Reflect on the sorts.**
   Enter sorts in the word study notebook. For example, a page could be devoted to words like *ran* (CVC), *game* (CVCe) and *far* (R- influenced CVC pattern).
5. **Study a second long vowel.**
   If students have acquired accuracy and fluency in the sorts of one long vowel, study a second long vowel. Begin the study of the second long vowel by comparing the orthographic patterns of these two long vowels. Here are two examples across vowels: *chain* and *feet* are both

CVVC vowel patterns; the CVV pattern is evident in these long vowels: *pay, pea, pie, toe.*

Fundamental Vowel Contrasts During the Within Word Pattern Stage

Vowel	Patterns					
Long a	CVCe name	CVVC nail break vein	CVV hay	Other they		
Long e	CVVC meal feet chief	CV me	CVV tea	Other these		
Long i	CVCe fine	-igh high	CVCC wild	CV my	CVV pie	Other sign
Long o	CVCe rode	CVVC boat	CVCC cold roll bolt post	CV go	CVV toe	Other snow comb
Diphthongs	oi, oy boil toy	ow now	ou loud			
Miscellaneous	oo noon	o to	ou could	oo wood		
Long u	CVCe mule rude	CVV blue	-ew grew	-ui juice		

Storing Teacher-made Sorts

Find a way to store the word sorts you make. A current favorite method is to use small library pockets for the words. The holder is sturdy enough so that a rubber band is unnecessary. Another popular method is to use boxes that checks come in from the bank.

GA Newspaper Word Hunt 7–6

Beginning Within Word Pattern; Long Vowels

Using a newspaper, teams are sent in search of various long vowel patterns (i.e., an "ai" team, an "ay" team, an "-aCe" team, etc.).

Words fitting the desired patterns are circled in crayon or highlighted and then written down. At the end of the search, words are read out for the class to check and to compare the length of lists, thus giving some indication of the more common patterns. The words may also be written out on a separate sheet of paper.

Variations

As noted in Chapter Six, students can hunt for sight words, similar vowel patterns, words to which inflected endings or plural forms may be added, or compound words.

FIGURE 7–4 Train Station Game: Long Vowel Patterns

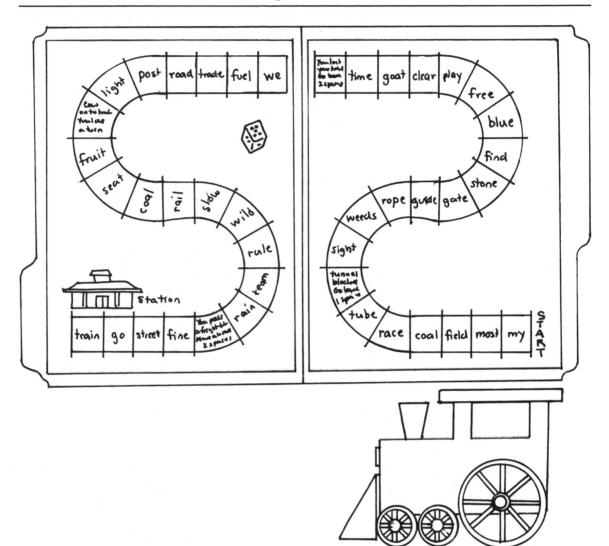

GA Train Station Game 7–7

Beginning Within
Word Pattern;
Long Vowels

This is an easy board game for up to 4 people used to emphasize automaticity with common long vowels.*

Materials

Use a basic pathway board, such as the one shown in Figure 7–4. There are four squares incorporated into the game board:

1. Cow on the track. Lose 1 turn.
2. You pass a freight train. Move ahead 2 spaces.
3. Tunnel blocked. Go back 1 space.
4. You lost your ticket. Go back 2 spaces.

---

*Thanks to Janet Bloodgood for this activity.

Procedures

Each child selects a marker. The first child then spins or rolls the die and places his marker on the appropriate space. She pronounces the word and identifies the vowel. In addition, she must say another word which contains the same vowel sound to stay on that space. Play continues in this fashion until someone finishes the course.

If students have studied the long vowel patterns within each long vowel, they can be asked to say what the pattern is, for example, "*nail* is a long *a* with a CVVC pattern (or an *ai* pattern)."

Word List

Here is a word list that you can use. There are dozens of other lists at the end of the chapter.

"a"	"e"	"i"	"o"	"u"
day	team	fine	go	rule
play	street	time	slow	fruit
gate	seat	light	post	fuel
race	we	my	goat	blue
mail	free	wild	gold	tube
rain	weeds	find	stone	
rail	field	sight	rope	
trade	clear	guide	coal	
freight			road	
			most	

Other words may be selected depending on the targeted feature.

 Turkey Feathers 7–8

Beginning Within
Word Pattern;
One Long Vowel

This is a game in which two players compare visual patterns across a single long vowel.*

Materials

Two paper/cardboard turkeys without tail feathers, such as the one in Figure 7–5; ten construction paper feathers; word cards representing the long vowel studied, for example, for long a, CVCe, -ai, and -ay. Word cards should have pairs, e.g., *cake/bake; mail/pail.*

Procedures

1. One player shuffles and deals five cards and five feathers to each player.
2. Remaining cards are placed face down for the draw pile.
3. Each player puts down pairs that match by pattern. For example *cake/bake* would be a pair, but *pain/sane* would not. Each time a pair is laid down, the player puts one feather on his/her turkey.
4. The dealer goes first, says a word from his or her hand, and asks the second player if he or she has a card that has the same pattern.
5. If player two has a card that matches the pattern, player one gets a feather; if not, player one must draw a card. If the player draws a card

---

*Marilyn Edwards developed this easy game and suggested this list of words.

FIGURE 7–5 Turkey Feathers: Comparing Vowel Patterns

which matches any word in hand, the pair can be discarded, and a feather is earned. Player 2 proceeds in the same manner.

6. The player using all 5 feathers first wins. If a player uses all his cards before earning 5 feathers, the player must draw a card before the other player's turn.

Variation

Upon using all 5 feathers, a player must correctly pronounce words. If a word is mispronounced, the player loses a feather and the game continues.

Word List

Refer also to the sorts at the end of this chapter.

CVVC	CVCe	CVV
-ai	-aCe	-ay
brain	grade	gray
rain	shade	tray
pain	came	spray
gain	game	clay
drain	bake	sway
main	shake	stray
snail	lake	may
pail	cake	stay
jail	place	
tail	lace	
sail	bare	
fail	share	
	care	
	flare	

GA The Racetrack Game   7–9

Players move around a track and match words in their hand with words on the track. This is a great way to examine long vowel patterns. A race track template can be found at the end of Chapter Six, and a sample gameboard appears in Figure 7–6.*

Procedures

This game, for 2 to 4 players, is played on an oval track divided into 20 to 30 spaces. Different words are written into each space that follow particular patterns. For example, *night, light, tie, pie, kite, like, my, fly, wish, fist, sit,* and *dig* could be used on a game designed to practice patterns for long and short i. A collection of 40 to 50 cards is prepared with words that share the same patterns. A number spinner or a die are used to move around the track.

1. Shuffle the word cards and deal six to each player. Turn the rest face down to become the deck.
2. Playing pieces are placed anywhere on the board and moved according to the number spinner or die.
3. When a player lands on a space, she reads the word and then looks for words in her hand that have the same pattern. For example, a player who lands on *boil* may pull *coil* and *foil* from her hand to put in the winning pile.
4. The cards placed in the winning pile are replaced by drawing the same number from the deck before play passes to the next player.

FIGURE 7–6 Racetrack Games Are Popular, Easy to Make, and Play

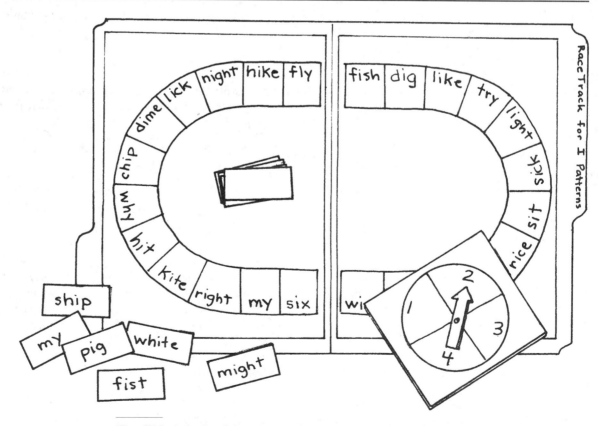

*Darrell Morris developed this game and has written extensively on word sort games (Morris, 1982; 1992).

5. If a player has no match for the pattern, she must draw a card anyway.
6. The game is over when there are no more cards to play. The winner is the player with the most word cards in her winning pile.

The Classic Card Game 7–10

Beginning Within Word Pattern; Long Vowels

This card game is a favorite for 2 to 5 players; 3 is optimal. Use the word sorts at the end of this chapter as well as words from students' word banks. This game is a McGuffey classic that has been recorded by Cindy Aldrete-Frazer. The many variations show how versatile this game is.

Procedures

1. Seven cards are dealt to each player. For most players, it is difficult to hold the cards in one hand as a fan. Players usually agree to lay them out and not to look at each other's words.
2. Roll the dice to see who goes first.
3. The first player places a card down, reads the word, and designates the vowel pattern to be followed, e.g., "rain"– "ai".
4. The next player places a card down with the "ai" pattern and reads it out loud.
5. The play continues going around the circle until all of the players are out of "ai" pattern word cards.
6. Players pass if they do not have a word card to match the category.
7. Players forfeit a turn if they do not read their contribution correctly.
8. The player who last played the pattern card gets to begin the new round. This player chooses a different card from his or her hand, with the new vowel pattern to be followed.
9. The object of the game is to be the first player to play all your cards.

Variations

1. Students who do not have a match can be forced to draw a card from the remaining cards until a match is found.
2. Wild cards can be added so players can change categories in mid-stream.
3. Write words arranged by pattern in the word study notebooks.
4. The rules of the game can be expanded to include parts of speech (i.e. nouns, adjectives, verbs).
5. Use words from the previous week's spelling words.

Word Sort™ 7–11

Beginning Within Word Pattern; Long Vowels

There is a computer sort that can be used for accuracy and fluency throughout the Within Word Pattern stage. It is available from:

Henderson Educational Software
1215 Inglecress Lane
Charlottesville, VA 22901

When using this software, students have their own word study sorts on a disk. Students can play for 15 minutes, stop, and then come back to the next sort the next day.

A management system is on the teacher's guide and disk. Analyses of students' sorts and printouts of class profiles are possible. Students enjoy this independent activity.

GA | Letter Spin

7–12

Beginning Within
Word Pattern;
Long Vowels

Players spin for a feature and remove pictures or words from their game boards that match the feature. For pictures, the features are sounds (long o, short o, long i) and for words, the features are patterns (o, oa, o-e, ow).*

Materials

1. A spinner divided into 3 to 6 sections and labeled with the pattern to be practiced.
2. A collection of picture or word cards.
3. Playing boards are divided like a tic-tac-toe board. 9" x 9" is a good size for 3" x 3" pictures (see Figure 7–7).

Procedures

1. Players draw cards and turn them face up on their boards or in a three by three array if students do not have playing boards.

FIGURE 7–7 Letter Spin Game: Finding Words to Match the Spinner

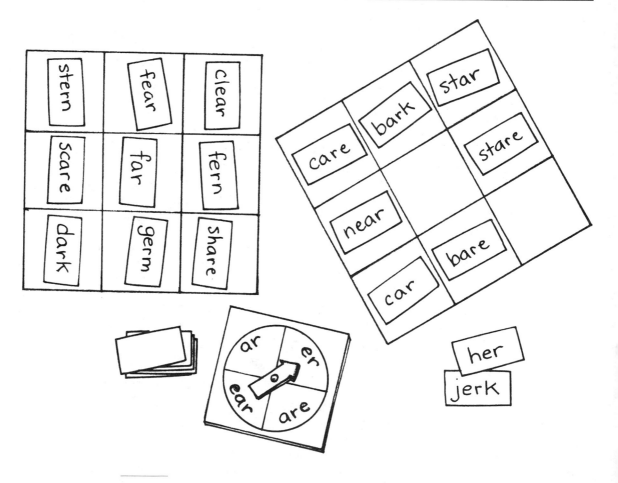

*Francine Johnston suggested this game.

2. The first player spins and removes all those picture or word cards that fit the sound indicated by the spinner. The cards go into the player's "point pile." That same player draws enough cards from the pile to replace the gaps in the playing board before play moves to the next player.
3. Play continues until a player has removed all cards and there are no more to be drawn as replacements. The winner is the player who has the most cards in her point pile.

Variations

1. This is a Tic-Tac-Toe version: Players prepare boards as described above but when they spin they can turn face down one picture that has that feature. The winner is the one who turns down three in a row.
2. This game can be used to study initial sounds, and blends. The spinner and the pictures change accordingly.
3. A large cube (1 inch square would do) is used like a die instead of a spinner. Use sticky dots to label the sides with the different features.

 Board Game with *Sheep in a Jeep*   **7–13**

Beginning Within
Word Pattern;
Long e

This activity uses *Sheep in a Jeep* by Nancy Shaw and illustrated by Margot Apple. This is a game for two people to examine two CVVC patterns (i.e., -ee- and -ea-).*

Procedures

1. After reading *Sheep in a Jeep,* players move to the board game and place game markers at the start position (see Figure 7–8).
2. One player spins and moves that number of spaces on the board.
3. The player reads the word on the space. A player moves back a space if the word landed on is read incorrectly.
4. Players alternate turns. The first player to the finish wins.

Variations

1. Players can move two or three times around the board.
2. Students hunt for these words or words which follow the same patterns in other texts.
3. Students spell the words.

Middle Within Word Pattern Activities

Students have made a pass through 2 or 3 long vowels and their orthographic patterns. At this point, students are comparing patterns across vowels. In addition, students examine the endings of words, and compare short and long vowel words that end in slightly different ways (e.g., tea**ch** to chur**ch**). Word study of the rest of the long vowels is pursued, and students work for fluency and automaticity in sorting the long vowels patterns and playing the board games below.

---

*Alison Dwier-Seldon developed this game.

FIGURE 7–8 Board Game for *Sheep in a Jeep*

GA Jeopardy® Game   7–14

Middle Within
Word Pattern;
Consonnant
Blends and
Digraphs

In this game, students sort for words that end in -*ch* and -*tch*;. Four or five students can play. A poster board is divided into a 5" x 5" array such as the one shown in Figure 7–9.*

Procedures

1. For added support to this game, students sort the words first.
2. One player is the moderator.
3. Roll the die to determine who goes first.
4. Game begins by the player picking a category and amount for the moderator to read, for example, "I'll take short vowels for 100."
5. Moderator reads the clue and the player must respond by phrasing a question and spelling the word:

   Moderator: "When struck it produces fire."

   Player: "What is match? m-a-t-c-h."

6. Player receives a card if the answer was correct. This player chooses another clue. (Player can only have 2 consecutive turns.) If player misses, the player to the left may answer.
7. Game continues until all the clue cards are read and won or left unanswered.
8. Players add their points, and the one with the highest amount wins.

---

*This game was contributed by Charlotte Tucker.

FIGURE 7–9 Word Jeopardy®, Game: "I'll take Long Vowels for 100."

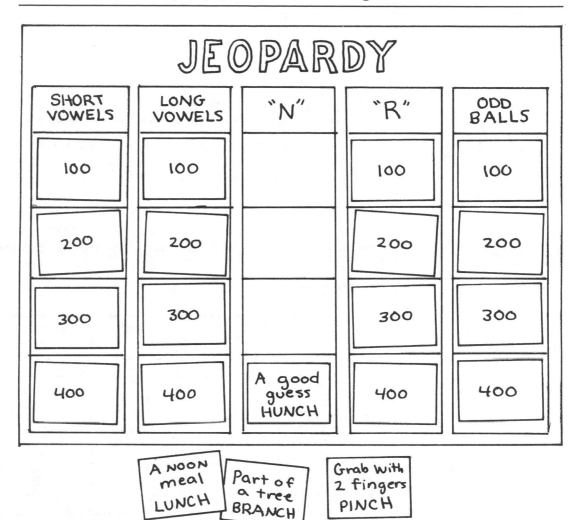

Word List

Here are some lists of words to use as clues. Students enjoy writing the clues.

"R"	"N"	Short Vowels	Long Vowels	Odd Balls
march	bench	stitch	beach	much
porch	branch	sketch	reach	such
birch	bunch	catch	teach	rich
church	crunch	patch	coach	touch
perch	munch	match	peach	watch
search	pinch	stretch	screech	which
arch	punch	clutch	roach	crouch
torch	clench	fetch		pouch
	hunch	hatch		
	lunch	match		
		pitch	pooch	
		scratch	smooch	
		snatch		
		witch		

batch
ditch
dutch
itch
latch
switch

 ## Word Study Scattergories®

7–15

Middle Within
Word Pattern;
Review of Vowel
Patterns

This is an independent activity for 2 to 4 students for review of patterns. Students make a list of words that follow a pattern (-*at* / *flat*). Students read their answers and earn a point when their word is different than the other players.*

Materials

Prepare game cards such as the one below that could be used for 5 games. There is also a blank answer provided that could be used for 3 games.

GAME CARD

ONE	TWO	THREE	FOUR	FIVE
1. at	1. et	1. ig	1. og	1. ug
2. ad	2. en	2. in	2. ot	2. ut
3. an	3. est	3. it	3. op	3. us
4. al	4. el	4. ing	4. ope	4. ute
5. ame	5. ea	5. ice	5. or	5. ew
6. ai	6. ear	6. ite	6. oo	6. ur
7. ay	7. ee	7. ile	7. oi	7. ue
8. ar	8. ie	8. igh	8. ow	8. ui
9. aw	9. ew	9. ir	9. ou	9. un
10. atch	10. er	10. y	10. oy	10. ush

BLANK ANSWER SHEET

ONE	TWO	THREE
1.	1.	1.
2.	2.	2.
3.	3.	3.
4.	4.	4.
5.	5.	5.
6.	6.	6.
7.	7.	7.
8.	8.	8.
9.	9.	9.
10.	10.	10
TOTAL		

*Brenda Reibel adapted Scattergories® by Milton Bradley Company for this fast moving word study game.

Procedures

The game is played in 3 rounds.

1. Each player has a Scattergories Game Card and an Answer Sheet like the one above.
2. The timer is set for two minutes.
3. All players quickly fill in the first column of their answer sheet using the patterns in the first column of the game card. Answers must fit the category and must use the vowel pattern given.
4. Scoring a Round: Players in turn, read their answers aloud for number 1. Players correct their own answer sheets by circling an acceptable answer that DOES NOT match any other player's answer. Continue reading answers until all 10 categories have been scored. Score 1 point for each circled answer. Record the score at the top of the column of the answer sheet.

Here is an example of one student's answers:

Pattern from the Game Card		Answer Sheet	
1.	-at	1.	flat
2.	-ad	2.	glad
3.	-an	3.	plan
4.	-al	4.	final
5.	-ame	5.	blame
6.	-ai	6.	gain
7.	-ay	7.	stay
8.	-ar	8.	farther
9.	-aw	9.	claw
10.	-atch	10.	match

5. Starting a New Round: Set the timer again; continue playing using the same category list as in the previous round. Fill in the next column with new answers.
6. Winning the Game: After 3 rounds have been played, players total the 3 scores on their answer sheets. The player with the highest score is the winner.
7. Rules for Acceptable Answers: The exact same answer CANNOT be given twice in one round: You cannot answer PUSH for -us and -ush.
8. Challenging Answers: While answers are being read, other players may challenge their acceptability. When an answer is challenged, all players vote on whether it is acceptable. Players who accept the answer give a thumbs-up sign. Players who do not accept the answer give a thumbs-down sign. Majority rules. In the case of a tie, the challenged player's vote does not count.

Variation

Create other cards to use to play word study Scattergories.

GA | Building Word Categories   7–16

Middle Within Word Pattern; Review of Vowel Patterns

Word cards are the playing cards in this matching game. Up to four students practice grouping short and long vowel words by pattern (sight, sound, meaning). Older students like this game because they use their poker terms.*

---

*Fran deMaio recorded the directions to this traditional game.

Materials

A deck of 45 cards is needed. The patterns can vary. A good starting combination is a blend of 5 cards of each short vowel (CVC) and 5 cards of each long vowel except for CVC (e.g., *Pete*).

Procedures

1. Five cards are dealt to each player. Players look in their hands for patterns (families).
2. Unwanted cards are discarded, and new cards are drawn to keep a hand of five cards. For example, *bone, phone, rat, pet, rake* could be one player's hand. This player may want to discard *rat, pet,* and *rake,* and draw three other cards to create a better hand, possibly.
3. Each player has a chance to draw up to four cards from the deck one time to create a better hand.
4. The possible combinations are a pair (*hat, rat*); two pairs (*hat, rat, bone, tone*); three of a kind (*bone, phone, tone*); four of a kind (*phone, bone, tone, cone*); three of a kind plus a pair (*bone, phone, tone, hat, rat*); or five of a kind (*phone, bone, tone, cone, drone*). (In poker this former combination is a full house, and five of a kind is like a flush.)
5. Determining winners: Five of a kind beats a three of a kind with a pair, four of a kind, three of a kind, two pairs, and a pair. Four of a kind beats everything except five of a kind. Two pairs beats three of a kind and a pair. Three of a kind beats two pair and a pair wins if it is the highest matching family.

   In case of ties, players can draw from the deck until one player comes up with a card that will break the tie.

Variations

1. Using classification folders, students can sort the words in their hands.
2. Pictures can be sorted with the words.
3. Wild cards can be included.

 A ## Guess My Category!   7–17

Middle Within
Word Pattern;
Review of Vowel
Patterns

This game is for 2 to 5 players (3 is optimal) to study long vowel patterns.

Materials

Combine long vowel words from pages 285–292. 45 word cards are needed from the vowels students have studied.

Procedures

This is similar to the Classic Card Game above, but it's a little more complex and works best with students who have had some experience playing games. In this game, players guess the first player's category.

1. Seven cards are dealt to each player and the remainder are placed face down as a draw pile. Players lay out their seven cards. Players should always have seven cards. Roll the dice to see who goes first.
2. The first player turns up a card from the draw pile in the middle and looks for a word in his or her hand to match. If the player can match the guide word, the matching word is placed underneath the guide

word. This first player does *not* declare the category. To keep the starter from changing categories, he or she can write down the reason for the match. This player becomes the judge for other players.

3. The next player places a card down underneath the two words and reads the new word aloud. What happens if the person who set up the category does not think the next player put down an acceptable card? The person who established the category is the judge and can send a card back and give that player another chance. Mistakes by the judge are discussed at the end of the game.

4. The play continues going around the circle until players stop putting words down to fit the pattern. Players can pass when they wish.

5. The player who plays the last card reads the list and then has to Declare the Category. If the last player has correctly guessed the category established by the first player, then the last player gets to keep the words. If there is a mistake, the previous player gets a chance to declare the category.

6. Players are dealt enough cards to get them back to seven, and then the next player gets a chance to turn up a card from the pile and gets to make up a category.

7. The player with the most cards wins.

Variations

1. Add WILD cards to the pile. Wild cards can be used to change categories in mid-stream. The person who establishes a new category must guess the original category correctly. This player becomes the new judge.

2. The rules of the game can be expanded to include semantic and grammatical categories.

Late Within Word Pattern

Word study during this last third of the Within Word Pattern stage focuses on consolidating students' knowledge of long vowel patterns. Students work with four columns in their sorts, and they look at patterns across vowels. Students examine R-influenced vowels in depth, and they study some of the exceptional patterns. This section also includes semantic sorts. These activities focus on meaning connections and homophones, and gets students ready for the word study in the next chapter.

A ## Word Study UNO® 7–18

Late Within Word Pattern; Review of Vowel Patterns

This game uses word cards, and students group patterns together. This game is for 2 to 4 players.*

Materials

Make 6 **WILD** cards, 6 **SKIP** cards, 6 **DRAW 2** cards, and 27 word cards. Use the word lists at the end of this chapter. A list used in the example is provided below. If students were studying word families across vowels, then the following skip cars could be made:

---

*Rita Loyacono developed this word study version of the UNO® game.

Skip	-ane	Draw 2	-ane
Skip	-ale	Draw 2	-ale
Skip	-end	Draw 2	-end
Skip	-and	Draw 2	-and
Skip	-ent	Draw 2	-ent

Procedures

1. Model this game in small group. Cards are shuffled and dealer deals five cards to each player. The remaining cards are placed face down and the top card is turned face up.

2. Players alternate and *discard a card that changes only one letter at a time,* or by playing one of the special cards (SKIP, DRAW 2, WILD).

   Here is a good example: If the beginning card was *sent,* the player could discard *send, lent, bent,* or *rent.* If the player did not have one of those cards, or chose not to use one of those, she could discard "SKIP -ent" or "DRAW 2 -ent". The "SKIP -ent" card allows the player to play a second card. The "DRAW 2 -ent" card forces the other player to pick two cards from the pile until he has two -ent words, and he may not discard. The player who discarded the DRAW 2 card may then take another turn (if only two are playing).

3. SKIP, DRAW 2, and WILD cards may be used successively to move from one pattern to another. If the player cannot discard from his hand, he must draw from the pile. Unless it is a DRAW 2 situation, he may discard if the card drawn follows the pattern.

4. As players alternate turns, they are attempting to discard all their cards. When a player has only one card remaining, she must say, "UNO." If she forgets, and the other player sees that the opponent is down to one card, she calls the fact to her opponent's attention and the opponent must then draw another card.

5. The first player to "go out" wins the game.

Word List

Here is a possible list:

hind	hint	hunt	runt	bunt		
rent	bent	lent	sent			
bend	lend	send	band	land	sand	
hang	rang	bang	sang	hung	rung	ring
lane	sane	bale	sale			

A Open Sort of Long Vowels   7–19

This open sort is used to assess students' knowledge of the long i vowel patterns.

Ask students to sort words into 4 or 5 columns. The student can have a Miscellaneous column. Students who approximate the following arrangement have a good understanding of the various long i orthographic patterns:

CVV	-IGHT	CVCe	CVVC	CVCC
tie	night	dime	(giant)	find
lie	light	bride	(height)	mind
pie	right	time	(weight)	hind
buy	sight	line	(riot)	bind
	bright	mine		kind

rhyme	sign
	(signal)
	(signature)

Extensions

1. The words in parentheses are interesting as extensions.
2. Take the words from the Odd Ball column, and sort these words into smaller groups and add to the columns.

dirt	find	final	work
third	mind	mine	(fork)
bird	kind		(stork)
skirt			

3. Enter these sorts into sections of the word study notebooks.

A | Homophone Win, Lose, or Draw 7–20

Late Within Word Pattern; Homophones

Four or more students work in teams to draw and guess each others' drawings.*

Procedures

1. Students divide the group into two equal teams. Choose a pair of homophones (*sail/sale*).
2. One player from each team is selected as the artist for that particular homophone. The artist must draw a picture representing the given homophone which will elicit the homophone itself, the spelling *and* the meaning.
3. A point is awarded to the team that provides the correct information first. Play proceeds in the same fashion.

Word List

Here is a word list; also see the word lists at the end of this chapter.

sail / sale
hare / hair
pair / pear

Variation

Homophone hang-man may be substituted.

A | Sorting R-influenced Vowels 7–21

Late Within Word Pattern; R-influenced Vowels

The *r* has a distinct influence on the pronunciation of words. The words are not hard to read, but the sounds often differ from similar words, for example, *bar* and *bat*. In the word lists to follow, there are many sorts for r-influenced words.**

Procedures

1. Brainstorm r-influenced words. The best way to enter into the influence of "r" is to brainstorm or hunt for any and all words containing a single vowel followed by an "r" pattern. The only rule is that there can be no "e" at the end. Any word that your students can recognize is fair game. A student-generated word list might look like this:

---

*Barry Mahanes based this on the television show.
**Neva Viise contributed this sort from her work with adults.

FIGURE 7–10 An R-influenced Word Sort

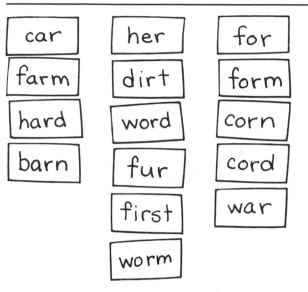

farm, nerd, firm, form, fur, far, perm, fir, for,
hard, herd, first, cord, word, war, hurt, turn,
dart, term, bird, dirt, world, born, curd

2. Start with a sound sort. Choose three words from the brainstorming which are distinguishable by sound. In the brainstorming used in this example, *far, perm,* and *for* represent three distinct sounds and could be used as the head of three columns. Use these words as "key" words for setting up categories for sorting.

3. Call out the other words, one at a time, and have students judge which category to place them in using sound as the sole criterion. After the students have made the decision as to which category, give one of them the word card to place in the proper column (see Figure 7–10). They will notice that most words which sound like *car* are consistently spelled only with the *ar* pattern.

far	perm	for
farm	nerd	born
car	her	form
hard	herd	world
dart	term	word
card	first	
barn	dirt	
bar	bird	
harm	turn	war
tart	burn	warm
part	curd	

 Terse Verse Rhyme 7–22

Late Within Word
Pattern; Vowel
Rhymes

In small groups, students think of rhyming pairs that describe an object, for example, "pink/sink", "bear/lair", "sled/bed".*

———

*Carolyn Melchiorre developed this extension.

FIGURE 7–11 Terse Verse: Create a Clever Rhyme

Procedures

Read *One Sun* to the group. Discuss the structure of the language and the book. Students will see how the author uses photographs to illustrate the "terse verse."

With the students, create a "terse verse." First, think of an object (i.e., sink, bear, bed). Then ask the group to think of rhyming words that correspond with the object (see Figure 7–11). Accept all responses and write them on a chart. Continue this process with the group until they are confident with the idea.

Students can create their own "terse verse" to challenge the group. They might opt to omit one word in the sequence:

There's a _____ in the pail. (whale)

The _____ is sad. (Dad)

Rhyming pairs collected from "terse verse" may be sorted by sound and pattern and may serve as the basis for other games.

Variation

1. Challenge students to draw a picture card and exchange with a friend who must figure out the terse verse.
2. For a real challenge, students use multisyllabic words.

 Contrasting Two Short Vowel Patterns   7–23

Late Within Word Pattern; Unusual Vowel Contrasts

Students examine short vowels that use a long vowel pattern (i.e., *head* and *bread*).*

Procedures

1. Show students the two patterns and place an example of each on the table, for example, *web* and *head*.

---

*Charlotte Jacobs developed this sorting game.

2. Give each student a card and ask them to place their cards underneath the correct column:
"Put your card under the correct word. Place your word card face down."
3. Ask a student to turn the cards of one column over, and have the group read the words as they appear.
4. Play again after shuffling cards.

Variations

1. Contrast this vowel pattern with the long vowel pattern (e.g., *bread* to *bead*). A third column, the long vowel CVVC pattern can be added. Use these words in this variation: bead, seat, freak, leak, meat, preach, steal, teach.
2. Can be played with one student or in a center with a pair.
3. Students can write words where they think they belong in their notebooks.

Word List

pet, fled, vet, sled, wren,
sped, shed, stem, red, web,
meant, breast, death, thread, head,
dead, bread, read, lead, spread

 ## Green Light! Red Light! A Sorting Game 7–24

Late Within Word Pattern; Review Vowel Patterns

This is a speed game for 2 or more players to review long vowel patterns.*

Materials

Word cards vary with the students' word studies. There must be at least 10 words for each player and 10 word cards for the draw pile.

Procedures

The object of the game is to be the first player to say "Red Light," write words on the chalkboard, and to score more points than other players. Players need to be attentive to challenge incorrect word sorting choices by others.

1. The leader writes the column pattern headings on the chalkboard. This is an example for long a word study:

Long a CVCe   Short a CVC   Long a CVVC   Short a CVCC

2. Players face the chalkboard, and each player is dealt 7 cards. The remainder are placed in the draw pile.
3. The leader writes numbers 1 through 5 at random under the word sort headings and says, "Green Light" as a signal for players to pick up their cards and search for words to match the numbered categories. For example, a leader may have numbered the patterns this way:

---

*Mary Ellen McGraw developed this game. She notes that this is more competitive than most games, and that it is enjoyed by many upper elementary and secondary students at this stage of development. Be sure that students are close in terms of development. She also noted that students liked to carry the game over from one day to another and wait a few days to declare a winner.

Long a CVCe	Short a CVC	Long a CVVC	Short a CVCC
2	5	1	3
		4	

4. The first player to find all 5 examples says, "Red Light." Searching halts. Other players turn their cards face down as this player goes to the board and writes the words beside the numbers. After writing all five words, the player reads aloud each heading as well as the words.

   The player then goes to the score section on the chalkboard and writes her name and score (5). The player discards the five cards and draws five from the draw pile. (After several rounds of play, the words in the draw and discard piles can be shuffled.)

5. Another player may challenge the word sort choices. This player goes to the board, points out any incorrect choices, and substitutes his/her words. The validity of the challenge is decided by the leader. The score is adjusted to account for corrections. For example, Jon has 5 points. Lisa correctly challenges 2 words. Lisa would have 2 points and Jon would be left with 3. The challenger must discard the used cards and draw an equal number of cards from the draw pile.

6. The leader starts another round by writing 1 through 5 at random under the headings. Play continues until all word cards are used or until time is called. The player with the most points is the winner.

A | Semantic Concept Sorts   7–25

Late Within Word Pattern; Semantic Sorts

This is a concept sort that focuses on the meaning of the words. This is a great game for content studies.

Procedures

1. Choose a topic. Topics can be chosen by students and can be related to content studies. Start with easy, familiar topics like sports and locations (countries, animal life, clothes, furniture, sports, modes of transportation).
2. Students brainstorm related words and write them down. Look for fluency of the brainstorming to assess success.
3. Students share their findings and see if they can come up with subcategories from their brainstorming. Categories can be circled by color or written over into columns.

Variations

1. Parts of speech can be sorted in this way (see Figure 7–12). For example, students can collect nouns, and then divide them into different types of nouns (e.g., things that move/animate vs. stationary/inanimate nouns).

cow	rock
boat	uranium
cats	plants

   When students look for differences in the concepts, they begin to debate. In just this easy example, one could argue that there is something quite active about both uranium and plants.

FIGURE 7–12 Grammatical Relations Can Be Examined in Semantic Sorts

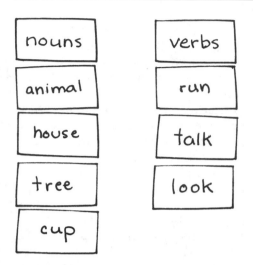

2. In an open sort, students sort a pack of pictures and develop their own categories.
3. Look in magazines, newspapers, and catalogs. Circle with a crayon words that express feelings, color words, people's names, or part of speech.

Pictures, Word Sorts, and Lists

Reminders

In the first part of this chapter, we have taken care to explain how the following materials are used in our teaching. Briefly, here are a few reminders.

1. Make copies of the pictures before you pick up scissors.
2. Students must be able to recognize the pictures and read the words easily.
3. Do not just plug students into these word sorts.

The sequence of word study we have presented is general. Based on students' development, we suggest that students study short vowels before long vowels. However, it is not clear what the order of vowels should be. In the previous chapter, it was suggested that short e not follow short a word study. We have found that the words are sometimes confused; this may be because both vowels are made towards the front of the mouth. Similarly, during the Within Word Pattern stage, it may be good to begin with long a followed by long o. The actual sequence depends upon the words students can read easily for word study. For example, if students have more sight words from short a and e than from short o, then it is better for short e to follow short a. The sequence of word study depends upon students' development and interests.

Long Vowel Pictures

The following long vowel pictures can be found in the collection of pictures for initial consonant sorts in Chapter Six.

Long a

gate	game	nail	paint	rake	vase	shave
chair	blade	plane	plate	scale	skate	train
grapes						

Long e

deer	jeep	key	leaf	seal	sheep	dream
wheel	sleeve	sleep	sweep	queen	tree	

Long i

nine	dice	smile	prize	drive	fire	tie
tire	price	cry	fly			

Long o

boat	goat	rope	hose	nose	comb	ghost
toes	float	globe	yoyo	snow		

Word Sorts and Lists of Long Vowels

There are over 80 teacher-made sorts to follow. They are designed to be made into teacher-made word sorts for students in the Within Word Pattern stage. And they are lists to use in games. The words are presented in columns to show the contrasts:

Short e	Long e
CVC	*CVVC*
<u>red</u>	<u>seat</u>

Only the underlined words are used as key cards at the top of each column. The codes in italics are for your reference.

Obviously, the cards are shuffled before they are used in open and closed sorts, and games. In closed sorts, the teacher shows students the categories they are to sort by. In open sorts, the students establish the sorts. The Odd Ball or Miscellaneous columns and words need to be added to these sorts. Here are the basic and easiest orthographic patterns for the five long vowels:

"a"	"e"	"i"	"o"	"u"
day	team	fine	go	rule
play	street	time	slow	fruit
gate	seat	light	post	fuel
race	we	my	goat	blue
mail	free	wild	gold	tube
rain	weeds	find	stone	
rail	field	sight	rope	
trade	clear	guide	coal	
freight			road	
			most	

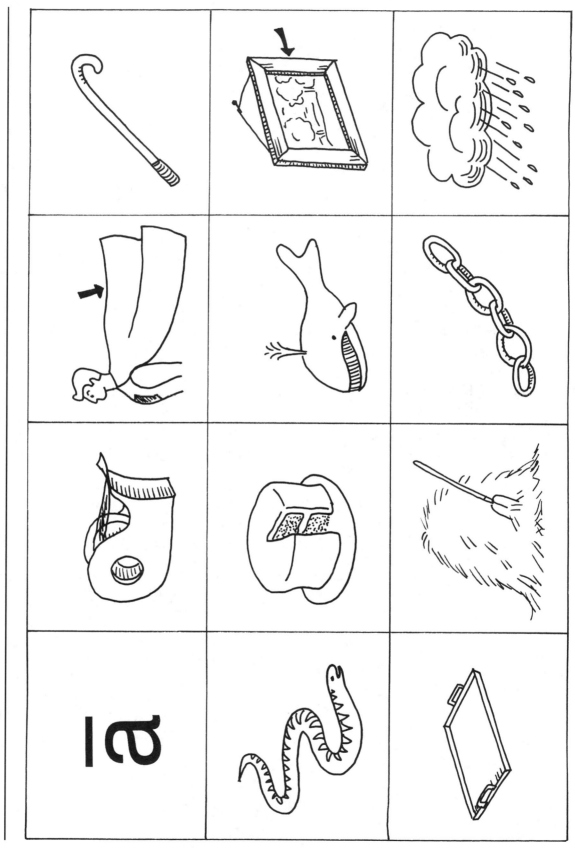

FIGURE 7–13 Long a Picture Cards

FIGURE 7-14 Long e Picture Cards

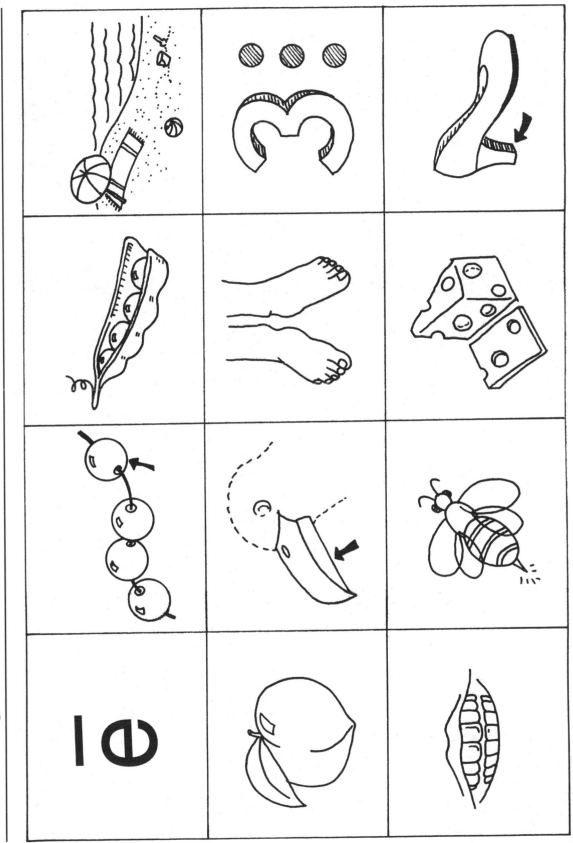

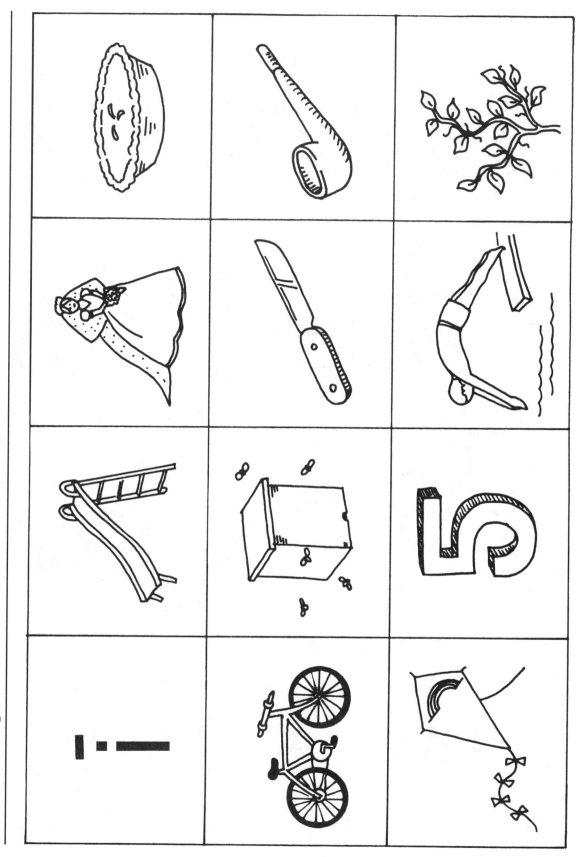

FIGURE 7-15 Long i Picture Cards

282

FIGURE 7-16 Long o Picture Cards

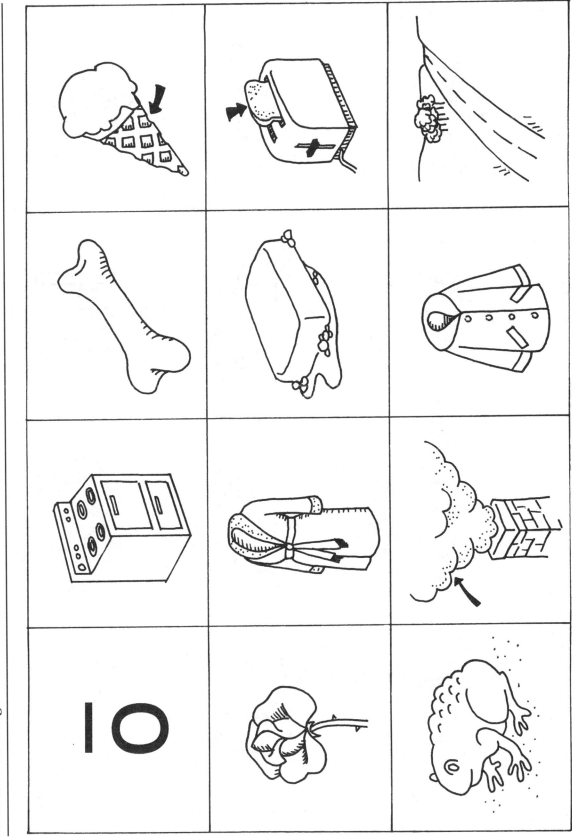

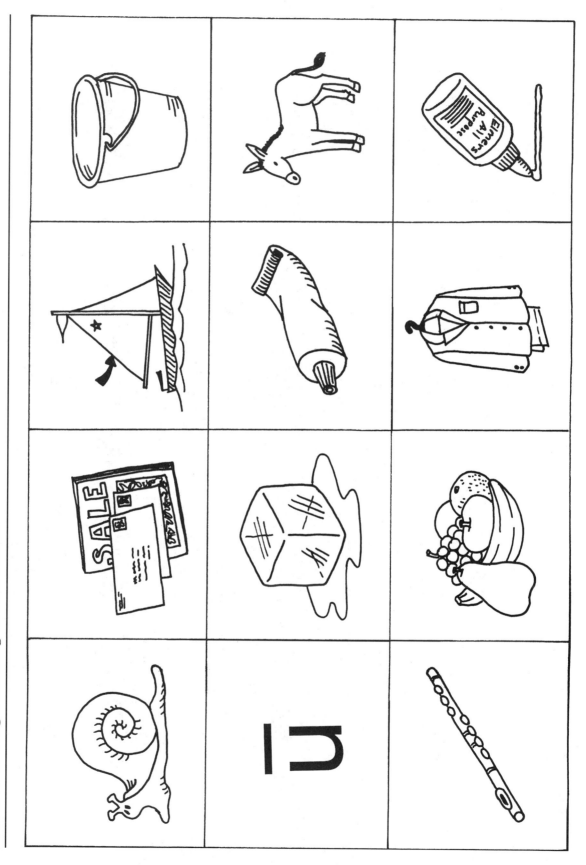

FIGURE 7–17 Long a and Long u Picture Cards

Long a Sorts

Short a/CVC/<u>bat</u>

at slam jacks wag clam strange
bag sat

Long a/CVCe/<u>plate</u>

ape pale race date paste wave
sale rate

Short a/CVC/<u>tank</u>

last has sack crab hand plant
fast wax

Long a/CVCe/<u>base</u>

base fame lame grave waste same
page slate

Long a/CVCe/<u>plane</u>

whale bathe flame crate stage
male chase plane base daze brake
tape ape

Long a/CVVC/<u>pail</u>

pain fail pail rail mail rain tail
faint

Long a/CVCe/<u>space</u>

came trace slave range babe lame
brave same plane hate sale ate

Long a/CVVC/<u>fail</u>

saint hail brain aid rail tail

Long a/CVCe/<u>plate</u>

wade safe cage bathe save waste
hate page fade pane pace wave
jade mane

Long a/CVVC/<u>bait</u>

pain mail grain hail gain snail

Short a/CVCC/<u>call</u>

talk wall chalk walk small tall
fall

Long a/CVVC/<u>rain</u>

train snail mail pain tail pail
sail

Long a/CVV/<u>may</u>

way stay play hay day say gray

Miscellaneous

have said was

Short a/CVC/<u>fan</u>

rap patch jacks lap crab ask

Long a/CVCe/<u>same</u>

pane scale face shape fade male
late mane shake

Long a/CVVC/<u>tail</u>

fail plain brain snail maid nail

Long a/CVCe/<u>cave</u>

paste base strange gaze grace
range

Long a/CVVC/<u>jail</u>

gain hail faint rain sail chain
maid praise aid

Long a/CVV/<u>day</u>

day tray pray lay slay jay

Long a/CVCe/<u>strange</u>

paste frame daze same crane

Long a/CVVC/<u>plate</u>

gain saint paint aid snail hail
faint main pain maid gain

Long a/CVV/<u>hay</u>	stray play say day ray slay
Short a/CVC/<u>jam</u>	snap dash hand fast sack wag dash
Long a/CVCe/<u>fame</u>	blame tame face mate stage rake fame
Long a/CVVC/<u>bait</u>	rain grain vain main claim brain gain
Long a/CVCe/<u>rage</u>	cave fade hate ape
Long a/CVVC/<u>rain</u>	jail rain paint faint straight mail aid
Long a/CVV/<u>pay</u>	hay stray clay way pay day ray sway
Short a/CVC/<u>strap</u>	cab has glad drag jay as
Long a/CVVC/<u>praise</u>	mail gain tail brain grain nail train claim paint gaint
Long a/CVV/<u>pay</u>	slay stay day stray
Long a/CVVC/<u>brain</u>	rain pain gain drain main snail pail jail tail sail fail
Long a/CVCe/<u>grade</u>	shade came game bake shake lake cake place lace bare share care flare
Long a/CVV/<u>tray</u>	gray spray clay sway stray may stay
Short a/CVC/<u>ram</u>	fad bat ask ax
Long a/CVCe/<u>grape</u>	bake clay pane trace flake state jade slave safe cage range scale
Long a/CVVC/<u>jail</u>	vain chain
Long a/CVV/<u>may</u>	way lay ray day
Short a/CVC/<u>Jack</u>	has rat snap pal map pad wag
Long a/CeiC/<u>weigh</u>	veil weight freight vein eight
Long a/CVCe/<u>scale</u>	daze stage crate flame gape whale bathe sale base male chase plane space brake tape cape grave same ate
Long a/CVVC/<u>jail</u>	rain mail nail fail pail saint rail pain
Long a/CVV/<u>ray</u>	tray hay lay stray day may pray
Long a/CVV/<u>hey</u>	prey grey they whey
Long a/CeiC/<u>weigh</u>	vein freight veil eight
Long a/CVVC/<u>great</u>	steak break

Long e Sorts

Short e/CVC/<u>**red**</u>	bet fell set net fed bled send pen led fed
Long e/CVVC/<u>**seat**</u>	beat real team lean reach peal deal sea real steal steam peal clean
Short e/CVC/<u>**men**</u>	bent stem red pet clench fled cent peel wed well
Long e/CVVC/<u>**peek**</u>	screen peep teeth greet yes peek sheel deep sheet speed week
Long e/CVVC/<u>**meal**</u>	peat heap cheap deal team dream bean defeat seat
Long e/CVVC/<u>**feet**</u>	kneel glee sweet creep squeeze free feel needle street reed keeper beet
Short e/CVC/<u>**pet**</u>	fence send hem bless bell crept length
Long e/CVVC/<u>**deed**</u>	speech steel sheet sweet screen deed seed speed fetch keeper preen squeal tea
Long e/CV/<u>**me**</u>	we be he she
Short e/CVC/<u>**bell**</u>	wren lens fed bell jet tent pet nest bend tense
Long e/CVVC/<u>**creek**</u>	greet seed feet three seek need peel
Long e/CV/<u>**we**</u>	me be she
Short e/CVC/<u>**west**</u>	yet slept left bless sketch
Long e/CVVC/<u>**lean**</u>	leak knead defeat bead mean lean sneaker wheat east please pea eat
Long e/CV/<u>**he**</u>	he she be me we
Short e/CVC/<u>**red**</u>	wren lest guest pet kept pled
Long e/CVVC/<u>**lean**</u>	please leash plead
Long e/CVVC/<u>**reef**</u>	reef feel preen feed bleed three screen teeth
Long e/CV/<u>**be**</u>	he we me keeper
Short e/CVC/<u>**mess**</u>	less pest bent tell shell test help scent peck wren stretch length
Short e/CVVC/<u>**dead**</u>	thread bread spread deaf tread breath head death
Short e/CVC/<u>**mess**</u>	crest best less rest fell well kept

Short e/CVVC/<u>head</u>	dead breath deaf ahead tread dread death
Long e/CVVC/<u>street</u>	neat sneaker meal treat heap mean feature bleed speak queen sheet fleet peat
Short e/CVVC/<u>speck</u>	wept led sent bell fell crest when test neck stretch
Long e/CV/<u>me</u>	we she me be
Long e/CVVC/<u>beet</u>	green geese teeth creep street seed need
Long e/CVVC/<u>field</u>	cheif yield thief grief niece
Short e/CVVC/<u>thread</u>	bread death head
Long e/CVVC/<u>clean</u>	squeal reach squeak wheat stream leak cream
Long e/CVVC/<u>need</u>	seed sneeze needle deed green steep feet sleeve beet street teeth
Short e/CVC/<u>set</u>	yes tense tell vest
Short e/CVVC/<u>bread</u>	tread spread deaf breath
Long e/CVVC/<u>stream</u>	seat heap meat seal treat feature tease sneak
Long e/CVVC/<u>deep</u>	peep teeth fleet free

Long i Sorts

Short i/CVC/<u>hip</u>	bit risk thrill spit twin string smith lip
Long i/CVCe/<u>ride</u>	hike slice life nice spine ripe price write
Short i/CVC/<u>this</u>	fish cling brisk drip smith bin fifth rich shrimp drink
Long i/CVCe/<u>pile</u>	spite stride quite prime write bike slice rise tire wire
Short i/CVC/<u>big</u>	big pin chin sit dig this did trip with stick kick
R-influenced/CVCr/<u>far</u>	bird third first dirt
Long i/CVCe/<u>dime</u>	bite while drive five white dime fine hide
Long i/-igh/<u>light</u>	right night wild
Short i/CVC/<u>pig</u>	swift kick wig fist mitt pin fifth knit swim trim drink
Long i/CV/<u>fly</u>	apply try by fry fly reply nearby cypress skyline cycle

Short i/CVC/<u>**fin**</u>	slit crib dish sink
Long i/CVCe/<u>**side**</u>	tribe glide spite prime wipe while like nice fire stride fire
Long i/CV/<u>**try**</u>	fly nearby cycle skyscraper skyline
Short i/CVC/<u>**rich**</u>	miss spit win wrist fit wish trick drip dish witch fig if
Long i/-igh/<u>**sight**</u>	night blight bright fright right fight glight might
Short i/CVC/<u>**lift**</u>	gift wrist drift sift
Short i/CuiCC/<u>**quill**</u>	built quilt build
Long i/CVCC/<u>**child**</u>	wild mild
Long i/-igh/<u>**might**</u>	knight tight sight light blight slight
Short i/CVC/<u>**bill**</u>	drill jill gill till spill mill
Short i/CuiCC/<u>**built**</u>	build guilt
Long i/CVCC/<u>**wild**</u>	mild child
Long i/CVV/<u>**fried**</u>	dried lie lied died cried tie
Short i/CVC/<u>**mix**</u>	drill gift sting lid thick sink
Short i/CuiCC/<u>**built**</u>	build quill quilt guilt
Long i/CVV/<u>**die**</u>	pie tie tried lied
Long i/CVCC/<u>**mind**</u>	bind pint child blind
Long i/-ight/<u>**might**</u>	flight fright sight bright
Short i/CVC/<u>**fig**</u>	this his quick sixth fig shrimp its
Long i/CVCe/<u>**life**</u>	wire five rise crime hive lice drive rice pride price life tire
Long i/-igh/<u>**sight**</u>	tight night fight bright
Long i/CV/<u>**by**</u>	try skyline spy sky supply skyscraper cypress
Long i/CVCe/<u>**tribe**</u>	vine crime pride kite dive mine mice
Long i/-ight/<u>**might**</u>	light flight night bright fright blight
Short i/CVC/<u>**lift**</u>	stick bit think
Long i/CVCe/<u>**smile**</u>	five vine wide nice stride pride smile strike
Long i/-igh/<u>**fright**</u>	might
Long i/CV/<u>**my**</u>	fry by apply spy supply dry skyline

Short i/CVC/<u>rib</u>	pit crisp pig lip list chin hitch string clip split hiss
Long i/CVCC/<u>mind</u>	kind wild find child mild blind bind
<u>**OddBall**</u>	bridge hinge
Long i/CVCe/<u>mice</u>	mice file dive tribe twice spite hike size fife mine tide wife dime tire ice
Long i/CVCC/<u>kind</u>	find mild grind pint mind child
Long i/CVCe/<u>nine</u>	spine line hike spite hire hide pine life ride tribe drive pipe wise
Long i/-igh/<u>bright</u>	night knight might
Long i/CVCC/<u>wild</u>	pint kind mind bind mild
Short i/CVC/<u>bin</u>	ping dig chip kick in
Long i/CVCe/<u>vine</u>	time fife shine write vine wife rice fire
Long i/-igh/<u>might</u>	knight flight might blight
Long i/CVCC/<u>bind</u>	blind grind hind pint wild

Long o Sorts

Short o/CVC/<u>dot</u>	hot box lock fond shot doll Bob crop
Long o/CVCe/<u>bone</u>	home slope note vote hose clove stroke smoke
Short o/CVC/<u>lot</u>	jog knock sock box hot shop hop top mop lot fox
Long o/CVCe/<u>slope</u>	hole stroke rose froze grope chose slope bone globe drove note
Short o/CVC/<u>not</u>	stomp chop stock throb hop shock prop shop from on ox off
Long o/CVCe/<u>pose</u>	froze home rode throne rove drove broke cove pose
Short o/CVC/<u>box</u>	job dot rock
Long o/CV/<u>go</u>	so no
Short o/CVC/<u>mop</u>	dot block knob notch mop top shot on pot ox
Long o/CVCC/<u>goal</u>	boat coast coal goal float soap road coach moan toast cloak loaves

Short o/CVC/<u>spot</u>	lock Bob box pop plot got notch bronze
Long o/-ow/<u>stow</u>	tow mow crow know blow flow row throw
Short o/CVC/<u>spot</u>	lock top mop rock flock gosh knob fox fond
Long o/-ow CVCC/<u>stow and folk</u>	crow mold bold know grow slow ghost throw bolt
Short o/CVC/<u>hot</u>	drop shock mop plot hop bomb block Tom
Long o/-ow/<u>stow</u>	snow tow growth throw grow slow flow stow
Short o/CVCe/<u>chose</u>	note stroke froze vote quote broke smoke wove
Long o/CVVC/<u>loaf</u>	coast bloat moan loaf load coal foam cloak
Short o/CVCC/<u>lock</u>	shock rock clock fond sock gosh doll
Long o/CVCC/<u>jolt</u>	fold colt host scold post gold bolt
Long o/CVCe/<u>broke</u>	bone clove broke home those drove phone
Long o/CVV/<u>hoe</u>	toe Joe woe doe

Long u Sorts

Short u/CVC/<u>bun</u>	club fuss hosh punch judge dump trust pup
Long u/CVV/<u>Sue</u>	blue glue due true
Short u/CVC/<u>dusk</u>	jump mutt dusk sum crust trust bump nudge
Long u/CVVe/<u>fume</u>	June cute lute cube tube crude prune dude
Long u Patterns:	
CVV/<u>blue</u>	glue clue blue true
CVV/<u>flew</u>	chew brew screw slew stew
CVCe/<u>cube</u>	huge June prune dune flute chute
CVVC/<u>fruit</u>	bruise juice suit cruise
Short u/CVC/<u>such</u>	sum cub lug plumb junk
Long u/CVCe/<u>tube</u>	fume dide prude rude lute
Long u/CVV/<u>due</u>	Sue blue glue

Long u/CVV/<u>knew</u>	new slew grew drew screw
Short u/CVC/<u>hug</u>	jump cut munch bus stump just drum spun
Long u/CVVC/<u>cruise</u>	fruit suit juice bruise
Short i/CuiCC/<u>guilt</u>	built quilt build quill
Short u/CVC/<u>bug</u>	slug rug gum sun strung clump plum
Long u/CVCe/<u>fume</u>	prune cube tune huge June cute duke
Long u/CVV/<u>due</u>	blue clue Sue true

Less common Vowels

Long o/CVV/<u>toe</u>	foe hoe woe Joe
Long o/CVV/<u>blow</u>	tow mow growth crow
Long u/CVV/<u>Sue</u>	glue true blue clue
Long u/CVV/<u>blew</u>	stew chew grew drew
Short u/CVC/<u>lung</u>	chunk pup mush pluck rust shrub crush fuss
ōō/CVCe/<u>dune</u>	huge lute tune rude duke dune prune
ōō/CVV/<u>few</u>	dew cluew flew drew new stew grew
ōō/CVV/<u>glue</u>	true due blue clue
ōō/CVVC/<u>suit</u>	juice cruise fruit bruise
ōō/CVCe/<u>tune</u>	plume June
ōō/CVV/<u>few</u>	new few blew grew slew crew
ōō/CVV/<u>glue</u>	blue true clue due
o Spellings	
ōō/CooC/<u>food</u>	cool soon noon too
Odd Balls/to	do two who
ōō/CouCC/<u>would</u>	should could
CooC/<u>good</u>	look book foot wood
o Spellings	
ōō/CooC/<u>boot</u>	roof tool fool broom school booth
Odd Balls	whose truth youth you through soup
oo/CooC/<u>brook</u>	look took stood wood hook

Diphthongs io & ou

CVV/<u>toy and coin</u>	Roy boy joy foil miose point boil spoil voice
CVV/<u>clown</u>	town gown down howl prowl crowd vowel frown
CVV/<u>sound</u>	mouth doubt bounce mount scout loud couch round

Homophones

blue, blew	plane, plain	aid, aide
tow, toe	bare, bear	haul, hall
one, won	seem, seam	stake, steak
dye, die	hay, hey	sore, soar
days, daze	cite, sight	symbol, cymbal
eye, I	threw, through	pole, poll
been, bin	cent, scent	piece, peace
sail, sale	hair, hare	past, passed
gate, gait	knew, new	main, mane
jeans, genes	son, sun	medal, meddle
pail, pale	stair, stare	forth, fourth
red, read	pear, pare, pair	creek, creak
way, weigh	heard, herd	ant, aunt
four, flower	hour, our	flair, flare
Mary, marry, merry	rough, ruff	strait, straight
read, reed, Reid	know, not	sweet, suite
your, you're	lie, lye	mist, missed
no, know	their, there, they're	wear, where, ware
mail, male	see, sea	sore, soar
sow, sew, so	waist, waste	fir, fur
to, too, two	shoe, shoo	died, dyed
great, grate	led, lead	manor, manner
right, write	poor, pour	flee, flea
rain, reign	due, do, dew	pier, peer

R-influenced Vowel Sorts

Some of the R-influenced sorts below are included in the individual long vowels study above. A closed word sort with the columns *rat cake bar* is included in the beginning long vowel studies.

Here are the most basic r-influenced word patterns: **ar/farm; er/nerd; ir/bird; ur/burn.**

R-blends/CVC/<u>grill</u>	crush fry price bruise cream cry draw trap wrap
R-influenced/CVrC/<u>girl</u>	curl first purse burn service dark tarp worn

R-Influenced Short vowel Sort:

CVC/<u>car</u>	farm far barn hard card warm

CVC/<u>her</u>	nerd perm herd term fern firm first bird dirt fur burn hurt turn word world worm
CVC/<u>for</u>	form acorn corn cord scorn
Short a/*CVC*/<u>far</u>	tar star jar bar car scar
Long a/*CVCe*/<u>dare</u>	spare bare stare snare care square
CVr/<u>car</u>	farm lard barn dart
<u>W</u> *Influence*/<u>war</u>	warm hard card ward
"ar"/*CVC*/<u>hard</u>	charm bark farm scarf barn yarn dart start shark smart
"ar"/*CVVC*/<u>hearty</u>	heart hearth earn earl earth
"er"/*CVVC*/<u>pearl</u>	learn search heard
"ar"/*CVC*/<u>card</u>	shark car march sharp cart bark farm hard
"ar"/*CVVC*/<u>heart</u>	hearty hearth
Long a/*CVCe*/<u>dare</u>	scare rare spare flare mare stare
Long a/*CVVC*/<u>pair</u>	fair hair stair chair
"er"/*CVC*/<u>her</u>	herd nerd perm
Long e/*CVVC*/<u>hear</u>	clear beard spear near gear hear fear ear
Long e/*CVVC*/<u>steer</u>	cheer near steer
"ir"/*CVC*/<u>fir</u>	dirt flirt firm sir whir stir
Long i/*CVCe*/<u>fire</u>	spire sire mire tire wire hire dire flier plier
"er"/*CVC*/<u>her</u>	word worm would herd
"or"/*CVC*/<u>cord</u>	form born scorn cord corn acorn adorn warm
R-influenced o:	
CVC/<u>for</u>	cord short sword horn form fort short worn dorm sport corn port sort torn orb
CVVC/<u>four</u>	court course
CVCe/<u>fore</u>	core horse shore chore
CVVC/<u>hoarse</u>	boar soar
<u>W</u> *influenced* /<u>work</u>	worse worth worm world word
"er"/*CVC*/<u>hurt</u>	purr turn bureau curd lurk hurt church burst curl churn
Long u/*CVCe*/<u>cure</u>	pure lure curse purse sure

R-influenced in 1st or 2nd Syllable

cirlce	insert
thirty	black bird
birthday	blue bird
bird house	shepherd
whirlwind	western
kerchief	preserve
permit	deserve
mermaid	northern
certain	modern
Jersey	concert
merchant	concern
perhaps	lantern
nervous	expert
perfect	eastern
servant	
service	

Two-syllable ur words

during	disturb
purpose	surround
hurtle	surprise
purple	purchase
burrow	burro
Thursday	turkey
gurgle	hurrah
turnip	surface

Blank word study sheets

Use the blank word study sheet, in Figure 6–62, for small group word study. Students also use them to create their own sorts. Two word study sheets that we created for students in the Within Word Pattern stage appear in Figures 7–18 and 7–19.

FIGURE 7–18 Long a Sort for Middle Within Word Pattern

CVVC/Long a	CVV/Long a	CVC/Short a, l-influenced	Miscellaneous Words
rain	may	call	sail
pain	tail	pail	hay
train	have	play	say
stay	way	gray	wall
day	mail	talk	small
walk	tall	chalk	was
fall	snail	said	

FIGURE 7-19 Long i Sort for Middle Within Word Pattern

CVC/Short i	CVCe/Long i	C-ight/-ight pattern	CVC/R-influenced
big	dime	light	fir
sit	dig	this	did
trip	with	stick	kick
bite	while	drive	white
five	chin	hide	fine
bird	third	first	dirt
pin	night	right	wild

Word Study for Intermediate and Specialized Readers and Writers in the Syllable Juncture and Derivational Constancy Stages

Beginning in second and third grade, for some students, and in fourth grade for most, cognitive and language potential allows children to make new and richer connections among the words they know and the words they will learn. As we teach our students at these levels, *we* often find the whole enterprise of learning about words to be fascinating—as well as never-ending. As we first noted in Chapter 2, this awareness sustains *our* interest and delight in words and in what our students will be learning about words.

> Most students do not discover the powerful relationships between spelling and vocabulary on their own.

Most students in the intermediate grades need to be shown how to examine the words they are learning in ways that will help them read, write, and spell much more effectively. On their own, most students do not see the patterns of spelling and meaning that link thousands of words within meaning "families," and they do not realize how productive the relationship between spelling and vocabulary can be.

At the intermediate and middle grade levels, word study should be fun, but it should also be systematic, and it should be related effectively to the reading and writing that students are doing. It should also come to emphasize how the structure or spelling of words is a direct clue to learning and remembering the meaning of words. The intermediate and middle grades are a critical time for consolidating knowledge about the spelling of words with knowledge about how this spelling represents meaning.

In this chapter we will be exploring how we can establish a firm foundation in spelling at the Syllable Juncture and Derivational Constancy levels as we facilitate students' move into understanding the role of *structure* and *meaning* in the spelling system.

Literacy Development and Instruction

Reading and Writing

The intermediate stage is a time of expanding reading interests and fine-tuning of reading strategies (see Figure 8–1). With respect to words and their structure, there is still considerable fine-tuning that will be necessary.

FIGURE 8–1 Synchrony Among Reading, Writing, and Spelling Development

Stage IV: Syllable Juncture	Stage V: Derivational Constancy

Reading

1. Intermediate ————————➤ Specialized
   Reads fluently, with expression
   Prefers silent reading
   Acquires a variety of reading styles and experiences
   Explores widely in different genre
   (Ages 10 and Up)

Writing

2. Intermediate ————————➤ Specialized
   Fluent writing
   Building expression and voice
   Exploring widely different styles and genre
   Writing reveals personal problem solving and personal reflection

Orthographic Knowledge and Spelling —————————————————➤

Syllable Juncture	Derivational Constancy
cattel, cattle	cattle
sellar, cellar	cellar
plesor, plesure	pleasure
comsion, commoshun	comotion, commotion
reversbul	reversable, reversible

In previous developmental stages of word knowledge, the challenges posed by what the children are reading stem more from children's level of word knowledge than from their background knowledge about the topic or genre. At the intermediate and specialized levels, the challenges they encounter in reading will come more from the *conceptual* load in whatever they are trying to read (Bear, 1991b). The nature of students' word knowledge allows them to read more fluently, exercising and expanding their increasing level of cognitive and language sophistication.

Students will be reading, writing, and thinking about polysyllabic words for quite some time before they have developed into intermediate readers and writers whose word knowledge is characterized by what we have termed Syllable Juncture. Because the knowledge of within-word pattern has become so automatic, reading and writing are much more fluent. With respect to orthographic knowledge, the foundation has been firmly laid at the Within Word Pattern stage for examining these patterns as they occur within polysyllabic words. The examination of polysyllabic words and attending to the spelling of each syllable through spelling builds a more efficient word identification routine for reading because it leads to a more developed knowledge of word structure. The ability to perceive syllables rapidly within polysyllabic words will contribute to reading efficiency, and the ability to understand the conventions that determine what happens at the juncture, or coming together, of syllables will facilitate spelling efficiency.

The type of word knowledge that underlies mature reading and writing includes, of course, an ever-expanding conceptual foundation and the addition of words that represent this foundation. In particular, mature readers have available at some level an appreciation for the role of the classical legacy in English vocabulary—those word elements that reflect their Greek and Latin

Exploration of polysyllabic words builds *reading* efficiency as well as *spelling* efficiency.

In polysyllabic words, Syllable Juncture readers "pick up" *syllables*—Derivational Constancy readers "pick up" *morphemes*.

origins in their spelling. Notably, these word elements are the important morphemes out of which thousands of words are constructed. In most instances, these words are derived from a single base or root morpheme through the addition of *affixes*—prefixes and suffixes. Readers at this level have constructed another layer of information about words that allows them to perceive polysyllabic words at a fairly sophisticated level as they read. Whereas the Intermediate reader (Syllable Juncture) picks up *syllables* in such words, the Mature reader (Derivational Constancy) picks up *morphemes* (Taft, 1991; Templeton, 1992). For example, an Intermediate reader attempting to read the word *morphology* would most likely analyze it syllable by syllable, picking up the letter sequences *mor - pho - lo - gy*. The Mature reader would most likely pick up the letter sequences *morph - ology,* which cross syllable boundaries.

Literacy Learning and Instruction

Word study at the Intermediate and Specialized levels should demonstrate to students how their word knowledge can be applied to advance their spelling knowledge, their vocabulary, and their strategies for figuring out unknown words. At the intermediate and middle grades, then, the following principles should guide our instruction:

✦ Students should be actively involved in the exploration of words; if they are, then they are more likely to develop a positive attitude towards word learning and a curiosity about words.

✦ Students' prior knowledge should be engaged; this is especially important if they are learning the specialized vocabulary in different disciplines or content areas.

✦ Students should have many exposures to words in meaningful contexts, both in and out of connected text.

✦ A sequence of structural elements—syllables and morphemes—should be followed, and the ways in which these elements combine should be taught.

Applying Word Knowledge in Context

Because spelling and vocabulary knowledge underlie the efficient application of word analysis in reading, let's look specifically at the strategy for approaching new words in reading.

When an unknown word is important to the overall meaning of what students are reading, we encourage students to try the following steps:

Contextual clues and word knowledge work *together* in the identification of unknown words.

1. Try *context* first to see if you can get a sense of the word.
2. However, you will probably need to examine the word for meaningful parts—base, root, prefixes, or suffixes:
   a. If there is a prefix, take it off first.
   b. If there is a suffix, take it off second.
   c. Look at the base or root to see if you know it or if you can think of a related word (a word that has the same base or root).
   d. Reassemble the word, thinking about the meaning contributed by the base or root, the suffix, and then the prefix—this should give you a more specific idea of what the word is.
3. Now try out this meaning in the sentence; check if it makes sense in the context.
4. If the word still does not make sense, or if you were unable to break the word down into affixes and base—*and* if it is still critical to the meaning of the overall passage—then look it up in the dictionary.

Here's how we might model this process for students, engaging in a type of "think-aloud" with the following text, displayed on a transparency:

> To say that Kim was *disillusioned* when at last she saw their vacation island would be putting it mildly. It did not look like the travel poster at all—there wasn't much of a beach, and what there was seemed to have stringy seaweed all over it. A cold wind blew without letup.

> "I don't know this word [pointing to *disillusioned*], so I'll think about the context. It sounds like Kim isn't happy—she was expecting something else, whatever it was like in the poster—but here she's found a disappointing beach with stringy seaweed all over it. And, to top it off, it's cold! So, this word [pointing again to *disillusioned*] may have something to do with being unhappy. Let's think about the word—it looks like there's a prefix, *dis-*. That leaves *illusioned,* and -*ed* is a suffix, so I'll take that off. That leaves *illusion.* I've heard of that—I think it's like when something isn't real. *Dis-* usually means "not" or the opposite of something. So, Kim was "not illusioned"? Hmm . . . let's see if that fits with the context . . . she expected something else, but it was not the way the island *really* was—kind of like her expectation was an illusion, not real.

It may seem like a lot of work when we talk through this process for students and then help guide them through it. Like the development of any other skill or complex of skills, it does take some time at first. However, it's critical that we introduce, model, and reinforce this process for students, because as they move through the grades and read more widely, they will encounter many new terms that are *not* highlighted and supported by a rich context (Just & Carpenter, 1987). This strategy will not only get them through the text but become the most effective means of developing and extending their vocabulary knowledge.

You will notice that authors of many textbooks try to provide a rich context to support new vocabulary as well as highlighting important new terms for the reader. While we need to teach students about these features, we also need to provide them with the strategy we've just discussed so that they can grow confidently and competently into independent word learners. But as we've seen, this strategy depends critically on the students' knowledge of word structure. Adams (1990) best emphasized this importance:

> . . . learning from context is a very, very important component of vocabulary acquisition. *But this means of learning is available only to the extent that children . . . bother to process the spelling—the orthographic structure—of the unknown words they encounter.* Where they skip over an unknown word without attending to it, and often readers do, no learning can occur. *Acquisition of the meaning of a word from context depends on the linkage of the contextually evoked meaning with the structural image of the word"*

> (p. 150, emphasis added)

Characteristics of Orthographic Development
Syllable Juncture

As we first discussed in Chapter 2, children have examined single-syllable patterns at some length by now. At the Syllable Juncture phase, we will help them see that these single-syllable patterns also apply in polysyllabic words. This directly benefits their spelling knowledge, but it also directly facilitates their reading efficiency by supporting rapid identification of longer words.

While students are now spending time examining and consolidating their word knowledge at the syllable level, part of this focus will naturally include attention to base words and simple prefixes and suffixes—the "meaning" or *morphemic* aspects of the syllables. This examination provides the fundamental grounding in understanding how these important word parts combine to create words and their meaning. It is very important to emphasize that we will not engage Syllable Juncture learners in extensive morphemic analysis—that will come later in the Derivational Constancy stage. So, at the Syllable Juncture stage, it is important that students encounter and learn to read many, many words that are constructed from morphemic elements (for example *unlock* = un + lock; *likable* = like + able; *examination* = examine + ation)—but we will not explore most of these important morphemic features in depth until later.

Understanding of syllable juncture begins with students' beginning grasp of what happens when inflectional endings are added to single-syllable words. Edmund Henderson made a simple yet elegant observation regarding orthographic knowledge at the Syllable Juncture stage: "The core principle of syllable juncture is that of doubling consonants to mark the short English vowel" (1990, p. 68). When you have a short vowel preceding the juncture in a polysyllabic word, in other words, the vowel will usually be followed by at least two consonants (ba**sk**et, po**pp**ing). Children lay the foundation for grasping this principle when they are aware of these two things:

1. They know that, when adding *-ed* or *-ing* to a CVC-pattern word, they double the final consonant.
2. When adding *-ed* or *-ing* to a CVCe-pattern word, they drop the *e*. As we have seen, for most children this understanding begins to develop later in the second grade year.

Table 8–1 presents some representative errors by students in third and fourth grade who are in the Syllable Juncture stage. In addition to examining the juncture of syllables, students should examine unaccented syllables because they often misspell the vowel in these syllables (for example, ORGAIN). They also examine less common vowel patterns as they occur in two-syllable words (*early*, n*eigh*bor).

> Core principle of syllable juncture is that of doubling consonants to mark the short English vowel.

TABLE 8-1 Examples of Spelling at Grades Three and Four

Word	*Examples of Spelling Errors*
Grade Three	*Grade Three*
crawl	croll, craul
dollar	dallar, doler
uesful	usful, usfull
circle	circel, circile
early	erly, eirly
keeper	keper, kepper
Grade Four	*Grade Four*
barber	barbar
helmet	helmit, helment
skipping	skiping
ugly	ugley
hurry	heary, hurrey
traced	traissed
parading	peradding, parrading
damage	damige, damadge

On the Grade Three list, notice the misspellings of *crawl,* a less-frequent vowel pattern (we examined these in Chapter 7); misspellings for *dollar* reflect the ambiguity of the final vowel sound or the uncertainty about whether to double the *l.* At fourth grade, unaccented syllables lead to misspellings for vowels (BARBAR, HELMIT) and syllable junctures (SKIPING, PERADDING/PARRADING).

As teachers, we need to help students in grades three and up see how this *doubling* and *"e"-drop* principle applies *within* polysyllabic words as well. "Consonant doubling . . . is not just limited to adding *-ed* and *-ing.* It is the basic juncture principle for all words of two or more syllables" (Henderson, 1990, p. 70). In addition to consonant doubling and e-drop, students will also deal with vowel spellings in both accented and unaccented syllables, as well as some persistently challenging consonant spellings.

Derivational Constancy

Spelling / Meaning Principle: Words that are related in meaning are often related in spelling, despite changes in sound.

Beginning in the intermediate school years, most students are capable of understanding that the way words are spelled can provide clues to their meanings. This is where we begin by exploring spelling/meaning relationships, helping students become consciously aware of the spelling/meaning principle as it applies in English: *words that are related in meaning are often related in spelling as well, despite changes in sound* (Chomsky, 1970; Templeton, 1983). Because of the semantic relatedness of words that follow these patterns, intermediate students should overcome many of their spelling problems by trying to think of a related word when troubled with a particular spelling. For example, if they are uncertain about the spelling of the schwa in the second syllable of *competition,* they can think of the related base word *compete,* which offers a clue.

This spelling/meaning principle applies to literally thousands upon thousands of words. Beginning at this level, students can now move significantly beyond the expectation that spelling should directly and consistently represent the *sound* of words. Instead, they may fully appreciate how spelling represents *meaning* and does so with surprising consistency. Table 8–2 presents examples of misspellings from Derivational Constancy spellers in Grades 5 and 6.

At first glance, misspellings at the Derivational Constancy stage appear similar in type to those at the Syllable Juncture stage: Errors occur at the juncture of syllables and with the vowel in unaccented syllables.

TABLE 8-2   Examples of Spelling at Grades 5 and 6

Word	*Examples of Spelling Errors*
Grade 5	*Grade 5*
enclosed	inclosed
confession	confesion, confestion
installment	enstalment
correction	corection
Grade 6	*Grade 6*
prohibition	prohabition
accomplish	acomplish
responsible	responsable
irrelevant	irelevent
composition	compasition
changeable	changable

Derivational Constancy learners explore *how* Greek and Latin roots, bases, and affixes combine.

Earlier, at the Syllable Juncture stage, students' exploration of words has established a secure foundation for exploring and understanding morphemes and morphemic analysis at the Derivational Constancy stage. Students will explore how these morphemic elements combine—usually Greek and Latin bases, roots, and affixes—and they will see how this knowledge can be applied flexibly across reading and writing tasks.

Word Study Instruction: Syllable Juncture

Sequence of Word Study

The sequence for word study during this stage is presented in Figure 8–2. There are activities for word study which focus on each of these patterns. Some important features of the suggested sequence are examined in more detail following this table.

Open and Closed Syllables

Open syllables end with a long vowel sound; *closed* syllables end with a consonant sound.

To double or not to double? Answering this important question depends on whether you're dealing with an **open** or a **closed** syllable. Open syllables end with a long vowel sound (*labor, reason*) and *closed* syllables contain a short vowel sound that is closed by two consonants (*rabbit, racket*). Let's see how this works at a basic level first: When students in second and third grade examine what happens when *-ed* and *-ing* are added to short- and long-vowel pattern

FIGURE 8–2 Sequence of Word Study: Syllable Juncture

◆ Plural endings
◆ Compound words
◆ Open and closed syllables: Simple inflectional endings
◆ Homophones
◆ Open and Closed Syllables: The VCCV and VCV Patterns
◆ Changing final y to i
◆ Accent
◆ Spelling patterns for the /cher/ sound, /ər/ sound, and the /əl/ sound at the end of words
◆ Simple prefixes and base words

Concept of prefix. Begin with base word discussion plus the following prefixes:

Fourth Grade:
    un- not
    dis- not, away
    in- not [Note: There are other meanings for in-, but this is the most frequent and occurs more often in words students at this level are reading]
    non- not
Fifth Grade
    re- again
    en-/em- in, into
    over- over, too much
    mis- bad, badly
◆ Simple suffixes and base words
    1. Concept of suffix (no spelling change; -er, -s, -ed, -ing, -ness)
    2. Spelling change: consonant doubling, e-drop, *y* to i—this provides "setting" for introduction of spelling/meaning patterns later on in the Derivational Constancy stage (adding derivational suffixes such as *-ion, -ity, -ian,* etc.)

words, they are learning the basics of open and closed syllables—of syllable juncture. Consider these examples:

hop + ing = ho**pp**ing   hope + ing = ho**p**ing
strip + ing = stri**pp**ing   stripe + ing = stri**p**ing

For the speller, then, knowing about open and closed syllables can answer the "to double or not to double" question: When you are uncertain about whether to double the consonants at the juncture of syllables, say the word and listen to the vowel sounds. If you hear a long sound, the syllable is open and will be followed by a *single* consonant. If you hear a short vowel sound, the syllable will need to be closed by *two* consonants—otherwise, the vowel would be long. To use our example: If you are writing about how a rabbit moves along the ground (hopping) and do not double the *p*, you'll wind up with an entirely different meaning (hoping).

Whereas *within-word* patterns include the vowel and what follows within a single syllable, *syllable* patterns extend across the juncture—the point where syllables join—thus including parts of two syllables. The two most common syllable patterns are the closed VCCV pattern (sk**ippi**ng, **garde**n) and the open VCV (b**esi**de, h**opi**ng; though it is not as frequent as the open VCV pattern, there is a "closed" VCV pattern: s**eve**n, c**abi**n). In addition to syllable patterns, the notion of open and closed syllables will be extremely helpful for learners at this stage.

At this stage of word knowledge, therefore, students will need to get a functional sense of how spoken and written syllables operate, and they will benefit from thinking about *accent* in polysyllabic words. Let's begin by talking just about spoken syllables and how speech is a clue to spelling.

Now, for the moment you'll have to pretend that you've forgotten those rules about where to divide a word into syllables because these rules depend on *seeing* the word, and we're going to be talking about *sound* as a clue to spelling. This is fairly easy to understand when you think of a word like *market*, which follows a VCCV pattern. Pronounce the word and listen to each syllable; this will provide you with the information about the probable spelling of the two consonants at the juncture of the first and second syllables. The challenge comes when you hear only *one* consonant sound, but wonder whether the consonant is doubled.

Yes, there are exceptions—words such as *cabin* and *cover,* for example. Because students have examined how the syllable patterns *usually* work, however, these exceptions will be easier to remember. For example, as we'll see below, when words are sorted according to syllable pattern, these exceptions can be examined and possible explanations explored. As Henderson observed, ". . . therein lies the key to memory. One remembers only those things one has attended to. Poor spellers do not know where to look. Syllable-sorting tasks develop the habit of looking where it counts" (1990, p. 151).

Accent

Accent can be a squishy phenomenon for a lot of people. We feel this is usually because of how accent is often handled instructionally. Let's define it first and then see why it merits some attention in thinking about words.

Just as when we stress or *emphasize* the most important part of a point we are making to a friend, so do parts of words—syllables—get accented or emphasized more than others. Dictionaries show us how to do this, of course, with accent marks after syllables. Just as with open and closed syllables, however, we should initially work from *sound* rather than print. Start with your first name (if it contains two or more syllables) or the name of a friend. When you pronounce it, where are you putting most emphasis? Which syllable seems to sound louder than the others? If your name is "Molly," you prounounce it as MOLLee—not moLEE. If your name is "Jennifer," you say JENifer, not jeNIfer or jenniFER.

Now try this with certain homographs whose meaning changes with a shift in accent:

You give someone a PRESent, not a presENT.

You reCORD a message, you don't RECord it.

You are conTENT when you are with someone you care deeply about, not CONtent.

Thinking about accent as it works with names and then with certain homographs should help solidify this concept for you. This is also the sequence you should follow with your students, beginning in the upper elementary grades.

So, why is accent important? When examining words of more than one syllable, knowing about accent helps students identify what they know about the spelling of a polysyllabic word and what they *don't* know: what they will need to pay particular attention to. Take a word like *market*. When students pronounce it, they realize they know the spelling of the accented syllable (*mark*) yet may be uncertain about the vowel spelling in the second (unaccented) syllable. When students grasp the concept of an *accented* syllable, therefore, they also learn about the other side of this concept: the *un*-accented syllable. This awareness is important because the unaccented syllable is the one in which the spelling of the vowel (the schwa) is unclear—so students will need to pay close attention to it. As we'll see a little later, the spelling of the schwa in the unaccented syllable can often be explained in terms of meaning, but sometimes not—as in these simpler, VCCV- and VCV-pattern words.

> Understanding *accent* helps students identify what they *know* about the spelling of a polysyllabic word and what they *don't* know and need to attend to.

Lower-Frequency Vowel Patterns

There are a number of vowel patterns within polysyllabic words that are not sorted out until the upper elementary years. For example, you will find students working through the following:

✦ /oi/ as in enj**oy**, embr**oi**der
✦ /ər/ as in mot**or**, doll**ar**, quick**er**, teach**er**, sail**or**
✦ /ch ə r/ as in lec**ture**, punc**ture**

> Some vowel patterns still challenge students.

As we saw in Chapter 7, you will help your students discover how; by paying attention to the *position* of many ambiguous vowels, they can often determine which spelling pattern occurs most often. For example, *aw* and *oy* usually occur at the end of words or syllables (str**aw**, b**oy**cott), while *au* and *oi* are found within syllables (f**au**lt, v**oi**ce).

Spelling patterns for the /əl/ and /ər/ sounds at the end of words must either simply be remembered or examined in terms of their meaning:

✦ Wint**er**, mot**or**, lun**ar** must be remembered (after examining them in terms of accent and what must be particularly attended to—as we discussed above).
✦ Bett**er**, long**er**, soon**er** all denote a comparison of some type, so / ə r/ will in these instances be spelled **er**.
✦ Bak**er**, farm**er**, and teach**er** use -*er* to denote "someone or something who does something"; words that have come from Latin use -*or* to denote this: profess**or**, generat**or**.

Bases and Affixes

Research in vocabulary instruction has underscored the critical importance of students' understanding how prefixes and suffixes combine with base words and word roots to create new words. This understanding can help students analyze unknown words they encounter in their reading and lead to a rich expansion and elaboration of their vocabularies. Attention to the spelling and the meaning of these word parts reinforces this understanding. We begin to facilitate students' examination of these features when students are farther along in the Syllable Juncture phase.

Teacher Modeling How to Think About Word Structure and Spelling

In this section we'll present two scripts that illustrate a teacher modeling how to examine important features of words. The first script shows how we can help students focus on what they need to attend to in examining many polysyllabic words; the second models the "combinatorial" features of bases and affixes.

> During Syllable Juncture students begin to explore *how* meaningful word parts combine.

✦ While standing at an overhead projector, the teacher begins:

"Kids, a number of you have been trying out words in your writing that end with an 'er' sound. This sound can be spelled different ways, so I'd like to focus on thinking about the spelling for a moment. Now, here's how one of you spelled the word 'tractor' in your writing [writes *tracter* on the transparency]. Let's see, now. You correctly spelled *t, r, a, c, t,* and *r*. You knew almost *all* of the word! Here's the only letter that caused some problems [pointing to *e*]. Actually, the letter right here should be *o*. You can't hear this sound clearly, so you need to remember this spelling. Concentrate on this letter as you examine this word and some other words this week that end with the /er/ sound. Remember, this one letter is all you have to remember because you already know how to spell the rest of the word."

This simple, straightforward explanation does two important things:

1. It demonstrates to children how much they *already know* about spelling a particular word—spelling is not an "all or none" affair where you "get a word wrong"; usually you will get most of the word *correct,* and as teachers, we need to remind and reassure students about this.
2. It demonstrates to children what they need to focus on when they look at a word; because they already know most of the word, they need attend to the part that is still challenging.

✦ A fundamental objective at this level is to help students become aware of *how* affixes and base words combine. Part of our instruction involves teaching the terms **prefix** and **base** or **root word**, and then explicitly addressing the most frequently-occurring prefixes. Here's how we might first introduce this fundamental "combinatorial" aspect:

"I've underlined one of the words in this sentence: *They had to redo the programs after they were printed with a spelling error.* What does 'redo' mean? Yes, Adrienne?"

"When you have to do something over again?"

"Okay! So you already had done something once, right? Now, let's cover up this first part of the word [covers *re*]. What word do we have? Right—*do.*

"Now, let's look at these words:

join
tell
organize

When we join the prefix 're' to each of them, what happens? Right! We are going to be doing these things *again*—we can *re*join a group, *re*tell a story, *re*organize our classroom" [teacher writes the prefix *re* in front of each base word as she pronounces the new word].

The teacher then asks the students what they think the prefix *re* means. After a brief discussion, she asks a student to look up the prefix in the dictionary.

This type of discussion is so very important when we are first engaging students in examining words this way. Knowing how prefixes, suffixes, and base words "go together" is a powerful tool for vocabulary development, spelling, and figuring out unfamiliar words during reading.

Activities for Students in the Syllable Juncture Stage

A variety of activities can be used to solidify understanding of the particular word knowledge task. Here we will outline *word sorts, word hunts,* and *writing sorts* as they apply for students in the Syllable Juncture stage.

GA Word Sorts 8–1

As at earlier stages, *word sorts* are extremely effective for exploring, comparing, and contrasting word features.

Syllable Juncture word features may be introduced through teacher-directed small or whole group word-sorting activities where words containing the target feature(s) are compared and contrasted with words that do not.

Procedures

1. Display the two words that contain the features that you would like the students to address. (Words can be written on large cards with magnetic tape placed on the back for a magnetic blackboard or written on chart paper and placed in a location that everyone can see.)
2. Once the two exemplars have been introduced, randomly provide a few other words that contain the same features. Have the students pronounce the other words and study them carefully.
3. Encourage students to discover on their own what particular feature the words have in common (sound, spelling pattern, or meaning).
4. After a number of students have discovered the common feature, choose some of them to physically move (if they are written on cards) or write the words under the corresponding exemplar.
5. Briefly discuss the common features and perhaps begin a theory for what is occurring.

GA Word Hunts 8–2

Word hunts reinforce and extend students' understanding of syllable and meaning patterns in words.

We have discussed word hunts earlier in this book; here we outline their organization and extend the focus to *meaning* features.

Procedures

1. Have students hunt for words with the same features in books, magazines, and newspapers.

309

2. Students record their words in a special word study notebook.
3. Most students enjoy the excitement of knowing that there is a time limit on the word hunt—that it is a race against time.
4. Following the word hunt, bring the class or group back together and record all the words that were found.
5. Discuss and check each word with the students, and have them verify if it contains the feature of the exemplar.
6. Words that do not follow the stated pattern of the feature under discussion should not be discarded. These words should be placed in a "Miscellaneous" column, studied closely, and discussed. Through these discussions other patterns, features, exceptions, and word meanings are discovered.

Variations

Word sorts can again play a role as a follow-up on word hunts:
1. Students write words that are collected from the word hunt on small tagboard word cards or on a sheet partitioned into boxes which may be cut up for sorts.
2. The word cards are sorted into columns by the features under discussion. The teacher or a partner can check the sort for accuracy.
3. Sorts can be timed, performed with partners, and practiced at home.
4. Students work with a given feature and set of word cards until the set can be sorted accurately and without delays between cards.

In all cases, students should be encouraged to arrive at a generalization for the particular features under investigation—how and why do the words work as they do? Other reinforcement activities may be used as needed to add variety to the tasks and increase fluency.

GA Writing Sorts 8–3

Mastery of a given word feature can be determined by asking the student to do a *writing sort*.

Procedures

Early/Middle
Syllable Juncture

1. Students are asked to divide a sheet of paper into the required number of columns—2, 3, or 4.
2. The teacher provides words with the features under study to serve as exemplars at the head of each column.
3. Students then sort into appropriate columns and spell correctly the features under investigation in the words that the teacher calls out to the class or group.
4. Words in this task should contain the same features under study but should not be words that have been included in the previous sorting activity.

A Plural Sort 8–4

Early/Middle
Syllable Juncture

In this activity, students use a classification to look for -*s* and -*es*.*

---

*Amy M. Dixon developed this activity.

Procedures

1. Demonstrate how to use a sorting folder divided into 3 columns: "One cap, two caps; I hear 's' on the end of cap. One box, two boxes; I hear an 'es' on the end of box." Place the word card under the appropriate heading on the soring folder.
2. Use the word cards presented below. Each student is given a handful of word cards. Students read their word cards, say the plural form, and place the cards under appropriate headings on the folder.
3. Students group words in the *-es* column by spelling pattern (*x, s, ss, sh, ch, tch endings*) to discover word endings that need es- in the plural form.

Columns: *-s*   *-es*   Miscellaneous

Word Lists

cap	ax	bun	box
cow	mix	chick	bus
hill	pass	cliff	glass
park	dress	farm	dish
bump	crash	friend	brush
string	peach	path	bench
bath	watch		

Variations

1. After the task is introduced by the teacher, students can complete it individually.
2. Students can sort and write words needing *-es* endings in their word study notebooks. Students add new words to each category.

 Compound Words   **8–5**

Early Syllable Juncture

By exploring compound words, students can develop several types of understandings: First, they learn how different words can combine in different ways to form new words—this is the beginning understanding of the "combinatorial features" of English words. Second, they lay the foundation for explicit attention to *syllables,* because so often compound words comprise two smaller words, each of which is a single syllable. Third, students reinforce their knowledge of the spelling of many high-frequency, high-utility words in English, because these words constitute so many *compound* words.

Compound words lay the foundation for understanding how word meaning is created and how syllables work.

Procedures

1. Share some common compound words with the students, for example *cookbook* and *bedroom*. Discuss their meaning, pointing out how each word in the compound contributes to the meaning of the whole word.
2. With the words presented below, conduct open sorts with a small group; then have the students do open sorts working in pairs.
3. Arrange single-syllable words in two columns, and challenge students to create as many compound words as they can—some will be legitimate, real words—and others will be words that do not yet exist, but they *could*. Students may write sentences using the "pseudo" words, illustrating their meaning.
4. An interesting variation is for students to explore how many compound words can be made from one word. For example, *any* plus *time, one, how, one, body,* and so forth.

Word List

anyone, someone, somehow, baseball, sunshine, daytime, nighttime, football, daylight, somebody, nobody, airplane, somewhere, outside, anybody, someday, campfire, high school, race track, everything, earthquake

 A ## "Double Scoop": Inflectional Endings 8–6

Early/Middle
Syllable Juncture

This game will help children develop automaticity in writing words with inflectional endings. It is appropriate for small groups of 2 to 4 students.*

Materials

Gameboard (see Figure 8–3), playing pieces, spinner or die, board for writing answers and sentence cards as shown here:

The bunny was *hopping* down the garden. *Hopping*

FIGURE 8–3 Double Scoop Gameboard

*This activity is provided to us courtesy of Barbara Santos.

Procedures

1. Players put their pieces on the sun to start.
2. Player 1 reads a sentence card and repeats the underlined word.
3. Player 2 will then write the word that is repeated under the appropriate heading on the writing board.
4. The caller then checks the opponent's answer by comparing it to the sentence card. If it is correct, the writer spins and moves that number of spaces on the playing board.
5. The players then switch roles—one becomes the reader and the other becomes the writer.
6. The first player to reach the double scoop of ice cream wins.

Variations

Sort just the sentence cards by whether or not the final consonant is doubled before the ending is added: hoped   pinned

 Freddy, the Hopping, Jumping, Diving Frog 8–7

Early/Middle
Syllable Juncture

In this game for 2 to 4 players, students sort words that end in *-ing* according to these three categories:*

No Change	**Double**	**E-Drop**
jumping	hopping	diving

Procedures

1. Use a "follow the path board" marked with these labels: "Double", "No Change", and "E-Drop". (For an example, see the gameboard in Figure 6–15, p. 184)
2. Roll die to determine who goes first. Play proceeds clockwise.
3. Place drawing cards face down in the center of the board.
4. Player 1 draws 1 card, reads the card aloud, and moves to the closest space that matches the features of the word. For example, if the player draws *hopping,* the player moves to the nearest space that says "Double."
5. If a player draws a penalty or advancement card, follow directions on the card.
6. Cards are discarded on the discard folder according to "Double", "No Change" and "E-Drop".
7. Upon reaching the home lily pad, a player must correctly read the words on the discard folder in order to win. If the player misreads a word, he or she must move back 5 spaces, and play continues.

Word List

No Change	**Double**	**E-Drop**
pushing	bragging	trading
pumping	sunning	diving
jumping	hopping	gliding
kicking	running	riding

Marilyn Edwards developed this game.

finding	shopping	hoping
croaking	flopping	sliding
floating	swimming	
sleeping	plopping	

Penalty or Advancement Cards

1. You have the strongest legs. Jump ahead to the next lily pad.
2. Skip 2 spaces if you correctly pronounce the "e-drop" words on the discard folder.
3. Your croaking made me lose sleep. Move back 2 spaces.
4. You ate too many flies. Move back 2 spaces.

Variations

1. Discard by sorting "No Change" words by sound.
2. Determine the pattern for these.
3. Write uninflected forms on cards (i.e., *hop, jump, dive*), have players decide how the form should be spelled, and move to the appropriate place. Include an answer sheet with words in alphabetical order to check if there is a disagreement.

 Spelling "ed" and "t" endings   **8–8**

Early/Middle
Syllable Juncture

In these three sorts, students look at past tense spelling patterns.*

Procedures

1. Establish the three categories for words that end in *-ed*: hopped/**t**, stated/**ed**, grinned/**d**. Here are the words sorted into the three categories:

"t"	"ed"	"d"
stopped	traded	mailed
mixed	dotted	broiled
dropped	arrested	raised
dressed	treated	smiled
chased	patted	tried
trapped	batted	grabbed
cracked	divided	cared

Students try to find common features with each list. Notice that most "ed" words which sound like "t" have a base word that ends in k, p, s, or x. In contrast, the base words in the next category combine with the ending to form two or three syllables. These words can be easily recognized by the "d" or "t" ending on the base word. The last category includes base words with a variety of endings. The base word combines with the ed ending to form a single syllable word with a distinctive "d" sound at the end.

2. In this sort, students sort for word endings.

"t"	"ed"
knelt	chased
sent	stopped

---

*Karen Broaddus developed this activity.

thought	shopped
crept	dressed
dealt	picked
lent	hoped
taught	mixed
fought	cracked
swept	baked

3. Ask the students to name the present tense verb for each past tense verb. Place word cards by each column so that the students can make comparisons. If the student is having difficulty producing the present tense verb, use sentences as models (i.e., Mary **swept** the house yesterday, but today Mary needs to **sweep** the house again.) The cards should look like this:

knelt (kneel)	chased (chase)
sent (send)	stopped (stop)
thought (think)	shopped (shop)
crept (creep)	dressed (dress)
dealt (deal)	picked (pick)
lent (lend)	hoped (hope)
taught (teach)	mixed (mix)
fought (fight)	cracked (crack)
swept (sweep)	baked (bake)
caught (catch)	dropped (drop)
brought (bring)	trapped (trap)

4. Compare the lists. Most students will easily see that the first column with "t" endings contains verbs where the past tense verb is a completely different word from the present tense verb. In the second column, the students might notice that the "ed" ending is added to the present tense to form the past tense verb, and that you can always find the complete present tense verb in a past tense verb.

5. Ask students to circle the present tense within each of the past tense words in the second column.

6. Ask students to search for the one exception to this pattern in the sort. Most students will discover the present tense verb *deal* in *dealt,* but usually students can remember this exception by the change in vowel sound.

 Homophone Rummy   **8–9**

| Middle Syllable
| Juncture |

This activity is suitable for 2 to 6 students. The object of the game is to discard all of the cards in one hand as well as to get the most number of homophone pairs or points.

Materials

Several decks of homophone pairs (52 cards, 26 pairs if using a mixed sort; as many pairs as possible if sorted by sound and/or syllable/accent.)

Procedures

1. All words must be known as sight words. These words are placed on note card strips (see Figure 8–4). There should be alternative decks of

*Janet Bloodgood developed this activity.

FIGURE 8–4 Word Cards for Homophone Rummy

cards from which to draw in case there are words that are not part of a child's automatic sight vocabulary.

2. Each player is dealt 10 cards (2 players); 7 cards (3 to 4 players); 6 cards (5 to 6 players).

3. Each player checks his own hand for already-existing pairs. Once a pair is discovered, the meaning for each word is given in order to receive points. In giving definitions, the players may use the actual word in a sentence to show the meaning until they become well versed in homophone definitions; then, they must give a definition of the word separate from its use in a sentence or a synonym for the word. Each pair receives one point; any other additional homophone for the pair receives one additional point.

4. The remainder of the deck is placed in a central location as the drawing pile in which the first card is turned up.

5. The person on the left of the dealer goes first. And each player draws from the drawing pile or the discard line and retains pairs which he receives. Each player must discard one card. NOTE: If a card is taken from the discard line, all cards appearing below the card wanted also have to be taken. Also, the top card *must* be used.

6. The game is over when one player is rid of all his cards. That person yells "RUMMY." Then the pairs are counted up.

Variations

1. Rather than having a random mix of homophone pairs, the decks can be divided into a "homophones by sound" or "homophones by syllable accent." This creates an opportunity to examine homophones by both sound and spelling patterns as well as syllable and accent patterns. Each deck of cards can consist of 2 to 4 contrasting sound patterns or syllable/accent patterns which the children have to sort.

2. A player can be challenged by someone else disagreeing with his definitions. The person who challenges looks up the words in the dictionary. Whoever is right gets to keep the pair.

3. Each player can play off of other players' cards, receiving additional points for each homophone found.
4. If a player has a card that can be added to a set or sequence but does not realize it and discards it, another player detecting what happened can pick up the card discarded, and add it to a sequence. That player then gets to discard one of his own cards.
5. *Homophone synonyms* can be played off of this game. For each homophone, a child has to come up with at least one synonym. For example, if the pair was *through* and *threw,* synonyms corresponding to this pair might be finished and pitched.

HOMOPHONE WORD LIST

ant	Ann	tax	cash	fair
aunt	an	tacks	cache	fare
passed	rap	maze	sail	gate
past	wrap	maize	sale	gait
great	air	ate	break	hey
grate	heir	eight	brake	hay
mail	main	pale	pear	steak
male	mane	pail	pair	stake
			pare	
there	way	bear	tale	hair
their	weigh	bare	tail	hare
they're				
pray	rain	wear	ail	bale
prey	rein	ware	ale	bail
	reign			
praise	days	main	sleigh	base
prays	daze	mane	slay	bass
faint	wait	plain	vail	wade
feint	weight	plane	veil	weighed
wave	nave	red	led	wet
waive	knave	read	lead	whet
cell	bell	bred	tread	guessed
sell	belle	bread	tred	guest
rest	be	beech	need	deer
wrest	bee	beach	knead	dear
jeans	peace	sea	week	creek
genes	piece	see	weak	creak
meet	seem	real	peel	peak
meat	seam	reel	peal	peek
				pique

team	heel	leak	sees	sheer
teem	heal	leek	seas	shear
peer	cheap	feat	flee	hear
pier	cheep	feet	flea	here
ring	sweet	tea	teas	tear
wring	suite	tee	tease	tier
we	weave	we'd	bin	him
wee	we've	weed	been	hymn
wit	cent	scents	mist	tents
whit	scent	cents	missed	tense
		sense		
guilt	in	knit	tick	hi
gilt	inn	nit	tic	high
die	lie	by	night	right
dye	lye	buy	knight	write
		bye		
I'll	sight	I	time	rye
aisle	site	eye	thyme	wry
isle	cite	aye		
style	might	climb	find	side
stile	mite	clime	fined	sighed
tide	vise	not	all	paws
tied	vice	knot	awl	pause
born	chord	foul	mall	mourn
borne	cord	fowl	maul	morn
pour	rot	bomb	ball	bald
pore	wrought	balm	bawl	balled
browse	course	boy	socks	no
brows	coarse	buoy	sox	know
role	four	hole	road	so
roll	fore	whole	rowed	sew
				sow
board	bold	horse	bow	sore
bored	bowled	hoarse	bough	soar
boar	soul	lone	sown	or
bore	sole	loan	sewn	ore
pole	chalk	close	doe	fourth
poll	chock	clothes	dough	forth

groan	load	oh	rows	thrown
grown	lode	owe	rose	throne
told	son	plum	some	rung
tolled	sun	plumb	sum	wrung
one	brewed	brews	chews	coop
won	brood	bruise	choose	coupe
crews	flew	knew	loot	root
cruise	flu	gnu	lute	route
		new		
threw	do	to	blue	you
through	due	too	blew	ewe
	dew	two		
fir	per	wood	birth	
fur	purr	would	berth	

A	**Syllable Sorts**	**8–10**

Middle Syllable Juncture	This activity is suitable for small groups, and its purpose is to look at patterns in words when students are deciding how to divide words into syllables. This sort compares VCCV words (*tender*) and doublets that also follow this pattern (*kitten*), as shown in Figure 8–5. Before doing a sort such as this one, a teacher would have provided activities such as clapping words and asking how many syllables there are as well as saying words and having students listen for the number of syllables. It is important for the students to attend to sound first and then focus on pattern in words.

Materials

File folder and word cards; label the folder as shown in Figure 8–5.

Procedures

1. The teacher explains to the group that she is going to place each word card under the pattern that it matches. She asks the group to attend to pattern as she says each word. She also tells the students that the patterns they are looking at will help them better remember the spelling of these words by noticing where the words are divided into syllables.
2. She then shuffles the word cards and says each word as she places it in the appropriate column, for example, *lum–ber, mar–ket, dol–lar, din–ner.*
3. After the teacher has sorted the words, she asks the students how the words in column one are alike. She encourages the students to look at patterns in column one, and then asks them if anyone noticed where the words were "divided" when she pronounced them. Then she goes to column two and guides the students' examination in the same fashion.
4. On their own, students can sort these words until they are comfortable with the pattern.

FIGURE 8–5 Sample File Folder for Syllable Sorts

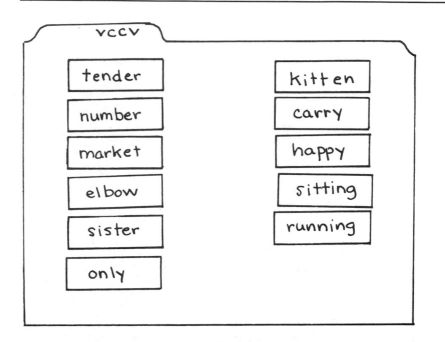

5. The teacher could then lead a closed sort and have the students write the words down on a paper they have labeled with two columns, *lumber* and *sitting*.
6. On another occasion, the teacher could call out the words and the students would write them in the appropriate column in their word study notebook.

Word List

number market member elbow basket sister center only
until circus signal canvas dollar setter cellar dinner
bottom yellow carry happy running sitting bunny happen

Additional Words

current canyon harvest attend common suppose allow
barber plastic hollow organ compose lumber carpet
perfect master thirty survive fellow

Variations

1. Use the VCCV-pattern words and, together with the following V/CV-pattern words, sort according to V/CV or VC/CV pattern (exemplars, for example, may be *canvas* and *basic*).
   baby hoping writer before begin beside
   basic even waving bacon chosen moment
   raking human pilot silent season navy
   music female stolen robot prefer

Guide the students through these questions: In which pattern is the first vowel usually short? Why? In which pattern is the first vowel usually long? Why?

2. Sort the preceding V/CV words with the following VC/V words:
   cabin planet finish robin magic limit cousin prison
   habit punish cover manage medal promise closet camel

 ## A | Base Word/Suffix Sorts: Changing "y" to "i"   8–11

Late Syllable
Juncture

The purpose of this sort is to look at patterns in words when students are deciding when *y* changes to *i* and when it remains the same. It works well with small groups.

Materials

File folder and word cards; the inside of the file folder is labeled with *carry* and *carried* as column heads.

Procedures

1. The teacher explains to the group that she is going to place each word card under either the base word or the related word. After the teacher has sorted the words, she asks the students why they think the spelling of the base word changed when -*ed* or -*es* was added.
2. On their own, students can sort these words until they are comfortable with the pattern. The teacher could then lead a closed sort and have the students write the words down on a paper they have labeled with two columns, *penny* and *pennies*.
3. On another occasion, the teacher could call out the words, and the students would write them in the appropriate column in their word study notebook.

Word List:

carry, carried, story, stories, hurry, hurried, penny, pennies
bunny, bunnies, pony, ponies, party, parties, baby, babies
city, cities, family, families, empty, emptied

Variations

1. Now explore single-syllable base words that end in *y*.
   dry, dried, cry, cries, try, tried, fly, flies
2. Add the following base and related words to words from the previous sorts; why *doesn't* the *y* change to *i*?
   turkey, turkeys, donkey, donkeys, chimney, chimneys
3. Sort base words and related words to which the suffixes -*er* and -*est* have been added:
   tiny, tinier, tiniest; pretty, prettier, prettiest; crazy, crazier, craziest
   early, earlier, earliest; happy, happier, happiest
4. In some words, such as *tiny* and *baby,* the spelling of *y* does *not* change when suffixes beginning with *i* are added. Present the following words, ask the students why they think the spelling doesn't change, then go on a word hunt to find other examples:
   tiny, tinyish; baby, babyish; copy, copyist

A "Stressbusters"

Late Syllable
Juncture/Early
Derivational
Constancy

The purpose of the game is to determine the correct placement of accent or stress in a given word. Students, in pairs, can play the game after they have conducted their initial sorting of the words by accent pattern under the teacher's guidance.*

Materials

Prepared game cards made from the attached list of words; "Stressbusters" game board (see Figure 8–6); game pieces; dictionary; word list showing accent in given words.

Procedures

As students identify the placement of accent, they will do the following:

1. If the accent falls in the beginning syllable and is correctly identified, the player moves the penny one space; if the accent falls in the second syllable and is correctly identified, the penny is moved two spaces; if accent is on the third syllable, the penny is moved three spaces.

FIGURE 8–6 Stressbusters Gameborad

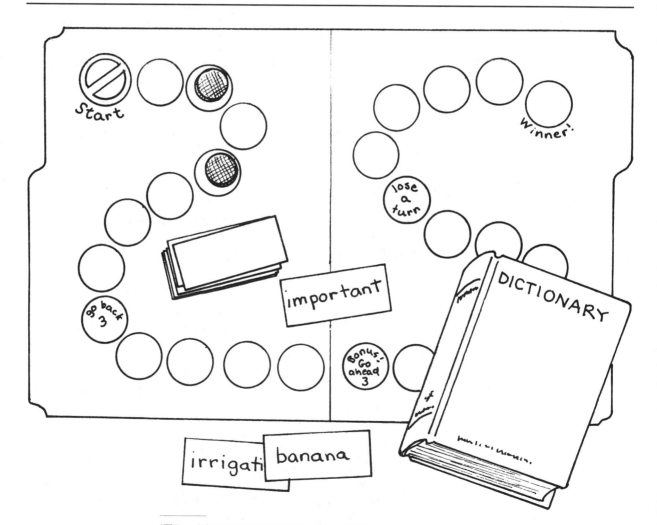

---

*This activity comes to us courtesy of Brenda Reibel.

2. Player One takes a card from the game card stack. Player One identifies if the accent falls on the first, second, or third syllable. If Player One is unchallenged, she moves the correct number of spaces depending on where the accent falls. If there is *more* than one accented syllable *and the player realizes this* (as in *CONstiTUtion*), the player may choose which syllable he/she will "count"; the player may decide that *constitution* should count for three spaces.

3. Player Two then takes a card from the game card stack, identifies the accent, moves the correct number of spaces depending on where the accent falls.

4. The game continues until one player reaches the finish circle.

5. CHALLENGING ANSWERS: Game players may challenge acceptability of accent answers. When an answer is challenged, the challenger looks the words up in the dictionary to determine the accented syllable. If the challenger is correct, he or she gets to move the game piece forward one, two, or three places, depending on where the accent falls. If the player is correct, and the challenger is wrong, the challenger must move back one space.

Words that are accented on the third syllable are also accented on the first syllable. These words may be challenged. If a player moves his piece one space for the word *constitution,* for example—not realizing it is also accented on the third syllable—the other player could then challenge. An incorrect challenge, however, costs the challenger the corresponding number of spaces (if the challenger thinks the word is accented on the second syllable and is incorrect, she must move back two spaces; if she thinks the accent is on the third syllable and is incorrect, she moves back three spaces).

Word List of Accented Syllables

First Syllable	Second Syllable	Third Syllable
anything	December	constitution
somebody	November	population
beautiful	October	planetarium
families	September	Sacramento
grandfather	uncommon	Tallahassee
January	unusual	understand
libraries	unwanted	imitation
Wednesday	protection	regulation
wonderful	reduction	California
populate	romantic	definition
acrobat	unable	diagnosis
Albany	providing	hippopotamus
amateur	vacation	irrigation
aptitude	whoever	Mississippi
architect	accountant	declaration
artery	agility	exclamation
avalanche	amphibian	
calculator	apprentice	
cantaloupe	asparagus	
comedy	attorney	
customer	computer	
engineer	election	
evidence	endurance	
forestry	executive	
generator	erosion	

improvise	ignition
iodine	judicial
meteorite	mechanic
navigator	banana
average	department
camera	important
carpenter	deliver
colorful	remember
everything	whenever
colorful	tomorrow
gasoline	abilities
everywhere	apartment
hamburger	companion
	condition

A You're Up 8–13

Late Syllable
Juncture

The purpose of the game, which should be played with 5 students, is to contrast the spellings for the "ure" sound: *ure* as in *picture* and *cher* as in *preacher,* as well as other incidents of the suffix "ure." The format is similar to the television Password® game.

Materials

Scoring pad and pencil; stopwatch; password covers (like a tachistoscope) such as the one in Figure 8–7.

Procedures

1. One student is designated as the Recorder, while the other four pair up into two teams of two players. Each team decides who is Player A and Player B. The recorder, who also serves as referee and time keeper, flips a coin to see which team will go first.

FIGURE 8–7 Password Cover for You're Up

2. Both players are given the password holders with the first word to be played showing through the window (see Figure 8–7). (Both teams are given the same words.)

3. Player A from the team that won the coin toss begins by giving his partner a **one word clue** as to the password on the card. This clue **may not** be any part of the word to be guessed, or contain the password in any form. Player B has one attempt to guess the password. If s/he does not guess the correct word, the other team has a chance.

4. Again Player A gives the clue and Player B must try to guess. Play moves back and forth between teams until one team guesses the password. If both teams have given 5 clues and the password is still not guessed, the referee throws the word out, and Players B are given the second word, with the second team's Player B leading off with a one-word clue to his or her partner.

5. Each time a team successfully guesses a word, they receive one point. If the same player that guessed the word can also **spell** the word, he receives another point (total of 2). If the player cannot spell the word, the opposing team has a chance to do so with whichever player was **guessing** the clues. The team with the most points wins.

6. For the teacher to assess students' knowledge of the targeted feature, and in the interest of fairness, the Recorder is to write down the given clues on a sheet provided with the words played. The Recorder also acts as referee and time keeper, making sure only **one word clues** are given and that those clues are in keeping with the rule. Keeping time involves allowing each team 15 seconds total for giving clues and guessing the password during each round, as well as a 15-second limit to spell the word.

Variations

1. Have students create their own Password cards with this feature, or another, for their fellow students to use.

2. This game could also be played with *ant/ent* words, providing an engaging way to practice spelling these words as well as sharpen vocabulary.

Word Lists

Two Syllables

chər	shŏor	jər	yŏor
culture	assure	conjure	endure
capture	ensure	injure	failure
creature	insure		obscure
denture	pressure		secure
feature	seizure		
fixture	fissure		
fracture	brochure		
future			
gesture	**zhər**	**cher (for contrast)**	
juncture			
lecture	leisure	archer	
mature	measure	bleacher	
mixture	closure	butcher	
moisture	pleasure	catcher	
picture	treasure	Fletcher	

pasture	marcher
posture	moocher
puncture	poacher
nature	preacher
nurture	rancher
rapture	scorcher
sculpture	searcher
stature	stretcher
stricture	teacher
texture	watcher
tincture	
torture	
venture	

Three Syllable

chər	shər/zhər	jər	yŏor
adventure	enclosure	procedure	manicure
departure	exposure		insecure
furniture	reassure		sinecure
indenture	composure		
premature	disclosure		
signature			
immature			
miniature			
overture			
aperture			

A | ## "The Apple and the Bushel" Game | 8–14

Middle/Late
Syllable Juncture

The purpose of the game is to help students differentiate between -*le* and -*el* endings. A prerequisite skill is the ability to sort rapidly words with -*le* and -*el* endings. Small groups can participate with ease in this activity.*

Materials

1. The Apple and Bushel game board (see Figure 8–8).
2. Game marker for each player.
3. Word cards with -*le* and -*el* ending left off. (Optional additional cards: words with -*le* and -*el* left on.)

Procedures

1. Students sort words with -*le* and -*el* endings to review (optional step).
2. Students roll die to determine order of turns.
3. Student draws card from pile and reads word out loud.
4. Student moves his marker to nearest -*le* or -*el* ending that would complete his word. (If there is disagreement among players about the correct ending, then they should consult the dictionary.)
5. The game continues until one player reaches the bushel. (Note: To get *in* the bushel, a -*le* word must be drawn. If a player draws an -*el* word, he must move backwards and continue playing from that space.)

---

*This activity is courtesy of Charlotte Tucker.

FIGURE 8–8 Apple and Bushel Gameboard

Variations

Students may sort word cards as they draw them from the pile. This will reinforce the spelling patterns.

Word List

apple	angel
little	model
rattle	gravel
settle	travel
meddle	camel
cattle	motel
nibble	level
pebble	hotel
maple	
cable	excel
table	pretzel
fable	bushel
handle	damsel
gentle	compel
candle	
durdle	
curdle	
turtle	
peddle	
angle	

GA "Words that Grow from Base and Root Words" 8–15

Late Syllable
Juncture

In this game, students see *directly* how words "grow" from base words.

Materials

Posterboard of tree (see Figure 8–9); base word cards; grease pencil.

Procedures

1. Select a base word card from the deck.
2. Place the base word or root card at the base of the tree, and think of as many forms as possible.
3. Write the words on individual branches.
4. Display the word-tree in the classroom for several days, then wipe off, and begin again with the introduction of new base word.

Variations

After making the words, students may use them individually in sentences and/or discuss their meanings. Confirm with the dictionary.

FIGURE 8–9 Word Tree: Words that Grow from Base and Root Words

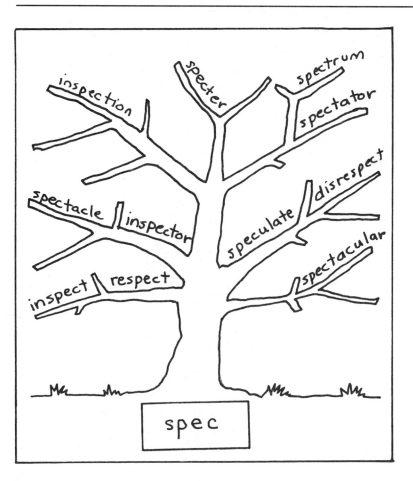

GA Additional Word Study Activities for Syllable Juncture Students   8–16

Late Syllable
Juncture

The following suggested activities may be teacher-directed and/or student-selected. They are conducted with the list or group of words the student is currently studying:

✦ Choose 5 words from your list. Circle the base word in each.
✦ Write a rhyming word for as many words on your list as possible.
✦ Make appropriate words on your lists plural.
✦ Choose 5 words on your list. For each word make as many new words as possible using the same letters.
✦ Choose 8 list words and mark the short, long, and silent vowels within each word.
✦ Circle any prefixes you find in the words on your list.
✦ Underline any suffixes you find in the words on your list.
✦ Choose three words on your list. Change at least one letter to create a new word.
✦ Add a prefix and/or suffix, when possible, to words on your list.
✦ Search for your words in several different sources, for example, *TV Guide,* newspapers, magazines, trade books, and so forth. Keep a tally of the number of times you find each word.
✦ Choose 8 words which contain dipththongs and digraphs.
✦ Decide upon 3 topics which will include most of your words. Group your words according to these categories.
✦ Separate your words into 2 lists according to the first vowel, whether it is long or short.
✦ Classify your words according to subject area: art/math/science/language/social studies.
✦ A word sort that pulls together much of the exploration you have been doing with 2-syllable words is a *three-step* sort. In this type of sort, a group of words is sorted according to three different criteria:

1. First, sort the words according to which syllable is accented.

   a / way'   ze' / bra

   to / day'   fe' / ver

2. Second, sort according to the *sound* you hear in the accented syllable. For example, *long* vowel vs. *short* vowel:

   lazy   ladder

   climate   better

3. Third, sort the sounds according to the *pattern* in the accented syllable. For example, syllable-final long vowel pattern vs. syllable-medial long vowel:

   today   remain

   climate   impeach

Word Study Instruction: Derivational Constancy

Sequence of Word Study

The
*Spelling/Meaning
Connection* lays
the foundation for
extensive
exploration of
Greek and Latin
word elements.

The sequence for derivational constancy begins with a straightforward exploration of the spelling/meaning connection. The study moves to Greek and Latin word elements, to predictable spelling changes, and then on to another look at prefixes. The sequence is presented in Table 8–3, which is followed by some reminders for word study at this stage.

There are some basic points to keep in mind regarding students' word study at this level (Templeton, 1989, 1992):

1. Words and word elements selected for study should be **generative,** which means that whenever possible we teach about words in meaning "families." This highlights the awareness that particular patterns of relationships can be extended, *generalized,* to other words. For example, an awareness of the long-to-short vowel alternation pattern in the words pl**ea**se and pl**ea**sant can generalize to words such as w**i**se-w**i**sdom and c**a**ve-c**a**vity.

2. The words that we initially select for exploration by our students should be selected based on how obvious their relationship is. For example, we will teach clearly-related words such as *represent/misrepresent* before teaching about words that are less clearly related, such as *expose/exposition*.

3. We should plan on using both teacher-directed instruction and student discussions.

Now let's examine more closely some important aspects of the sequence presented in Table 8–3—the spelling/meaning connection and Greek and Latin word elements.

> Students' word study should be *generative,* move from concrete to abstract, and be appropriately guided by the teacher.

TABLE 8–3   Sequence of Word Study: *Derivational Constancy*

The Spelling/Meaning Connection

Words that are related in meaning are often related in spelling as well, despite changes in sound.

1. ***Consonant Alternations*** in which the spelling of the base word remains the same, despite the change in sound. Work with known words first:

a. silent/sounded	sign/signal
	condem<u>n</u>/condem<u>n</u>ation
	sof<u>t</u>en/sof<u>t</u>
b. /t/ to /sh/	connec<u>t</u>/connec<u>t</u>ion
	selec<u>t</u>/selec<u>t</u>ion
	attrac<u>t</u>/attrac<u>t</u>ion
c. /k/ to /sh/	musi<u>c</u>/musi<u>c</u>ian
	magi<u>c</u>/magi<u>c</u>ian

2. ***Vowel Alternation*** patterns:

a. Long to short	pl<u>ea</u>se/pl<u>ea</u>snt
	cr<u>i</u>me/cr<u>i</u>minal
b. Long to schwa	comp<u>e</u>te/comp<u>e</u>tition
	def<u>i</u>ne/def<u>i</u>nition
	res<u>i</u>de/res<u>i</u>dent
c. Schwa to short	loc<u>a</u>lity/loc<u>a</u>l
	leg<u>a</u>lity/leg<u>a</u>l
	rela<u>t</u>ivity/rela<u>t</u>ive(relation)
	met<u>a</u>llic/met<u>a</u>l

Greek and Latin Word Elements

a. Start with Greek number prefixers *mono-* (one), *bi-* (two), *tri-* (three), and move to the Greek roots *tele-* (far, distant), *-therm-* (heat), *-photo-* (light), and *astr-* (star)

b. Move to frequent Latin roots with the aim of gaining a working understanding of a few frequent roots with relatively constant meanings: *-tract-* (drag, pull); *spect-* (look); *-port-* (carry); *-dict-* (to say); *-rupt-* (to break); and *-scrib-* (to write).

c. Explore additional Latin and Greek prefixes (building on those already taught at the Syllable Juncture phase):

TABLE 8–3   (continued)

Prefix	Meaning
inter-	between
intra-	within
super-	over; greater
counter-	opposing
ex-	out
fore-	before
post-	after
pro-	in front of, forward
co-/com-	together
sub-	under
pre-	before
con-	with
anti-	against
demi-	half
semi-	half
quadr-	four
pent-	five

d. Explore common Greek suffixes that students will frequently encounter:

-crat / -cracy:	rule (*democracy*—rule by the *demos*, "people")
-emia:	condition of the blood (*leukemia*—the blood has too many white [*leuk*] blood cells)
-ician:	specialist in (*dietician*)
-ine:	chemical substance (*chlorine, benzedrine*)
-ism/-ist:	belief in, one who believes (*communism/ communist, captialism/capitalist*)
-logy / -logist:	science of, scientist (*geology*—science of the earth, studying the earth; *geologist*—one who studies the earth)
-pathy / -path:	feeling, suffering, disease, (*sympathy*— feeling with; *osteopathy*—disease of the bones)
-phobia:	abnormal fear (*claustrophobia*—fear of being closed in or shut in [*claus*])

Predictable Spelling Changes: Consonants and Vowels

a.	t/c	silen*t*/silen*c*e
b.	d/s	explo*d*e/explo*s*ion
		ero*d*e/ero*s*ion
		deci*d*e/deci*s*ion
c.	Long to short	v*ai*n/v*a*nity; cons*um*e/cons*ump*tion
d.	Long to schwa	expl*ai*n/expl*a*nation; excl*ai*m/excl*a*mation; re*cei*ve/re*cep*tion; per*cei*ve/per*cep*tion

Absorbed or "Assimilated" Prefixes

These are prefixes whose spelling and sound have been "absorbed" into the spelling and sound of the base or root to which they are affixed:

   a. start with prefix + base (in + mobile = immobile; ad + count = account)
   b. move to prefix + root (ad + cept = accept; in + mune = immune)

Spelling/Meaning Connection

Very often there is a direct visual link between the spelling of related words and their related meanings. This spelling/meaning connection provides us with the opportunity to help students learn a *strategy* for examining words that are related in spelling and meaning as well as to help them become aware of the several different spelling/meaning *patterns* that characterize so many words in English.

For example, consider the "silent/sounded consonants" pattern: consonants that are silent in one word are "sounded" in a related word, as in the words solem**n** and solem**n**ity. Rather than trying simply to remember the spelling of one silent consonant in one word, students are given the following strategy: "To remember the spelling of a word with a silent consonant, try to think of a related word in which the consonant is sounded."

Another pattern is that of the spelling of the schwa, or least-accented vowel sound in words such as prohibition, adaptation, and genetic. This spelling becomes obvious when we pair these words with related words in which the corresponding vowel sound is clearly heard:

proh**i**bition	ad**a**ptation	g**e**netic
proh**i**bit	ad**a**pt	g**e**ne

Again, here is the strategy that is reinforced: "To remember the spelling of the schwa in a word, think of a related word in which the same vowel has the long or short vowel sound."

Students benefit most from their study of the spelling-meaning connection when these patterns are presented in an instructionally solid sequence. For example, related words that illustrate **vowel alternation** begin with straightforward long-to-short vowel changes such as ign*i*te/ign*i*tion and hum*a*ne/hum*a*nity; it's easier for students to understand this pattern before they explore in depth the long-to-schwa vowel changes as in imp*o*se-imp*o*sition. Later, students will examine patterns in which there is a significant spelling change within related words, but this change is predictable; for example, re*tain*/re*ten*tion, de*tain*/de*ten*tion. Students are conceptually primed for examining these words because they understand the spelling/meaning patterns presented earlier. The same sequence holds for **consonant alternation**: The earlier patterns in which the sound changes while the spelling remains constant in (si**g**n/si**g**nal) lay the groundwork for later *predictable* spelling alternations (divi**d**e/divi**s**ion; confiden**t**/confiden**ce**).

The spelling/meaning connection plays a very important role in expanding students' vocabularies. Once students understand how the principle operates in known words, we show them how it applies in unknown words. For example, let's say a student has used the word *solemn* in his writing—he knows the meaning of the word and understands it when he runs across it in his reading—but he misspells it as SOLEM. We would then show him the related word *solemnity*. In so doing, we have the opportunity to address two important objectives: First, the reason for the so-called "silent" *n* in *solemn* becomes clear—the word is related to *solemnity* in which the *n* is pronounced. Second, because students already know the meaning of *solemn,* they are able to understand the meaning of the new but related word *solemnity*—we have just used the spelling system, in other words, to expand the student's vocabulary.

The spelling/ meaning connection helps students become better spellers and expand their vocabularies.

Greek and Latin Elements

After exploring a number of spelling/meaning relationships and playing with the meaning changes accompanying the addition and deletion of affixes to known base words, students may be ready to explore the incredibly rich terrain of *word roots*—elements from Greek and Latin. They nestle within a word and are the meaningful anchor to which prefixes and suffixes may attach. It is important to remind students, moreover, that spelling still visually represents the meaning of these elements and preserves the meaning relationships among

Exploring Greek and Latin word elements lays the groundwork for understanding core concepts in science, social studies, and math.

words that at first may appear quite different, as for example in **jud**ge, prejud*ice* and ad**jud***icate*.

Students need to learn these two things:

1. *How* these elements work—how they combine—within words.
2. *What* are the specific, frequently-occurring Greek and Latin roots.

This initial understanding will help tremendously later on when students realize how many of these elements occur in the vocabulary terms that represent core concepts in science, social studies, and math.

We suggest that these Greek and Latin elements be sequenced according to the abstractness of their meaning, from concrete to more abstract. For example, the Greek roots *phon* (sound), *auto* (self), and *graph* (writing) are introduced before Latin roots because their meaning is more apparent and the way in which they combine with other elements is more understandable. Because Latin roots are usually more abstract, they are presented a little later: *spect* (to look); *scrib* (to write), *rupt* (to break; burst). In this chapter we will offer several affixes and roots for study; our offering is by no means exhaustive: There are many, many more out there—but we have selected those that occur most frequently in the reading material that intermediate and middle grade students are most likely to encounter. Thus, they occur often enough to warrant our direct attention *and* exploration of them, and how they combine provides a powerful foundation and productive strategy for continuing vocabulary and spelling growth.

A final word about these elements and how they combine: We should point out to students that they will be finding the effects of these combinations everywhere they look. For example, while browsing in the electronics store at the mall they will encounter a brand name based on the combination of these elements, as, for example, in *Magnavox*— "large voice."

Absorbed prefixes are addressed quite late in the instructional sequence because they depend upon considerable prior knowledge about other basic spelling/meaning patterns, upon processes of adding prefixes to base words, and upon simple Greek and Latin stems. They should be presented for the first time in the context of *base words:* <u>con</u>- + <u>respond</u> = co<u>rr</u>espond; <u>in</u> + <u>mo</u>bilize = i<u>mm</u>obilize. Once understood in these types of words, they may be taught in the context of *word roots:* <u>ad</u> +<u>tain</u> =a<u>tt</u>ain; <u>com</u> + <u>rode</u> = co<u>rr</u>ode.

Teacher Modeling

"Walking through words" helps students understand how derivational relationships work.

In this section we'll present vignettes illustrating how we can model and walk students through important features of derivational word knowledge.

Describing the Spelling/Meaning Connection

The teacher writes the word pair *compose* and *composition* on the chalkboard. Underlining the letters *compos* in each word, she asks the students, "Do these letters stand for the same sounds in both words, or different sounds? . . . In 'compose,' the *o* in the second syllable has a long vowel sound, doesn't it? It changes to a 'schwa' sound in the second syllable of *composition*. We say that these two words are related in *meaning* and in *spelling,* even though these letters stand for different sounds.

"Keeping this fact in mind can help you spell a word you may not be sure of, like *composition*. Why? Because that schwa sound in the second syllable of the word doesn't give you any clue to the spelling. Schwas are like that—they can be spelled with any one of the vowel letters, but the sound won't give you a clue. You've got a powerful strategy you can use, though: By thinking of a *related* word, like *compose* you can get a clue. You can clearly hear the vowel sound in the second syllable of *compose*—it is an 'o' and you know how to spell it—so that is your clue to the spelling of the schwa sound in 'composition.'

"Remember, *words that are related in meaning are often related in spelling as well.* So, by thinking of a word that is related to one you're trying to spell, you will often uncover a helpful clue to the spelling."

<u>Describing How Latin Roots 'Work'</u>

Here's an explanation of the Latin word root -*fract*-: The teacher has written the words *fracture* and *fraction* on the board:

"Kids, we know what these two words are and what they mean. They both come from a Latin word, though, that meant 'to break.' Can you see how the meaning of each of these words comes from this root? Let's take *fracture* first—when James broke his arm last fall, we talked about his *fracture.* When you first started learning about numbers that were smaller than whole numbers, you learned about *fractions,* which literally mean 'breaking down' whole numbers into smaller parts."

<u>Describing the Process of Prefix Assimilation ("Absorbed" Prefixes)</u>

"Jared, you checked the prefix *in-* in the dictionary yesterday and were a little perplexed! You discovered that it said that this prefix is also spelled *il, im,* and *ir.* It seems a little peculiar, doesn't it? Well, let's look at why this is so.

Show students *how* the process of *prefix assimilation* works—a process that is widespread and a powerful clue to spelling and vocabulary.

"Let's take the word *immobile.* Actually, it's constructed from the prefix *in,* meaning 'not,' and the base word *mobile,* which means 'capable of moving.' When we put *in* and *mobile* together, two things happen. First, the word parts combine to mean 'not mobile'— not capable of moving. Second, notice that the spelling of the prefix *in* has changed to *im.* Let's think about why this happened.

"A long time ago, someone realized that instead of always saying something was 'not mobile' they could simply combine the prefix *in* with the word *mobile* to create a new word that meant 'not mobile.' Now, try pronouncing the word like it was pronounced when it first came into existence—*in*mobile. Does that feel kind of weird? Does your tongue kind of get stuck on the beginning of 'mobile'? Mine sure does! Well, the same thing happened to speakers a long time ago—it became easier for people to leave out the 'n' sound when pronouncing the word. The sound of the 'n' became 'absorbed' into the 'm' sound at the beginning of the base word *mobile.* Before long, the spelling of the *n* changed to indicate this change in pronunciation—but it's important to remember that this letter didn't disappear. They knew it was necessary to keep the two letters in their prefix to indicate that it was still a prefix. If the last letter of the prefix had been dropped, then the meaning of the prefix would have been lost.

"Here are some other words that have 'absorbed' the *in* prefix into the base word [writes the words *immeasureable, immodest,* and *immortal* on the board]. These started out as *in*measureable, *in*modest, and *in*mortal."

The next step, in this lesson or on the following day, is to show how *in-* changes to *ir-* when combined with a base that begins with *r* (*irresponsible*) and how it changes to *il-* when combined with a base that begins with *l-* (*illiterate*). Other absorbed prefixes may be studied as they arise. Students will come to realize that the process of prefix assimilation or absorbed prefixes is quite widespread in the language.

<u>Describing the Effects of Accent and Consonant Doubling</u>

"Okay, we've got a few words here to sort. Notice that all of them end with 'ed.' But when we look at the base word, we see that in some cases the final consonant has been doubled before adding 'ed,' and in others it has stayed the same. Sort the words into two columns—those that are doubled and those that are not—and let's see if we can figure out what's going on here."

occurred	benefited
submitted	orbited
referred	conquered

The generalization towards which we are working in the sort is this: If the second syllable of the base word is accented, double the final consonant before adding -ed (and -ing as well). If the second syllable is *not* accented, then do *not* double the final consonant. Follow up the sort by pointing out the following bit of history:

"Here's something interesting: Have you ever noticed, for example, how the British and Canadians spell a word like 'benefited'? They double the final 't'! Actually, in just about every situation where we in America do *not* double the final consonant, people in other English-speaking countries *do*. Do you know who we can blame for making it so that Americans have to think about whether or not to double. . .? Would you believe it was *Noah Webster*? Yes! The man who brought us our dictionary!

"Actually, what Webster wanted to do was make English spoken and written in America different in many ways from English spoken in Britain. When he did this, America wasn't getting along too well with Britain—after all, we had fought a war to become independent not long before! So, in his dictionary of *American* English—the first of its kind—Webster decided to change many spellings. One of the most obvious was to take out the 'u' in words such as 'honour' and 'behaviour' [writes these on the board]. He also switched the 're' in words such as 'theatre' and 'centre' [writes these on the board]."

What this teacher has done is to bring a human side to an otherwise rather puzzling phenomenon. There is a *reason* why most words are spelled as they are, and very often there is an historical story behind a spelling. Sharing such information with students helps them to remember many spellings because they can associate them with a memorable story.

Word Study Notebooks

Many of the activities presented below involve students' word study notebooks. There is, however, a specific strategy we encourage older students to learn and apply (Gill & Bear, 1989). With the word study notebook close at hand, we urge students to get in the habit of doing the following:

1. While you are reading, place a question mark above words you find difficult, and place a question mark in the margin for easy reference. When

Students learn how syllable structure and *accent provide clues to consonant doubling—as well as* why *this process came about.*

Through a focus on definition, word structure, and context, word study notebooks *become powerful vocabulary builders.*

you are through reading or studying, go back to your question marks. Read around the word, and think about its possible meaning.

2. Write the word, followed by the sentence it came from, the page number, and an abbreviation for the title of the book. (There will be times when the sentence is too long. Write enough of the sentence to give a clue to meaning.) Think about the word's meaning.

3. Look at the different parts of the word—prefixes, suffixes, and root word. Think about the meaning of the affixes and root.

4. Think of other words which are like this one, and write them underneath the part of the word which is similar.

5. Look the word up in the dictionary, read the various definitions, and in a few words record the meaning (the one that applies to the word in the book you are reading) in your notebook or on a card. Look for similar words (both in form and meaning) above and below the target word, and add them to the list you started in item number four above.

6. Look at the origin of the word, and add it to your entry if it is interesting.

A realistic goal is to collect ten words a week. These words may be brought up in class and shared. In addition, record words that consistently present spelling challenges in the notebook or on the cards. For each word, think of words that are related to this particular word—again, as in number 4 above.

Let's summarize the process:

1. Collect the word.
2. Record the word and sentence.
3. Look at word parts and think about their meaning.
4. Record related words.
5. Study the word in the dictionary, and record interesting information.
6. Review.

Here's an example:

1. [Word]   ORTHOGRAPHY
2. [Sentence]   "English orthography is not crazy, and it carries the history of the word with it." p. 22, *Sounds of Language*
3. [Look at word parts] ortho   graph ("may have something to do with writing")
4. [Think of possible related words]

ortho	*graphy*
orthodontist	graphic
orthodox	
orthographer	[Note: These are
orthographist	added from Step 5]
orthomolecular	
orthodox	

5. [Definition] "a method of representing the sounds of a language by letters; spelling"
[Note: The third definition fits most nearly the meaning of *orthography* as it was used in the sentence. The first two meanings are "1. the art or study of standard spelling. 2. The aspect of language study concerned with letters and spelling," (*The American Heritage College Dictionary* (1993), p. 965).
6. [Origins]   ortho: correct   graph: something written

Activities for Students in the Derivational Constancy Stage

Early
Derivational
Constancy

Materials

Word sort lists (see below)

Procedures

To understand *-ion* and *-ian* endings, one must return to the base word or word root in the examples illustrated in the following lists—the clue, as each category below reveals, lies in the spelling of the base or root. Closed word sorts can be created by combining any two or more categories from these lists and hunting down similar features of pattern or sound. Following are the several categories of base and derived word in which *-ion* or *-ian* has been added, together with the generalization that applies to each:

1. Words ending with **"te"**

separate	separation
fascinate	fascination
educate	education
complicate	complication
gencrate	generation
navigate	navigation
vegetate	vegetation

   This is a simple addition; the e drops, the "t" is retained, and the word adds *-ion*. (Note: Words ending in "t" without the "e" perform the same: "erupt" to "eruption".)

2. Words ending with **"ce" (or "ct")**

introduce	introduction
produce	production
reduce	reduction
extinct	extinction
act	action
contract	contraction
conduct	conduction
affect	affection

In "ce" endings, the e drops and *-tion* is added. In "ct" words, both letters are maintained and the ending *-ion* is added giving "ce" and "ct" words identical endings (tion). (Note: *"pronounce/pronunciation"* is a variant, though it follows its own pattern—as in *renounce/renunciation* and *announce/annunciation*.)

3. *Words ending with **"se"** and **"ss"***

convulse	convulsion
repulse	repulsion
express	expression
profess	profession

Words with "se" endings drop the e and maintain the *-sion*. Words with "ss" endings maintain the double "s". (Note: When "t" occurs at the end of a word, preceded by a vowel, the "t" changes to "s" and *-sion* is added, resulting in a doubled "s": *permit/permission; remit/remission*.)

Middle
Derivational
Constancy

4. Words ending with **"de"** or **"d"**

include	inclusion
explode	explosion
delude	delusion
persuade	persuasion
erode	erosion
collide	collision
extend	extension
comprehend	comprehension
succeed	succession
proceed	procession

BUT

intend	intention
contend	contention
attend	attention

Words with "de" endings go to *-sion* as do most "d" endings. It may be necessary to give special attention to the "d" endings which go to *-tion* since there seems no rule to distinguish words such as "extend to extension" from "attend to attention". (Note: When "de" goes to "s", the "s" is sounded as "z" as in "inclu"z "ion". This is caused by the open vowel preceding the *-sion* since it also applies to words such as *occasion*.)

Middle
Derivational
Constancy

5. All other **"e"** endings:

admire	admiration
perspire	perspiration
determine	determination
observe	observation
illumine	illumination
imagine	imagination
inspire	inspiration
realize	realization
starve	starvation

NOTE:

compose	composition
expose	exposition
depose	deposition
relax	relaxation
exclaim	exclamation
reclaim	reclamation

All other "e" endings drop the "e" and replace it with "a," giving an added syllable to the word. In the case of "se" endings preceded by a long vowel, the "e" is replaced with an "i". This dropping of the long vowel marker is also true in words like *exclaim* where the "i" is dropped and the "a" is added. (NOTE: In *relax* to *relaxation*, the "x" is a letter which behaves according to its own rules. Perhaps "x" at the end of words cannot take an "e," but sometimes, as in this case, behaves as if it had.)

Middle Derivational Constancy

6. Words ending with **"y"**

apply	application
occupy	occupation
satisfy	satisfaction

To develop patterns for these words, it may be necessary to examine additional derivatives such as *apply* to *applicable* to *application*. Since the accent moves in these words, consideration of various derivatives can aid in spelling (the second syllable of application is spelled with an "i" since it comes from *apply*).

Middle Derivational Constancy

7. Words ending with **"cian"**

magic	magician
beauty	beautician
statistic	statistician
music	musician
physic	physician
diet	dietician

It becomes obvious that all of these *-cian* words represent people. In most cases they stand for "one who creates." The same is true of words such as *guardian*.

A **"Is It '*sion*' or '*tion*'?"** 8–18

Early Derivational Constancy

This activity will involve students in small groups or two teams of two each, examining words to determine clues for the spellings *-tion* and *-sion*.

Materials

Small cards on which to write the base words and their derivations; each team or group needs a sheet divided into two columns, labeled on the left column "We Think," and on the right column "Because"; stop watch or timer.

Procedures

1. Each team gets a stack of cards to sort (the same words are in each stack, written in two colors to keep separate).
2. The teams separate and sort the cards into what they think are appropriate categories (no previous hints about how to do this sort should be given).
3. After looking closely at the words sorted, each team individually fills out their "We Think" sheets with generalities that they notice about when words took the *-tion* or the *-sion* ending.
4. After the teams have filled out their "We Think" sheets and supported their generalized rules under the "Because" section, the teams have a meeting of the minds to compare findings.
5. After the teams have come to a mutual generalization about the spelling patterns of base words that add either *-tion* or *-sion,* they do a final word sort—against the clock and each other.

Variations

This activity will work with other base words and derivations. Also, this activity may be used with a larger group. A variation may be to have the students look for other words with *-tion* or *-sion* endings, determine the base or root, and then determine whether it fits the spelling generalization the team came up with. This gives students the opportunity to keep a running record in their word study notebook and to monitor their generalization to see if it continues to work for new words that are encountered.

Word List

Words may be selected from categories 1 through 6 in the "-*ion* or -*ian*" activity above.

GA | Greek and Latin Word Parts: Science Vocabulary   8–19

Early/Middle
Derivational
Constancy

As we mentioned earlier, Greek and Latin word parts form a large part of the new vocabulary that students encounter in the intermediate years and beyond. This is most apparent at first in the area of science. Students can see how these parts occur in a number of words, and that these parts so very often represent consistent meanings. After word parts are examined in several terms, students can list the elements—and words in which they are found—in their word study notebooks. They can hunt for these elements in words in their texts and add these words to their lists.

This activity works best after students have been introduced to a number of word roots and examined how they "work" in words. The teacher should precede this activity with a walk-through for Latin and Greek elements (see pp. 330–334). Students, alone or in small groups, may sort words by root, using words that contain the most frequently-occurring roots (see accompanying word list).*

Materials

File folders with Greek and Latin elements listed at top of inside flap; word cards to be sorted.

Procedures

Have students sort three or four roots at a time. Write each root on a card with its origin and meaning on the back. Words can be sorted by following these directions:
1. *Sort* the words, matching them with the Greek or Latin word part they contain.
2. *Say* the words; students should use general knowledge about the meanings to guess what the Greek or Latin word part means. Ask these questions:

  ◆ What do all of the words have in common?
  ◆ How are they related?

3. Students should check the back of the word card to see if their guess about the meaning is correct. What part of the meaning stays *constant* among the related words?
4. Record the words, by word part, in word study notebooks.

Word List

astro- [Greek "astron," *star*]: astronomer, astronaut, astrology, astrolabe
bio- [Greek "bios," *life*]: biology, biome, biosphere, biotic

---

*This activity was developed by Patsy Stine and Amy Dixon.

-chlor- [Greek "khloros," *greenish-yellow*]: chlorophyll, chloroplast, chlorine, chlorella

eco- [Greek "oikos," *house*]: ecology, economy, ecosystem, ecotype

hydro- [Greek "hydor," *water*]: hydrophobia, hydrology

hypo- [Greek "hypo," *under*]: hypodermis, hypodermic, hypothermia, hypotension

photo/phos- [Greek "phos," *light*]: phosphorescent, photography

vor- [Latin "vorax," *devour*]: voracious, omnivore, carnivore

Variations

After the students automatically respond to the meaning of about a dozen Greek and Latin word parts, they may work cooperatively as a group to sort words according to their roots. Then, they may categorize the words according to the area of science in which they might be used— "plant words," "animal words," "environment words," "space words."

A **"Greek and Latin Jeopardy®"** 8–20

Middle/Late Derivational Constancy

A total of six students are involved in this game. Three students are the "contestants," while one student is in charge of the answers and questions; one student is the scorekeeper, and one person can be the judge in case of the need to question a decision.*

Materials

Enlarge the "Latin Root Jeopardy®" and "Double Latin Root Jeopardy®" boards in Figures 8–10 and 8–11. (Using an overhead projector will make the task much easier.) Cut on the lines so that each square is separate from the others. Fix them in the correct order, using a small piece of tape on either side (so they will stick to the board) with the side on which only the number is written is facing out. Turn over the square that is requested during the playing of the game so the answer can be read.

Procedures

The teacher will probably need to go over the rules of the game first.

1. The game is modeled after the *Jeopardy* television game. The answer will appear when it is turned over in this version. The players must phrase their answers in the form of a question.
2. The game consists of three rounds: Jeopardy, Double Jeopardy, and Final Jeopardy.
3. The first player to respond correctly with the question to an answer chooses the next question.
4. Questions are chosen by category and point amount (see Figures 8–12 and 8–13). The leader then reads the question to the players.
5. Point amounts are used rather than dollar amounts as on television.
6. The first player responding correctly adds the point amount of the question to his or her total. An incorrect answer means that amount is subtracted.
7. When it is time for the "Final Jeopardy" question, here is the procedure: Players see the category, but not the answer. They then decide how many of their points they will risk. When they see the answer, they have thirty seconds to write the question. If they are correct, they

---

*Helen McMullen developed this word study game.

add the number of points they risked to their total; if incorrect, that number of points is subtracted from their total.

Answer: Coming from the Latin root meaning "great," its defiinition means "generous in forgiving."

Question: What is *magnanimous?*

Word List

In the word lists, we have used modern English spellings of roots and their contemporary meanings, rather than tracing the evolution of each root from its original spelling and literal meaning in Latin.

TABLE 8–4   Additional Latin Roots

aud: to hear
audible, inaudible, audience, auditory, audio, audition, auditorium

bene: well, good
benefit, beneficial, benevolent, benefactor, benediction

cred: to believe, to trust
credit, credible, credence, discredit

dict: to say
dictate, diction, dictator, dictionary, contradict, contradiction, indict, benediction

duc: to lead
conducive, deduce, deduct, educate, induce, introduce, produce, reduce, aquaduct

fac: to do, to make
fact, factual, factory, faciliate, manufacture, benefactor

flec/flex: to bend
reflection, deflect, flexible

form: shape
formation, formative, deform, formula

fract: to break
fracture, refract, fraction

ject: throw
reject, projectile, eject, inject

jud: judge
judgment, prejudice, adjudicate

junct: to join
juncture, junction, conjunction

port: to carry
import, export, transport portable

rupt: to break
abrupt, corrupt, disrupt, eruption, interrupt, bankrupt, rupture

scrib/script: to write
inscribe, transcribe, transcript, manuscript, prescription, describe

sect/sec: cut
dissect, intersect, insect, midsection

spect: to look
spectator, inspect, prospect suspect

spir: to breath
respiration, inspire, conspirators

st/sta/stat: to stand
stable, station, constant, establish, statue, arrest, constitute, institute, obstacle

stru: to build
construct, instruct, destruct

tang/tact: to touch
tangible/intangible, tangent, contact, tactile

trac/tract: to drag, pull
trace, track, tractable, tractor, detract, extract distract

vid/vis: to see
video, invisible, television

vert/vers: to turn
revert, inversion, vertical, convert

voc: voice, to call
vocal, advocate, vociferous

FIGURE 8–10   Latin Root Jeopardy® Board

LATIN ROOTJEOPARDY®

SPECT (to look)	FORM (shape)	PORT (to carry)	TRACT (draw or pull)	DICT (to say, speak)
100 One who watches; an onlooker	100 One "form" or style of clothing such as is worn by nurses	100 Goods brought into a country from another country to be sold	100 Adjective: having power to attract; alluring; inviting	100 A book containing the words of a language explained
200 The prospect of good to come; anticipation	200 One who does not conform	200 One who carries burdens for hire	200 A powerful motor vehicle for pulling farm machinery, heavy loads, etc.	200 A speaking against, a denial
300 To regard with suspicion and mistrust.	300 To form or make anew; to reclaim	300 To remove from one place to another	300 The power to grip or hold to a surface while moving, without slipping	300 A blessing often at the end of a worship service
400 Verb: to esteem Noun: regard, deference Literally: to look again	400 To change into another substance, change of form	400 To give an account of	400 An agreement: literally, to draw together	400 An order proclaimed by an authority
500 Looking around, watchful, prudent	500 Disfigurement, spoiling the shape	500 A case for carrying loose papers	500 To take apart from the rest, to deduct	500 To charge with a crime

FIGURE 8–11 Double Latin Root Jeopardy® Board

DOUBLE LATIN ROOT JEOPARDY®

CRED (to believe)	DUCT (to lead)	FER (to bear)	PRESS (to press)	SPIR (to breathe)
200 A system of doing business by trusting that a person will pay at a later date for goods or services.	200 A person who directs the performance of an choir or an orchestra.	200 (Plants) able to bear fruit; (Animals) able or likely to conceive young.	200 A printing machine.	200 An immaterial intelligent being.
400 A set of beliefs or principles.	400 To train the mind and abilities of.	400 To carry again; to submit to another for opinion.	400 Verb; to utter; Noun; any fast conveyance.	400 To breathe out; to die.
600 Unbelievable.	600 To enroll as a member of a military service.	600 To convey to another place, passed from one place to another.	600 To press against, to burden, to overpower.	600 To breath through; to emit through the pores of the skin.
800 Verb, prefix meaning "not", word means to damage the good reputation of.	800 The formal presentation of one person to another.	800 Endurance of pain; distress.	800 State of being "pressed down" or saddened	800 To breath into; to instruct by divine influence.
1000 An adjective, prefix "ac", word means officially recognized.	1000 An artificial channel carrying water across country.	1000 Cone bearing, as the fir tree.	1000 To put down, to prevent circulation.	1000 To plot; to band together for an evil purpose.

FIGURE 8–12   Questions for Latin Root Jeopardy and Double Latin Root Jeopardy

Questions for Latin Root Jeopardy	*Questions for Double Latin Root Jeopardy*

Spect

1. What is spectator?
2. What is expectation?
3. What is suspect?
4. What is respect?
5. What is circumspect?

Cred

1. What is credit?
2. What is creed?
3. What is incredible?
4. What is discredit?
5. What is accredited?

Form

1. What is uniform?
2. What is nonconformist?
3. What is reform?
4. What is transform?
5. What is deformity?

Duct

1. What is conductor?
2. What is educate?
3. What is induct?
4. What is introduction?
5. What is aqueduct?

Port

1. What is import?
2. What is porter?
3. What is transport?
4. What is report?
5. What is portfolio?

Fer

1. What is fertile?
2. What is refer?
3. What is transfer?
4. What is suffering?
5. What is coniferous?

Tract

1. What is attractive?
2. What is tractor?
3. What is traction?
4. What is contract?
5. What is subtract?

Press

1. What is press?
2. What is express?
3. What is oppress?
4. What is depression?
5. What is suppress?

Dict

1. What is dictionary?
2. What is contradiction?
3. What is benediction?
4. What is edict?
5. What is indict?

Spir

1. What is spirit?
2. What is expire?
3. What is perspire?
4. What is inspire?
5. What is conspire?

Variations

The gameboard may be copied and given to players who work alone. A sketch of the gameboard may be drawn on the chalkboard with the point amount in the square. Mark off the square chosen before the question is read by the leader from her copy. "Daily Doubles" may be included, if desired (the number of points for an answer is doubled, and if correct, added to the player's score; if incorrect the doubled number of points is subtracted from the player's score).

FIGURE 8–13   Alternate Items for Latin Root Jeopardy

Latin Root Jeopardy
(Alternate Items)

1. *valeo* – to be strong, to be worth
    a. noun–the worth of thing in money or goods
    b. noun–courage or bravery
    c. verb–to value at less than the real worth
    d. adj.–brave, full of courage
    e. adj.–priceless, precious
2. *signum, signi* – to sign, to seal
    a. to write one's name on–verb
    b. a person's name written by himself–noun
    c. a thing or happening that shows, warns, or points out–noun
    d. to be a sign of, to mean–verb
    e. a seal or other mark stamped on a paper to make it official–noun
3. *nomen, nominis* – name
    a. to name as a candidate for election–verb
    b. a person who is nominated–noun
    c. in name only–adj.
    d. a system of names, as those used in studying a certain science–noun
    e. showing the subject of a verb, or the words that agree with the subject–noun
4. *rumpo, ruptum* – to break
    a. to burst forth, as lava from a volcano–verb
    b. to break in between–as in conversation–verb
    c. to part violently–verb; a hernia–noun
    d. a rending asunder, something you don't want in the classroom–noun
    e. to defile, to taint–verb
5. *struo, structus* – to build
    a. noun–a building
    b. adj–"good" or criticism
    c. noun–ruin
    d. verb–to teach or train
    e. noun–that part of the building above the foundation

Questions for Latin Root Jeopardy
(Alternate Items)

1. *valeo*
    a. What is values?
    b. What is valor?
    c. What is undervalue?
    d. What is valiant?
    e. What is invaluable?
2. *signum*
    a. What is sign?
    b. What is signature?
    c. What is signal?
    d. What is signify?
    e. What is signet?
3. *nomen*
    a. What is nominate?
    b. What is nominee?
    c. What is nominal?
    d. What is nomenclature?
    e. What is nominative?
4. *rumpo*
    a. What is erupt?
    b. What is interrupt?
    c. What is rupture?
    d. What is disruption?
    e. What is nominative?
5. *struo*
    a. What is structure?
    b. What is constructive?
    c. What is destruction?
    d. What is instruct?
    e. What is superstructure?

A "Hidden" Greek Roots 8–21

Middle/Late
Derivational
Constancy

This is a more advanced activity with Greek roots for 1 to 3 students.

Materials

Greek root reference sheet; Greek root word cards; definition cards; dictionary.

Procedures

1. The teacher initiates discussion and background material for Greek Root Word activity.
2. The teacher and/or students prepare word/definition cards.
3. Then using the Table of Greek Roots as a guide, student(s) sort word cards by:

   ✦ Greek word families
   ✦ Greek word card/definition card match
   ✦ Through discussion and use of dictionaries, students may "discover" related word families.

Variations

One variation is the card game "It's All Greek to Us." The deck is composed of Greek Word Cards. Two to four players may participate, one of whom will serve as "Game Master" and hold and read definition cards.

1. The Game Master shuffles word cards, deals 10 cards per player, and places remaining word cards face down in front of players.
2. Players refer to the Table of Greek Roots (Table 8-5) and their ten cards, as Game Master reads definition card. If a player is holding a card to match the definition, he places it below the corresponding Greek Root. Upon discarding, players must draw one word card from remaining deck. If no player can respond to the defnition, the Game Master places the definition card on the bottom of his cards for rereading later in the game. If a player successfully responds and matches a word card and definition, the Game Master places that definition card to the side.
3. When word card deck is depleted, player who discards all word cards first is the winner.

Definition Cards

Adj.	1. Of long duration, continuing, constant
	2. Prolonged
Adj.	Arranged in order of time of occurrence
N.	The representation of something as existing or happening at other than its proper or historical time; anything out of its proper time
N.	The medical study of the physiology and pathology of the skin
N.	The outer, protective, nonvascular layer of the skin
N.	A design composed of one or more letters, usually the initials of a name
Adj.	Without variation or variety; repetitiously dull
Adj.	1. Bold and definite in expression or action
	2. Accentuated; definite
V.	To speak of God (or something sacred) in an irreverent or impious manner
N.	The substitution of an inoffensive term for one considered offensively explicit
Adj.	Devoted to or appreciative of music
N.	1. A listing of the order of events and other pertinent information for some public presentation

TABLE 8–5 Greek Roots

aer: air
aerial, aerate

agog: leader
demagogue, pedagogue, synagogue

angel: messenger
evangelist, angelic

aster/astr: star
asteroid, astronomer, astronomy,
asterisk

auto: self
autograph, autobiography

chron: time
chronic, chonicle, chronology,
synchrony

derm: skin
epidermis, dermatology

gram: thing written
diagram, monogram, telegram

graph: writing
autograph, biography, photograph,
telegraph

hydr: water
hydrant, hydrology, hydroplane

logo: word, reason
logic, analogy, catalogue, prologue

meter/metr: measure
metric, barometer, diameter,
geometry, perimeter, symmetry

micro: small
microscope, micrometer

mono: one, single
monotone, monastery, monk

od/hod: road, way
episode, method, methodical, exodus,
episode

phe/phem: to speak
blaspheme, emphasis, euphemism

phil: love
philanthropy, Philadelphia,
philosophy, philharmonic

phon: sound
telephone, phonics, symphonic,
euphony

photo/phos: light
photograph, telephoto,
phosphorescent

pol/polis: city, state
police, metropolis, politics,
cosmopolitan

scope: instrument for viewing
microscope, telescope,
kaleidoscope

techn: art, skill, craft
technical, technology, polytechnic

therm: heat
thermometer, thermostat, thermal,
exothermic

zoo: animal
zoo, zoology

---

	2. a. A procedure for solving a problem
	b. Coded for a computer
Adj.	1. Of or pertaining to written or pictorial representation
	2. Described in vivid detail
N.	The process of rendering optical images on photosensitive surfaces
N.	A movement away; a departure, usually of a large number of people
N.	A means or manner of procedure; especially, a regular and systematic way of accomplishing anything
N.	An outlet from a water main consisting of an upright pipe with one or more nozzles or spouts
Adj.	Of, involving, moved, or operated by a fluid, especially water, under pressure
Adj.	1. Showing consistency of reasoning
	2. Able to reason clearly
N.	A statement of acknowledgement expressing regret or asking pardon for a fault or offense
N.	A short addition or concluding section at the end of any literary work or play

N.   An instrument for measuring atmospheric pressure, used in weather forecasting and in determining elevation

N.   1. a. *Mathematics*–A closed curve bounding a plane area
    b. The length of such a boundary
    2. *Military*–A fortified strip or boundary protecting a position

N.   A long speech or talk made by one person

N.   Exclusive possession of our control over anything

N.   A succession of sounds or words uttered in a single tone of voice

N.   The composition of printed material from movable type

N.   Public park or institution in which living animals are kept and exhibited to the public

N.   The biological science of animals

N.   An irrational fear of animals

N.   Science that deals with microorganisms, especially their effects on other forms of life

N.   A diminutive, representative world

N.   A film upon which documents or photographs are greatly reduced in size

N.   The scientific study of one of the universes beyond the earth, especially the observation, calculation, and theoretical interpretation of the position, dimensions, distribution, motion, composition, and evolution of celestial bodies and phenomena

Adj.   1. Of or pertaining to astronomy
    2. Inconceivably large; immense

N.   The story of a person's life written by himself; memoirs

N.   A person's own signature or handwriting

V.   To dip or immerse in water or to sprinkle water on (a person) during a baptismal ceremony

V.   To expose to the circulation of air for purification

Adj.   1. Of, in, or caused by the air
    2. Reaching high into the air; lofty

N.   A leader who obtains power by means of impassioned appeals to the emotions and prejudices of the populace

N.   Schoolteacher; educator

N.   The suffering of intense physical or mental pain

N.   One who opposes and actively competes with another; adversary

Adj.   Of, or pertaining to, consisting of, or belonging to angels

N.   The zealous preaching and dissemination of the gospel, as through missionary work

N.   A star-shaped figure (*) used in print to indicate an omission or a reference to a footnote

N.   The study of the nature of God and religious truth

N.   Disbelief in or denial of the existence of God

N.   One who denies the existence of God

V.   To write something with a typewriter; to typewrite

Adj.   Exhibiting the traits or characteristics peculiar to its kind, class, group, or the like; representative of a whole group

N.   1. City of Brotherly Love
    2. Large metropolitan city in Pennsylvania

N.   The effort or inclination to increase the well-being of mankind, as by charitable aid or donations

Adj.   Occurring at the same time

N.   The study of language as a systematically composed body of words

N.   The study of the position and aspects of heavenly bodies with a view to predicting their influence on the course of human affairs

Adj.   1. Too small to be seen by the unaided eye

	2. Exceedingly small, minute
N.	A small tube in which patterns of colors are optically produced and viewed for amusement
Adj.	Doubting; questioning; disbelieving
N.	The systematic procedure by which a complex or scientific task is completed
Adj.	Pertaining to or dealing with many arts and sciences
N.	Beautiful handwriting
Adj.	Of or pertaining to, or having the nature of sound, especially speech sound
N.	1. Harmony, especially of sound or color
	2. Anything characterized by a harmonious combination of elements
Adj.	1. Common to the whole world
	2. At home in all parts of the earth, or in many spheres of interest
N.	1. A major city
	2. A large urban center of culture, trade, or other activity
N.	The fortified height or citadel of a city

 "Joined at the Roots": A Categorization Activity 8–22

| Middle/Late Derivational Constancy | This activity may be a very effective extension of students' exploration of Latin and Greek roots. It is appropriate for individuals, buddies, or small groups. |

Materials

Word sort board; word cards; word study notebook.

Procedures

1. The teacher begins by modeling how to place words with appropriate roots under a particular category, for example, "speaking and writing," "building/construction," "thinking and feeling," and "movement." She then involves the students in the categorization.
2. Once students have grasped how this categorization scheme "works," they can work in small groups or in pairs: Each group or pair will take a different category and sort words whose roots justify their membership in that category.
3. Lists can be written down in word study notebooks and brought back to the larger group to share and discuss. (NOTE: Several of the words to be sorted may be placed under different categories.) Following are some examples of categories and a few illustrative words.

Word List

Building/ Construction	Thinking and Feeling	Movement	Travel
technology	philanthropy	synchrony	astronaut
construct	philosophy	fracture	exodus
tractor		attraction	

Government	Speaking and Writing
economy	autobiography
demagogue	photograph
politics	catalogue
	emphasis

A | "Is it -able or -ible?" 8–23

Middle/Late Derivational Constancy

This may be done as a class activity from the board or in a small group. This study should follow an examination of *-sion, -tion,* and *-cian* since many of the principles examined relate to both and are explained in more detail in the previous study.

Materials

The features to be examined must be controlled; students in the early derivational stage need only examine the first three or four concepts; older, more experienced students may consider the less frequent patterns. A suggested order follows:

1. If the ending follows a full word it is *able;* if it follows a root which is not a full word it is *ible*.

depend	dependable
expend	expendable
pass	passable
profit	profitable
break	breakable
agree	agreeable
predict	predictable
perish	perishable
accept	acceptable
remark	remarkable
read	readable
laugh	laughable
profit	profitable
punish	punishable
cred-	credible
aud-	audible
ed-	edible
plaus-	plausible
vis-	visible
feas-	feasible
compat-	compatible
terr-	terrible
horr-	horrible
poss-	possible
indel-	indelible
leg-	legible

2. If a word ends in a silent "e" drop the "e" and add *-able*.

presume	presumable
pleasure	pleasurable
desire	desirable
dispense	dispensable
blame	blamable
use	usable
excuse	excusable
love	lovable
deplore	deplorable
compare	comparable

3. However, a soft "g" or "c" (*gem, cite*) cannot precede an "a" (*gate, cat*); therefore, to maintain the soft sound, words ending in "ce" or "ge" keep the "e" before adding *-able*.

notice	noticeable
peace	peaceable
marriage	marriageable
bridge	bridgeable
manage	manageable
change	changeable
notice	noticeable
service	serviceable

4. Soft "c" or "g" endings without silent "e" must, for the same reason as in item number three, go to *-ible*.

negligible	invincible
eligible	irascible
intelligible	crucible
tangible	legible

5. It follows that words ending with a hard "g" or "c" sound must take an *-able* ending.

navigable	applicable
indefatigable	amicable
despicable	irrevocable
impeccable	

6. A few words ending in silent "e" do not retain the "e," and therefore they also must go to *-ible* to maintain the soft "c" sound.

convince	convincible		
induce	inducible		
reduce	reducible		
force	forcible		
produce	producible		
expand	expanse	expansion	expansible
defend	defense	defensive	defensible
reprehend		reprehensive	reprehensible
respond	response	responsive	responsible
sense		sensitive	sensible

Because *-able/-ible* is a very complex issue, it is possible to find exceptions or low frequency patterns. It is interesting to compare and contrast these words and discover or hypothesize reasons for these findings. Since very few children (or adults) will ever totally conquer the mysteries of *-ible/-able,* it is useful to note that more words end in *-able,* and so, if in doubt, use *-able.*

7. Related words: Many root words (verbs) become nouns by adding some form of *-ion.* If the *-ion* form of the word ends in *-ation,* the *-ble* form will be *-able.* This is a very helpful rule since *-ation* endings all include the long "a" sound.

irritate	irritation	irritable
demonstrate	demonstration	demonstrable
estimate	estimation	estimable
tolerate	toleration	tolerable
separate	separation	separable
	duration	durable
impregnate	impregnation	impregnable
commend	commendation	commendable
inflame	inflammation	inflammable

vegetate	vegetation	vegetable
educate	education	educable
navigate	navigation	navigable
admire	admiration	admirable
observe	observation	observable
reclaim	reclamation	reclaimable
apply	application	applicable

8. In the same way, if the *-ion* form derived from the verb root does not include *-ation,* the *-ble* form will be *-ible.*

collect	collection	collectible
access	accession	accessible
contract	contraction	contractible
suppress	suppression	suppressible
repress	repression	repressible
exhaust	exhaustion	exhaustible
reduce	reduction	reducible
produce	production	producible
express	expression	expressible

This is a strong "rule" and overrides the simpler idea that roots which are made up of whole words go to *-able*. There are, however, exceptions to this rule involving root words which end in "ct" (*correct* to *correctable; detect* to *detectable; predict* to *predictable*). The "ct" endings must, therefore, be noted and memorized.

9. When a root ends in "ss" or "ns," the ending is *-ible*. Often the root actually ends in "t" (*permit*) or "d" (*comprehend*) and follows the same pattern as the movement to the *-ion* or *-ive* endings.

permit	permission	permissible
admit	admission	admissible
dismiss	dismissal	dismissible
transmit	transmission	transmissible
comprehend	comprehension	comprehensible

A	**Which Suffix?**	**8–24**

Middle/Late Derivational Constancy	This activity is an excellent follow-up to previous work with base words, roots, and suffixes. It is appropriate for individuals, buddies, or small groups. The suffixes included are: *-ible/-able* (use words in previous activity), *-tion/-sion* (use words from lists on pages 337–339), *ence/-ance, -ary/-ery* (see lists following this activity).

Materials

Word sort board, word cards, word study notebook.

Procedures

1. The teacher chooses how many suffixes to place at the top of the word sort board. (NOTE: Several of the words to be sorted may be placed under different suffixes, for example *permit:* permiss*ible,* permis*sion*) Each card has the base word written on one side and the same word with allowable suffixes on the other side.
2. The teacher mixes up the word cards and places the deck with base words face up. The children in turns choose the top card and decide which suffix category it belongs in.

3. After all the cards are placed, the students record in their word study notebooks what they think the correct spelling of the word is.

4. After recording all the words, the children turn the cards over to self-check the correct spelling.

Variation

Students can work as buddies to explore a particular suffix "team" (for example, -*tion* and -*sion*) to see what generalization(s) may underlie the use of a suffix.

A | Defiance or Patience 8–25

Middle/Late
Derivational
Constancy

"Defiance" (if using the *ant/ance/ancy* family) or "Patience" (if using the *ent/ence/ency* family) is simply a version of Go Fish for three to five players. The object of the game is to make as many groups of two, three, or four cards of the same derivation and to be the first to run out of cards.

Materials

Two decks of 52 blank cards, as close to regular card size as possible. Use the list of words below, as well as roots when applicable. To prepare for the game, select words from the list of your choice in groups of two, three, and four until you have a total of 52 words. Do not split any groupings, as this may be misleading. Write these words across the upper width of the cards and your deck is prepared.

Pre-Game Warm Up

Before playing Defiance and/or Patience, students should engage in a word study activity that addresses both categories of *ant/ance/ancy* and *ent/ence/ency* words. A suggested order follows:

Sort I: *ent* vs. *ant*
Sort II: Add the related -*ence* and -*ance* words. Sort *ent/ence* vs. *ant/ance*. Then match *ent/ence* pairs and *ant/ance* pairs.
Sort III: Add the related -*ency* and -*ancy* words. Sort *ent/ence/ency* vs. *ant/ance/ancy*. Then sort *ent/ence/ency* triples, followed by *ant/ance/ancy* triples.
Sort IV: Add those words that do not come in triples, but simply in pairs for both word families.
Sort V: Add roots to any of the pairs or triplets, sorting first by the -*ant* or -*ent* category, then by groups of two, three, or four in the same derivational family.

Procedures

1. Each player is dealt 5 cards from the deck. The player to the left of the dealer begins the game. He may first lay down any existing groups of two, three, or four that he has in his hand. Then he may ask any other player for a card of a certain derivation that he holds in his hand: "Matthew, give me all of your *resistance*." (This could result in gaining *resistance, resistant, resistancy* or *resist*.)

2. If a player does not have cards with the feature being sought, s/he responds, "Be Defiant" or "Be Patient" depending on which game is being played.

3. At this, the asking player must draw another card from the deck. If the card is of the same family they were seeking, they may lay down the match and continue asking other players for cards. However, if the card is not of the correct derivational group, play passes to the person on their left and continues around the circle in the same manner. If the drawn card makes a match in the asking player's hand, but was not that which was being sought, he must hold the pair in hand until his turn comes up again. Of course this means there is a risk of another player taking the pair before play rotates back to him/her.
4. Play ends when one of the students runs out of cards. The player with the most points wins.
5. Players may play on other people's card groups, laying related cards down in front of themselves, however, not in front of the player who made the original match.
6. Singles played on other people's matches   1 point
    Pairs   2 points
    Triples   6 points
    Groups of Four   10 points
    First player to run out of cards   10 points

Variations

1. "Defy My Patience" could be the version that mixes sets of words from both lists to create a *ent/ant* deck.
2. "Challenge My Patience" or "Defy My Challenge": In this version, during scoring before everyone throws down their hand, students should write down on secret slips of paper any additional words for groups they have laid down, which have not been played. Before hands are revealed, these lists should be shared, and an additional point added to every player's score for each related word they wrote. If other players doubt the authenticity of a word claimed by an opponent, someone may **challenge** the word. The challenger looses a point if the word is valid, or gains a point if it is not. The player, likewise, counts the word if it is valid, or loses a point if the challenger proves him wrong.
3. Students should be encouraged to come up with their own derivational families to be added to this game or another feature to be substituted for the ANT/ENT contrast.

Word List

ENT	ENCE	ENCY	OTHER
patient	patience		
silent	silence		
impatient	impatience		
present	presence		
evident	evidence		
iridescent	iridescence		
incident	incidence		
adolescent	adolescence		
diligent	diligence		
prominent	prominence		
florescent	florescence		
absent	absence		

pendent		pendency	
innocent	innocence		
turbulent	turbulence	turbulency	
belligerent	belligerence	belligerency	
translucent	translucence	translucency	
confident	confidence		confide
obedient	obedience		obey
different	difference		differ
magnificent	magnificence		magnify
violent	violence		violate
coincident	coincidence		coincide
phosphorescent	phosphorescence		phosphorous
reverent	reverence		revere
subsequent	subsequence		sequel
competent	competence	competency	compete
excellent	excellence	excellency	excel
independent	independence	independency	depend
dependent	dependence	dependency	depend
convenient	convenience	conveniency	convene
persistent	persistence	persistency	persist
correspondent	correspondence	correspondency	correspond
resident	residence	residency	reside
equivalent	equivalence	equivalency	equal

ANT	ANCE	ANCY	OTHER
constant		constancy	
tenant		tenancy	
vagrant		vagrancy	
dormant		dormancy	
distant	distance		
grievant	grievance		grief
instant	instance	instancy	
fragrant	fragrance	fragrancy	
valiant	valiance	valiancy	
brilliant	brilliance	brilliancy	
buoyant	buoyance	buoyancy	buoy
vibrant	vibrance	vibrancy	vibrate
vacant		vacancy	vacate

Three Syllables

attendant	attendance		attend
assistant	assistance		assist
important	importance		import
defiant	defiance		defy
arrogant	arrogance		arrogate
dominant	dominance		dominate
ambulant	ambulance		ambulate/tory
ignorant	ignorance		ignore
vigilant	vigilance		vigil
significant	significance		signify
elegant	elegance	elegancy	
hesitant	hesitance	hesitancy	hesitate
reluctant	reluctance	reluctancy	reluct

expectant	expectance	expectancy	expect
radiant	radiance	radiancy	radiate
abundant	abundance	abundancy	abound
resistant	resistance	resistancy	resist

A | Beginning to Explore Assimilated Prefixes: *ad-, com-, and in-* 8–26

Materials

1. Chalkboard, magnetic tape, word cards, word study notebook.
2. Word cards for individual sorting activity (see list in Table 8–6).
3. Sorting folders with given exemplars for sort.

Late Derivational Constancy

Procedures

1. The teacher introduces the three prefixes. She places the exemplars on the board in three columns.
2. The teacher takes a list of word cards with magnetic tape and has students read each card and place the card in the appropriate column (see Figure 8–14).
3. The teacher should discuss any word meanings, if necessary, and how the prefix changes the meaning of the base word. She then asks the class if they can think of why the prefix spelling changes in certain words.
4. The students write the words in their word study notebooks under the appropriate exemplar.
5. After all example words have been studied, mix the cards, and have students sort as a small group or individually.

TABLE 8–6 Assimilated Prefixes and Their Assimilations

ad- (to, toward)	in- (not, into)	com- (with)	ob- (against, toward)
ac- accompany, account, accustom, accommodate af- affirm, affix, affront, affluent ag- aggression, aggrieve, aggravate al- allay, allocate, allot, alleviate an- announce, annotate ar- arrange, arrest, array as- assign, assort, assure, assimilate at- attend, attune	il- illiterate, illegal, illuminate, illegitimate im- immature, immigrant, immobile, immortal, immediate ir- irresponsible, irradiate, irregular, irreligious, irrational	col- collaborate, colleague, collide, collocate, collect con- connect, connote cor- correspond, correct	oc- occur, occult of- offend op- oppose, oppress

	ex-(out)	per-(through)	dis-(opposite)
sub- (under) suc- suceed, sucess suf- suffix, suffuse sup- support, supplant, suppress	ec- ef- efface, effect, efferent	pel-	dil- dif- diffuse, different

FIGURE 8–14 Exploration of Assimilated Prefixes: ad-, com-, in-

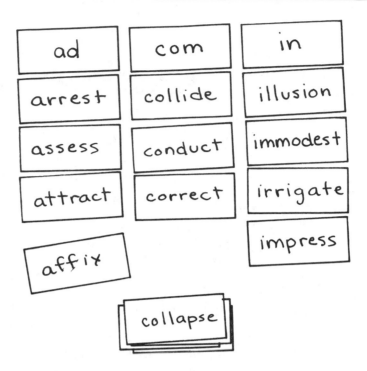

6. Have students go on a word hunt for words with these assimilated prefixes, and add to the word study notebook.

| A | "Assimile" | 8–27 |

Late Derivational
Constancy

Setting: 2-6 players *

Materials

Game board modeled after "Monopoly" (see Figure 8–15); dice; game playing pieces; colored blank word cards with base words written on each ("Chance" cards); deck of assimilated prefix base words (only readily-apparent base words such as *accompany;* see list below); sheet of paper and pencil or pen for each player (to use in spelling words).

Procedures

This game is modeled after Monopoly®.

1. Assimilated prefix base words (readily apparent base words) are placed face down around the board. A particular prefix is chosen to be focused on, and this is placed face up in the center of the board. "Chance" cards (colored cards with base words written on them) are also placed in the middle. Chance cards are a "chance" to think of one's own assimilated prefix word using the base word on the card and any assimilated prefix. Chance cards are picked up every time a player passes 'GO.'

---

*Telia Blackard contributed this activity.

FIGURE 8–15 Assimile Gameboard

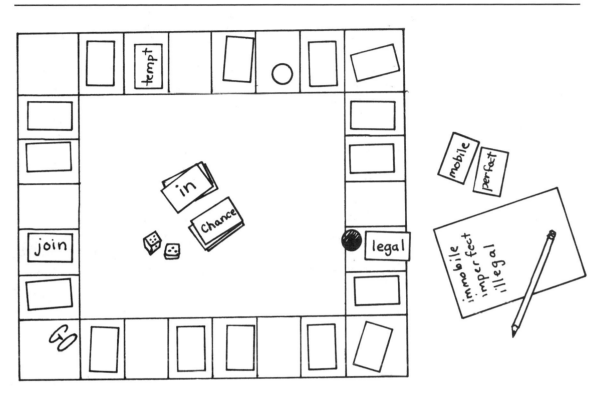

2. Players roll the dice to see who goes first. The player with the highest number rolls again and moves the number of spaces on the board.

3. Upon landing on a particular space, the word card is turned up, and the player has to determine whether this word can be assimilated to the prefix in the center of the board. If the card can be made into a word, the player attempts to both say the word and to correctly spell it. If the player is able to correctly spell the word, he receives 1 point and is also allowed another turn. (The word card is actually removed and retained by the player.) If the word cannot be assimilated, it is kept on the board face up (this word will not be played again). However, if the word can be assimilated, but the player misspells the word, the card is turned back over to be played later in the game.

4. If the player is unable to come up with a word (for whatever reason), he forfeits his turn, and the next player tries his luck.

5. The game is over when all cards that can be played are played, and the winner is the one with the most correctly spelled words.

Variations

A separate set of "Community Chest" cards using all of the original assimilated prefixes can be placed in the middle of the board, and this can be drawn from after each round of turns. This ensures that all prefixes are studied. ("Community Chest" cards will have the prefixes *ad-, in-, com-, ob-, sub-, ex-, per-, dis-*.) If this method is played, then word cards which cannot be played with one particular prefix are turned back over until able to be played.

Rolling Prefixes 8–28

Late Derivational
Constancy

Materials

Create a deck of 32 word cards of assimilated prefixes (8 sets of four). Each group of four should consist of a mixed sort from each of the seven sets of assimilated prefixes: *ad-, in-, com-, ob-, sub-, ex-, dis-*. One set will have to be a "wild set" (words which have the aforementioned prefixes).*

Procedures

1. After the initial sorting of assimilated prefixes, each player is dealt eight cards—3 cards to each player on the first round, 2 cards to each player the second round, and 3 cards to each player the third round.
2. The player on the dealer's left starts the game by putting a card face up in the center of the table. It doesn't matter what the card is, but the player must read the word and state what the prefix is.
3. The next player to the left and the others that follow, attempt to play a card of the same "suit" as the first one put on the table ("suit" meaning having the **same** prefix). Everyone must read his or her word and state the prefix.
4. If everybody follows suit, the cards in the center of the table are picked up after all the players have added their cards, and are put to the side. No one scores.
5. The game continues in the same fashion until someone is unable to follow suit. When this occurs, the player can look through her hand for a "wild card" and play it, changing the suit for the following players.
6. A player may change suit in this manner at any point in the game if she so chooses. For example, a player may play the word *collide* fix *com-*), and the next player may either play a *com-* prefix word (such as *concoct*) or a word with *com-* elsewhere in the word, such as *accommodate.* If the player chooses *accommodate,* the prefix the following player must concentrate on is *ad-* or a form of *ad-*. Players must be familiar with all types of assimilated prefixes.
7. If a player is unable to follow suit, she must pick up the center deck of cards. The player who picks up the cards begins the next round. The game continues this way until someone gets rid of all his or her cards. When this happens the game ends.

Variations

1. At first, players may not wish to state the original prefix of the words.
2. Multiple decks of assimilated prefixes can be made, allowing for variation.
3. Instead of ending the game after one person gets rid of all her cards, the game can continue by the winner of the first round receiving one point for each card that the other players hold in their hands at the end of the game.

---

*This was adapted from the game "Rolling Stone" from *Games and Fun with Playing Cards* by J. Leeming.

Additional Word Exploration for Derivational Students

Word Origins

Exploring the origins of words and the processes of word creation provides a powerful knowledge base for learning spelling and vocabulary, as well as for facilitating more effective reading and writing. **Etymology**, the study of word origins, may develop into a lifelong fascination for many students. Many times the spelling of a word may appear odd, but an understanding of its origin provides the most powerful key to remembering the spelling. Knowing that so many words have come from mythology, literature, and historical events and figures provides important background knowledge for students' reading in the various content areas. Sensitivity to and interest in word origins, in other words, will provide invaluable insight into the concepts and content of much of our students' continuing education.

Words from Mythology

We'll share just a few of the notables here, while referring you to probably the best book on the subject for intermediate students and older—Isaac Asimov's *Words from the Myths* (1960). This excellent book is still in print.

Hypnos: The Greek god of sleep, from which comes our word *hypnosis.*

Titans: These were a race of giants (hence our word "titanic") who ruled the world before the Greek gods and goddesses took over. They warred with the gods and lost; their fate was eternal punishment of some sort or another.

Atlas: One of the Titans, Atlas', punishment was to support the world on his shoulders. A picture of this was often included in the early books of maps, so over time such books came to be called *atlases.*

Luna: Goddess of the moon, we derive our words "lunacy" and "lunatic" from her. At one time people believed the moon had the power to drive some people out of their minds.

Hercules: The strongest of the Greek heroes, he gave us our word "herculean," meaning very powerful. We often speak of "herculean" tasks, which means they are very difficult and trying. Hercules had to perform several seemingly impossible tasks (for example, one was the slaying of a nine-headed monster, the *Hydra*—when one of its heads was severed, two grew in its place).

Places, Things, Actions

Places, things, and actions are often named for their characteristics or for some individual. Students' interest in word origins is often sparked by finding out where place names come from. Consider the states: *Vermont,* for example, comes from French and means "green mountain"; *Nevada* is Spanish and means "snowy," after the Sierra Nevada mountain range; *Minnesota* comes from a Native American word meaning "cloudy water," describing a flooding river; *Virginia* was named for Elizabeth I, England's "Virgin Queen" (Ayers, 1986).

When places, things, and actions are named after an individual, they are called **eponyms** (from Greek *epi-*, "after," + *onoma*, "name"). Here is a sampler of some common eponyms:

bloomers	Amelia Bloomer, an American feminist in the late nineteenth century
boycott	Charles Boycott, whose servants and staff refused to work for him because he would not lower rents

| guillotine | Joseph Guillotin, a French physician and the inventor of the device |
| magnolia | Pierre Magnol, French botanist |

The following resources include lists and information about eponyms:

Dale, D., O'Rourke J., Bamman, H. (1971). *Techniques of Teaching Vocabulary.* Palo Alto: Field Educational Enterprises.

Terban, Marvin. *Guppies in Tuxedos: Funny Eponyms.* New York: Clarion.

How Words Are Used

Writers who use words effectively usually have a solid awareness and knowledge of the sound, structure, and meaning of words. This is why they can select and link together those words that work most effectively in a particular context. Similarly, readers who read most effectively have a solid awareness of sound, structure, and meaning. And ultimately, of course, this is our concern: How words are put into play—how writers use them to craft images, to engage feelings, and to prompt action. Here we are moving into areas beyond the scope of this book, but we cannot leave our exploration of the sound, structure, and meaning of words without at least mentioning how writers put words to use— and the vocabulary we can use to describe this use of words. We should help students see how this is done, identify instances of effective word use, and learn the terms that help us talk about this usage: denotation/connotation, simile and metaphor. (There are more, but these are the most common and most important for intermediate and middle level students to know).

> *Students develop appreciation for how words are used to craft images, engage feelings, and prompt action.*

Words have **denotative** meanings—what they literally mean or refer to. They also have **connotative** meanings—what they *suggest* to us, how they make us feel—the associations we bring to them beyond their literal meanings. For example, it makes a difference if we refer to a person as "old" or as "elderly"; *elderly* has a kinder, more respectful association than were we to refer to someone simply as *old.* Both words literally refer to or denote an older person, but we select one over the other in most contexts because of its more effective *connotative* meaning.

Simile and metaphor are much more common than we realize in our language. Students can learn the straightforward definitions: **simile** expresses a comparison using the terms *like* or *as.* In *Timothy of the Cay* (1993), Theodore Taylor writes in the first person of how young Phillip was rescued from the cay on which he had been stranded, and how "I'd been brought aboard from the rescue boat, naked as a plucked pigeon. . ." (p. 2). Taylor has used a *simile* to describe Phillip's condition.

Metaphor also expresses a comparison, but without the words *like* or *as.* In *On My Honor* (1986), Marion Dane Bauer offers the following description as young Joel finally staggers onto the riverbank after nearly drowning:

> *When the river bottom came up to meet his feet, he stood. The sky was an inverted china bowl above his head* (p. 33).

Of course, the sky is not *literally* an inverted china bowl; we understand this is a comparative description. The starkness of the image—a white glare after he had been struggling underwater—also captures Joel's sense of being caught in a nightmare from which he cannot escape: He has just realized that his friend Tony, who has also been swimming in the river, has probably drowned.

Scott O'Dell, in *Black Star, Bright Dawn* (1989), describes Bright Dawn's realization that she is caught in a whiteout while on the grueling Iditarod Dog Sled Race in Alaska:

There was nothing to see except swirling curtains of white cotton. There was no sky above me, no ice beneath my feet (p. 83).

O'Dell does not have to say "The snow was *like* 'swirling curtains of white cotton.'" We know he is talking about the snow, and his description is the more effective because he states it directly.

When students explore metaphor, they come to the realization that almost all language is in fact metaphorical. *Eye,* for example, can literally mean the organ used for seeing or it can metaphorically mean "wisdom." We should emphasize to students, though, that our purpose in helping them explore metaphor is to identify instances where metaphor has been used to express something in a fresh, new way. We should not linger too long at this level; rather, we should turn students' attention back to *applying* this awareness in their writing and in their appreciation of what they read.

A Concluding Observation

Words are the heart and soul, the building blocks, of the language. We know full well that they live their lives most fully and happily in context (Lewis, 1957). But we also know that readers' and writers' fuller appreciation of these contextual lives depends in large part on a solid understanding of the sounds, patterns, and meanings that their appearance suggests. All that we have shared with you in this book assumes that your students are surrounded by books and by writing in the classroom and are encouraged to explore through reading and writing. Given this encouragement, the word explorations, word sorts, word *play* in which you engage your students will help empower them to make the most of their reading and writing endeavors.

Appendix:
Children's Literature for Word Study

Ahlberg, J. & Ahlberg, A. (1978). *Each peach pear plum.* New York: Viking Press.

Anglund, Joan Walsh. (1960). *In a pumpkin shell.* (Alphabet Mother Goose). San Diego, CA: Harcourt Brace.

Anno, Mitsumasa. (1975). *Anno's alphabet.* New York: Crowell.

Asimov, I. (1960). *Words from the myths.* Boston: Houghton Mifflin.

Aylesworth, J. (1992). *Old black fly.* Illustrated by Stephen Gammell. New York: Scholastic.

Azarian, M. (1981). *A farmer's alphabet.* Boston: David Godine.

Barchas, S.E. (1975). *I was walking down the road.* Illustrated by Jack Kent. New York: Scholastic.

Base, Graeme, (1986). *Animalia.* New York: Harry Abrams.

Baskin, Leonard. (1972). *Hosie's alphabet.* New York: Viking Press.

Bauer, M. D. (1986). *On my honor.* New York: Clarion

Bayor, J. (1984). *A: My name is Alice.* Illustrated by Steven Kellogg. New York: Dial.

Benjamin, A. (1987). *Rat-a-tat, pitter pat.* Photographs by Margaret Miller. New York: Crowell.

Blake, Q. (1989). *Quinton Blake's ABC.* New York: Knoff.

Bruna, D. (1977). *B is for Bear: An ABC by Dick Bruna.* New York: Methuen.

Cameron, P. (1961). *I can't said the ant.* New York: Coward-McCann.

Carle, E. (1974). *My very first book of shapes.* New York: Harper Collins.

Cherry, L. (1988). *Who is sick today?* New York: Dutton.

Chess, V. (1979). *Alfred's alphabet walk.* New York: Greenwillow Books.

Cole, J. (1989). *101 Jump-rope rhymes.* New York: Scholastic.

Cole, J. & Calmenson, S. (1990). *Miss Mary Mac and other children's street rhymes.* Illustrated by Alan Tiegreen. New York: Scholastic.

Crew, D. (1968, 1986). *Ten black dots.* New York: Scholastic.

Dahl, R. (1982). *The BFG.* New York: Trumpet Club.

Eichenberg, F. (1952). *Ape in a cape.* New York: Harcourt Brace.

Falls, C.B. (1923). *ABC book.* New York: Doubleday

Florian, D. (1990). *A beach day.* New York: William Morrow.

—. (1990). *City street.* New York: William Morrow.

—. (1989). *Nature walks.* New York: William Morrow.

—. (1987). *A winter day.* New York: William Morrow.

Gág, W. (1933). *The ABC bunny.* Hand Lettered by Howard Gág. New York: Coward-McCann.

Galdone, P. (1973). *The three billy goats gruff.* New York: Clarion Books.

Garten, J. (1994). *The alphabet tale.* New York: Greenwillow.

Geisert, Arthur. (1986). *Pigs from A to Z.* Boston: Houghton Mifflin.

Hague, K. (1984). *Alphabears: An ABC book.* Illustrated by Michael Hague. New York: Holt, Rinehart & Winston.

Heller, R. (1993). *Chickens aren't the only ones.* New York: Putnam.

Hennessy, B. G. (1989). *The missing tarts.* New York: Scholastic.

Hoban, T. (1978). *Is it red? Is it yellow? Is it blue?* New York: Greenwillow Books.

Hoffman, P. (1990). *We play.* Illustrated by Sara Wilson. New York: Scholastic.

Langstaff, J. (1974). *Oh, a hunting we will go.* New York: Atheneum.

Lionni, L. (1969). *Alexander and the wind-up mouse.* New York: Pantheon.

Macmillan, B. (1990). *Play day.* New York: Holliday House.

—. (1990). *One sun: A book of terse verse.* New York: Holliday House.

Martin, B. (1983). *Brown bear, brown bear, what do you see?* New York: Henry Holt.

Martin, B., and Archambault, J. (1989). *Chicka chicka boom boom.* Illustrated by Lois Ehlert. New York: Simon & Schuster.

Martin, J. (1991). *Carrot parrot.* New York: Simon & Schuster.

Martin, J. (1991). *Mitten Kitten.* New York: Simon & Schuster.

McPhail, D. (1991). *David McPhail's animals A to Z.* New York: Scholastic.

McLenighan, V. (1982). *Stop-go, fast-slow.* Chicago, IL: Children's Press.

Musgrove, M. (1976). *Ashanti to Zulu: African traditions.* Illustrated by Leo and Diane Dillon. New York: Dial.

O'Dell, S. (1989). *Black star, bright dawn.* Boston: Houghton Mifflin.

Owens, Mary Beth. (1988). *A caribou alphabet.* Brunswick, ME: Dog Ear Press.

Pallotta, J. (1989). *The yucky reptile alphabet book.* Illustrated by Ralph Masiello. New York: Trumpet Club.

Parish, P. (1981). *Amelia Bedelia.* New York: Avon.

Raffi (1985). *One light, one sun.* Universal City, CA: Troubadour Records.

Raffi (1976). *Singable songs for the very young.* Universal City, CA: Troubadour Records.

Schwartz, A. (1989). *I saw you in the bathtub.* New York: Harper Collins.

Seuss, Dr. (1974). *There's a wocket in my pocket.* New York: Random House.

Sharmat, M. *Gregory the terrible eater.* New York: Four Winds Press.

Shaw, N. (1986). *Sheep in a jeep.* Boston: Houghton Mifflin.

Shaw, N. (1992). *Sheep on a ship.* Boston: Houghton Mifflin.

Slepian, J. & Seidler, A. (1967). *The hungry thing.* Illustrated by Richard E. Martin. New York: Follet.

Slepian, J. & Seidler, A. (1990). *The hungry thing returns.* New York: Scholastic.

Slepian, J. & Seidler, (1987). *The cat who wore a pot on her head.* New York: Scholastic.

Steig, W. (1978). *Amos and Boris.* New York: Farrar, Straus and Giroux.

Straus, B. & Friedman, H. (1987). *See you later alligator: A first book of rhyming word play.* New York: Trumpet Club.

Taylor, T. (1993). *Timothy of the cay.* San Diego, CA: Harcourt Brace.

Terban, M. *Guppies in tuxedos: Funny eponyms.* New York: Clarion.

Thornhill, J. (1988). *The wildlife A-B-C: A nature alphabet book.* New York: Simon & Schuster.

Wallner, J. (1987a) *City mouse–country mouse.* New York: Scholastic.

Wallner, J. (1987b). *The country mouse and the city mouse and two more mouse tales from Aesop.* New York: Scholastic.

Wells, N. (1980). *Noisy Nora.* New York: Dial Press.

White, E.B. (1945). *Stuart little.* New York: Harper Row.

Withers, C. (1948). *Rocket in my pocket.* New York: Holt, Rinehart.

Wood, A. (1988). *Elbert's bad word.* New York: Harcourt Brace.

Yektai, N. (1987). *Bears in pairs.* New York: Macmillan.

Glossary

absorbed/assimilated prefixes The spelling and sound of the consonant in a prefix has been "absorbed" or assimilated into the same spelling and sound at the beginning of the base or root to which the prefix is affixed (e.g., *ad* + *tract* = *at*tract)

affixation The process of attaching a word part, such as a prefix or suffix, to a base word, stem, or root.

alphabetic A writing system containing characters or symbols representing sounds.

alphabetic layer of instruction The first layer of word study instruction focusing on letters and letter-sound correspondences.

alternation patterns The regular pattern of change in moving from one form of a word to another. *Admire-admiration, perspire-perspiration, declare-declaration* form a consistent pattern of change in moving from one form of the word to another.

analytic approach An approach to phonics instruction that separates a whole word into its constituent parts for further study.

articulation How sounds are shaped in the mouth during speech. To invent spellings, the ways sounds are articulated guides some invented spellings. Some confusions are made in spelling based on similarities in articulation (e.g., *ir* for *dr*).

aural Perceived by the ear, through listening.

base word A word to which prefixes and/or suffixes are added. For example, the base word of *unwholesome is whole.*

beginning period of literacy development A period of literacy development that begins when students have a concept of word and can make sound-symbol correspondences. This period is noted for disfluent reading and writing, and Letter Name spelling.

biological forces The physical endowments of the human brain which control the coordination of thousands of muscles necessary for speaking and listening.

blind sorts A word sort in which the pupil does not look at the word being sorted. Key words are written above each category to cue analogy (*See key words*). A word is called out and the pupil decides which category it belongs to based on the word's sound and memory for its spelling pattern.

center work Work completed independently in prepared areas within a classroom.

circle work   Group work conducted under the teacher's direction.

closed sorts   Word sorts that classify words into predetermined categories.

closed syllable   A *closed* syllable ends with or is "closed" by a consonant sound. In polysyllabic words, a closed syllable contains a short vowel sound that is "closed" by two consonants (*rabbit, racket*). (*See open syllable*)

cognitive forces   Mental processes through which knowledge is acquired.

compound words   Words made up of two or more smaller words. A compound word may or may not be hyphenated, depending on its part of speech.

concept of word   The ability to match spoken words to printed words as demonstrated by the ability to point to the words of a memorized text while reading. This demonstration must include one or more two-syllable words.

connotation/connotative   The *associative* meaning of words—what words suggest to an individual and how they make an individual feel. For example, the word "sick" to a particular individual may suggest extreme discomfort and depression; to another, the word may suggest "bad taste," as in a "sick" joke. (*See denotation/denotative*)

consonant alternation   The process in which the pronunciation of consonants changes in the base or root of derivationally-related words, while the spelling does not change. For example, the silent-to-sounded pattern in the words sign and signal; the /k/ to /sh/ pattern in the words musi̱c and musici̱an.

cut and paste activities   A variation of picture sorting in which students cut out pictures from magazines or catalogues and paste them into categories.

denotation/denotative   The *literal* meaning of words; what words refer to. For example, the word "sick" refers to or denotes the condition of "not being well." (*See connotation/connotative*)

Derivational Constancy spelling stage   The last stage of spelling development in which spellers learn about derivational relationships preserved in the spelling of words. Derivational refers to: a) The process by which new words are created from existing words, chiefly through affixation; b) The development of a word from its historical origin. *Derivational Constancy* refers to spelling patterns that remain the same despite changes in pronunciation across derived forms. *Bomb* retains the *b* from *bombard* because of its historical evolution.

Developmental Classroom Profiles   A class roster arranged by developmental spelling stages. These profiles are used to plan small group word study activities.

developmental level   One of five stages of spelling development: Preliterate, Letter Name, Within Word Pattern, Syllable Juncture, or Derivational Constancy.

Directed Reading-Thinking Activities (DRTAs)   A strategy for developing comprehension processes during reading. The strategy is a variation of a predict-read-prove routine.

directionality   The left-to-right direction used for reading and writing English.

draw and label activities   A variation of picture sorting in which students draw pictures of things which begin with the sounds under study. The pictures are drawn in the appropriate categories and labeled with the letter(s) corresponding to that sound.

emergent period of literacy development   A period of literacy development ranging from birth to beginning reading. This period corresponds to the Preliterate stage of spelling development.

eponyms   Places, things, and actions that are named after an individual.

etymology   The study of the origin and historical development of words.

frustration level   A dysfunctional level of instruction where there is a mismatch between instruction and what an individual is able to grasp. This mismatch precludes learning and often results in frustration.

generative An approach to word study that emphasizes processes that apply to *many* words, as opposed to an approach that focuses on one word at a time.

group concept sort A concept sort conducted cooperatively as a whole class or group.

homographs Words that are spelled alike, have different pronunciations and different meanings, e.g., "*tear* a piece of paper" and "to shed a *tear*"; "*lead* someone along" and "the element *lead*."

homophones Words that sound alike, are spelled differently, and have different meanings, e.g., *bear* and *bare*, *pane* and *pain*, and *forth* and *fourth*.

independent level That level of academic engagement in which an individual works independently, without need of instructional support. *Independent level* behaviors demonstrate a high degree of accuracy, speed, ease, and fluency.

individual sorting Picture sorting or word sorting conducted individually.

instructional level A level of academic engagement in which instruction is comfortably matched to what an individual is able to grasp.

instructional pacing The schedule of instructional delivery over time. The pacing follows the developmental sequence presented by a student. Instructional pacing is considered in the assessment process.

instructional placing The point where instruction begins in a scope and sequence. *Instructional placing* implies that not all students begin at the same place.

invariance spelling features which do not vary, but remain constant.

juncture *Syllable juncture* refers to the transition from one syllable to the next. Frequently this transition involves a spelling change such as consonant doubling or dropping the final *e* before adding *-ing*.

key pictures Pictures placed at the top of each category in a picture sort. *Key pictures* act as headers for each column and can be used for analogy.

key words Words placed at the top of each category in a word sort. *Key words* act as headers for each column and can be used for analogy.

Language Experience An approach to the teaching of reading in which students read about their own experiences recorded in their own language. Experience stories are dictated by the student to a teacher who writes them down. Dictated accounts are re-read in unison, in echo-fashion, and independently. Known words are lifted out of context and grouped by various phonic elements.

Letter Name spelling stage The second stage of spelling development in which students represent beginning, middle and ending sounds of words with phonetically accurate letter choices. Often the selections are based on the sound of the *letter name* itself, rather than abstract letter-sound associations. The *letter name* H ("aitch"), for example, produces the "ch" sound, and is often selected to represent that sound rather than the abstract "huh".

meaning layer of information The third layer of English orthography including meaning units such as prefixes, suffixes, and word roots. These word elements were acquired primarily during the Renaissance when English was overlaid with many words of Greek and Latin derivation.

medial The vowel sound in the middle of words or syllables.

metaphor A word or phrase that means one thing is used, through implication, to refer to something else. For example, "His remark created a *blizzard* of controversy." (*See simile*)

mock linear Writing characteristic of the Emergent period of literacy development in which the linear arrangement of written English is mimicked in long rows of letter-like shapes and squiggles.

nasals A sound produced when the air is blocked in the oral cavity but escapes through the nose. The first consonants in the words "Mom" and "No" represent *nasal* sounds.

nonstandard spelling   Incorrect spelling. Standard spelling is the accepted spelling. Dictionaries provide standard spelling.

onset   The *onset* of a single syllable or word is the initial consonant(s) sound. The *onset* of the work "sun" is /s/. The *onset* of the word "slide" is /sl/.

open sorts   A type of picture or word sort in which the categories for sorting are left open. Students sort pictures or words into groups according to the students' own judgment. *Open sorts* are useful for determining what word features are salient for students.

open syllable   An *open* syllable ends with a long vowel sound (*labor, reason*). (*See closed syllable*)

orthography/orthographic   *Orthography* refers to the writing system of a language, specifically, the correct sequence of letter, characters, or symbols.

pattern   Letter sequences that function as a unit and are related to a consistent category of sound. Frequently these *patterns* form rhyming families, as in the *ain* of *Spain, rain*, and *drain*.

pattern layer of information   The second layer or tier of English orthography in which patterns of letter sequences, rather than individual letters themselves, represent vowel sounds. This layer of information was acquired during the period of English history following the Norman Invasion. Many of the vowel patterns of English are of French derivation.

Personal Readers   Individual books of reading materials that Beginning Readers can read with good accuracy. Group Experience Charts, Dictations and rhymes comprise the majority of the reading material.

phoneme   The smallest unit of speech that distinguishes one word from another. For example, the **t** *of* **tug** and the **r** of **rug** are two English phonemes.

phonemic awareness   Refers to the ability to consciously separate individual sounds in a spoken language. Phonemic awareness is often assessed by the ability to tap or push a penny forward for every sound heard in a word like cat: /c/ /a/ /t/.

picture sort   A categorization task in which pictures are sorted into categories of similarity and difference. Pictures may be sorted by sound or by meaning. Pictures can not be sorted by pattern.

picture sorting activities   Various categorization games and routines using picture cards. Picture sorting activities are all variations on the process of compare and contrast.

preconsonantal nasals   Nasals that occur before consonants, as in the words *bump* or *sink*. The vowel is nasalized as part of the air escapes through the nose during pronunciation. (*See nasal*)

prefix   An affix that is attached to a base word or word root.

Preliterate spelling stage   The first stage of spelling development before letter-sound correspondences are learned and coordinated with printed word boundaries. This spelling stage coincides with the emergent period of literacy development (*see emergent period of literacy development above*).

progressive skill development   A progression of word study activities that increases in thinking skills: The lower levels of word study activity require only recognition or recall of the spelling features studies. The higher levels of word study require students to judge (as in discriminate) and apply what they have learned.

prosody/prosodic   The musical qualities of language, including intonation, expression, stress, and rhythm.

rimes   A rime unit is composed of the vowel and any following consonants within a syllable. For example, the rime unit in the word "tag" would be -*ag*.

r-influenced vowels   In English, when an *r* colors the way the preceding vowel is pronounced. For example, compare the pronunciation of the vowels in *bar* and *bad*. The vowel in *bar* is influenced by the *r*.

root word   This term is most often used as a synonym for "base word."

scaffold   A form of support. The familiar structures of oral language offer a form of support for beginning readers.

seat work   School work that is completed independently at the student's own desk. Students are already familiar with whatever *seat work* is assigned.

simile   Two unlike things are explicitly compared, usually with the words *like* or *as*. For example, "Her tousled hair was like an explosion in a spaghetti factory." (*See metaphor*)

sound board   Charts used by Letter Name spellers that contain pictures and letters of the basic sound-symbol correspondences (e.g., the letter b, a picture of a bell, and the word bell. Individual copies of sound boards are given to students for easy reference, and sound board charts are posted so students can refer to them when they write. Sound boards are provided in Chapter 6 and 7 for initial consonants, consonant blends and digraphs, short and long vowels.

sound sort activities   Activities which ask students to categorize pictures or words by sound as opposed to visual patterns.

spectrograph   A record of sound levels present in speech. We can see how speech is organized in contours through a spectrograph.

speed sorts   Pictures or words that are sorted under a timed condition. Students try to beat their own time.

spelling   The construction of words with letters in a standard order. A synonym for orthography (*See orthography*).

standard spelling   Correct spelling. The accepted spelling found in publishing.

syllabary   A list or set of written characters, each one symbolizing a syllable. In the emergent period of literacy development, children often use a syllable strategy in which a consonant stands for entire syllables.

Syllable Juncture spelling stage   The fourth stage of spelling development which coincides with intermediate reading. *Syllable Juncture* spellers learn about the spelling changes which often take place at the point of transition from one syllable to the next. Frequently this transition involves consonant doubling or dropping the final e before adding -ing (*see juncture*).

syllables   Units of spoken language that consist of a vowel that may be preceded and/or followed by several consonants. *Syllables* are units of sound and can often be detected by paying attention to movements of the mouth. Syllabic divisions indicated in the dictionary are not always correct since the dictionary will always separate meaning units regardless of how the word is pronounced. For example, the proper syllable division for the word *naming* is **na-ming.** However, the dictionary divides this word as **nam-ing** in order to separate the -ing.

synchrony   Occurring at the same time. In this book, stages of spelling development are described in the context of reading and writing behaviors occurring at the same time.

synthetic approach   An approach to phonics instruction that begins with individual letter-sounds that are blended together to form a word. *Synthetic phonics* starts with the parts and builds up to the whole. Analytic phonics starts with the whole and breaks down into parts (*see analytic approach*).

tacit   Tacit knowledge is knowledge that is usually obtained through activity and without conscious reflection.

tracking   The ability to fingerpoint read a text, demonstrating concept of word.

transitional stage of literacy development   A period of literacy development when learners are becoming fluent in reading easy materials. Silent reading becomes the preferred mode. There is some expression in oral reading. This stage is between the beginning and intermediate stages of literacy development. This period corresponds to the Within Word Pattern stage of spelling development.

uvula   A piece of cone-shaped fleshy tissue that hangs down from the roof of the mouth above the back of the tongue. Nasal sounds produced by *n's* and *m's* are produced by the *uvula* blocking the air passing through the nasal passage (*see nasal*).

vowel   A speech sound produced by the easy passage of air through a relatively open vocal tract. *Vowels* form the most central sound of a syllable. In English, *vowel* sounds are represented by the following letters: *a,e,i,o* and *u,* and sometimes *y.*

vowel alternation   The process in which the pronunciation of vowels changes in the base or root of derivationally-related words, while the spelling does not change. For example, the long-to-short vowel change in the related words crime and criminal; the long-to-schwa vowel change in the related words impose and imposition.

Vygotsky   A Russian psychologist known for a social-constructivist view of child language, cognitive development, and learning (*see Zone of Proximal Development*).

Within Word Pattern spelling stage   The third stage of spelling development that coincides with the transitional period of literacy development. *Within Word Pattern* spellers have mastered the basic letter-sound correspondences of written English, and they grapple with letter sequences which function as a unit, especially long vowel patterns. Some of the letters in the unit may have no sound themselves. These "silent" letters, such as the silent *e* in *snake* or the silent *i* in *drain,* serve as important "markers" in the pattern.

word cards   Known words are written on 2" × 1" pieces of card stock. Words students can recognize with ease are used in word study games and word sorts.

word hunts   A word study activity in which students are sent back to texts they have previously read to *hunt* for other words that follow the same spelling features examined during the word or picture sort.

word root   A Greek or Latin element to which affixes are attached, for example, *-cred-, -dict-, -fract-, -phon-.* A word root usually cannot stand alone as a word.

words   A unit of meaning. A word may be a single syllable or a combination of syllables. A word may contain smaller units of meaning within it. In print, a word is separated by white space. In speech, several words may be strung together in a breath group. For this reason, it takes a while for young children to develop a clear concept of word (*see concept of word*).

word sort   A basic word study routine in which students group words into categories. Word sorting involves comparing and contrasting within and across categories. *Word sorts* are often cued by key words placed at the top of each category (*see key words*).

word study   *Word study* is a learner-centered, conceptual approach to instruction in phonics, spelling, word recognition, and vocabulary.

word study notebooks   Notebooks used by students to record their sorts and collect words that follow patterns. Word study notebooks are organized around the orthographic features students are studying. Within Word Pattern students have sections of their notebooks dedicated to long vowel sounds and patterns. Students in the Syllable Juncture stage have sections dedicated to lists of different prefixes and suffixes (e.g., *-es* words and *-tion* words). Derivational Constancy students collect words by their common meanings (e.g., words that have *ter* in them: *terrain, terrestrial*).

writing sorts   A *writing sort* often follows a word sort. Students write key words as headings of columns. Word cards are jumbled up and called out. Students write the words they hear under the appropriate key word and column (*see blind sorts and key words*).

zone of proximal development (ZPD)   A term coined by the Russian psychologist Vygotsky referring to the ripe conditions for learning something new. A person's **ZPD** is that zone which is neither too hard nor too easy. The term is similar to the concept of instructional level (*see instructional level*).

References

Adams, M.J. (1990). *Beginning to read: Thinking and learning about print.*
Cambridge, MA: MIT Press.

Ashton-Warner, S. (1963). *Teacher.* New York: Simon & Schuster.

Ayers, D.W. (1986) *English words from Latin and Greek elements.* (2nd ed.).
Tucson, AZ: University of Arizona Press.

Baretta-Lorton, M.L. (1968). *Math Their Way.* Reading, MA: Addison-Wesley.

Barnes, G. W. (1989). Word sorting: The cultivation of rules for spelling in
English. *Reading Psychology, 10,* 293–307.

Barone, D. (1989). Young children's written responses to literature: The relationship between written response and orthographic knowledge. In S. McCormick
& J. Zutell (Eds.), *Cognitive and social perspectives for literacy research and instruction* (pp. 371–380). Chicago, IL: National Reading Conference.

Barone, D. (1990). The written responses of young children: Beyond comprehension to story understanding. *The New Advocate, 3*(1), 49–56.

Bear, D. (1988). *"On the hurricane deck of a mule": Teaching adults to read using
language-experience and oral history techniques,* a manual distributed by the
Nevada Literacy Coalition & University of Nevada-Reno, Reno, NV. (ERIC
Document Reproduction Service No. ED 294-155.)

Bear, D. (1991a). Copying fluency and orthographic development. *Visible
Language, 25*(1), 40–53.

Bear, D. (1991b). "Learning to fasten the seat of my union suit without looking
around": The synchrony of literacy development. *Theory Into Practice, 30*(3),
149–157.

Bear, D. (1992). In S. Templeton & D. Bear (1992). (Eds.), *Development of orthographic knowledge and the foundations of literacy: A memorial Festschrift for
Edmund H. Henderson* (pp. 137–186). Hillsdale, NJ: Lawrence Erlbaum.

Bear, D. & Barone, D. (1989). Using children's spellings to group for word study
and directed reading in the primary classroom. *Reading Psychology, 10*(3),
275–292.

Bear, D., Truex, P. & Barone, D. (1989). In search of meaningful diagnoses:
Spelling-by-stage assessment of literacy proficiency. *Adult Literacy and Basic
Education, 13*(3), 165–185.

Bear, D. & Cathey, S. (November, 1989). *Reading fluency in beginning readers
and expression in practiced oral reading: Links with word knowledge.* Paper
presented at National Reading Conference, Austin, TX.

Bear, D., Templeton, S., & Warner, M. (1991). The development of a qualitative inventory of higher levels of orthographic knowledge. In J. Zutell & S. McCormick (Eds.), *Learner Factors / Teacher Factors: Issues in Literacy Research and Instruction: Fortieth Yearbook of the National Reading Conference* (pp. 105–110). Chicago: NRC.

Beck, I. L., & McKeown, M. (1991). Conditions of vocabulary acquisition. In R. Barr, M. L. Kamil, P. Mosenthal, & P. D. Pearson (Eds.), *Handbook of reading research* (Vol. 2) (pp. 789–814). White Plains, NY: Longman.

Beers, J. W., & Henderson, E. (1977). A study of developing orthographic concepts among first graders. *Research in the Teaching of English, 11,* 133–148.

Cathey, S.S. (1991). Emerging concept of word: Exploring young children's abilities to read rhythmic text. Doctoral dissertation, University of Nevada. Reno, UMI #9220355.

Chomsky, C. (1970). Reading, writing, and phonology. *Harvard Educational Review, 40,*(2) 287–309.

Chomsky, C. (1971). Write first, read later. *Childhood Education, 47,* 296–299.

Chomsky, N. & Halle, M. (1968). *The sound patterns of English.* New York: Harper & Row.

Clay, M. (1975). *What did I write?.* Exeter, NH: Heinemann.

Cole, M., & Scribner, S. (1978). *Mind in society.* Cambridge, MA: Harvard University Press.

Crystal, D. (1987). *The Cambridge encyclopedia of language.* New York: Cambridge University Press.

Cummings, D. (1988). *American English spelling.* Baltimore, MD: John Hopkins University Press.

Cunningham, P. (1988). Names—A natural for early reading and writing. *Reading Horizons, 28,* 114–122.

Cunningham, P. (1991). *Phonics they use: Words for reading and writing.* Boston: Allyn & Bacon.

Cutler, A., Mehler, J., Norris, D. & Segui, J. (1987). Phoneme identification and the lexicon. *Cognitive Psychology, 19,* 141–177.

Dale, D., O'Rourke J., & Bamman, H. (1971). *Techniques of teaching vocabulary.* Palo Alto, CA: Field Educational Enterprises.

Delpit, L.D. (1988). The silenced dialogue: Power and pedagogy in educating other people's children. *Harvard Educational Review, 58,* 280–298.

Ferreiro, E. & Teberosky, A. (1982). *Literacy before schooling.* Portsmouth, NH: Heinemann.

Fromkin, V. & Rodman, R. (1993). *An introduction to language* (5th ed). Fort Worth, TX: Harcourt Brace Jovanovich College Publishers.

Ganske, K. (1994). *Developmental spelling analysis: A diagnostic measure for instruction and research.* Unpublished doctoral dissertation, University of Virginia, Charlottesville.

Gelb, I.J. (1963). *A study of writing* (2nd ed.). Chicago: University of Chicago Press.

Gibson, J.J. & Yonas, P.M. (1968). A new theory of scribbling and drawing in children. In *The analysis of reading skill: A program of basic and applied research* (Final Report, Project No. 5-1213, Cornell University and the U.S. Office of Education). Ithaca, NY: Cornell University, pp. 335–370.

Gill, C. (1980). An analysis of spelling errors in French. (Doctoral dissertation, University of Virginia, 1980). *Dissertation Abstracts International, 41*(09), 3924A. (University Microfilms No. 79–16, 258).

Gill, J.T. (1992). Focus on research: Development of word knowledge as it relates to reading, spelling and instruction. *Language Arts, 69,*(6), p. 444–453.

Gill, J. & Bear, D. (1988). No book, whole book, and chapter DR-TAs: Three study techniques. *Journal of Reading, 31*(5) 444–449.

Gill, J. & Bear, D. (1989). *Directions for upper level word study.* Unpublished paper.

Gillet, J. & Kita, M.J. (1978). Words, kids, and categories. *The Reading Teacher, 32,* 538–542.

Goswami, U. & Bryant, P. (1990) *Phonological skills and learning to read.* E. Sussex, UK: Lawrence Erlbaum Associates, LTD.

Hall, M. (1980). *Teaching reading as a language experience.* Columbus, OH: Merrill.

Henderson, E. (1981). *Learning to read and spell: The child's knowledge of words.* DeKalb, IL: Northern Illinois Press.

Henderson, E. (1990). *Teaching spelling* (2nd ed.). Boston, MA: Houghton Mifflin.

Henderson, E. (1992). The interface of lexical competence and knowledge of written words. In S. Templeton & D. Bear (Eds.), *Development of orthographic knowledge and the foundations of literacy: A memorial Festschrift for Edmund H. Henderson* (pp. 1–30). Hillsdale, NJ: Lawrence Erlbaum.

Henderson, E., Estes, T., & Stonecash, S. (1972). An exploratory study of word acquisition among first graders at midyear in a language experience approach. *Journal of Reading Behavior, 4,* 21–30.

Henderson, E. H., & Templeton, S. (1986). The development of spelling ability through alphabet, pattern, and meaning. *Elementary School Journal, 86,* 305–316.

Invernizzi, M. (1993). Orthographic development within the emergent reading stage. Paper presented at the Early Childhood Association annual conference.

Invernizzi, M., Abouzeid, M., & Gill, T. (1994). Using students' invented spelling as a guide for spelling instruction that emphasizes word study. *Elementary School Journal, 95*(2), 155–167.

Jacobson, M. (1982). In E. Henderson, et. al. *Teachers' edition: Houghton Mifflin Spelling.* Boston, MA: Houghton Mifflin.

Just, M. & Carpenter, P. (1987). *The psychology of reading and language comprehension.* Boston: Allyn & Bacon.

Kamhi, A.G. & Catts, H.W. (1991). Language and reading: Convergences, divergences, and development. In A.G. Kamhi & H.W. Catts (Eds.), *Reading disabilities: A developmental language perspective,* (pp. 1–34). Boston: Allyn & Bacon.

Koch, K. (1970). *Wishes, lies, and dreams: Teaching children to write poetry.* New York: Harper and Row.

Lenneberg, E. (1967). *Biological foundations of language.* New York: Wiley.

Liberman, I. & Shankweiler, D. (1991). Phonology and beginning reading: A tutorial. In L. Rieben & C. Perfetti (Eds.), *Learning to read: Basic research and its implication.* Hillsdale, NJ: Lawrence Erlbaum.

Lieberman, P. (1991). *Uniquely human.* Cambridge, MA: Harvard University Press.

Malinowski, B. (1952). The problem of meaning in primitive languages. In C.K. Ogden & I.A. Richards (eds.), *The meaning of meaning* (10th ed). New York: Harcourt.

McIntosh, M. & Bear, D. (December, 1993). *The development of content-specific orthographic knowledge: A look at vocabulary in geometry.* Paper presented at the 43rd Annual National Reading Conference, Charleston, SC.

Morais, J., Cary, L., Alegria, J., & Bertelson, P. (1979). Does awareness of speech as a sequence of phonemes arise spontaneously? *Cognition, 7,* 323–331.

Morris, D. (1980). Beginning readers' concept of word. In E. Henderson & J. Beers (Eds.), *Developmental and cognitive aspects of learning to spell,* 97–111. Neward, DE: International Reading Association.

Morris, D. (1981). Concept of word: A developmental phenomenon in the beginning reading and writing process. *Language Arts, 58*(6), 659–668.

Morris, D. (1982). "Word sort": A categorization strategy for improving word recognition ability. *Reading Psychology, 3,* 247–259.

Morris, D. (1992a). *Case studies in teaching beginning readers: The Howard Street tutoring manual.* Boone, NC: Stream Publications.

Morris, D. (1992b). Concept of word: A pivotal understanding in the learning to read process. In S. Templeton & D. Bear (Eds.), *Development of orthographic knowledge and the foundations of literacy: A memorial Festschrift for Edmund H. Henderson.* (pp. 53–77). Hillsdale, NJ: Lawrence Erlbaum.

Morris, D. (1993). Concept of word and phoneme awareness in the beginning reader. *Research in the Teaching of English, 17,* 359–373.

Nessel, D. & Jones, M. (1981). *The Language-Experience Approach to reading.* New York: Teachers College Press.

Read, C. (1971). Pre-school children's knowledge of English phonology. *Harvard Educational Review, 41*(1), 1–34.

Read, C. (1975). *Children's categorization of speech sounds in English.* Urbana, IL: NCTE Committee on Research, *17.*

Read, C. & Hodges, R. (1982). Spelling. In H. Mitzel (Ed.), *Encyclopedia of Educational Research* (5th ed.). New York: Macmillan.

Read, C., Zhang, Y., Nile, H., & Ding, B. (1986). The ability to manipulate speech sounds depends on knowing alphabetic reading. *Cognition, 24,* 31–44.

Richgels, D. (1995). Invented spelling ability and printed word learning in kindergarten. *Reading Research Quarterly, 30*(1), 96–109.

Roberts, B.S. (1992). The evolution of the young child's concept of word as a unit of spoken and written language. *Reading Research Quarterly, 27*(2), 125–138.

Schlagal, R. (1992). Patterns of orthographic development into the intermediate grades. In S. Templeton & D. Bear (Eds.), *Development of orthographic knowledge and the foundations of literacy: A memorial Festschrift for Edmund H. Henderson* (pp. 31–52). Hillsdale, NJ: Lawrence Erlbaum.

Scragg, D. (1974). *A history of English spelling.* New York: Barnes & Noble Books, Manchester.

Snow, C. E. (1983). Literacy and language: Relationships during the preschool years. *Harvard Educational Review, 53*(2), 165–189.

Southworth, F. & Chander, D. (1974). *Foundations of literacy.* New York: The Free Press/Macmillan.

Spenser, B. (1989). *The development of the young child's concept of word: A longitudinal study* (Monograph). Newark, DE: International Reading Association.

Stanovich, K. (1986). Matthew effects in reading: Some consequences of individual differences in the acquisition of literacy. *Reading Research Quarterly, 21,* 360–406.

Stauffer, R. (1980). *The language-experience approach to the teaching of reading,* 2d ed. New York: Harper and Row.

Stever, E. (1980). Dialect and spelling. In E. H. Henderson & J. W. Beers (Eds.), *Cognitive and developmental aspects of learning to spell English* (pp. 46–51). Newark, DE: International Reading Association.

Strickland, D. & Morrow, L. (1989). Environments rich in print promote literacy behavior during play. *Reading Teacher, 43,* 178–179.

Sulzby, E. (1986). Writing and reading organization. In W. H. Teale & E. Sulzby (Eds.), *Emergent literacy: Writing and reading,* pp. 50–89. Norwood, NJ: Abex.

Taft, M. (1991). *Reading and the mental lexicon.* London: Lawrence Erlbaum Associates.

Temple, C. (1978). An analysis of spelling errors in Spanish. Doctoral dissertation, University of Virginia.

Templeton, S. (1976, December) *The spelling of young children in relation to the logic of alphabetic orthography.* Paper presented at the 26th annual convention of the National Reading Conference, Atlanta, GA.

Templeton, S. (1983). Using the spelling/meaning connection to develop word knowledge in older students. *Journal of Reading, 27(1)* 8–14.

Templeton, S. (1989). Tacit and explicit knowledge of derivational morphology: Foundations for a unified approach to spelling and vocabulary development in the intermediate grades and beyond. *Reading Psychology, 10,* 233–253.

Templeton, S. (1991a). Teaching and learning the English spelling system: Reconceptualizing method and purpose. *Elementary School Journal, 92,* 185–201.

Templeton, S. (1991b). *Teaching the integrated language arts.* Boston, MA: Houghton Mifflin.

Templeton, S. (1992). Theory, nature and pedagogy of higher-order orthographic development in older children. In S. Templeton & D. Bear (Eds.), *Development of orthographic knowledge and the foundations of literacy: A memorial Festschrift for Edmund H. Henderson* (pp. 253–278). Hillsdale, NJ: Lawrence Erlbaum.

Templeton, S. & Bear, D. (eds.), (1992a). *Development of orthographic knowledge and the foundations of literacy: A memorial Festschrift for Edmund H. Henderson.* Hillsdale, NJ: Lawrence Erlbaum.

Templeton, S. & Bear, D. (1992b). Teaching the lexicon to read and spell. In S. Templeton & D. Bear (Eds.), *Development of orthographic knowledge and the foundations of literacy: A memorial Festschrift for Edmund H. Henderson* (pp. 333–352). Hillsdale, NJ: Lawrence Erlbaum.

Templeton, S., & Spivey, E. M. (1980). The concept of "word" in young children as a function of level of cognitive development. *Research in the Teaching of English, 14*(3), 265–278.

Treiman, R. (1985). Onsets and rimes as units of spoken syllables: Evidence from children. *Journal of Educational Psychology, 77*(4), 417–427.

Treiman, R. (1991). The role of intrasyllabic units in learning to read. In L. Rieben & C. A. Perfetti (Eds.), *Learning to read: Basic research and its implications* (pp. 149–160). Hillsdale, NJ: Lawrence Erlbaum.

Tunmer, W. E. (1991). Phonological awareness and literacy acquisition. In L. Rieben & C. A. Perfetti (Eds.), *Learning to read: Basic research and its implications* (pp. 105–120). Hillsdale, NJ: Lawrence Erlbaum.

Venesky, R. (1970). *The structure of English orthography.* The Hague: Mouton.

Vygotsky, L.S. (1962). *Thought and language.* Cambridge, MA: MIT Press.

White, T. G., Power, M. A., & White, S. (1989). Morphological analysis: Implications for teaching and understanding vocabulary growth. *Reading Research Quarterly, 24,* 3, 283–304.

Wilde, S. (1991). *You kan red this!* Portsmouth, NH: Heinemann.

Worthy, J. & Viise, N. (1993). "Can we know what we know about children in teaching adults to read?" Unpublished paper.

Wysocki, K., & Jenkins, J. R. (1987). Deriving word meanings through morphological generalization. *Reading Research Quarterly, 22,* 66–81.

INDEX